The Best Family Destinations

WITHDRAWN

FamilyTravelForum.com with Kyle McCarthy

ALPHA

A member of Penguin Group (USA) Inc.

ALPHA BOOKS

Published by the Penguin Group

Penguin Group (USA) Inc., 375 Hudson Street, New York, New York 10014, USA

Penguin Group (Canada), 90 Eglinton Avenue East, Suite 700, Toronto, Ontario M4P 2Y3, Canada (a division of Pearson Penguin Canada Inc.)

Penguin Books Ltd., 80 Strand, London WC2R 0RL, England

Penguin Ireland, 25 St. Stephen's Green, Dublin 2, Ireland (a division of Penguin Books Ltd.)

Penguin Group (Australia), 250 Camberwell Road, Camberwell, Victoria 3124, Australia (a division of Pearson Australia Group Pty. Ltd.)

Penguin Books India Pvt. Ltd., 11 Community Centre, Panchsheel Park, New Delhi—110 017, India

Penguin Group (NZ), 67 Apollo Drive, Rosedale, North Shore, Auckland 1311, New Zealand (a division of Pearson New Zealand Ltd.)

Penguin Books (South Africa) (Pty.) Ltd., 24 Sturdee Avenue, Rosebank, Johannesburg 2196, South Africa

Penguin Books Ltd., Registered Offices: 80 Strand, London WC2R 0RL, England

Copyright © 2011 by Kyle McCarthy

International Standard Book Number: 978-1-61564-047-8
Library of Congress Catalog Card Number: 2010908790

13 12 11   8 7 6 5 4 3 2 1

Interpretation of the printing code: The rightmost number of the first series of numbers is the year of the book's printing; the rightmost number of the second series of numbers is the number of the book's printing. For example, a printing code of 11-1 shows that the first printing occurred in 2011.

Printed in the United States of America

Publisher: *Marie Butler-Knight*
Associate Publisher/Acquiring Editor: *Mike Sanders*
Senior Managing Editor: *Billy Fields*
Development Editor: *Jennifer Moore*
Senior Production Editor: *Janette Lynn*
Copy Editor: *Lisanne V. Jensen*

Cover Designer: *Bill Thomas*
Book Designer: *Trina Wurst*
Indexer: *Tonya Heard*
Layout: *Ayanna Lacey*
Proofreader: *John Etchison*

For my family, who has taught me so much about what makes travel fun.

Contents

Appendixes

Introduction

If you have one child or many or have just been put in charge of organizing the family reunion, you've probably realized that some aspects of vacation planning are harder than they need to be.

That's why we've included a wide variety of what we call the "best" destinations and reviewed them in enough detail so you and your family can decide together whether they sound like the best for you.

As frequent family travelers ourselves, we know how much we've benefited from the tips and suggestions passed on by other families who have been there and done it before us. That's the kind of useful information we hope to share with you, in a simple and easy-to-use format.

How This Book Is Organized

Because many of you will plan road trips (and will need an attraction or two to pacify backseat travelers) or may look for a quick weekend away to escape the grind of school and work, we have organized the book into "parts" by the following major geographic regions:

> **Part 1: The Northeast:** Connecticut, Delaware, Maine, Maryland, Massachusetts, New Hampshire, New Jersey, New York, Pennsylvania, Rhode Island, Vermont, and Washington, D.C.

> **Part 2: The South:** Alabama, Arkansas, Florida, Georgia, Kentucky, Louisiana, North Carolina, South Carolina, Tennessee, Virginia, and West Virginia

> **Part 3: The Midwest:** Illinois, Indiana, Iowa, Kansas, Michigan, Minnesota, Missouri, Nebraska, North Dakota, Ohio, South Dakota, and Wisconsin

> **Part 4: The Southwest:** Arizona, New Mexico, Oklahoma, and Texas

> **Part 5: Mountain States:** Colorado, Idaho, Montana, Utah, and Wyoming

Part 6: The West: California, Nevada, and Hawaii

Part 7: The Northwest: Alaska, Oregon, and Washington

Part 8: Mexico

Part 9: Canada

At the beginning of each part, we've included a map with all of our destinations identified to help you plan an efficient itinerary.

Getting the Most from This Guidebook

In our experience, the "best" family destination is a subjective choice based on your family's needs for a given vacation period. What makes the 200 or so destinations we've included in this book so special is their capacity to entertain, educate, and amaze all visitors, with a special knack for engaging kids.

As you read, you'll notice that we selected our favorites in each region and grouped them by theme:

- **City Style**   best for an exciting city getaway

- **Cultural Appeal**   best museum, event, or bit of America, or folk culture

- **Living History**   best at illustrating history in a fun way

- **At the Beach**   best beaches for kids

- **Amusement Parks**   best midways, theme parks, and water parks

- **Outdoor Adventures**   best nature, ecological, and recreation areas

Within each theme, every destination review highlights its unique attributes, what ages it's appropriate for, the best season to visit, and money-saving tips. The names of our favorite sights and nearby special attractions are **bolded,** and all the contact information you need to make plans is included.

So please don't take the 200 or so destinations we highlight as the very best for you; learn more about them, discuss them with your family, and use them to plan your itinerary.

Helpful Sidebars

We've added the following sidebars with even more information:

VACATION PLANNING TIPS

In these boxes, you'll find advice from other travelers you can use to plan a better itinerary or make better choices about the destination.

FELLOW TRAVELERS SAY ...

In these boxes, you'll find quotes from journals, travel blogs, and posts from the Family Travel Forum community websites: www. FamilyTravelForum.com, www.travelBIGO.com, and www. FamilyTravelBoards.com.

TRAVELERS BEWARE!

Here, you'll find hints to keep you out of trouble. Fortunately, there aren't too many of these.

FUN FACTS

Here, you'll find unusual factoids you can share with the kids—and maybe, if you're lucky, you'll avoid hearing the familiar refrain, "Are we there yet?"

One Last Thing ...

One thing we've learned in our years of traveling is that, at every age and stage of life, kids' needs and interests change. So we ask that you involve everyone in the family when planning your next trip—and no matter how much time you have, cut your schedule in half. While kids' needs may change, having time to enjoy each other without rushing off to the next attraction will always be what family vacations are all about.

We hope you'll use this guidebook in the years to come, whether you're planning a trip for relaxation, hoping to enrich your kids' curriculum, or just need a fun diversion on the way to Grammy's.

Please keep in touch by writing us in care of the publisher or emailing us at FTF@familytravelforum.com with your suggestions and comments on how to make this guidebook better for the next edition!

Acknowledgments

First, I'd like to thank my co-author, FamilyTravelForum.com, for the vacation stories and travel tips shared by millions of families in its travel community over the years. Special thanks go to the Family Travel Forum staff—especially editors Fran Falkin and Jillian Ryan—who worked long and hard with me to select the very best family destinations. We could never have assembled so much wisdom about family travel without their energy and input and the help of FTF interns Lee Dunlap, Emily Yanez, Maureen Linehan, Mia Kunst, and Regan Bozman. I'd also like to express my appreciation for the guidance of Mike Sanders and his staff at Alpha Books and development editor Jennifer Moore, who made this book "idiot-proof." And last, but certainly not least, to my own family who gave up several school vacations to help me get this manuscript in on time so you could have it to plan your own family vacation.

Trademarks

All terms mentioned in this book that are known to be or are suspected of being trademarks or service marks have been appropriately capitalized. Alpha Books and Penguin Group (USA) Inc. cannot attest to the accuracy of this information. Use of a term in this book should not be regarded as affecting the validity of any trademark or service mark.

The Northeast

The modern history of the Northeast dates to the Pilgrims, who set sail for northern Virginia aboard the *Mayflower* on September 6, 1620. About nine weeks later, they spied the North American continent around Cape Cod and, sailing south to Virginia, were caught in rough seas. Fearing for their lives, the Pilgrims turned back and settled in Plymouth. Nearly four centuries later, the Northeast region includes the populous states of Connecticut, Delaware, Maine, Maryland, Massachusetts, New Hampshire, New Jersey, New York, Pennsylvania, Rhode Island, Vermont, and Washington, D.C. As the birthplace of much of American history, the Northeast is one of the nation's busiest four-season tourist destinations, with great cities, cultural marvels, beautiful beaches, amusement parks, and towering mountains for outdoor adventure.

In Part 1, you'll find family fun among the Federal buildings and national monuments and read about too many attractions to see in any one vacation—so study the map and plan carefully.

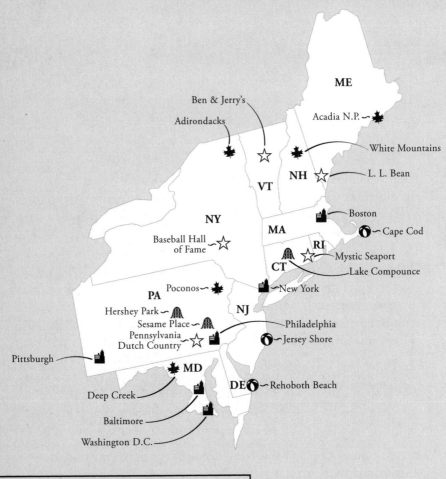

ME

Ben & Jerry's

Adirondacks

Acadia N.P.

White Mountains

VT

NH

L. L. Bean

NY

Boston

Cape Cod

Baseball Hall
of Fame

MA

RI

CT

Mystic Seaport

Lake Compounce

Poconos

New York

PA

NJ

Hershey Park

Sesame Place

Philadelphia

Pennsylvania
Dutch Country

Jersey Shore

Pittsburgh

MD

DE

Rehoboth Beach

Deep Creek

Baltimore

Washington D.C.

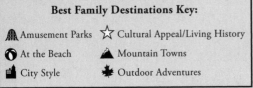

Best Family Destinations Key:

- Amusement Parks
- ☆ Cultural Appeal/Living History
- At the Beach
- ▲ Mountain Towns
- City Style
- ❦ Outdoor Adventures

City Style

In This Chapter

- Baltimore's crab cakes and Camden Yards
- The Ivy League meets the Revolution in Boston
- New York City, crossroads of the world
- Philadelphia, the nation's birthplace
- Pittsburgh's family-friendly destinations
- Power meets politics in Washington, D.C.

To some, the urban sprawl of almost 58 million people in the New York-Philadelphia-Baltimore-Washington corridor is a turn-off. Even dignified Boston and colorful Pittsburgh can be intimidating if you don't like the hustle and bustle of cities. But to others, the excitement of these ethnically diverse and culturally rich metropolises is the key ingredient for the perfect family destination.

Keep in mind that these cities are some of the most expensive destinations in the United States, so we've mentioned many of our favorite free activities and festivals so you can get the most from your hard-earned vacation budget.

Baltimore, Maryland

Baltimore is a relatively compact Eastern seaboard city that welcomes families to explore its maritime heritage, historical attractions, ethnic diversity, arts, and culture. At the heart of this city's renaissance is

Inner Harbor, a successful cultural addition to what was an under-used historic waterfront. **Harborplace,** the central shopping and restaurant complex, is certain to keep your family engaged. Make your first stop the **Baltimore Visitor Center** to purchase a **Baltimore Harbor Pass** and use it on the water taxi that connects Inner Harbor to more than 30 museums, attractions, and neighborhoods.

Inner Harbor highlights include the iconic **National Aquarium in Baltimore,** home to 16,500 animals and sea creatures inhabiting a multi-story tank. Favorite family attractions include a live dolphin show and the 4D Immersion Theater. The **Maryland Science Center** is a great place for the young Einsteins in your crew; kids will also love the IMAX theater, live science demonstrations, and hands-on activities. History buffs will want to step aboard the **USS Constellation** to learn about naval history on this Civil War–era sloop. For some mealtime fun, check out the ESPN Zone at the **Power Plant,** a recycled industrial building housing a fantastic entertainment complex including a restaurant, sports bar, and inter-active game room.

VACATION PLANNING TIPS

Come and enjoy the flavors of Baltimore at the world's largest fresh food center, **Lexington Market,** at 400 West Lexington Street. As they have since 1782, merchants are happy to tell you about their specialties at 130 stalls serving a wide variety of goods, including fresh seafood, homemade chocolates, ice cream, baked goods, Kosher corned beef, and fresh meats and produce. You'll find weekly entertainment on Saturdays and special festivities during the holidays.

Nearby **Port Discovery** is a children's museum devoted to kids ages 2 to 10. A short stroll from Inner Harbor is **Oriole Park at Camden Yards,** the official home of the Baltimore Orioles. This famous base-ball stadium combines modern features with a nostalgic "retro" feel; the one and a half–hour guided tour takes you to the press room, scoreboard control room, and the dugout. Next door, **Sports Legends at Camden Yards** is a fun museum featuring artifacts and interactive exhibits about Baltimore sports; kids can even try on uni-forms in the "Locker Room." Upstairs is **Geppi's Entertainment Museum,** a unique facility dedicated to the 230-year history of popular culture and a fun place to reminisce with kids. Included are the first long-gone characters used in toy manufacturing, plus Buster Brown, Felix the Cat, and Howdy Doody up to modern icons like 007, Barbie, and SpongeBob. Die-hard Babe Ruth fans should follow the baseballs painted on the street leading to the **Babe Ruth Historic Birthplace and Museum** three blocks away.

Museum lovers will find plenty to keep them busy. **Fort McHenry,** best remembered as the inspiration for "The Star-Spangled Banner," is under the aegis of the National Park Service and offers a free film, daily flag change, Ranger-led activities, and cannon-firing demonstrations. The **B&O Railroad Museum,** home to the oldest, most comprehensive collection of railroad artifacts in the Western Hemisphere, is housed in the historic 1884 Baldwin Roundhouse. Seasonally, families can enjoy a train ride on the first commercial railroad track in America, and a delightful model train is on display year-round.

The **National Museum of Dentistry** is an offbeat but fun museum. The only one of its kind, it offers many interactive displays, including "32 Terrific Teeth," a must-see for kids of all ages. Art lovers won't want to miss the renowned **Baltimore Museum of Art,** which houses the world's largest collection of works by Henri Matisse. The **American Visionary Museum** displays whimsical and unusual artwork created by self-taught artists.

Baltimore is proud of its diversity, and **Baltimore's Heritage Walk** tours several neighborhoods, showcasing more than 20 of the city's most distinct landmarks, historical sites, and neighborhoods. The Baltimore Black Heritage Tours company runs guided visits to sites of the Underground Railroad, historic churches and restaurants, as well as tours of the **Eubie Blake National Museum** and the **National Great Blacks in Wax Museum.** The **Reginald F. Lewis Museum of Maryland African American History and Culture,** the East Coast's largest museum focusing on the history and contributions of African Americans, has interactive learning centers, a theater, and a recording/listening oral history studio. The **Jewish Museum of Maryland** offers changing exhibits and programs about the Jewish community as well as guided tours of two restored historic synagogues. East of the Inner Harbor, Baltimore's **Little Italy** is an ideal place for families to stroll, dine on pasta and crab cakes, and drink a little vino while experiencing this vibrant neighborhood.

Guided tour options abound. The **Ride the Ducks of Baltimore** uses a 1945 Army DUKW (or amphibious vehicle nicknamed "duck"), for a unique 80-minute romp through the streets and off the shore, past some famous landmarks. A traditional London open-top, double-decker bus makes stops at 16 attractions, and you can hop on and off whenever you like.

The Baltimore Visitor Center
1-877-BALTIMORE
www.baltimore.org, visitmaryland.org

Boston, Massachusetts

Boston is truly one of the most glorious American cities and offers many treats for traveling families. Its history was written with the settling of the United States and the War for Independence. Children are fascinated by the tales—the Tea Party, the armed conflicts, and the lanterns in the church tower—and present-day Boston offers many pleasures as well.

The big historic hits are found on a walking tour of **The Freedom Trail.** Along its two and a half–mile long, red-brick road are 16 historical sites, including the **Paul Revere House,** built in 1680, and the **Granary Burying Ground,** the resting place of many patriots (including Paul Revere, John Hancock, and Samuel Adams) as well as Elizabeth Vergoose, better known as Mother Goose. Follow the bricks inlaid in the street to visit the **Old North Church** and its famous tower ("one if by land, two if by sea"), **Bunker Hill, Faneuil Hall,** the **USS** *Constitution,* and more. The Trail is busy with guided groups led by costumed interpreters, but you can follow it on your own by starting at the Visitors Center at **Boston Common.**

FUN FACTS

The **Public Garden** in Boston Common is home to the city's **Swan Boats,** the inspiration for Robert McCloskey's book *Make Way for Ducklings.* Your 15-minute ride provides a stunning view of the city plus the treat of sharing a boat with a lovely white swan.

Neither history nor fun end on The Freedom Trail, so branch out and explore the **Boston African-American National Historic Site,** which comprises the largest area of pre-Civil War black-owned structures in the United States. The roughly two dozen sites on the north face of **Beacon Hill** were the homes, businesses, schools, and churches of a thriving community known for its abolitionist leadership and as a sanctuary for fugitive slaves before and during the Civil War. Free guided tours of the site are offered from the Park Service visitors' center in the Abiel Smith School; afterward, drop by the **Museum of African American History** on Joy Street. Don't miss this opportunity to explore the charming, narrow lanes of the wealthy Beacon Hill neighborhood that makes you feel like you've traveled back in time to the eighteenth and nineteenth centuries.

At the **Boston Harbor,** you can also see where the most famous tea party in history took place. When it reopens in summer 2011, you'll be able to tour authentic replicas of the *Brig Beaver II, Dartmouth,* and *Eleanor,* the cargo ships docked in the harbor that historic night when protestors dumped 342 chests (more than 123,000 pounds) of tea in the briny bay.

The Esplanade park on the banks of the **Charles River** offers a variety of opportunities for family-friendly outdoor activities, including walking and biking paths, sailboat rentals, plus several different play areas along the river. For those looking to rest their feet, benches offer ample opportunities to relax and watch Ivy League rowers hone their skills. You can circle back to Boston Common, the oldest public park in the United States. Over the years, it has been used for public hangings and other forms of punishment; today, visitors can join the thousands of locals who enjoy picnics while listening to concerts or cooling off at the frogless Frog Pond. Winter months bring ice skating on the pond; you can rent a pair of skates from a nearby vendor.

For spectacular city views, head over to the **Skywalk Observatory.** Visitors ride 50 floors to the top in a mere 32 seconds—and on a clear day, you can see all the way to the mountains of New Hampshire and the beaches of Cape Cod.

Home to many of the world's great universities, Boston is a mecca for college tours and culture-seekers. The dynamic duo of deeply interesting and fun museums, the **Harvard Museum of Natural History** and the **Peabody Museum of Archaeology and Ethnology,** are situated together on the classic grounds of Harvard University in Cambridge, a short ride on the elevated train (the T), from Boston. Kids will love the rooms filled with preserved animal specimens and fossilized dinosaur skeletons. One of the most interesting permanent exhibits is the Ware Collection of Glass Flowers, consisting of 3,000 meticulously authentic glass reproductions of flowers and flower parts. Family programs and story time sessions are offered on Saturdays and Sundays.

The Boston art museums, **The Museum of Fine Arts** and the **Gardiner Museum,** have world-renowned collections and are well worth a visit if the young ones have the patience. For restless kid days, head straight to the fine **Boston Children's Museum,** which belongs to the "please touch" school. Children can see themselves on TV in "Arthur's World," climb aboard a life-size boat, scale towers and tubes, or perform in a live theatrical show. Younger children flock to the museum's PlaySpace. The **Museum of Science** is one of the country's most renowned museums, housing more than 400 interactive exhibits with live animal presentations, weather-making exhibits, lightning bolt demonstrations, a Discovery Center for preschoolers, planetarium and Omni IMAX theater, plus a walk-through butterfly garden. Kids can even create their own fish in the Virtual Fishtank.

Located on Central Wharf, the **New England Aquarium** greets visitors with seals and sea otters in its outdoor pool. Inside, another 7,000 fish and aquatic animals inhabit a huge cylindrical tank you can view from a spiral ramp. For a family field trip, join a **whale-watching cruise** aboard the *Voyager III* to the Stellwagen Bank Marine Sanctuary, a rich feeding area for whales, dolphins, sea birds, and other marine life. Naturalists and educators are on board, and reservations are strongly recommended for this three- to four-hour trip.

FELLOW TRAVELERS SAY ...

"Loved the city: the **DuckTour** was a cut above, thanks to the deadpanning driver; we had fun shopping on Charles Street and Newbury Street, and there is a great playground and wading pool on Boston Common. Also took the shuttle to Harvard Square—very busy. Small thing: the DuckTour company charges extra for online bookings."

—M. E., www.FamilyTravelForum.com

Satisfy your shopping urges at the famous **Faneuil Hall Marketplace,** which includes the renovated produce hall of **Quincy Market,** where you'll find many of the smaller national chains along with an impressive array of local eateries and drinkeries. For a more local shopping experience, head to **Newbury Street** in Back Bay below Beacon Hill. Antique stores, boutique clothing stores, art galleries, and cafés line several blocks adjacent to the T-stop.

Greater Boston Convention & Visitors Bureau
1-888-SEE-BOSTON
www.bostonusa.com, www.massvacation.com

New York, New York

Few forget their first trip to the Big Apple, one of the world's great cities. Within New York City's five boroughs—Manhattan, Brooklyn, The Bronx, Queens, and Staten Island—families can find hundreds of attractions and activities that they'd have to travel far and wide to experience elsewhere. That's why careful planning and comfortable shoes are so important.

The iconic **Empire State Building,** at 102 stories, is once again the city's tallest building and the star of more than 60 films. During your stay, be sure to glance up each night and see what color her crown is; if it's illuminated red and green in July, you can be sure a Christmas-themed movie is being filmed in town. Kids 36" or taller will enjoy the immersive, 30-minute **New York Skyride** virtual tour on the second floor; a combo pass includes both admissions. Many visitors prefer the **Top of the Rock,** the observation deck above midtown's **Rockefeller Center** office complex. Here, other skyscrapers are in-your-face close, and it's a more complete tour—with a background film, kids' play area, open-top elevator to the 67th floor, and three levels of open air and enclosed viewing terraces.

FUN FACTS

Parents might want to watch *Guys and Dolls, An Affair to Remember,* or *Sleepless in Seattle*—classic films set at the Empire State Building—before they visit. More action-packed, kid-friendly movies shot there include *King Kong, Last Action Hero, Independence Day,* and *Elf.*

The subject of skyscrapers brings us to the **World Trade Center** and former Twin Towers that collapsed after the September 11, 2001, terrorist attacks. At **Ground Zero,** the city has erected a small information booth, and guided tours are available daily. You can see the slow progress that has been made in rebuilding the area and visit a gallery devoted to the victims of the tragedy.

As worldwide symbols of freedom, the **Statue of Liberty** and **Ellis Island Immigration Museum** are must-see attractions. The statue and the fascinating exhibits within her pedestal on 12-acre Liberty Island are open to visitors. Twelve million immigrants came through Ellis Island before settling in America between 1892 and 1954, and the museum's multimedia displays allow visitors to search for their records.

VACATION PLANNING TIPS

You can reserve your ferry seats to the Statue of Liberty in advance online at www.statuecruises.com and purchase advance tickets to Lady Liberty's crown and museums at www.nps.gov/stli. Be sure to get to the ferry early, however, because security lines are long. Don't carry unnecessary items, as all bags are searched. Take advantage of free Park Ranger walks, audioguides geared to children, and special needs tours. If you're short on time, you can admire the Statue of Liberty from a passing ferry, a cruise tour, or a shorefront promenade in lower Manhattan.

Many of New York's cultural institutions offer free-entry days or evenings, free one-hour guided tours geared toward families, and special workshops on weekends. Check their websites and plan your itinerary around these offerings to save a bundle on admission fees.

The **American Museum of Natural History,** where actor Ben Stiller supposedly spent his *Night at the Museum*, is a must-see for its collection of life-size dinosaur skeletons, original dioramas depicting the world's habitats, and futuristic planetarium. Also, don't miss the dinosaur-shaped chicken nuggets served in all the museum restaurants. The **Metropolitan Museum of Art** contains more than two million works of art from across the globe and the centuries, but you'll never see them all. Instead, follow its clever Museum Kids scavenger hunt and play in the Arms and Armor wing. Some kids will relate to the contemporary art on display at the **Guggenheim Museum** (the Frank Lloyd Wright–designed "flower pot" on Fifth Avenue) and at the **Whitney Museum** of twentieth-century American art, film, and video. The best known of the modern museums is MOMA, the **Museum of Modern Art,** which showcases 150,000 paintings, sculptures, photography, drawings, films, and more. MOMA's guides do a great job helping kids appreciate contemporary art.

A melting pot, New York City culture comes in many flavors. Some of the city's historical, multi-ethnic neighborhoods include the **Lower East Side,** whose struggling immigrant histories are brought to life in the fascinating **Lower East Side Tenement Museum;** New York's thriving **Chinatown,** where you can join walking tours focused on food, culture, or cuisine; **Harlem** for a sweet potato pie or Wednesday's **Amateur Night at the Apollo; Brooklyn Heights,** home to celebrities from the late Norman Mailer to Beyoncé; Hasidic **Williamsburg** and the Russian enclave of **Brighton Beach** in Brooklyn; and The Bronx's Italian **Arthur Avenue,** the 300-acre **Bronx Zoo** and, of course, **Yankee Stadium.** The 2009 World Series champs play in a brand-new stadium, but the Bombers took Monument Park, with the team's 16 retired numbers and their corresponding placards, with them. The New York Mets, Knicks, Rangers, Giants, Jets, and other sports teams play in different venues in Manhattan, Queens, and even New Jersey—all of which have daily tours. Most visitors touch ground on remote Staten Island only to get off and back on the free **Staten Island Ferry,** which provides the best view of the Statue of Liberty

Outdoor adventures abound, even in a city that never sleeps. Kids love Manhattan's famous **Central Park,** especially if explored creatively. Jog; rent bikes; join a free birder's tour; don inline skates; board a rowboat, gondola, or horse-drawn carriage; or hire one of the city's bicycle-powered pedicabs. There's a wonderful urban zoo, playgrounds, children's petting zoo, great hotdogs, a historic **Carousel,** free outdoor movies, concerts, dance performances, incredible dog-watching, and two ice skating rinks (one becomes a pool in summer, but it's way too crowded to really enjoy). The

Central Park Visitor's Center, located mid-park around 65th Street, can provide information on current park programs.

The High Line, originally a nineteenth-century elevated freight line, reopened as a park in June 2009. This creative public space runs from Gansevoort to 20th Street in Manhattan's Chelsea neighborhood and affords strolling families unparalleled Hudson River and skyline views. Keep in mind that each of the boroughs has its own major parks, and Brooklyn, Queens, and **Governor's Island** have waterfront promenades with **Manhattan skyline views.** For the best beaches, locals take the subway to **The Rockaways** in Queens or to the famous **Coney Island** in Brooklyn. Its boardwalk, amusement park, and the original Nathan's hotdog stand are still there.

If **Wall Street** makes New York City a financial capital and **Broadway** makes it a performing arts mecca, then surely **Times Square** makes it the tops in fun. Running from 42nd to 48th Streets along Broadway (closed to traffic) and 7th Avenues are an amazing array of electronic displays, themed shops with costumed mascots out front, wild street performers, celebrities grabbing lunch, sleight-of-hand hustlers, and favorite kids' attractions such as **MTV,** the **Toys"R"Us** megastore with its own Ferris wheel, **Madame Tussaud's,** the **Disney Theatre,** and nearby the **Intrepid Sea-Air-Space Museum** moored in the Hudson.

FUN FACTS

New York has a $5 billion film and TV industry. To see a little bit of Hollywood in the Big Apple, join a themed tour and see where "Law & Order," "Friends," "Spider-Man," and more were filmed, or order tickets to live shows such as "The Today Show," MTV, "Saturday Night Live," "The Daily Show with Jon Stewart," and others by requesting them through each network's website.

Although we think New York is a great family destination, the city can be overwhelming. We suggest beginning your trip with a guided tour to get your bearings; several competitors sell two-day hop-on, hop-off **double-decker bus tours** with multilingual guided narration. A totally free option is **The Big Apple Greeters,** local volunteers (usually with big personalities) who take you around to sites of your choice and introduce the cheap forms of public transportation. **Sightseeing cruises** are a popular alternative, especially in New York's hot and humid summers. Some favorites include an amphibious truck-boat tour, a super-speed boat cruise on the Hudson River, a bright yellow water taxi, and—of course, the granddaddy of all—**The Circle Line** three-hour humorously narrated tour of Manhattan.

NYC & Company Official NYC Visitor Information
212-484-1200
www.nycgo.com, www.nyc.gov/visitors

Philadelphia, Pennsylvania

The Liberty Bell and deliciously famous cheese steaks aren't the only reason to visit Philadelphia. Founded in 1669, the city is a sightseeing dream for families.

Your kids are sure to enjoy an entertaining (and little do they know, educational) trip to The City of Brotherly Love. Whether exploring colonial history or mimicking Rocky Balboa by running up the steps of the **Philadelphia Museum of Art,** Philly has always been a great family destination. Getting around is easy, too. **Philadelphia Trolley Works** runs guided tours of all the landmarks in this compact city with an all-day hop-on and -off option.

A walking tour through the **Old City** is the best way for the family to gather an impression of Colonial Philadelphia. **Franklin Court,** an unusual subterranean museum built under the excavated remains of Benjamin Franklin's first permanent home, offers insights into his life and the inspirations for his many inventions. You can meet "Betsy" at the **Betsy Ross House**—and, in summertime, look for the costumed re-enactors at free storytelling benches at 13 locations around Historic Philadelphia.

The **Independence National Historical Park,** in the heart of the Old City, is the site of the **Liberty Bell** and **Independence Hall,** where the Declaration of Independence was debated and adopted and the United States Constitution was signed by the Founding Fathers. Older kids will enjoy the evening **Lights of Liberty,** a light-and-sound show in which they can trade iPods for headsets and walk around the illuminated monuments while listening to recreations of key moments during the nation's founding.

FELLOW TRAVELERS SAY ...

"We toured Independence Hall and the Liberty Bell. These were actually pretty cool places, and our tour guide managed not to bore us to death. I was expecting the Liberty Bell to be this huge, grand, spectacle, but in fact, it is just a normal-looking bell with a crack. When you imagine these things while reading textbooks, it is completely different than when seeing it in real life ... it was a lot more fun and exciting than I expected."

—H. B., www.travelBIGO.com

The contemporary **National Constitution Center** honors and explains America's guiding document through engaging multimedia exhibits and artifacts. **The National Liberty Museum** is an interactive showplace featuring 350 exhibits about famous American heroes. Kids can even practice for their constitutional right in a simulated voting machine designed with them in mind.

The newest historic sites to open on Independence Mall are the **President's House Commemorative Site,** which features the remains of the home where U.S. Presidents George Washington and John Adams lived with nine house slaves who served them while in office, and the **National Museum of American Jewish History,** which chronicles the lives of American Jews throughout U.S. history.

The magnificent 642-room **City Hall**—the largest, tallest, and most expensive city hall in the country—is well worth a visit. A golden 37-foot-tall statue of William Penn, city founder, prominent Quaker, and champion of democracy, tops the hall. Until 1987, when a modern skyscraper rose nearby, there was an agreement that no building should be taller than the top of Willy Penn's head. Today, center-city Philadelphia is known for its outstanding contemporary architecture and the creative reuse of its many National Historic Landmark buildings.

Another icon, historic **Reading Terminal Market** (established in 1892), is the place for families on a budget to sample diverse gastronomic pleasures—from cheese steaks to Bassetts ice cream to Amish pretzels with mustard—in food-obsessed Philly. It's fun to roam the more than 80 food stalls and peruse shops selling funky jewelry and crafts.

FUN FACTS

In 2003, Oprah Winfrey declared **Delilah's** Mac 'n' Cheese (made from scratch with Gruyère and Asiago cheeses) to be the best in America. Once you get a table at this Reading Terminal Market stall, be sure to have Delilah's fried chicken, Virginia ham, collard greens, banana pudding, and—our favorite—homemade strawberry lemonade.

Even if your kids haven't studied American History 101 yet, Philly offers many fun attractions bound to engage children of all ages. Our youngest loves the **Please Touch Museum,** designed for children ages 7 and younger. Its new location in Memorial Hall, Fairmount Park, is spectacular, and the toddler play areas have tripled in size. **The historic Philadelphia Zoo,** quite a walk away in Fairmount Park, is home to 1,700 animals and has a toddler-friendly Children's Zoo.

After your visit to the zoo, stroll over to Boathouse Row and watch the dozens of rowing crews plying the Schuylkill (pronounced SKOO-kul) as well as the park's **Waterworks,** a National Historic Engineering Landmark and the first steam-pumping station of its kind in the United States.

Budding scientists will be blown away at the **Franklin Institute of Science Museum,** dedicated to one of the city's most famous minds. Exhibits include a walk-through human heart and the chance to sit in the cockpit of a T-33 jet trainer. Outside, the Science Park has a fun, interactive play area.

At the **Academy of Natural Sciences,** kids will love the vast collection of dinosaur bones and fossils, including the T. Rex and its larger challenger, Giganotosaurus. Kids can even search for real fossils at the "dig." You can explore the nautical world at the **Independence Seaport Museum,** offering model ships, wartime memorabilia, and submarine tours along the Delaware River.

Two unusual museums for school-age children include the **Mutter Museum,** an incredible (if gory) collection of preserved brains, body parts, medical exhibits, and artifacts that span the history of medical science; and the **Mummers Museum,** devoted to the extravagantly costumed Mummers who parade up Broad Street every year on New Year's Day. Kids are encouraged to compose their own push-button medleys and dance in their own parade.

Philadelphia Convention and Visitors Bureau
215-636-3300
www.philadelphiausa.travel, www.visitphilly.com

Pittsburgh, Pennsylvania

Formed at the head of three rivers snaking through the Pennsylvania hills, the City of Steel rivals its sister metropolis, Philadelphia, in cultural diversity, museum attractions, shopping, and cuisine.

Pittsburgh's East side is a culinary wonderland for the hungry tourist—particularly the **Strip District** area, where shop after shop produces sumptuous and inviting smells of local and not-so-local eats. Once spanned by industrial and warehouse spaces, the Strip District today features trendy nightclubs, open-air food stalls, and small restaurants including the famous **Primanti Brothers,** where sandwiches the size of your face are packed with French fries, coleslaw, and almost every topping imaginable. After refueling, you can shop for all manner of goods including vibrant, hand-woven Peruvian tapestries and wood-carved Dia de los Muertos figurines. Located north of the Strip District in Lawrenceville (or *Lola* to its residents), this recently up-and-coming section features the **16:62 Design Zone,** a 56-block area full of shops with unique home furnishings, antiques, and objets d'art.

FUN FACTS

The phrase, "Don't throw the baby out with the bath water" purportedly originated at the **Lawrenceville Bath House,** where area residents would form a line to wash up: men first, women and children next, and then babies. By the time the babies would reach the bathhouse to be washed, the much-used water would be so dirty that they could hardly be seen, thus the phrase was born.

Entering the heart of the East Side toward the **University of Pittsburgh** and **Carnegie Mellon University,** the **Carnegie Museum of Natural History** allows curious guests to touch an ancient dinosaur bone, explore room after room of dazzling rocks and gemstones, and climb into a massive, vibrating replica of a whale's heart. At the **Pittsburgh Zoo & PPG Aquarium,** watch as polar bears dive and gracefully swim past the huge aquarium tank window. Plan to spend a portion of your day at the **Phipps Conservatory and Botanical Gardens,** featuring a maze of trees and plants interspersed with beautiful hand-blown glass sculptures by Dale Chihuly.

Across the Allegheny River on the north side of the city, Pittsburgh's downtown **Cultural District** has five theaters—including the grand **Benedum Center for the Performing Arts** and **Heinz Hall**—for live performances of ballet, theater, opera, Broadway, symphony, and contemporary dance. Sports fans can gawk at the impressive **Heinz Field** and **PNC Park**—home to the Steelers and the Pirates—while the more artsy types may do their own gawking at retro paintings and unusual portraits at the **Andy Warhol** and **Mattress Factory** museums. Nearby, the **Pittsburgh Children's Museum** provides a full day's worth of entertainment with its many high-tech learning activities as well as a floor reserved entirely for aquatics. Also on the north side, the **National Aviary** allows kids to learn about the facility's collection of more than 500 rare birds and even features an African Penguin exhibit; its Kids' View Tube gives children a unique underwater perspective and even lets them pop up between the penguins in domed bubbles.

While the steel mill is certainly an iconic Pittsburgh image with which we can all identify, the south end of Pittsburgh possesses the famous **Duquesne Incline,** commanding a spectacular view of the city from Mt. Washington. Farther southeast from the incline along the **Monongahela River,** the area along East Carson Street known as the **South Side Works** is home to a movie theater and countless bars, restaurants, and specialty stores. If shopping is your thing, **Station Square** has all you need for Steelers apparel, jewelry, and more. Next to a promenade featuring rainbow-colored flowing fountains and sitting areas with riverside views of the city, the

Hard Rock Café is a fun place to grab some grub and take in rock-and-roll memorabilia lining the walls. For those seeking a thrill or two, the summer months bring to life the area's amusement parks, **Kennywood** and **Sandcastle Waterpark**—both located farther down on the south side along the Monongahela River.

While public buses and the city's subway, the T, are great ways to get around the city, all sorts of guided tours are available, including the amphibious **Just Ducky Tours** for the kids, historic **Trolley Tours** downtown, and scenic rides on the *Gateway Clipper* sightseeing paddle wheeler.

FUN FACTS

During your visit, be on the lookout for the locally renowned dialect of Pittsburgh's long-time residents, known as Yinzers. Speakers use the expression "yinz" just as a Southerner uses "y'all" (for example, "Are *yinz* goin' downtown?").

Greater Pittsburgh Convention & Visitors Bureau
1-800-359-0758
www.visitpittsburgh.com, www.pavisnet.com/allegheny/

Washington, D.C.

Washington, D.C., capital of the United States and keeper of its past and future, has never been as exciting for family visitors as with Barack Obama serving as its 44th President.

Whether your family wants to explore some of the best museums in the nation, experience grand monuments that commemorate past leaders, or simply discover the metropolis that is the heart of the U.S. government, you can do much of it for free—because tax dollars support what goes on in D.C.

You can see 1600 Pennsylvania Avenue from afar, but interior tours of **The White House** are only conducted twice daily Tuesdays through Saturdays. After a post–September 11, 2001, boost in security, The White House requires groups to submit a request six months in advance through their congressional representative. If you are lucky enough to get clearance, marvel at the beautiful assortment of furniture and art that has been collected by first families for more than 200 years. And of course, marvel at being inside The White House!

At the **National Archives,** get some face time with the documents that serve as the backbone of U.S. democracy. In the Rotunda of the Exhibition Hall are the Charters of Freedom: the Declaration of Independence, the Constitution, and the Bill of Rights. For anyone who has spent time studying the early history of the U.S. government, this can be a stirring experience.

If you need to convince your kids to go to any of the 17 **Smithsonian Museums** that are sprinkled throughout the city (all easily accessible by the great Metro system), just mention the Ben Stiller comedy *Night at the Museum: Battle of the Smithsonian.* A favorite of those interested in planes or space travel is the National Air and Space Museum. From the 1903 Wright Brothers flyer to the *Apollo 11* command module, you'll see tons of fun and interactive exhibits. After more than 15 years of planning, the National Museum of the American Indian presents a fascinating exploration of Native American struggles, with displays of artifacts documenting their lives. Although not exactly a museum, the **National Zoo** is also a member of the Smithsonian Institute. Established in 1889, the zoo is home to more than 2,000 animals of 400 different species—many rare or endangered, including the Giant Panda.

Washington's beautiful monuments honor the heroes of our nation, and there are hundreds of memorials in all shapes and sizes scattered throughout the city. Our two favorites are centrally located on the Mall. The **Washington Monument** rises 555 feet above ground, and a quick elevator ride to the observation deck offers a magnificent view of the entire city. To the east, across the **Reflecting Pool** and the **National World War II Memorial,** is the stunning neo-classical structure that surrounds a larger-than-life statue of one of our nation's most beloved men, Abraham Lincoln. The grandeur of the **Lincoln Memorial** seldom fails to render visitors silent for a few moments. Inside, read the Gettysburg Address inscribed in the limestone structure—and be sure to look closely at Lincoln's head. (Occasionally, birds make their nests upon it.)

If your family takes an interest in Lincoln, head to **Ford's Theatre,** the site where John Wilkes Booth assassinated the nation's sixteenth president on April 14, 1865. In the basement of the theater, a small museum contains a variety of historic artifacts and interactive exhibits that illustrate Lincoln's presidency and the Civil War. Across the street is the Petersen House, where Lincoln died hours after being shot.

Although technically located outside D.C., **Arlington National Cemetery** is a must-see for all visitors to our nation's capital. As the resting place for more than 300,000 American citizens, it includes veterans from every war (Revolutionary through Iraq). Overlooking the Potomac River, the most popular stops include the Kennedy graves, the Tomb of the Unknowns where visitors can watch the changing of the guard, and Robert E. Lee's former residence, Arlington House. The grounds are spread over 200 acres, so families may want to take a guided trolley tour to limit walking.

If time permits, kids will love to see where money comes from at the **Bureau of Engraving and Printing.** Another favorite is the **Postal Museum,** where they can climb aboard an original Pony Express mail wagon. Among hundreds of commercial attractions, the **International Spy Museum** and the **Newseum** are most fun for families interested in contemporary culture with kids older than eight. Keep in mind that weekends and summertime, when the legislature is out of session, are the best value times to visit.

Washington, D.C. Convention and Tourism Corporation
1-800-422-8644
www.washington.org, www.washingtonpost.com/gog/dc-visitors-guide.html

Cultural Appeal

In This Chapter

- Cooperstown, birthplace of America's favorite pastime
- Vermont's most famous ice cream factory
- L.L. Bean's family-friendly store and more
- Marine life and seafaring history in Mystic Seaport
- Pennsylvania's Amish strongholds

The Northeast is the cradle of American culture as we know it today, but in addition to all the history and monuments to democracy, this region boasts some really offbeat and unusual attractions. Use the map at the beginning of this part to plot your road trip carefully, and you can weave in some fun, kid-friendly breaks on your way between historical destinations. You'll be a hero with the backseat crowd.

Baseball Hall of Fame, Cooperstown, New York

There's no fan attraction in the same league as the **National Baseball Hall of Fame,** a stadium-size, multimedia showcase for the personal memorabilia of baseball's greats. The museum was built in an era when Abner Doubleday's nearby field was thought to be the birthplace of America's favorite pastime—a claim no one defends anymore. Nonetheless, Cooperstown remains a magnet for Little

Leaguers around the world who imagine themselves being inducted into the Hall of Fame's hallowed halls.

Your littlest ones will enjoy **The Sandlot Kid's Clubhouse,** where chairs are shaped like baseball mitts and loaner books on baseball abound. You'll find the requisite video screens showcasing famous plays in famous games as well as hands-on exhibits where kids can push a button, swing a bat, or admire collectible baseball cards. **The "Baseball at the Movies" exhibit**—where most nonfans will linger—documents more than 150 Hollywood films about the sport. A permanent exhibit about Hank Aaron, from childhood through his stellar Major League and post-baseball career, opened in 2009 to much acclaim. The big Baseball Hall of Fame gift shop is packed with MLB merchandise, but you may prefer to send the kids out to Main Street to browse the dozens of baseball card shops, where a little allowance goes a long way toward beginning their collection.

FELLOW TRAVELERS SAY ...

"Now, most people think of New York and immediately think dirty city, but Cooperstown made me realize that New York also contains an immense amount of beautiful landscape."

— R. P., www.travelBIGO.com

Cooperstown itself is a walkable village surrounded by "gentleman" farms located in central New York's scenic Leatherstocking Region. Plan a weekend at any time of year to visit the Farmers Museum, a recreation of an 1845 farmstead where delightfully tiny "heritage" animals are bred for history museums around the country. The **Fenimore Art Museum,** once the estate of James Fenimore Cooper (author of *The Last of the Mohicans,* set in this area) has an impressive collection of American art. In summer, when mobs crowd the sightseeing trolleys, you can head to **Lake Otesaga** for a swim or picnic on the grounds of the world-famous **Glimmerglass Opera** and catch a performance.

While locals refer to the wide variety of visitors as the "Cabernet Sauvignons versus the Budweiser Crowd," we think any type of family will fall under Cooperstown's small-town spell. Note that the annual HOF Induction Weekend, usually in late July, is the most crowded and most expensive time of year to visit.

National Baseball Hall of Fame and Museum
25 Main Street
Cooperstown, NY 13326
1-888-HALL-OF-FAME
www.baseballhall.org, www.thisiscooperstown.com

Ben & Jerry's and the Green Mountains of Vermont

What family doesn't love **Ben & Jerry's,** the all-natural ice cream with wildly imaginative mixings that are constantly evolving with the times? From the folks who brought you flavors such as Cherry Garcia (vanilla whipped with nuts and cherries in honor of The Grateful Dead's Jerry Garcia) and Chocolate Chip Cookie Dough came Hubby Hubby (peanut butter cookie dough with fudge and pretzels) to celebrate Vermont's same-sex marriage law. Here's your chance to go behind the scenes, see how ice cream is made, and meet the cows who make it possible. And everyone who takes the tour of Ben & Jerry's Waterbury, Vermont, factory gets a sample.

The Ben & Jerry's guided factory tour, one of the top tourist attractions in the state, takes less than an hour. First comes a short film introducing founders Ben Cohen and Jerry Greenfield, who turned a $5 correspondence course on ice cream making into a very successful, socially conscious business (now owned by Unilever). From the glassed-in mezzanine, you'll be able to see the shiny steel vats churning away as a guide explains how ice cream is produced. Try to visit weekdays when flavors are being made; weekend tours rely on an entertaining video to explain the process. Last stop is the **Flavoroom** for samples of the day's ice cream.

This is a fun half-day outing for kids and adults. A gift shop stocks an amazing array of cow-themed items. Outside the factory, there's a shop selling ice cream (of course) and other refreshments, a playground, cows in the pasture, a picnic area, and a coloring station.

Kids can color a postcard and write home about their visit, then join the adults for a nostalgic tour to honor the departed victims of poor mixing and marketing in the Flavor Graveyard.

FUN FACTS

Founded more than three decades ago, Ben & Jerry's continues to operate according to its mission statement, which emphasizes product quality, economic reward, and a commitment to the community. How can you not buy a scoop from the company that says, "Our focus is on children and families, the environment, and sustainable agriculture on family farms"?

If you like peaceful country roads, use Ben & Jerry's as a stop on an extended road trip in the region. Other stops in Waterbury include the **Cold Hollow Cider Mill,** where you can watch cider being pressed, and the **Waterbury Center State Park** where, if the weather is nice, you can get some lakefront "beach" time. In summer, the lush Green Mountains attract families to its many lakes, fishing streams, and mountain biking and hiking trails. In the fall, the two-lane blacktops slow to a crawl with leaf-peepers. Winter brings snow sports fans heading to the three peaks at **Stowe** (a top-notch mountain resort with a funky chic town and gourmet eateries) and **Okemo** (a resort known for its superior kids' skiing and snowboarding schools).

About an hour away, **Burlington** is not only a very fun college town, it's also a great base for visits to the extraordinary American folk and farm arts on display at the **Shelburne Museum;** the amazing flagship **Burton Snowboards shop;** pretty **Lake Champlain;** and the **Vermont Teddy Bear Factory.**

Ben & Jerry's Factory
1281 Waterbury-Stowe Road
Waterbury, VT 05676
1-866-BJ-TOURS
www.benjerry.com, www.vermontvacation.com

L.L. Bean of Freeport, Maine

Legendary outdoor outfitter **L.L. Bean** has had its flagship store on the main street of Freeport, Maine, since 1917, but it is the millions of catalogs sent to homes across America that have made this original shop—with a giant hiking boot guarding the entryway—a mecca for outdoors lovers.

L.L. Bean aims to serve all aspects of the lifestyle embraced by anyone who's into nature. The flagship store reflects this by providing cool ways to test the merchandise as well as weekly musical performances and demonstrations of unusual new tools and camping items. Recognizing how busy today's families are, this huge, multi-wing store is open 24 hours a day, seven days a week, every single day of the year.

L.L. Bean offers activities for every age group, from infant and toddler story times to walking-stick lessons. Free "how-to" clinics are held several times a day on Fridays, Saturdays, and Sundays year-round. If the kids want to learn more about selecting a proper-fitting daypack to carry their schoolbooks, this is the place. The entire family can get tips on pitching tents, starting a campfire, and getting the most from a portable GPS device.

The outdoor outfitter hosts free outdoor concerts, kid-oriented festivals, and one-day adventure clinics where families can learn a new sport or skill. No pre-planning is required; you can walk in and sign up for an inexpensive introductory lesson in kayaking or canoeing, or try cross-country skiing or snowshoeing, as L.L. Bean Walk-On Adventures change seasonally. Most clinics are open to ages 8 and older, but some—like the popular skeet shooting option—require kids to be at least 12. The eight-week Northern Lights Celebration held each winter includes free carriage rides in the parking lot, campfires, and hot chocolate.

Beyond the store, Freeport is one big outlet shopping mall, so we prefer to base a long weekend stay in nearby **Portland,** a culturally rich city that suits families. Plan to spend half days at the wonderful **Children's Museum & Theatre of Maine**—or, with older kids, drop by the **Portland Museum of Art.** Nearby on Monument

Square is a fun indoor public market where local farmers and bakers sell their goods; this is a perfect place to pick up lobster sandwiches and other picnic fare for the family. The market moves outdoors during the summer. **Smiling Hill Farm** is one vendor that welcomes families to visit its 500-acre property, with a petting zoo and ice cream shop to go along with its fresh produce. The old-fashioned **Palace Playland** midway and sandy beach at **Old Orchard Beach** make for a fun and inexpensive summertime outing.

L.L. Bean
95 Main Street
Freeport, Maine 04033
1-877-755-2326
www.llbean.com, www.visitmaine.com

Mystic Seaport and Essex, Connecticut

Founded in 1654, the seafaring town of Mystic was once the shipbuilding capital of New England. Although those days are gone, quintessential Mystic still boasts its historic old charms. We love to visit the 19-acre **Mystic Seaport: The Museum of America and Sea,** the largest maritime museum in the nation. It's chock-full of hands-on, interactive displays, and children love to climb aboard any of the historic ships on display.

For an added fee, families can sail along the Mystic River on the 102-year-old *Sabino,* one of the world's oldest coal-fired wooden steamboats. Or you can observe ship restoration up close in the Preservation Yard, where the 340-ton *Charles W. Morgan,* the world's last wooden whaling ship, is getting a makeover.

FUN FACTS

Connecticut's long history with the sea includes the *Amistad* incident of 1839, which began when 53 West Africans who had been illegally kidnapped were sold as slaves in Cuba. In transit to a sugar plantation, the captive Africans seized their ship, the cargo schooner *La Amistad,* which was eventually towed to New London, Connecticut, where the Africans were jailed. Former President John Quincy Adams eloquently argued their case before the Supreme Court, and two years later the 35 who survived were freed and returned to Africa.

When director Steven Spielberg chronicled this historic event in *Amistad,* he filmed scenes set in the ship's hold in the blubber room of the Mystic Seaport whaler, *Charles W. Morgan.* Today, *Amistad*—a re-creation of the original and the official state flagship—sails around the world to publicize human rights issues and may be in Mystic when you visit.

Back on land, check out the authentic nineteenth-century seafaring village that features 30 restored buildings. Shops and businesses include a bank, press and printing office, chapel, drugstore, lighthouse, and general store. After exploring the village, the youngest sailors in the family will be happy to know there are plenty of kids-only activities.

At the Discovery Barn, kids eight and older can play old-fashioned card games and learn how captains used flags to communicate at sea. The entire family will enjoy the entertaining 30-minute children's show "Tales of a Whaler" that teaches the basics of whaling. A special children's museum and play area are also on the premises.

Once you've discovered how life was for people living on and by the sea, it's time for kids to learn about marine life underwater at the **Mystic Aquarium.** Featuring nearly 5,000 creatures, the aquarium is home to more than 340 species of marine animals. Exciting exhibits allow guests to get up close and personal with penguins, beluga whales, and exotic fish. With daily feedings and shows performed in the 1,200-seat Marine Theater, families can watch the antics of the sea lions: Coco, Surfer, and Boomerang. Kids can get their hands wet interacting with animals at the Discovery Labs or join the challenge at the adventure-packed XD Motion Theater and learn the darkest secrets of the deep ocean.

After these attractions, families can opt to stroll through the quaint historic streets of Mystic and have a bite to eat at the famous **Mystic Pizza** from Julia Roberts' 1988 film. If you are on a mission to see more of the olden days, head 30 miles west to Essex to check out the **Essex Steam Train and Riverboat.** Take the two and a half–hour journey by rail and sea to witness the gorgeous country landscapes and views of the Connecticut River. As the steam from the train billows overhead, you'll feel as though you have truly traveled back in time to experience original New England.

Mystic Seaport: Museum of America and the Sea
75 Greenmanville Avenue
Mystic, Connecticut 06355
1-888-973-2767
www.mysticseaport.org, www.ctvisit.com

Pennsylvania Dutch Country

The Amish people emigrated from Switzerland to the United States at the end of the seventeenth century to escape religious persecution in their homeland. As German (Deutsch) speakers, those who settled in Lancaster County became known as the Pennsylvania "Dutch." Their population has grown throughout the years, and in several small towns you can witness the simple lifestyle of this traditional community.

Stepping back in time, you will see farmers working the land as their forefathers did, without motorized equipment or modern conveniences. Drive past corn and tobacco fields, classic barns and silos, and see cows grazing on rolling hillsides. Horse-drawn buggies transport the local residents, and roadside farm stands run on the honors system!

FUN FACTS

The Pennsylvania Dutch maintain unique customs they've had since before America's independence. For example, although most of the buggy carriage tops are a somber gray, other colors indicate membership in various clans within the community.

A good place to begin your tour is **The Mennonite Information Center.** This educational center offers an overview of the lives and beliefs of the Amish people in the 30-minute movie, *Who Are the Amish?* and a walk-through exhibit about both the Amish and Mennonite sects. You can take part in informative tours with a local guide and find listings of working farms that rent guest rooms, a real treat for kids, who will enjoy milking the cows and collecting fresh eggs from the chicken coop each morning.

Busy Lancaster is in the heart of Amish Country. Stop at the **Pennsylvania Dutch Visitors Center** for information and maps of this eighteenth-century town. Don't miss the **Central Market,** the country's oldest farmer's market, in operation since the 1730s and held every Tuesday, Friday, and Saturday. Here, you can purchase regional produce, flowers, meats, candies, jams, baked goods, and Amish crafts and meet and speak with farmers, bakers, craftspeople, and their families. A real tot pleaser to let off steam is **Dutch Wonderland,** with its 43 acres of rides, including two kid-friendly coasters and a water play area.

Nearby, in the town of Intercourse, don't miss browsing in **The Old Country Store** for the creations of 300 local Amish and Mennonite craftspeople, including pottery, fabrics, and Amish dolls as well as books about the culture. Upstairs, you'll find **The Quilt Museum,** which exhibits an extraordinary collection of antique (pre-1940) Amish and Mennonite quilts as well as more contemporary creations. The gift shop is a favorite stop for quilters and quilt lovers.

Two other interesting stops are **The Old Candle Barn,** where you can watch old-fashioned candle dipping on a self-guided factory tour, and **Lapp's Coach Shop,** where you can purchase locally made furniture and handcrafted toys, rocking horses, and birdhouses. In Bird-in-Hand, your family can climb onto a horse-drawn Amish carriage at **Abe's Buggy Rides.** This is a fun way to tour the area's farms and explore Lancaster County's Amish history.

In the center of Pennsylvania Dutch Country, the town of Strasburg is a haven for the train buffs in your family. The **Strasburg Railroad,** founded in 1832, became the first tourist railway in the country when it began its operations in 1958. Climb aboard *The Paradise* for a 45-minute, 9-mile ride in restored Victorian-era coaches pulled by a huge coal-burning steam locomotive all the way to Paradise, Pennsylvania. Full-day, hop-on/hop-off passes allow the family to ride several steam trains pulling open-air, dining, lounge, or historic parlor cars. June, September, and December bring special rides on a visiting **Thomas the Tank Engine;** reserve ahead to meet one of the preschool set's most popular heroes.

At the Railroad Museum of Pennsylvania, you can explore the immense **Railroaders Hall,** which contains more than 100 locomotives and rail cars, including a reproduction of the 10-ton John Bull steam engine—the only operational piece of equipment in the museum. The nearby **National Toy Train Museum** is headquarters of the Train Collector's Association, which preserves the five wonderful toy train displays covering locomotive history from the mid-1800s to the present.

Pennsylvania Dutch Country Welcome Center
501 Greenfield Road
Lancaster, PA 17601
1800-PA-DUTCH
www.800padutch.com, www.visitpa.com

At the Beach

In This Chapter

- Cape Cod's beach playground
- Busy boardwalks and fun amusement parks on the Jersey Shore
- Enjoy the nostalgia, discount shopping, and fresh salt air at Rehoboth Beach, Delaware

Granted, the Northeast—with a cold climate during the majority of the year—may not seem like the ideal beach destination. But during the warmer summer months, the shoreline has numerous delightful sandy beaches for your family to discover and enjoy. You can't go wrong escaping to any of the beaches previewed in this chapter.

Cape Cod, Massachusetts

Along the tusk of the rearing mammoth's head that protrudes from Massachusetts' southeast coastline, the **Cape Cod** peninsula invites all families—from the Kennedys to current presidents and day trippers from the mainland—to enjoy its 100-plus beaches, ocean-front sand dunes, and the diverse wildlife of the Cape Cod National Seashore. The majority of the park's most popular features are off Route 6 from **Eastham** to **Provincetown.** Throughout your tour, you will see many examples of the single-story, white clapboard houses with shutters and steep-pitched roofs that define the Cape Cod style.

VACATION PLANNING TIPS

The **Old Harbor Life-Saving Station** in Provincetown, built in 1897, is one of the few surviving life-saving stations. Thursday evenings in summer, it displays rescue equipment and hosts re-enactments by the National Park Service staff of the historic Breeches Buoy rescue drill.

While this region offers an abundance of outdoor recreation—including trail hiking, biking, and water sports—we rate Cape Cod's numerous beaches among the best places in the United States to relax and read a book. Eastern beaches facing the Atlantic boast the biggest (and coldest) surf, while southern **Nantucket Sound**–side beaches enjoy warmer water. Cape Cod's population of 250,000 swells to a million and a half in summer, many heading to popular locations outside the National Seashore boundaries such as **Craigsville Beach** in Centreville and **Harding's Beach** in Chatham.

On the peninsula's west coast facing Cape Cod Bay, **Gray's Beach** in Yarmouth Port and **Paine's Creek Landing and Beach** in Brewster both harbor a diverse collection of coastal plant and marine life, including fiddler and horseshoe crabs. Young children can explore the rock jetties. The **Zooquarium** features sea lion shows, a petting zoo, and hands-on activities. The **Cape Cod Museum of Natural History,** only open in the summer, is located in Brewster.

Just before the "elbow" of the cape turns northward lies **Bass River Beach,** also known as Smuggler's Beach—a swimmers' and boaters' paradise. In addition to bumming around the beach, families can taste the local culture on a cranberry bog tour in **Harwich** or surrounding areas (harvest lasts from mid-September to late October). The Atlantic beaches along the National Seashore's north and east coasts provide a more traditional experience; lifeguards are on duty only from late June to late August. At **Nauset Light Beach,** where families can spot the endangered piping plovers in spring, the **Three Sisters Lighthouses** proudly help mariners differentiate between the **Highland Light** in Truro and the **Chatham Light's Two Towers** to the south.

At the northernmost tip of the cape sits **Head of the Meadow Beach** in Truro, known for its ocean graveyard of old shipwrecks. Part of the Cape Cod National Seashore, this beach reveals picturesque sand dunes and glacial cliffs that exceed heights of 100 feet in some spots. For older kids and adults, the **Off-Road Corridor** from Race Point Lighthouse in Provincetown to Head of the Meadow Beach is a mecca for permitted off-road vehicles; rental cars are not allowed.

Recognized as a top gay- and lesbian-friendly destination, the bustling village of Provincetown features several family beaches, great restaurants, whale-watching excursions, dune tours, and arts festivals. Housing twentieth-century American art collections, the **Provincetown Art Association and Museum** is worth visiting after too many hours in the sun. Families can drive or fly to Cape Cod or catch public buses or ferries between Boston and Provincetown.

Cape Cod Chamber of Commerce
1-888-33-CAPECOD
www.capecodchamber.org, www.massvacation.com/capecod

The Jersey Shore, New Jersey

The 127 miles of gold-sand New Jersey shoreline flirting with the choppy Atlantic offers both busy boardwalks and peaceful quaysides, making it ideal for the entire family. (And you're unlikely to have the squabbles that plagued the cast of the popular MTV reality show *Jersey Shore.*)

Where else to begin your journey than the rock-and-roll town of **Asbury Park?**

FUN FACTS

Asbury Park is just north of Neptune City, the childhood stomping grounds of actors Jack Nicholson (*Mars Attacks!*) and Danny DeVito (*Reno 911: Miami*).

Colorful and alive with the arts, humble Asbury Park attracts music lovers as well as those who simply wish to stroll down the wide-open wooden boardwalk and lie on the beach listening to the sound of the Atlantic surf. A must-visit is the **Stone Pony,** opened in 1974 and better known for being the club where Bruce Springsteen, The Shore's most famous son, made his claim to fame.

For the gamer in the group, make a stop at the boardwalk's **Silverball Pinball Museum,** which has more than 6,000 pinball machines manufactured between 1933 and 1979. Among the wide variety of boardwalk shops, you can try your hand at glass blowing or rest your feet and take in a classic movie at the **ShowRoom.** Some of The Shore's best beaches are in Ocean County along the sliver peninsula that begins just south of Asbury Park at the **Point Pleasant Beach** boardwalk and extends past **Seaside Heights** to **Beach Haven.**

With a two and a half-mile–long boardwalk and eight miles of beach, the barrier island of **Ocean City** has a quaintness that continues to draw generations back to The Shore. For 85 years, **Gillian's Wonderland** has entertained families with rides and games for all ages, while other diversions include miniature golf, go-karts, arcades, and movie theaters. Special events are held throughout the summer at Ocean City's **Music Pier,** making it tough to book one of the small hotels and motels. **Margate,** sharing narrow **Absecon Island** with the famously not-family-oriented gamblers' destination of **Atlantic City,** is home to **Lucy the Elephant,** the 65-foot-tall wooden pachyderm built as a real estate development gimmick back in 1881. Protected on the National Register of Historic Places, she proudly guards the dunes and can be toured daily.

A New Jersey shoreline favorite is the town of **Avalon,** a more upscale destination featuring clean beaches, natural dunes, and a small, well-maintained boardwalk. A stone's throw away, **Wildwood** has options for every generation in the family, whether souvenir shopping along the two-mile boardwalk, spending a day at the boardwalk's water park, or even taking a relaxing ride on a pontoon boat.

FELLOW TRAVELERS SAY …

"There is so much to do on the beach. Wildwood even has a few amusement parks along their boardwalk. To assure a fun vacation with minimal sulking, make a point to let the children have their best friend tag along. Trips are always more fun when spent with a friend."

—N. S., www.travelBIGO.com

The picturesque, well-preserved, Victorian-era **Cape May,** a former whaling town at the southernmost tip of the New Jersey shore, offers scenic sightseeing on the town trolley and a climb up the 199 steps of the poetic **Cape May Lighthouse.** Between April and November (summer months are peak season), whale watchers embark to view whales and dolphins feeding in the coastal waters. **The Nature Center of Cape May** provides year-round natural history programs, including a hands-on Harbor Safari and a butterfly garden tour. When the pastel houses begin to blur and the narrow beach isn't enough, the **Cape May County Park and Zoo** features nearly 200 species of animals and a children's zoo.

Families from New York and Philadelphia drive to towns along the Jersey Shore by following the well-marked Garden State Parkway, but avoid this route on Friday and Sunday evenings. Most housing belongs to locals or weekend homeowners, so visitors will need to plan accommodations well in advance.

New Jersey Tourism
1-800-VISIT-NJ
www.visitmonmouth.com, www.visitnj.org

Rehoboth Beach, Delaware

Part of the Delaware Seashore State Park along the Atlantic Ocean, Rehoboth Beach is a very popular, soft-sand seaside getaway on a barrier island that stretches south through Ocean City, Maryland, and down to Chincoteague Island. Along with **Bethany Beach** and **Dewey Beach,** it is the frequent getaway of city dwellers who yearn to breathe fresh salt air. Rehoboth's appeal is truly nostalgic and cross-generational, as parents return to their favorite childhood spots with their own children. Visitors come from Wilmington, Baltimore, Philadelphia, and especially Washington, D.C.—hence its nickname "The Nation's Summer Capital."

The wide expanse of sand and water makes it a perfect playground for beach lovers. Take out the pails and shovels, and your tiny travelers will be in heaven. Older kids who love jumping in the waves can try to body surf, boogie board, or arrange for a surfing lesson— and the family can go clamming and crabbing together in search of dinner.

Rehoboth Beach boasts a mile-long boardwalk perfect for strolling past oceanfront amusement centers, mini-golf courses, fun souvenir shops, and kid-friendly eateries. Must-dos include buying saltwater taffy and stopping at **Thrasher's French Fries** for fresh, crispy potatoes covered in salt and vinegar—no ketchup allowed! Thrasher's fries are a Delaware tradition, and they're divine. The boardwalk is also the place to arrange boat rentals or to book a day cruise; other activities to look into are fishing, dolphin watching, and bike riding. Nearby **Lake Gerar** offers a nice playground for kids ages 2 to 10 and a fishing bridge for children. Take in the Saturday evening concerts and free movies at the **Rehoboth Beach Bandstand.**

Beyond the T-shirt and souvenir stores are bookstores, eclectic shops, and galleries specializing in handmade soaps, jewelry, specialty food items, and nautical-themed memorabilia. For serious shoppers, **Tanger Outlets** operates three separate malls in and around Rehoboth.

After a day at the beach, when everyone has showered the sand from their bathing suits, head to **Funland** for an old-fashioned good time. Its 18 rides, midway games, and an arcade with pinball and video machines will keep the kids happy for hours. Also, check out a play at the **Rehoboth Children's Summer Theatre.** Past performances have included *Jack and the Beanstalk* and *Cinderella.*

Rehoboth Beach-Dewey Beach Chamber of Commerce
501 Rehoboth Avenue
Rehoboth Beach, Delaware 11971
1-800-441-1329
www.beach-fun.com, www.rehoboth.com/community/
visitorservices.asp

Amusement Parks

In This Chapter

- All ages enjoy a Kiss at Hershey Park
- Visit Lake Compounce, the oldest American amusement park
- Enjoy Sesame Street's family-friendly thrills

Although the Northeast has never been known for its amusement parks, the region's play lands of pleasure still make for sanity-saving stops on "boring" family road trips. Note that most are open daily between May and October, with extra weekend openings during the shoulder seasons to catch holiday travelers.

Hershey Park, Pennsylvania

Anyone with a sweet tooth in your family will be satisfied in Hershey, Pennsylvania. A factory town founded in 1905 by Milton D. Hershey, the city is synonymous with the Great American Chocolate Bar. As the company grew to be a worldwide confectionery sensation, the town—with street names such as Chocolate and Cocoa avenues—has been transformed into a family destination with a sweet theme park.

Originally established in 1907 for factory employees to relax and picnic, **Hershey Park** now features more than 65 attractions. Guests can still enjoy authentic rides from Hershey's beginnings, including a 1919 handcarved carousel as well as Tidal Force, one of the world's largest and tallest splashdown rides. The park also has 11 thrilling roller coasters—Fahrenheit, the newest, boasts a 121-foot drop at a 97-degree angle—and younger children can hop on any of 20 kiddie rides. The entire family will love the Boardwalk, which has everything from the Ferris wheel to the Wildmouse to Dippin' Dots ice cream. And animal lovers can wander over to the adjacent ZooAmerica, which is included in admission to Hershey Park.

For many, the real motive for visiting Hershey is the milky Hershey confections. **Hershey's Chocolate World** offers a free tour that shows how tiny cacao beans are transformed into bars of chocolate. For an even more chocolaty experience, spend time with Hershey's resident bonbon expert Dr. Livingston McNib for an interactive chocolate-tasting experience. When you've completed all courses, you will receive a Master's in Chocolate Tasting from Hershey University.

The Hershey Story museum focuses on the history of the Hershey company. Inside, the Chocolate Lab gives visitors hands-on experience in making treats during which you can sample chocolate from Africa, Indonesia, and Mexico. While the kids are on their sugar high, take them on the guided **Hershey Trolley Works.** The singing conductor might be a bit hokey, but that's part of the fun as you tour around town in an old-fashioned trolley and look for the town's famous Kiss-shaped street lamps. Kids age 13 and older can accompany Mom to the day spa for a fruity facial or mani-pedi while she enjoys a chocolate massage.

Hershey Park
100 W. Hersheypark Drive
Hershey, PA 17033
1-800-HERSHEY
www.hersheypa.com

TRAVELERS BEWARE!

Families pushing strollers should know that Hershey Park is pretty hilly with lots of little inclines. A backpack or front child carrier will make it easier to tote little ones.

Lake Compounce, Connecticut

The nation's oldest amusement park, **Lake Compounce** in Bristol, Connecticut, has been in continuous operation since 1846 when then-owner, Gad Norton, conducted electricity experiments on the 23-acre lake. The event was well-publicized, and although the science aspect failed in the end, thousands of spectators came to witness Norton's demonstration. Once the property was open to the public, there was no stopping the crowds who came to swim and enjoy concerts in the lakeside gazebo. We love the authentic 1911 open-air trolley, the antique carousel, and the Wildcat, a wooden coaster that has been running in the park since 1927.

Don't let Lake Compounce's age fool you. The park's management has invested upward of $40 million in renovations and construction, making the 407-acre park as good as new with more than 50 rides and attractions. Voted the "World's #1 Wooden Rollercoaster," Boulder Dash reaches speeds of 65 mph and boasts a 115-foot drop. Thunder N' Lightning is a giant two-arm swing that catapults riders with four Gs of force. Much less extreme is Zoomer's Gas n' Go, a mini-Corvette ride that transports the entire family back to 1950s with drive-in movies and period gas stations and billboards.

Garfield's Circus World is dedicated to kids ages 3 to 10. Little ones can take a ride on the Caterpillar Train, fall from the sky in the mini Drop Zone, or soar above with the Flying Elephants. If your kids want to grow up fast, take them on miniature versions of Lake Compounce's bigger rides, including the kiddie coaster the Wildkitten.

The outdoor Splash Harbor water park features more than 15 water attractions, including a 60-foot New England lighthouse, slippery waterslides, tube rides, a wave pool, and other wet delights. And when it's time to unwind, the 800-foot lazy river is the perfect spot to take it easy.

Lake Compounce is only 20 miles from **Hartford** or 30 miles from **New Haven,** so most families come for the day. A Halloween favorite is the Haunted Graveyard. Only for the bravest family members, the spook-fest is New England's largest and features six haunted houses connected by terrifying trails. Our favorite feature at this park is the free soda—all day, every day, with unlimited refills—that will keep the thirsty kids (and your wallet) happy.

Lake Compounce Family Theme Park
822 Lake Avenue
Bristol, CT 06010
860-583-3300
www.lakecompounce.com, www.ctvisit.com

Sesame Place, Pennsylvania

We can tell you how to get, how to get to **Sesame Place**—the 14-acre water park located in Bucks County. Embracing the likes of Elmo, Big Bird, Bert, Ernie, and other famous characters from the much-loved PBS children's television show, Sesame Place brings *Sesame Street* to life for the entire family. Whether drifting down Big Bird's Rambling River or splashing around in the Teeny Tiny Tidal Waves, the park offers parents and kids alike a happy dose of fun.

Sesame Place is famous for its attractions designed especially for youngsters age 6 and under. Ernie has an interactive wet adventure where the little ones can crawl, jump, and play in water-spraying mazes. Cookie Mountain, a bright vinyl cone that may look puny to adults, is fun for little ones to scale; toddlers feel like champions once they reach the top. At Ernie's Bed Bounce, you can let the kids go crazy leaping on a huge mattress. And for the babies, the Rubber Duckie Pond is a shallow pool with a safe miniature slide.

The entire family can enjoy many rides together. At Elmo's World, families can explore a garden of giggles, venture into space, or climb aboard Elmo's Flyin' Fish. From Big Bird's 40-foot high balloon tower, families can see all the rides as they soar above the park. For those who love to get wet, there are plenty of waterslides—some perfect for a parent and child to ride together in a double tube. The Count's Splash Castle is a multi-level, interactive water play area with a 1,000-gallon tipping bucket, multiple waterslides, and 90 more features.

After exploring the famous neighborhood and Bert and Ernie's house at 123 Sesame Street, stop by one of the entertaining shows going on throughout the day. Meet the newest Sesame Place neighbor, Abby Cadabby, in her Treasure Hunt Show, hang out with Big Bird, or watch the entire *Sesame Street* cast prance down the street in the Rock Around the Block parade.

Dozens of nearby hotels sell weekend packages, and the great family-friendly city of **Philadelphia** (see Chapter 1) is just a half hour away.

Sesame Place
100 Sesame Road
Langhorne, PA 19047
215-752-7070
www.sesameplace.com, www.visitphilly.com

Outdoor Adventures

In This Chapter

- Acadia National Park's seaside cliffs and beaches
- Deep Creek Lake, a mid-Atlantic hidden gem
- The great outdoors Adirondack-style
- Playing in the Poconos
- The Granite State's White Mountains

The Pilgrims knew what they were doing when they turned north from Virginia to build the first settlement in the beautiful landscape of the northeastern part of the continent. From the harsh winds off Maine's Acadia National Park to the funky paintball play areas in the Poconos, you'll find scenic and fun outdoor adventures to suit every type of family and every age group.

Even if you'd prefer to stay in the minivan and tour the outlet malls or ride the subways and immerse yourself in great art, your fellow travelers in the backseat will relish a chance to get out into the great outdoors. In this chapter, we share our family's best destinations to let off steam and reconnect with nature.

Acadia National Park, Maine

The oldest national park east of the Mississippi, Acadia attracts families with its rugged beauty, crashing Atlantic Ocean surf, pine-clad granite peaks, and quaint New England villages. Of the park's 47,000 diverse acres, more than 30,000 are on **Mount Desert Island,** with much smaller parcels on Isle au Haut and the Schoodic Peninsula. Motorized vehicles are not permitted within the park, so you'll have to catch the **Island Explorer** propane-fueled bus (which runs along the coast from late June to October), hike or bike in, or take a horse-drawn carriage ride from one of the inns within its border.

If you're not camping, plan to settle in one of the many cozy B&Bs in **Bar Harbor** on Mt. Desert's eastern shore. You can make day trips to hike, photograph the striking tide pools that form near the shore, or mountain bike (rental bike shops are in town) along the park's 55 miles of carriage roads. Within Bar Harbor, families will find tasteful souvenir shops, restaurants featuring the state's famous lobster, a movie theatre, some museums, and a lot of small-town charm.

TRAVELERS BEWARE!

In summer, temperatures vary from 45°F to 85°F. Don't tell the kids this is a beach vacation! The park's craggy coastline leads to beautiful sand beaches, but the Atlantic is rough and freezing; swimming is only for the hardy.

In winter, fog and snow are common. The park remains open year-round, but most ranger-led facilities operate only from mid-May to mid-October. Although certain roads close when icy, snowmobiling and cross-country skiing are becoming popular winter activities in the park.

Acadia is known for its 120 miles of historic hiking trails, many cut by local outdoorsmen at the turn of the century. The stonework along their borders, as well as stone-lined carriage ways built by John D. Rockefeller, Jr. for the pleasure of riders, is well preserved and adds a measure of Old World dignity not found in any other national park. Hikers will find trails through the pine and spruce forests, ranging from easy to challenging. Experienced hikers may want to climb up to the steep slopes of **Cadillac Mountain** (1,530 feet), the highest point on the U.S. Atlantic coast; those with less experience can join rock-climbing classes.

Park rangers lead their own kid-friendly hikes and children's programs. Boat tours and excursions for whale watching, sailing, canoeing, or sea kayaking are best suited to older children. Backcountry camping is not allowed in Acadia, so if you're hoping to pitch a tent, you'll have to book a site in **Blackwoods** or the **Seawall Campground** months in advance (or even longer for summer weekend visits). For more information, stop by the Visitor Center (open April 15 through October) or pick up a copy of the park's free newspaper, *The Beaver Log.*

Acadia National Park
National Park Service
www.nps.gov/acad, www.visitmaine.com

Deep Creek Lake, Maryland

Sharing a mile-long stretch of shoreline with a state park, the man-made Deep Creek Lake in the narrow panhandle of Maryland offers a perfect combination of mountains and sea for a wide variety of outdoor activities. For experienced boaters, several companies at the **Deep Creek Marina** offer boat rentals (with lifejackets for all ages) on a first-come, first-served basis. Although it can get rather pricey, a relaxing day with the family spent on a Pontoon Bayliner or a wild ride on one of the many ski boats is worth the expense. There's more fun to be had on rental inner tubes, wakeboards, and other water toys, but make your rental reservations months in advance.

Hike **Deep Creek Lake State Park's** winding trails under the shade of large oak and hickory trees, explore the area, and try to spot a number of indigenous mammals including raccoons, opossum, and—for the occasional unlucky trekker—skunks. At the **Deep Creek Lake Discovery Center,** located at the southernmost tip of the forest, kids can become nature specialists and discover the area's countless critters and plant life in one of the center's learning programs. For an even deeper immersion, outfitters such as **Camp Earth** provide guided hikes, kayak tours, farm tours, and photography workshops with on-site naturalists.

FUN FACTS

In the summertime, visitors can climb the steps of the 90-foot **Thayerville Fire Tower,** installed in 1921 as one of the first fire towers in the state. It's also the last in operation, making the ranger-led tour of its tower especially interesting.

Before the kids begin to gripe and keel over from hiking exhaustion, head west and clop on over to the family-run **Circle R Ranch,** where you'll find beautiful Arabian, Paint, and Belgian horses and expert guides to take your family on an hour-long trail around the farm's old apple orchards. If the kids enjoyed the horse ride, perhaps they'll also like **Husky Power Dogsledding.** This outfitter gives families a personal experience with these energetic canines that pull your sled both through snowy terrain and through grassy hillsides (on wheels) during the off season.

A popular winter destination situated at the northernmost branch of Deep Creek Lake, **Wisp Mountain Resort** offers skiing, snowboarding, snowshoeing, hiking, and snowmobiling. You can even nip down to the lake for a few peaceful hours of ice fishing. Wisp's varied terrain includes kid-friendly bunny slopes as well as more experienced moguls. This popular mid-Atlantic resort also boasts a Frisbee golf course, a skate park, ATV tours, mountain bike trails, paintball, fly fishing, and kayaking. Just a stone's throw away from Wisp Mountain, the ultimate arcade and game park, **Smiley's FunZone,** offers families a chance to let loose with go-kart racing, miniature golf, laser tag, video games, pinball, and more.

Garret County Visitors Bureau
301-387-4386
www.visitdeepcreek.com, www.mdisfun.org

Lake Placid and the Adirondack Mountains

Located in the northernmost part of New York, this six-million-acre **Adirondack Park** mountain region offers a plethora of outdoor activities, scenic sights, and quaint towns with an always-welcoming ambiance. You may be familiar with the Adirondack style: picturesque split-log cabins with stone foundations and dark green shutters; enormous Great Camps with slate roof tiles and lawns bordered by pine forests; stuffed bear sculptures and carved decoy ducks; Native American–patterned wool blankets and coonskin caps; and Teddy Roosevelt seated on a wooden Adirondack chair overlooking **Saranac Lake.**

While each village has its own unique appeal, bustling **Lake Placid** has a relaxed, rustic charm that attracts visitors looking for an easy, old-fashioned escape. Comforts abound, as Lake Placid is home to the Adirondacks' largest array of places to stay, from quiet B&Bs to cozy cabins, trailer parks, and five-star resorts.

Lake Placid's setting around **Mirror** and **Placid Lakes** in the heart of Adirondack Park, a designated wilderness since 1892, means families will find an immense number of year-round activities. Outdoor lovers can choose from a number of attractions, including ice fishing, climbing, skating, hunting, swimming, mountain biking, bob-sledding, snowmobiling, whitewater rafting, hiking, and skiing at **Whiteface** or **Gore.**

Lake Placid was home to two Olympics and has many related venues. The **1932 and 1980 Winter Olympic Center and Museum** displays the legacy of these events in exhibits showcasing videos, athletes' uniforms and equipment, and historical information about the area's Olympic sites. If you're feeling a bit daring and can handle heights, the **Olympic Jumping Complex,** almost immediately visible upon entering the region, allows you to visit the 400-foot-tall ski jump tower and even provides a sky deck for spectators.

The history and arts of this long-established resort are found in the **Adirondack Museum on Blue Mountain,** which features

22 exhibits, restored buildings, extensive painting collections, delicate gardens, and exceptional stories of life, work, and play around **Lake Champlain** and **Lake George.**

FELLOW TRAVELERS SAY ...

"I think the greatest benefit is to be derived from being in the woods in early spring, when the pine, hemlock, and balsam first begin to bud out. I am told that at that time the atmosphere is especially sweet and healing. The fresh, pure, medicinal air of the Adirondacks is the best medicine in the world."

— J. W. F., quoted from "The Adirondacks as a Health Resort," 1886

Keene Valley, a neighboring town, is known for its well-stocked outdoor stores and numerous hiking trails, including the trail to summit **Mt. Marcy,** the highest in the state. (The 46ers Club is for hikers who've scaled all 46 of the park's High Peaks taller than 4,000 feet.) Another nearby town worth visiting is Saranac Lake, known for the winter-time ice castle and summertime boating excursions to spot local wildlife and examine the century-old Great Camps along its shore.

Adirondacks Region Economic Development Office
1-800-487-6867
www.visitadirondacks.com, www.iloveny.com

Pocono Mountains, Pennsylvania

Known to parents and grandparents as a honeymoon destination and to local teens for its paintball and go-kart facilities, the Pocono Mountains in northeastern Pennsylvania are a popular vacation spot. Yet, it was anthracite coal—not tourism—that shaped the area's history as a coal producer, railroad center, and land of opportunity for many European immigrants. In addition to history, the 2,400 square miles named by Native Americans "stream between two mountains" offers families more than 150 lakes, scenic drives, and verdant woodlands for year-round fun.

The rambling Pocono Mountains can be thought of as five distinct sightseeing and recreation areas. The **Upper Delaware River** region has more than 100 miles of trails for hiking, biking, and horseback riding. Summer months invite swimming, canoeing, and rafting along the river rapids and fishing along its banks. In winter, nature lovers and birders observe the area on snowshoes, cross-country skis, or snowmobiles. Spring is an ideal time to discover the state's tallest waterfall, **Raymondskill Falls,** just four feet short of those at Niagara Falls.

Learn about this center of anthracite mining by hiking a bit of the gentle **Delaware & Hudson Canal Towpath,** where rope ferries were once used to shuttle people and supplies between Pennsylvania and New York. The **Delaware Aqueduct** is the nation's oldest existing wire cable suspension bridge. Begun in 1848 to replace the rope ferries, it proved so successful that its designer, engineer John Augustus Roebling, was commissioned to design New York's Brooklyn Bridge.

The Poconos' Lake region is anchored by **Lake Wallenpaupack,** a manmade lake built in 1927. Over its 13-mile length are 6 public recreation areas, hundreds of acres of forest, wildlife, walking trails, campsites, and boat slips. There are also dozens of golf courses and a fun toddler outing, the **Stourbridge Line Rail Excursion.** The Delaware River region, also known as the **Delaware Water Gap National Recreation Area,** boasts 73 miles of prime Class I and II whitewater rapids—making it your family's destination for a refreshing float trip on inner tubes or a gentle, communal romp on a guide-led raft. In inclement weather, the **Pocono Environmental Education Center (PEEC)** has fun discovery programs.

Although most of the newer family resorts are in more rural areas of the Mountain Region, artsy **Stroudsburg** is a commercial center with many quaint B&Bs that welcome young children. Hikers can summit Big Pocono Mountain, then cool off in the Northeast's largest indoor water park resort. A **Great Wolf Lodge** day pass grants access to waterslides, a wave pool, and even an interactive tree house water fort with a dump bucket to soak unsuspecting family members.

The Lehigh River Gorge's hiking trails are part of 4,548-acre **Lehigh Gorge State Park,** well known for its deep gorge with steep walls, thick vegetation, rock outcroppings, and waterfalls. Instead of hiking, kids may prefer a smooth 16-mile riverfront ride aboard the 1920's Lehigh Gorge Scenic Railway. The region's Victorian-era town of **Jim Thorpe,** named for a native son who brought home gold at the 1912 Stockholm Olympics, is a good base to explore some historic sites, museums, and antique shops, and there are many picturesque B&Bs and restored country inns to lay down weary heads at night.

Pocono Mountains Visitors Bureau
1004 Main Street
Stroudsburg, PA 18360
1-800-POCONOS
www.800poconos.com, www.visitpa.com

White Mountains, New Hampshire

In the upper half of New Hampshire lies a quietly hidden treasure of protected wilderness, the **White Mountain National Forest.** Established in 1918, the National Forest has grown to almost 800,000 acres and now draws more than six million visitors each year. The scenery is breathtaking, and the appeal for adventurous families covers all seasons and many activities.

FUN FACTS

The White Mountains are covered with white-bark birch trees in summer and snow in winter, and they're fun to climb for a number of reasons:

- The peaks of the White Mountain's **Presidential Range** are named for Presidents Washington, Monroe, Eisenhower, Jefferson, and a number of other notable Americans (not all presidents).
- The region has 48 mountains at least 4,000-feet-tall.
- **Mt. Washington,** at 6,288 feet, is the tallest in the Northeast, and if you decide to drive the **Mt. Washington Auto Road,** you'll pass through four climate zones and a range of striking scenery.
- The historic (1869) **Mount Washington Cog Railway** to the summit is the second steepest railway in the world. There, take time to explore the **Mount Washington Weather Observatory.**
- Within the park are 1,200 miles of trails, 23 developed campgrounds, six ski touring areas, and four alpine ski areas.

The secret weapon of the White Mountains is the **Appalachian Mountain Club (AMC),** a 144-year-old environmental and educational organization. The AMC has built a remarkable network of lodges and huts, helps maintain miles of trails, and provides organized hikes and activities throughout the area.

AMC Lodges are modern, full-service hotels with dorm rooms for groups, and their staff can help families select age-appropriate lectures and hikes. Wonderful rustic **wilderness huts** are found throughout the far reaches of the trail system and provide bunkhouse-style facilities and hearty meals to weary hikers. Our family likes to start from a lodge (leaving heavier gear behind), then hike hut-to-hut for a few days. The AMC operates shuttle buses that bring hikers from their furthest points back to their point of origin. Reservations are necessary in the summer months for both lodges and huts.

Numerous attractions await outside the White Mountains forest. The 800-foot long **Flume Gorge** in **Franconia Notch State Park** provides a trail through a dramatic narrow chute shared with a raging stream. In summer, you'll also find the **Conway Scenic Railway,** the **Whale's Tale Water Park,** and—at **Attitash ski resort**—the mile-long alpine slide, lift-assisted mountain biking, and more. As you tour the region, don't miss the prosperous and charming town of **Littleton,** home to the amazing **Bishop's Ice Cream** and **Lahout's,** a great outdoor equipment store. North Conway is an outlet store mecca, and **North Woodstock** is another small town with a large variety of good restaurants.

In any season, the **Mount Washington Resort** is a luxurious getaway with stunning views. Built in 1902, it hosted the 1944 Bretton Woods Conference, with delegates from the Allied nations meeting to establish international monetary policy for the post–World War II period. Across the road from the Bretton Woods ski resort, Mount Washington Resort offers a year-round slate of activities, including a zip line, mountain biking, horseback riding, golf, and tennis as well as spa services.

VACATION PLANNING TIPS

Bretton Woods is New Hampshire's largest ski resort, and the extensive selection of beginner and intermediate trails make it an ideal family destination. The bustling town of Lincoln is centrally located between several ski areas, including Loon Mountain, Waterville Valley, and Cannon Mountain—all of which have well-regarded children's programs.

White Mountains
1-603-271-2665
www.visitwhitemountains.com, www.visitnh.gov

The South

For many travelers from outside the United States, the words "The South" will be forever tied to the Civil War that divided the country for much of the nineteenth century. But before and after that war, many generations of tourists had been drawn to the region by its warm climate and natural beauty.

Once the automobile (and later, cheap mass transportation) opened the South to full-scale tourism, the needs of the new American road tripper spawned a myriad of motels, manmade sights, and amusement parks. And Mickey Mouse began to narrow America's North-South divide.

Alabama, Arkansas, Georgia, Kentucky, Louisiana, North Carolina, South Carolina, Tennessee, Virginia, and West Virginia have joined the Sunshine State to attract families to their cities, offbeat cultural attractions, fantastic beaches, famous theme parks, and varied terrain for outdoor adventures.

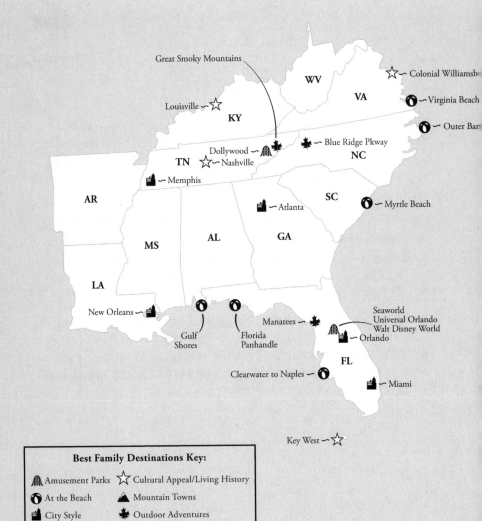

Great Smoky Mountains

WV

VA

Colonial Williamsb

Louisville ~ ☆

KY

Virginia Beach

Outer Bar

Dollywood ~ 🎢 🍁 ~ Blue Ridge Pkwy

TN

☆ ~ Nashville

NC

🏭 ~ Memphis

AR

SC

🏭 ~ Atlanta

Myrtle Beach

MS

AL

GA

LA

New Orleans ~ 🏭

Manatees ~ 🍁

Seaworld
Universal Orlando
Walt Disney World

🎢 ~ Orlando

Gulf
Shores

Florida
Panhandle

FL

Clearwater to Naples ~ 🌊

🏭 ~ Miami

Key West ~ ☆

Best Family Destinations Key:

🎢 Amusement Parks   ☆ Cultural Appeal/Living History

🌊 At the Beach   🍁 Mountain Towns

🏭 City Style   🍁 Outdoor Adventures

City Style

In This Chapter

- Getting to know more about Martin Luther King Jr. and Coca-Cola in peachy Atlanta
- Honoring the Blues, Elvis, and M.L.K. in Memphis
- Embracing Miami's Latin culture, Euro chic, and great beaches
- Living it up in New Orleans
- Going beyond the theme parks in Orlando

The major cities of the Southern United States hold a lot of appeal for families precisely because of their Southern charm and gentle ways. Waitresses say "Good Morning!" and museum guides speak slowly and clearly, albeit sometimes with a drawl. Hotel staffs are friendly, and prices are generally much lower than in other cities such as New York or San Francisco.

So if you're seeking an urban vacation—a destination with great museums, pockets of local culture, fine dining and nightlife, bargain shopping, and a distinctive role in American history—you can't go wrong with Atlanta, Georgia; Memphis, Tennessee; Miami, Florida; New Orleans, Louisiana; or Orlando, Florida.

Atlanta, Georgia

Considered the capital of the South and one of the most cosmopolitan cities in the country, Atlanta is home to two American
legends—Martin Luther King Jr. and Coca-Cola—as well as the
nation's largest aquarium.

The **Martin Luther King Center** on Auburn Avenue, open daily and
free of charge, was founded in 1968 to preserve King's teachings
and memorabilia from his nonviolent movement for peace, justice,
and equality. At his nearby birth home, visitors can peruse family
artifacts, dishes, and period furniture.

FUN FACTS

Auburn Avenue is where Atlanta's once-segregated African American
community set up its own businesses, congregations, and community
centers. The **Sweet Auburn District** is now a National Historic Landmark.
If you have older kids in tow, you can see this area on a fun **Segway tour.**

Coca-Cola, the world's best-known brand, is enshrined at the
recently expanded **World of Coca-Cola,** a surprising collection
of the beverage's worldwide sales and bottling memorabilia dating
back to 1886. There's also a thrilling 4-D theater, interactive displays, works by Andy Warhol and other great artists, and a tasting
experience where visitors can sample nearly 70 different Coca-Cola
products.

The state-of-the-art **Atlanta Aquarium,** with more than 100,000
animals inhabiting 8 million gallons of fresh water and seawater, has
been a sellout since opening. Book ahead and catch a themed Shark
or Penguin Family Tour for an in-depth, behind-the-scenes learning
adventure.

The city's wide cultural appeal ranges from paintings in the **High
Museum of Art** to rap music and broadcast media. The area code
"404" is home to rappers Ludacris, Outkast, Lil John, and TI, all
of whom often appear at local clubs. The world famous Cable News
Network gives a 45-minute **CNN Studio Tour** of its flagship station
that explains how news broadcasts and studio productions work.

Underground Atlanta is an unusual mall built around five downtown blocks that were buried below street level by a 1920s viaduct project. The restored buildings now house restaurants and shops. Sports are big here. Drop by **The Braves Museum,** and for certain games, you might score $1 bleacher tickets to see the Atlanta Braves play at Turner Field.

Atlanta's milder climate makes for outdoor adventures year-round. Most popular with local families is the historic **Stone Mountain Park,** where three Confederate heroes—Confederate President Jefferson Davis, General Robert E. Lee, and Lt. General Thomas "Stonewall" Jackson—are carved into an 825-foot-long granite wall covering 583 acres. You can hike right to the top of Stone Mountain and look over Georgia at 1,683 feet above sea level, then stay after sundown and watch a spectacular laser light show set to your favorite songs dance across the face of the mountain. Within the park's 3,200 acres, families will find swimming, fishing, tennis, golf, and opportunities to meet characters such as SpongeBob and Dora the Explorer.

Lemuel P. Grant gave **Grant Park** to the city in 1883, and in 1889, the Atlanta Zoo was established—followed a few years later by a Cyclorama depicting historical events. Kids will appreciate the park's playground, gazebo, pond, and live entertainment events. Stop at Piedmont Park and learn more about Atlanta's future development on a free, three-hour **Belt Line Tour** that describes how the Belt Line will connect green space, trails, public light-rail transportation, and more through 22 miles of once-abandoned railroads and historic neighborhoods.

FELLOW TRAVELERS SAY ...

"We explored the **Jimmy Carter Museum,** which was one of my favorite places. In the Carter Museum, I read all the events Mr. President Jimmy did in one day; the document was like a time journal. I saw the library where all the documents in Carter's reign are held. One of the displays that fascinated me the most was Carter's involvement in Africa ..."

—B. L., travelBIGO.com

For a day of hiking or leisurely strolls, try the 65-acre **Fernbank Forest** or visit the Fernbank Museum, which offers bird walks and educational strolls. There's also a Science Center and Observatory in the park. **Centennial Olympic Park,** built for the 1996 Centennial Olympics with funds raised by selling 686,000 inscribed bricks, hosts music events almost daily. In the hot, sticky summer, let the kids splash in the Fountain of Rings or the Children's Playground. Just outside town, the **Six Flags Over Georgia** amusement park has a variety of big coasters and a Thomas the Tank Engine–themed kids' area for younger siblings.

Families with children ages 2 to 8 will like **Imagine It! The Children's Museum of Atlanta.** Other toddler attractions can be found at the **Atlanta Botanical Garden,** which has a Dinosaur Garden with fossil digs, and the unique **Center for Puppetry Arts,** a museum full of puppets, including a collection from legendary Jim Henson, creator of the Muppets.

Atlanta Convention & Visitors Bureau
1-800-ATLANTA
www.atlanta.net, www.exploregeorgia.org

Memphis, Tennessee

Memphis is a hoot for a lot of reasons—Elvis, music, Elvis, ducks, Elvis, civil rights, and Elvis. In this Southern town on the banks of the Mississippi River, a rich musical history goes way beyond Elvis and is widely celebrated. Nashville may own country music, but Memphis is the blues—and from the blues came rock and roll, then came Elvis Presley, Otis Redding, and Al Green. This compact city delivers a great family weekend getaway that's especially fun for teens, and the Tennessee climate is relatively mild year-round.

Long before Elvis, there was W. C. Handy, an African American composer and musician who in the early 1900s moved to Memphis for the music, helped grow and change it, and even today is considered the "Father of the Blues." **Beale Street** was the epicenter of that musical genre and is still home to a number of bars, clubs, and terrific barbecue joints.

"After visiting Sun Records, we continued on to the world-famous Beale Street. On Beale Street, I heard authentic blues bands, which were amazingly great. It's the rocking beat of the blues that makes one feel ready to face life and to live it up. Beale Street was like one big party, and everyone was having a great time. Music was a 24-hour celebration here. While downtown, we took a carriage ride and our driver spoke to us about the history of Memphis and pointed out the great architecture."

—S. G., www.travelBIGO.com

Walking beyond the club area, visit the **W. C. Handy Memphis Home and Museum** to learn more about the man, or the **Memphis Rock 'N' Soul Museum,** where a century's worth of amazing musical history is presented in sound and video. The Smithsonian Institution and the National Museum of American History collaborated to create this permanent exhibit, which is well designed to engage kids who might be new to the sounds.

Your family's musical journey can also include **Soulsville: Stax Museum of American Soul Music,** which celebrates the soul music vein of Memphis. Its title refers to the long-gone **Stax Recording Studio,** where lots of music was laid down, including records by Otis Redding, Al Green, Aretha Franklin, Booker T and the MGs, and more. True music aficionados should make a pilgrimage to **Sun Studio,** where legend has it Elvis' first record was made, along with discs from Jerry Lee Lewis, Roy Orbison, and later B. B. King, Johnny Cash, and U2 among others. You can touch the microphone used by Elvis and never wash that hand again.

While you're downtown, don't miss a more somber but profoundly important site—the **National Civil Rights Museum**—housed in the remodeled Lorraine Motel, where Martin Luther King Jr. was gunned down on April 4, 1968. With the annual King Day Celebration held each January on the federal holiday and new theme exhibits for National Black History Month established each February, winter is a perfect time to explore this treasure. Other special events occur in early April on the anniversary of his assassination.

And then, it's time for **Graceland**—the home of Elvis Presley, the one and only legendary King of Rock and Roll, who in life and death has sold more than a billion records—more than any other recording artist. Graceland is the second most visited home in the United States, after the White House; join the crowds and see the entire place.

FUN FACTS

Who said, "Rhythm is something you either have or don't have, but when you have it, you have it all over"? You guessed right; that was Memphis' other king, Elvis Presley.

The Graceland Mansion Tour is a must-see attraction, but don't stop there. Buy the Platinum Tour and see the Automobile Museum, the two private jets, the Elvis in Hollywood Exhibit, the Private Elvis Exhibits (about his two years in the U.S. Army), Elvis Lives, and more; for double the ticket price, you'll get the Elvis Entourage VIP Tour with first-in-line privileges. Don't miss the gift shop offering a remarkable range of memorabilia. Even with bored kids (and that's unlikely), you'll need a half day to see it all; just keep in mind that the place really gets crowded during the weeks around January 8, the King's birthday, and August 16, the date of his death in 1977.

Before you leave town, treat the kids (and the kid in you) to the famous **Duck Walk at the Peabody Hotel.** A flock of five Mallard ducks spend their day in a fountain in the lobby of the historic Peabody Hotel. Great fanfare surrounds their daily entry: when the elevator doors open at 11 A.M., they waddle across the lobby to the fountain;. At 5 P.M., they waddle back to the elevator to return to their rooftop home. It's been a tradition since the 1930s and draws big crowds, so come early to get a good view. Some people stay at the hotel to enjoy repeat performances each day.

Memphis Convention & Visitors Bureau
901-543-5300
www.memphistravel.com, www.tnvacation.com

Miami, Florida

For decades, Miami has earned its reputation as the hottest of the hot spots in the country for both climate and fame. While many families are drawn by the year-round sunny climate, the warmth of this exotic region doesn't stop with the weather or the beautiful Atlantic beaches. This multi-cultural paradise offers eclectic attractions, lush tropical landscapes, great nightlife, fine dining, and a unique Latin heritage that vacationers can't help but embrace. There are many kid-friendly attractions, but parents can find fun as well.

Jungle Island is one of our favorite sights. Home to more than 2,000 exotic birds, including the parrots for whom it was originally named, it also entertains little ones with a petting zoo, a fun children's playground, and a Miccosukee Indian display. Low, child-high feeding stations are available for some hands-on action and adorable photo ops. Wildlife shows and interactive exhibits take place throughout the day. Beautiful botanical gardens serve as a gorgeous backdrop for a half-day visit and provide much-needed shade.

VACATION PLANNING TIPS

Some of our family's favorite things about Miami:

- Sightseeing cruise past stars' homes on the private islands of Biscayne Bay
- Having stone crab claws and Key lime pie at **Joe's Stone Crab**
- Watching the cruise ships leave the **port of Miami** on their way to the Bahamas
- Eating ice cream at **Bayside,** a waterfront mall, and watching the street performers
- Playing on the sweeping lawns of **Vizcaya** after touring the historic mansion
- Grabbing a stool at one of the Cuban joints near the beach and having conch fritters, café con leche or a sopa de mariscos (seafood soup) to get the real taste of the city

The **Miami Museum of Science and Planetarium** is a Spanish mission-style building, low-slung and surrounded by palm trees and bright bougainvillea. The museum has a state-of-the-art planetarium and a variety of rotating exhibits. The two big attractions for young children are the **Wildlife Center,** a rehabilitation haven for injured wildlife, and the **Smithsonian Expedition,** an interactive exhibit of early cultures of the Americas that includes a Caribbean village, Palapa houses, Olmec stoneware, Andean music performances, and an archeological "dig."

There's a real distinction between Miami, with its financial and business centers tucked into striking, contemporary high rises, and the elegant Mediterranean style **Coral Gables,** the trendy bohemian **Coconut Grove,** and the separate city of **Miami Beach,** which is on the Atlantic shoreline.

Near downtown Miami on Key Biscayne, **Miami Seaquarium** offers visitors an entertaining and educational experience. The region's tropical climate allows for year-round outdoor marine shows featuring dolphins, killer whales, and other sea acrobats. The Seaquarium also features sea turtles, seals, sea lions, and the endangered Florida manatee.

Key Biscayne is just south of the city and leads to the string of sandbars and coral isles of the Florida Keys. Like any Caribbean island, the Keys draw snorkelers and scuba divers—especially to **John Pennekamp Coral Reef State Park,** the country's first underwater preserve. It's located on **Key Largo,** and a visit—well worthwhile—is a full day's outing.

The **Everglades National Park,** the largest subtropical wilderness in the United States, boasts rare and endangered species. It has been designated a World Heritage Site, International Biosphere Reserve, and Wetland of International Importance (although low water levels at certain times of year mean there is very little wildlife to see). **Airboat tours** are noisy and invasive but an exhilarating way to see them. It takes a bit of a drive to get to the park's entrance, but you'll pass through some old-style Florida towns on the way.

    FELLOW TRAVELERS SAY ...

"Spending most of the day at the beach was on the top of our priorities. For anyone who's modest, South Beach is topless optional, and plenty of locals and tourists enforce the policy. It's easy to forget about the lack of swimwear after a dip in the ocean and relaxing with a cold drink."

—Susan F., www.travelBIGO.com

If you visit **South Beach** (also called SoBe), the city's hot spot, you might catch a glimpse of a celebrity—but more likely, you'll see lots of young, very attractive Euro and Latin American models. There's a certain sophistication and flair in the air that is only enhanced by the beauty of the Art Deco hotels along Ocean Drive. You can rent bikes or inline skates for cruising the beach or just sit in **Lummus Park** and watch everyone else ride or blade by.

Stop by the **Miami Design Preservation League** and **Art Deco Visitors Center** to pick up a walking map or an audio guide so the entire family can appreciate the many Art Deco landmarks, including authentic 1920s homes whose walls are made of crushed coral (a favorite nesting spot for spiders). Teens and design aficionados should not miss the world-class **FIU-Wolfsonian Museum,** an extraordinary collection of propaganda arts, posters, and industrial design of the nineteenth and twentieth centuries.

What sets Miami apart from other Southern cities is the celebration of the outdoors and nature. That tropical feeling—plus the laid-back lifestyle; rich cultural diversity in music, food, and traditions; and the apparent comfort of different generations relating easily and respectfully to one another—makes Miami genuinely friendly and welcoming to families.

Greater Miami Convention & Visitors Bureau
305-539-3000
www.miamiandbeaches.com, www.visitflorida.com

New Orleans, Louisiana

Known for Mardi Gras, for Jazz Fest, and for its vibrant multi-ethnic culture and music, New Orleans is the spot for a great family vacation. "The Big Easy" is a charming Southern belle boasting to-die-for cuisine, a wild array of entertainment, and a dark and intriguing history. Straddling the Mississippi River, still growing and recovering after the devastating Hurricane Katrina, NOLA is a must-see American city.

The oldest and most famous neighborhood in New Orleans, the French Quarter, was first settled in 1718. Spend some time in Jackson

Square, where you'll find **St. Louis Cathedral,** the oldest continually open cathedral in the United States, as well as the **Cabildo,** Colonial New Orleans' old city hall and the site of the signing of the Louisiana Purchase. **Bourbon Street** is the iconic thoroughfare of the Quarter, and the bar-lined blocks near Canal Street are often quite raucous at night. To visit during the day, walk away from Canal Street to explore the quieter and architecturally pristine back streets closer to Esplanade Avenue. Finally, after a stroll or carriage ride through the French Quarter, stop at Café du Monde for its famous beignets and rich chicory coffee. At night, take one of the popular Haunted Tours for another perspective.

TRAVELERS BEWARE!

Watch your wallet anywhere in the Quarter, as pickpockets are known to frequent here.

Beyond the Quarter, join a cemetery tour to see graveyards with tombs built above water-logged ground, or ride the cheap, old-fashioned streetcar (once named Desire, after the street) out St. Charles Street; the restored trolley takes you past Southern mansions on the palatial, oak-lined boulevards of the Garden District and Uptown.

New Orleans was the birthplace of jazz, which melded blues, gospel, and ragtime genres with improvisation. Your family can get a taste of this art form at **Preservation Hall,** the legendary music venue and home to its namesake band. The **New Orleans Jazz National Historic Park** offers self-guided audio tours about jazz history. The center offers free live jazz performances five days a week, and there are clubs all over town jumping with music every night.

The devastation of Hurricane Katrina in 2005 is now ingrained into the culture of New Orleans and the country. Widespread flooding destroyed thousands of homes and businesses, and many are still in need of repair. NOLA offers countless voluntourism opportunities to travelers looking to lend a hand. There are special Devastation Tours as well.

Mardi Gras, taking place each February or March but always the day before Ash Wednesday, is the most famous New Orleans event—though colorful and fun, the world-famous parades can be overwhelming for families. An easier experience is available year round at Mardi Gras World, where guests are invited to walk among the glamorous costumes and floats of Mardi Gras past.

Various outfitters offer tours of nearby restored plantations and sprawling, alligator-infested swamps. Tours of Barataria Preserve in **Jean Lafitte National Historic Park** take you into the habitats of alligators, egrets, raccoons, and a variety of snakes. Or enjoy a bit of nature in the city by heading to the **Audubon Aquarium of the Americas,** on the river near the Quarter, or the **Audubon Zoo** in the historic Uptown district, where visitors can say hello to Spots, the white alligator, or ride a safari simulator ride.

NOLA is also famous for its fantastic war museums. Its oldest, **The Confederate Museum,** is home to the country's second-largest collection of Confederate memorabilia. Don't miss **The National World War II Museum,** which includes historic war vehicles and boats (especially the locally built Higgins), along with actual soldiers' uniforms, weapons, and oral history stations.

New Orleans Convention & Visitor's Bureau
1-800-672-6124
www.neworleanscvb.com, www.louisianatravel.com

Orlando, Florida

Orlando, like a huge tourist magnet, attracts families from all over the world to central Florida to enjoy its warm and sunny climate. The city is best known for its theme parks, and with good reason: it's home to some of the best on Earth, covered in detail in Chapter 9. But Orlando also offers a fascinating and perhaps unexpected variety of natural, cultural, historical, and downright unusual activities. Savvy families who have "been there, done that" and spent a fortune on a theme park vacation often return to the city because airfare is cheap, bargains abound, and there's so much fun to be had within an hour's drive. The first stop for any family visiting Orlando should be www.orlandoinfo.com, where you can order a free **Magicard** with discounts on hotels, restaurants, and attractions.

> **FUN FACTS**
>
> You certainly won't be the only one visiting Orlando this year—it's the second most popular domestic travel destination in the United States after New York, with more than 50 million people visiting last year.

One attraction that we love in this city is the **Orlando Science Center,** the highlight of which is Body-Zone 3D, a movie that takes viewers wearing 3D glasses through the circulatory system with a red blood cell. Interactive displays on healthy living, a hands-on laboratory, a flight simulator, and a planetarium round out the experience. **Wonder Works** is a fantastic attraction that features an upside-down building, laser tag, and a comedic dinner show. Kids will love sitting in realistic cockpits of F18 fighter jets and pretending to fly them.

The **Charles Homer Morse Museum of American Art** in nearby **Winter Park** (where you can take a scenic boat tour past elegant nineteenth-century homes) features the world's most comprehensive collection of works by famed stained glass designer Louis Comfort Tiffany.

Slightly north of Orlando lies the **Central Florida Zoo.** Here you'll find demonstrations and feedings with elephants, cheetahs, and other creatures with tested visitor appeal as well as something distinctive in a smaller package: the state's only Insect Zoo. **Black Hammock Adventures,** just east of the zoo, offers free live alligator and bird exhibits. A favorite is watching trainers feed the 12-foot, 650-pound resident gator named Hammy. At the Lazy Gator Bar, guests can join the deck party every Friday and Saturday night and listen to free live music.

North of the zoo lies beautiful **Blue Spring State Park.** The main highlight is the manatees that winter there from mid-November through March. Ranger talks offer information and a Q&A about these gentle giants. When the manatees leave during the hotter months, humans can move back into the water for swimming, snorkeling, and tubing; to actually swim with a manatee, see Chapter 10.

Many families choose to stay in nearby **Kissimmee** due to its proximity to the theme parks and its budget motels, but it has its own attractions worth visiting. **Green Meadows Petting Farm** is great for kids and makes an especially fun side trip for urbanite families seeking some country air. Two-hour tours run continuously throughout the day, allowing visitors a hands-on visit with a variety of farm animals, including cows and ponies. For those who prefer an adrenaline-fuelled trip in a fast-moving boat, check out **Boggy Creek Airboat Rides.** Tours depart every half hour, and airboat passengers might see gators, bald eagles, and other wildlife amid the cypress-lined wetlands as they glide over the water. An attraction that offers an experience somewhere between a petting farm and an airboat ride on the adrenaline scale is the **Zipline Safari at Forever Florida.** All ages can have a blast soaring through the trees, getting a bird's-eye view of the natural plants and animals that call this huge nature preserve home.

VACATION PLANNING TIPS

From tapas at **Tu Tu Tango** to the fried fish at the **Bubba Gump Shrimp Company** or the prancing horses and princes at the **Arabian Nights** dinner theatre, there are a lot of out-there themed restaurants in Orlando. Perhaps the most fun for the family is the self-styled **World's Largest McDonalds** in a huge, two-story entertainment mall shaped like a box of French fries. Load up the kids with change so they can play arcade games and win redeemable tickets; the PlayPlace is free, and you'll find everything from tourist information to ice cream to hustling time-share salespeople within this unique facility.

For those who want to see some local wildlife, go no farther than **Gatorland.** This 110-acre theme park and wildlife preserve houses thousands of alligators and crocodiles. Families can get up close and personal in a safe environment while they learn about these mysterious beasts. In addition, the park is home to rare white alligators—four of only a few in the world. Rest your feet during the park's standard animal shows: Gatorland Jumparoo, Gator Wrestl-ing, and the Up-Close Encounters Show.

Just east of Kissimmee lies the wonderful **Reptile World Serpentarium.** This strange but locally treasured attraction is off the beaten path and cheap. Although probably not for the squeamish, the highlight of a visit to Reptile World is witnessing the daily scheduled "milking" of poisonous snakes for venom to be used in scientific research.

Dinosaur World, a collection of more than 150 life-size dinosaur replicas, is about an hour west of Orlando. Like its sister park in Kentucky, Dinosaur World Florida offers visitors an experience not unlike walking through a prehistoric picture book. There's also a "fossil dig" activity that lets kids find and take home their own small fossils. The pathways are paved, and although there are no food facilities, picnicking is allowed.

Located about 45 minutes east of Orlando at **Port Canaveral,** the **Kennedy Space Center** was built in 1967 for astronauts' families to view space center operations. Today it's open to the public with behind-the-scenes tours, interactive activities, a huge IMAX theater, and opportunities to meet an astronaut. Smaller children will have plenty to climb on between the Children's Play Dome and the Mercury, Gemini, and Apollo replicas in the Rocket Garden. If you're really lucky, you might be able to visit on the day of a space shuttle launch and buy a ticket for prime seating—but this will require serious advance planning!

Orlando, Florida
407-363-5871
www.orlandoinfo.com, www.visitflorida.com

Cultural Appeal

In This Chapter

- Colonial Williamsburg: a living history encounter for kids
- Louisville's friendly southern charm
- Nashville's musical roots
- Key West's laid-back attitude

Among the earliest tourists drawn to the South were the Spanish explorers under Ponce de Leon who, by 1565, had established St. Augustine, Florida, as the earliest European settlement. Waves of immigrants soon settled the fertile region, bringing varied traditions and home-country lifestyles to the area.

Colonial Williamsburg, Virginia

Upholding their mission to help the future learn from the past, the Colonial Williamsburg Foundation runs America's most famous and comprehensive living history museum, inviting families to step back into the time and place where the ideas of independence, democracy, and revolution were born. Located 150 miles south of Washington, D.C., and midway between **Richmond** and **Norfolk,** this city was the capital of the largest, most dominant British colony in the New World from 1699 to 1780.

Today, 301 acres with more than 88 original buildings and hundreds of reconstructed homes, shops, and public buildings welcome visitors to the eighteenth century. The key to capturing the minds of visitors is involvement, not just watching: families can learn about foods and customs by visiting trade shops and participating in a wide array of activities such as boot-, barrel-, furniture-, and wig-making; court proceedings, and dining in traditional taverns (a must).

You can learn about the contributions of slaves and gentry, attend speeches by "Thomas Jefferson" and "Patrick Henry," and question the principles that led to their call for independence. Evenings are for strolling candlelit streets and attending music, dance, and drama performances. Most activities will grab the attention of school-age children, and even your youngest kids will enjoy the surroundings.

 FELLOW TRAVELERS SAY ...

"Staying in one of the restored Colonial houses in Williamsburg, Virginia, is amazing. We have done this with our sons for years, and it's a favorite trip for our family. You get all the benefits of the renowned Williamsburg Inn (you check in there and have access to the inn's amenities/room service), but you stay in a restored house or tavern right in the historic area.

Especially in the fall, there's nothing quite like it with the trees ablaze with beautiful autumn colors, the smell of wood-burning fireplaces in the air, and hot cider and gingerbread cakes for sale by local trades people (dressed in authentic colonial attire). You can't help but be transported back to the early times of our country and the struggle for freedom and independence. It's first class and definitely worth doing!"

—C. W., www.FamilyTravelForum.com

Although the crowds are smallest from January to March, the weather can be cold and damp; spring and fall are the best times to visit. The Visitor's Center helps you make the most of your time and sells a two-day or unlimited-access annual pass—both good values.

Accommodations are available on-site or through the **Association of Williamsburg Hotels and Motels;** be sure to check out the discounted ticket packages they offer to Williamsburg-area attractions.

Although you should plan to spend at least two days at Colonial Williamsburg, you can stay very busy for several more days by visiting the nearby **Jamestown Settlement,** site of the first English settlement in America, and the **Yorktown Victory Center,** a museum of the American Revolution. Reward the kids with a fun day at **Busch Gardens Williamsburg.** Its European-themed architecture and formal landscaping make it one of the prettiest amusement parks—and the famous roller coasters like Griffon, Alpengeist, and Loch Ness Monster are outrageous.

Colonial Williamsburg
Williamsburg, Virginia
1-800-HISTORY
www.history.org, www.virginia.org

Louisville, Kentucky Horse Country

Sports families jockey on down to the place that is most famous for horses but that also celebrates chicken (the home of KFC), baseball, and boxing. Hugging the northern border of Kentucky, LEW-vill has many different pronunciations, but we can all agree that it's a fun family destination. To experience its scenic beauty, hop on the *Belle of Louisville* for a summer sightseeing cruise along the Ohio River. Elevator access to the second deck makes this ship particularly relaxing for seniors, and many locals throw birthday parties and reunions on board.

A must-see in Louisville is, of course, **Churchill Downs,** the oldest continuously operated thoroughbred racetrack in the United States. For the last 135 years, every first Saturday in May, Churchill Downs hosts the running of the Kentucky Derby—the greatest 2 minutes in sports. To get a hands-on experience, the **Kentucky Derby Museum** offers interactive exhibits, the official jockey scale for those lightweight riders, and walking tours of the track. Live racing takes place from late April to early July and from October to late November. Children are allowed to view the races, but betting is entertainment for adults only. If your family plans it right, you can get in on the festivities at the **Kentucky Derby Festival,** which takes place the two weeks prior to the race. Out of the many fun events, the biggest is **Thunder over Louisville,** the country's largest fireworks display.

Baseball fans will love visiting the Hillerich & Bradsby's **Louisville Slugger Bat Factory and Museum,** home to the world's largest bat.

The field across the street is home to the AAA team, the Louisville Bats. The **Muhammad Ali Center** provides an unusual learning experience for aspiring boxers, and kids can learn about Ali and many other notables. The interactive pavilions and multimedia presentations show visitors how "The Greatest's" six core values of respect, confidence, conviction, dedication, spirituality, and giving can make anyone a success.

Sure to please young non-sports fans, the **Speed Art Museum** boasts the Art Sparks Interactive Gallery, which features multi-media activities, an Electronic Art Room, and the wonderful Planet Preschool. **Museum Row** has several other attractions including Glassworks, the Frazier International History Museum, the Louisville Science Center & IMAX Theatre, the Kentucky Museum of Art and Craft, the Kentucky Center for Performing Arts, and the London Royal Armouries. The 70,000 pieces of arms, armor, and artillery dating from antiquity to the present represent one of the largest such collections outside England.

The **Louisville Zoo** appeals to all members of the family with its Tiger Tundra exhibit, scheduled giraffe and lorikeet feedings, and tiger training sessions. For a truly offbeat experience in Kentucky, journey south about 100 miles to impressive Mammoth Cave at **Mammoth Cave National Park,** where the family can take tours of the cave, go camping and horseback riding, and enjoy some boating or swimming.

Greater Louisville Convention & Visitors Bureau
1-800-626-5646
www.gotolouisville.com, www.kentuckytourism.com

Nashville's Country Western Scene

There's nowhere else on Earth with the sights and sounds that abound in the country music capital of Nashville. The "Buckle of the Bible Belt" has been home to television show hostess and actress Oprah Winfrey, the notorious Bettie Page, and pop star Miley

Cyrus. As we list our favorites in the city where music is sacred, you'll see where these stars drew inspiration.

FUN FACTS

Nashville was originally named Fort Nashborough after American Revolutionary War hero Francis Nash.

A visit to Nashville must begin at the newest theater for the **Grand Ole Opry,** home to the longest-running radio broadcast in the world. A six-foot circle of well-worn oak rests in the middle of the stage, cut right from the stage of the Opry's former home, the **Ryman Auditorium.** This historic slab allows visitors and performers to stand on the exact spot where country's legends once entertained. While the Ryman Auditorium wasn't the first home to the Grand Ole Opry, it was arguably its most memorable and historical venue. Today, the Ryman offers tours and country memorabilia and also showcases performers in several genres. Located in the sprawling Grand Ole Opry complex are the Gaylord Opryland Resort and **Opry Mills mall.**

Aspiring musicians should head to **The Musicians Hall of Fame and Museum,** the only museum in the world that recognizes the industry's backup talent. At **The Country Music Hall of Fame and Museum,** catch a glimpse of Elvis' gold Cadillac, a history of Hank Williams and his offspring of performers, and memorable clips from *Hee-Haw.* On Broadway between lively honkytonks, the **Hatch Show Print** shop lets visitors browse prints and watch new designs being created on old-fashioned presses. You'll see a collection of artists' prints from Duke Ellington to Leon Redbone hanging on their walls.

Cowboy Town caters to the cowfolk in all of us, taking visitors back in time for old-fashioned entertainment and fun. Explore Ramblin' Breeze's 116 acres just 10 minutes from downtown Nashville for Wild West gunfights, horseback riding, live cowboy music, and other wild outdoor activities. Go way back in time to the life-size replica of the historical **Parthenon.** Built in 1897 for Nashville's Centennial Exposition, the building also serves as a museum of Greek artifacts.

At **The Hermitage,** home of President Andrew Jackson, the history lovers in the family can explore the home of our nation's seventh President and learn about his family and life on the 1837 farm.

Smartly designed for kids, the **Frist Center for the Visual Arts** features hands-on learning opportunities as well as more than 30 interactive arts exhibits. Young guests can also learn about photography, architecture, and the essentials of art, including depth, color, light, and perspective. What the Frist does for creativity, the **Adventure Science Center** does for space explorers. If your preschoolers become too overwhelmed by museum visits, check out the **Nashville Zoo at Grassmere,** which houses leopard, cougar, porcupine, lemur, piranha, red panda, and many more scaly, furry, and feathered creatures.

To get around this Southern city in style, climb aboard a 300-foot paddlewheel riverboat, the *General Jackson Showboat,* for a cruise on the Cumberland River set to live music. Named after the first steamboat to operate on the Cumberland River in 1817, the modern version was christened in 1985.

Nashville Convention & Visitors Bureau
615-259-4730
www.visitmusiccity.com, www.tnvacation.com

Pirates of Key West, Florida

Situated like Jack Sparrow's footlocker at the southernmost point of the United States, Key West has been revered by generations of visitors as a safe haven for those who dare to go their own way. This is a come-as-you-are, anything-goes city, and that suits the locals just fine.

This close-knit community of castaways, which began as a Spanish colony more than 300 years ago, includes all your major tropical species—pagans and pirates, musicians and artists, plumed birds and marine life, and performing cats and dolphins. Key West has remained unique despite the commercial pressures of mass tourism—and in the process has become a bona-fide family destination, boasting myriad family-friendly and educational attractions. The beating heart of Key West, **Old Town,** is the sole Florida city to be listed on the National Register of Historic Places.

FUN FACTS

Fast Buck Freddie's on Duval Street has to be seen to be believed. Alert your teens! It has lots of tropic-themed keepers: wicker furniture, lamps with seashell bases, cookie jars shaped like Hawaiian dancers, underwear with a palm tree pattern, and lime green Izod boaters. It also carries incredibly elegant designer linen shirts and suits, an entire Tommy Bahama department for golfers, authentic handmade Guayabera shirts, an eclectic collection of flip-flops, and inexpensive evening wear. All ages will enjoy it.

Key West is a walking town; it's all about taking in the sights, eating key lime pie, and chilling. Be forewarned that sunken treasure and drunken pleasure hold equal sway, especially at dusk on **Mallory Square.** Many of Key West's performers and artisans display their wares along **Mallory Pier** during the must-see Sunset Celebration; some families prefer to see it from the decks of one of the historic schooners passing by.

This "rainbow" Florida Key city is especially welcoming to same-sex couple families, who will find many child-friendly things to do within a very accepting community of fellow travelers. The city's motto is "One Human Family," and TV celebrity Rosie O' Donnell has counted Key West—just 90 miles west of Cuba and 152 miles from Miami—as a favorite port of call.

Among other must-see sites are the **Ernest Hemingway Home & Museum,** where dozens of six-toed felines have run of the place— all descendants of a six-toed cat, Snowball, given to Hemingway by a ship's captain when he moved there. The city holds an annual festival called **Hemingway Days** that celebrates the Old Man's ties to his favorite home.

Sea-themed museums include the wonderful **Mel Fisher Maritime Heritage Museum,** housing the richest single collection of seventeenth-century maritime and shipwreck antiquities in the Western Hemisphere. Key West was a salvager's paradise in the

1850s, and its rise from rogues to riches make for great stories and displays full of doubloons.

Other more campy attractions include the **Key West Shipwreck Historeum,** where actors re-enact life at a wrecker's warehouse in 1856; and **Pirate Soul,** whose collection of authentic pirate artifacts will thrill younger children.

Not to be missed is the **Key West Butterfly and Nature Conservatory.** Suitable for all ages, the spacious glass-domed tropical butterfly habitat is home to more than 1,000 of these colorful creatures from nearly 50 diverse species. Note that Key West is especially busy on weekends, so you'll have to book one of the many family-welcoming B&Bs or small hotels in advance.

Key West Florida Tourism
1-800-352-5397
www.fla-keys.com/keywest, www.keywestattractions.org

At the Beach

In This Chapter

- The 200 miles of sandy shores along Florida's West Coast
- The Panhandle's green waters and beachfront parks
- The Gulf Shore's history, nature excursions, and beach
- Myrtle Beach's fun family attractions
- Sand dunes and pirate tales in The Outer Banks
- The boardwalk is the main attraction at Virginia Beach

With a warm climate within driving distance of millions of people, it makes sense that the South has developed family beach destinations geared toward a variety of styles and budgets. The beautiful, calm, and warm waters of the Gulf of Mexico make the plethora of beach resorts that line the coast of western Florida and southern Alabama an easy choice for families—especially those traveling with infants and toddlers.

Along the southern sector of the East Coast, we've picked three more great beaches on the Atlantic Ocean. Each provides the essential ingredients of a beach vacation—sun and sand—while adding fun attractions, amusement parks, nature preserves, and boardwalks to keep all ages busy. Read on to discover what makes them special and why their unique local flavors can't be found elsewhere.

Clearwater to Naples on Florida's West Coast

With so many to choose from along Florida's **Gulf Coast,** we've picked the best beaches between **Clearwater** and **Naples. Tampa** is the nearest airport serving the western seaboard, where beaches are ideal for families with younger children. The **Gulf of Mexico's** surf is calm most of the year, and the weather is almost always warm and sunny. Note that in the past, however, hurricane activity has peaked between July and September—bringing rain, wind, and rougher seas.

The central west Florida coast covers an eclectic region that mixes the old with the new. While there's a lot of history in small coastal towns, many modern attractions provide a variety of entertainment. Families with mixed interests will find fun for all.

Multifaceted **Clearwater Beach** is a barrier island surrounded by the spectacular Gulf of Mexico on the west and the **Intracoastal Waterway** on the east. The entire Clearwater area is rich in marine and bird life, with nature preserves and an extensive state park brimming with flora and fauna. As one of the most popular beaches in this area, your family adventure can begin and end here, on the beach, where many vendors offer parasailing, jet ski rentals, and deep-sea fishing excursions. Also, after five years of planning, the new beach walk is complete—revitalizing the community by providing a stretch of retail, entertainment, and hotel venues, with the pristine white sands and crystal-clear water of Clearwater Beach as its centerpiece.

St. Pete Beach has more of a cultural bent, with the **Florida International Museum** and the extensive **Salvador Dali Museum** located in the nearby city of **St. Petersburg.** If you prefer a more secluded beach, there are plenty to choose from minutes away. **Treasure Island, Redington Beach,** and **Madeira Beach** all offer the same quality beach vacation as St. Petersburg but without all the hustle and bustle. Don't forget to visit the celebrated **John's Pass Boardwalk** in Madeira Beach, known for its unique retail shopping and assorted restaurants. Madeira Beach is the water sports hub of St. Petersburg.

As soon as you drive past the famous pink landmark **Don Cesar Hotel** and enter the charming little town of **Pass a Grille,** you'll feel as if you have stepped into another world. The residents of this hidden paradise seem to maintain a laid-back and worry-free outlook on life, and by the time you leave, their attitude will have inevitably rubbed off on you.

Fort Desoto is both a park and a beach. This historical landmark offers nature trails, canoeing and kayaking areas, and fishing piers. You'll also find a number of grills, picnic tables, and park benches located a few feet from the beach, making this a perfect locale for an entire day at the beach.

Heading south along the coast brings you to one of the quieter beach regions. While many residents are retirees, this pampering resort paradise is anything but boring—with several family-friendly beaches and natural attractions. **Fort Myers Beach** has a sort of West Coast feel to it (we're talking the Pacific); this trendy city is more relaxed than anything. Offering an assortment of eateries and quality shopping venues, it's a budget-friendly town that ensures a fun time for the entire family. **Naples Beach** offers all the first-class amenities and posh resorts along its 11-mile stretch but also has a wild side: steps away from the island is the tropical wilderness of the **Everglades.** If taking a walk on the wild side isn't exactly your forte, Naples offers quality dining, shopping, and numerous golf courses where you can ensure your golf stroke is up to par with your buddies back home. **Sanibel Island** is known for its unique shelling opportunities and stretches of secluded beaches. This piece of paradise is the perfect place for those waiting all year for a little peace and quiet to rent a condo. (Note: to maximize your peace and quiet, you may want to leave your kids at home.)

Visit Florida
850-488-5607
www.visitflorida.com, www.visitstpeteclearwater.com

The Beaches of the Florida Panhandle

The Emerald Coast stretches for nearly 200 miles along northwest Florida's Gulf of Mexico shore and features picturesque beaches of soft, ivory sand; crystal clear water; and warm, gentle surf—perfect for young children. Outdoor fun abounds in 19 state and national parks that encompass more than a million acres of preserved land. Although the state's **Panhandle** occupies an 11,000-square-mile area, we recommend the central and western beaches stretching from **Port St. Joe** to **Pensacola.** Here are some of our favorites, as encountered along Route 98 driving east to west.

FUN FACTS

Because the sand and sea floor are made of glistening Appalachian quartz, the sand is really white and the Gulf waters appear green—thus giving this area its catchy nickname, the Emerald Coast.

Panama City Beach offers 27 miles of stunning sand and surf plus exuberance, style, and boatloads of activities. You'll never have a dull moment while exploring the family-friendly attractions, sensational dining, and exciting nightlife. From real-life pirate ships to hands-on animal parks and daring giant slingshots and go-kart tracks, the ambiance will excite kids until they're too exhausted to trek back home. You can visit Panama City's very own **Ripley's Believe It or Not Museum,** with 15 galleries of Ripley's unique works of art and a moving 4-D theater. Be warned: Panama City Beach is a very popular spring break getaway.

Grayton Beach is for families who might find Panama City and Pensacola (both cities with airports) too rambunctious. This laid-back beach is surrounded by quaint historic cottages and modern mini-mansions. Strolling along the 100-year-old roads, you get the sense that not too much has changed except the live music at the local favorite, **Red Bar.** You can pitch your tent in **Grayton Beach State Park,** where a coastal nature trail leads through scrub oaks and old gnarled magnolia trees. At its end, a public dock is available for the avid boater and/or fisherman, although surf casting is said to be very good. After a visit, your family may understand the town's unofficial slogan: "Nice dogs, strange people."

Destin, the area's best-known drive-to beach, attracts almost 80 percent of the Emerald Coast's annual visitors. Generations of Southern families have enjoyed Destin's sun, sand, and sparkling green waters and crowded the city's busy hotels, high-rise condominiums, and ice cream parlors each summer. The 2,400-acre gated community of **Sandestin,** farther west, is renowned for its first-class service, tennis, golf, children's activities, **Baytowne Wharf** shopping village, and fine restaurants. Similarly, **Fort Walton** has experienced more upscale development along its award-winning beach.

Pensacola Beach is calmer than Panama City, equally fun, and delivers more bang for the buck. Here, a variety of outdoor, indoor, and local attractions entertain all ages, and the nearby **Naval Air Station**—one of many military facilities along this coast—livens up the scene. Snorkeling, jet skiing, sailing, and deep-sea fishing have become favorite activities, and each has multiple outfitters located in town. If you prefer to stay above water, this interesting town has a wintertime PG-rated **Mardi Gras,** a daily polar bear dip, the **Blue Angels Flight Demonstration Team,** and live music at many of the New Orleans–themed restaurants. Accommodations catering to a family budget range from quaint B&Bs to small family-operated hotels—and, of course, resort condos and chain hotels located along the shoreline.

Emerald Coast Convention & Visitors Bureau
1-800-322-3319
www.destin-fwb.com, www.thebeachfla.com

Gulf Shores, Alabama

When we think of popular beaches, we often picture the ones swarming with college students. Yet Alabama's southern coast on the Gulf of Mexico offers a different, more economical choice for an ideal three-season beach getaway: Gulf Shores. The 30,000-acre island community is home to quiet sand beaches and gentle surf, mingled with a splash of Southern culture, history, wildlife, and fun recreational activities.

While families can amuse themselves at the beach with volleyball, sailing, windsurfing, or boating, it's the opportunities for viewing wildlife that sets this place apart. Dolphin watching is a popular activity, and viewers can get a more personal and up-close experience at the **Alabama Gulf Coast Zoo** animal park. Farther north, the **Weeks Bay Estuary Reserve** gives guests the opportunity to spot a few alligators. For those who would rather keep their distance from scaly monsters, the **Alabama Coastal Birding Trail**'s well-marked paths are a good alternative. The **Bon Secour National Wildlife Refuge** consists of 7,000 acres of pristine coastal ecosystems; before setting out to see the refuge's sea turtles, birds, and beautiful wild flowers, stop at the visitor's center to pick up a trail guide and plant and animal identification brochures for some family I-Spy fun.

The Gulf Shores and surrounding waters are historically significant as the site of very early sea battles. **Fort Morgan,** an architecturally unique fort constructed in 1834, lies a short distance away in **Mobile Bay,** Alabama, and is a great place for kids to learn the history of war from the 1800s up to World War II. If you need a break from the beach, take a 15-mile inland jaunt to picturesque **Magnolia Springs.** Steeped in Spanish, Creole, and Civil War history with live oak–canopied streets, this riverfront country town offers visitors the chance to enjoy a refreshing dip in the local mineral springs, a home-cooked meal, some fishing, or watching the motorboat mail carrier make deliveries in dockside boxes on the Magnolia River.

VACATION PLANNING TIPS

Historic Fort Morgan is the first and last landfall for migrating songbirds. For two weeks each April and October, skilled birdwatchers catch and band birds such as indigo buntings, warblers, and scarlet tanagers as they fly through the area. Children can "adopt" a bird and help release it during their Fort Morgan visit.

Family vacationers may want to skip the hurricane season (most active between August and October), but that's also the time when condo rentals are cheapest. Between November and March, the climate is pleasantly cool, and you might even get lucky and hit one of their 70° days. For indoor activity, there's always **Sawgrass Landing,** a shopping, dining, and entertainment complex with an adjacent fishing pier and water park. Don't miss the chance to sample authentically prepared Gulf Coast seafood such as catfish, crab cakes, soft-shell crabs, and gulf shrimp.

Alabama Gulf Coast Convention & Visitors Bureau
1-800-745-7263
www.gulfshores.com, www.alabama.travel

Myrtle Beach, South Carolina

Offering year-round oceanfront fun, this town's Southern hospitality makes it a wildly sought-after haven for family holidays. Don't forget to bring pails and shovels to build sandcastles along miles of broad, gold-sand beaches. Recreation includes waterskiing, wind surfing, kayaking, fishing, and three-season swimming. Cyclists can spend hours exploring extensive bike trails. If golf drives your family, test your skill on the lush fairways of more than 100 championship courses or enjoy the spirit of the game at one of 50 themed mini-golf courses.

While the Myrtle Beach region is packed with outdoor activities of all kinds, beach pleasures are its best feature. As the prime city along the **Grand Strand** (or **Long Bay**)—with more than 60 miles of uninterrupted beach from **Cape Fear, North Carolina,** to **Georgetown, South Carolina**—it attracts more than 10 million tourists, including spring breakers.

Myrtle Beach State Park, with campgrounds and nature trails, is one of the most popular summer beaches and opens the dunes to horseback riders from November to February. **Huntington Beach State Park,** a little more off the beaten path and known for its fishing, hiking, birding, and boating, is considered the best-preserved and cleanest beach on the Grand Strand.

VACATION PLANNING TIPS

Rain or shine, your family will enjoy many of these nonbeach attractions:

- **Broadway at the Beach** is a premier entertainment complex whose outposts include **MagiQuest,** a fantastic dragon-and-princess–inspired virtual reality challenge.
- **Ripley's Aquarium** offers an educational 1.2 million-gallon aquarium bisected by a 330-foot underwater tunnel that allows visitors to see sharks swim overhead.
- Kids can catch the infectious thrill of racing at **NASCAR Speed-Park.**
- Little ones will love the classic rides at **Pavilion Nostalgia Park.**
- **All Children's Park** in Surfside has a barrier-free playground designed for kids with special needs.
- The **Children's Museum of South Carolina** has a Magic School Bus.
- **Family Kingdom Amusement Park** is an old-fashioned midway with 30 rides and a water park.
- The brand-new, mile-long **Oceanfront Boardwalk and Promenade** in downtown Myrtle Beach, with its shops and restaurants, promises even more fun!

More "natural" entertainment is available at **Brookgreen Gardens** and its **Lowcountry Zoo,** home to a variety of creatures all in their natural habitats. Animal lovers will also enjoy **T.I.G.E.R.S. Preservation Station**—that is, The Institute of Greatly Endangered and Rare Species, a free-living tiger exhibit that features many different species of the large cat. Visitors get to hold their choice of baby tigers or apes. If you have baseball fans in the family, check out the **Myrtle Beach Pelicans,** the Minor League baseball team of the Atlanta Braves.

For those drawn to live entertainment, **The Palace Theatre** presents "Le Grand Cirque," the next generation of Cirque du Soleil, and the **Carolina Opry** has nightly shows covering the genres of rock, gospel, and country. Kids will enjoy some entertaining evenings: dinner and a live jousting tournament between mounted knights at **Medieval Times** or the friendly rivalry between the North and the South that plays out at **The Dixie Stampede.**

Myrtle Beach Area Visitor Information
1-800-356-3016
www.visitmyrtlebeach.com, www.discoversouthcarolina.com

Outer Banks & Kitty Hawk, North Carolina

Once isolated from the world, North Carolina's **Outer Banks** form a semi-circular arc of barrier islands—connected by a network of bridges and ferries—stretching into the Atlantic. The main attractions are the vast stretches of sandy beach, sculpted sand dunes, and the third largest wildlife refuge and estuary system in the world.

While most know the Banks from having watched tense, wind-blown reporters on TV shouting their hurricane reports from **Cape Hatteras** (the southernmost point), the 72-mile-long region is the nation's first national seashore and home of "America's Lighthouse." The 208-foot-tall, brick **Cape Hatteras Lighthouse,** dating from 1871, had to be relocated inland in 1999—but it's still impressive.

Beyond the broad beaches, many quality family adventures beckon. Kayaking eco-tours are a fun way to spend the afternoon, and with themed adventures families can encounter alligators and dolphins or even take a sunset or nighttime excursion. For stargazing, go to **Jockey's Ridge State Park** in **Nag's Head,** the tallest active sand dune in the eastern United States. Rumored to contain Blackbeard's buried treasure, kids will love exploring this mini Sahara that consists of more than six million dump-truckloads full of sand. Here, rangers have a Sunset of the Ridge program, a unique nighttime adventure for kids that involves identifying animal tracks and learning the lore of the dunes.

After tourism, fishing is the area's main industry. You can rent a boat for the day, then pick up a bucket of bait and some rods. Or head to the **Pea Island & Alligator River National Wildlife Refuge,** where children work with park rangers to unroll a seine net that drags the bottom of **Albemarle Sound.** They get to help pull up crabs, shrimp, pipefish, and croakers. Carefully, and with wet hands so as not to harm the creatures, participants untangle the sea catch while the ranger weaves fishing lore into the activity.

The site of Wilbur and Orville Wright's first attempt at flight, **Kitty Hawk,** is home to the **Exhibition Center at the Wright Brothers National Memorial.** The monument itself is a dramatic structure that soars upward from a grassy knoll, and the actual park houses the crude sheds in which the brothers lived and built their plane. Kids will love to learn about the Wright Brothers' experiments that started on December 17, 1903, when the improbable-looking, double-winged craft flew 120 feet and stayed off the ground for 12 seconds.

More than a half century later, these designs inspired the aircraft that would put astronauts in space.

Outer Banks Visitors Bureau
252-473-2138
www.outerbanks.org, www.visitnc.com

Virginia Beach, Virginia

Families have been flocking to the balmy shores of **Virginia Beach** for more than 115 years. With more than 35 miles of waterfront on the Atlantic at the mouth of **Chesapeake Bay,** a family vacation in this resort town means more than sand and surf.

FELLOW TRAVELERS SAY ...

"A trip to Virginia Beach is a trip of a lifetime. Can you imagine beautiful people, great shops, nice climate, and the main attraction, the beach? Perfect vacation spot for all."

—B. W., www.travelBIGO.com

Whether you're pushing a stroller or biking the boardwalk, exploring marshlands or admiring the 34-foot-tall cast bronze statue of **King Neptune** himself, there is truly something for everyone.

A classic day in Virginia Beach might consist of simple, lazy beach-lying on the 14 miles of free public beaches—so wide that even with the crowds, you'll always find a spot to lay down your towel. Parents can watch as the kiddies erect sandcastles and splash to their hearts' content. Boogie boarding, surfing, and kayaking are also popular activities.

A great location for the family to get in touch with nature, Virginia Beach has more than 18,000 acres of protected lands. **First Landing State Park** offers free monthly educational programs that include animal tracking, surf fishing, and hiking. Further south in **Sand-bridge** is the **Back Bay National Wildlife Refuge.** Home to a variety of endangered species, including wild horses, bald eagles, and loggerhead turtles, the 8,700 acres of beach, dune, and marsh landscapes are accessible for exploration.

A myriad of boats at **Rudee Inlet** operate cruise tours for dolphin and whale-watching, narrated by an educator from the **Virginia Aquarium and Marine Science Center.** This place is a must for families; Virginia's largest and most-visited aquarium, it features more than 700,000 gallons of water habitats and 300 hands-on exhibits. Now double in size, the new Restless Planet display houses more than 6,000 animals, including Komodo dragons, exotic cobras, and hedgehogs.

FUN FACTS

Be sure to stroll down the famous **Virginia Beach Boardwalk,** dating from 1888. Originally a five-block-long wooden promenade, the city spent $103 million to make it a concrete walkway and bike lane stretching 3 miles from the Rudee Inlet all the way to 40th Street. Keep your suits on, grab your flip-flops, and expect to see the following highlights:

- Puppeteers, jugglers, street performers, and other circus-variety entertainers performing on the sidewalks from 17th to 25th Streets
- A stage set up almost every 10 blocks for live musical entertainment and festivals year round
- **Beach Street USA** lit up at night to lure teens and partygoers
- The days of yore at the **Old Coast Guard Station,** a fascinating life-saving station at 24th Street

For a softer, gentler boardwalk experience, families can play miniature golf at the 18-hole **Jungle Golf** course, a Virginia Beach staple. Or if the Atlantic isn't wet enough, head to the **Ocean Breeze Waterpark,** a 19-acre slip-and-slide paradise with a million-gallon Runaway Bay wave pool, 16 waterslides, and a special pirate-themed section for the little ones.

Virginia Beach Convention & Visitor's Bureau
1-800-VA-BEACH
www.vbfun.com, www.virginia.org

Amusement Parks

In This Chapter

- Dollywood offers a variety of Southern amusements for the country western fan
- If you'd rather be under the sea, SeaWorld is your destination
- Ride the movies and learn how they're made at Universal Orlando
- Walt Disney World: the largest and most popular amusement park of them all, with good reason

When it comes to amusement parks, the South is *the* place to be, with its mini-cities packed with highly stylized roller coasters and multimedia attractions devoted to one theme or topic.

In our FamilyTravelForum.com online community, almost every family hopes to visit Walt Disney World and the other Orlando theme parks at least once during their kids' childhoods. That means a lot of households have the same vacation goals you do, and probably the same school breaks in which to do them. Here are a few tips that may help with your vacation planning:

Just because theme parks are marketed to all ages doesn't mean that everyone in the family will enjoy them. Your 14-month-old who loves Donald and Mickey cartoons may be terrified of costumed characters and get cranky from the heat, the long lines, and the hyper-excitement. Teens who hate cartoon characters may love the live shows yet fear roller coasters.

Try to visit these theme parks at the very beginning or end of school vacations (which vary state to state) or during the off seasons: January until mid-February, August, September, and from after Thanksgiving until mid-December. Lines are shorter then, and hotels, meals, and park tickets are cheaper.

Be prepared to wait in line. In our experience, it takes about 90 minutes of walking and waiting for each 2-minute ride. You won't get on more than two or three rides per day unless you plan ahead, mark up a park map, split up parents to accompany kids of different ages/interests, and use the park's free fixed-time entry passes or pay an extra fee for early admission or VIP status.

Weather matters. Many of these sky-high metal coasters will be closed during a rainstorm (count on daily showers in summer) or if lightning is nearby, so be prepared with a strategy (allowance, willpower, whatever) to spend time under cover in costly gift shops and souvenir stands. Carry a small backpack (it will be searched at the entry) with a towel and a change of clothes for everyone; lockers are widely available.

Be flexible. Each park has great shows and filmed attractions where parents can rest and kids can chill; we guarantee you won't get on every thrill ride of your dreams on this vacation.

Have fun. A theme park vacation is a big financial investment, which is why so many families save up to go to the best. And the Orlando parks, especially, offer just that.

Dollywood and Pigeon Forge, Tennessee

Home to Dolly Parton's **Dollywood** theme park and dozens of other country western–coated attractions, **Pigeon Forge** has become a huge vacation destination for families. Closely tied to its towering next-door neighbor and America's most visited national park, the **Great Smoky Mountains,** travelers pour into this bustling tourist gateway. Down-home country flavor is what it's all about, with a glitzy, neon-lit blanket thrown proudly over it. But just below the surface of Pigeon Forge is simple living, good times, patriotism, and a refreshing sense of Americana. Wandering up and down **The Parkway** is an adventure in itself; the town's main drag is lined with waterslides, go-kart tracks, arcades, and souvenir stands. Large, ornate theaters house resident country and western performers who entertain almost every night, all year long.

FELLOW TRAVELERS SAY ...

"We used to go [to the Great Smoky Mountains] for two weeks at a time and ... spent a lot of time in **Gatlinburg** and Pigeon Forge, and especially Dollywood! There's so much to do for young and old alike. Dollywood alone has so much stuff to offer, with outstanding shows, awesome rides, really great food, crafts, and shops."

— Dfrag, www.FamilyTravelBoards.com

Native daughter Dolly Parton grew up in humble surroundings in the Great Smoky foothills. After hitting it big, she returned to Tennessee to establish charitable foundations that work directly with Smoky Mountain communities. Dolly made her biggest move in 1986 when she took more than 118 acres belonging to an old theme park. Today, Dollywood is Tennessee's most popular manmade tourist attraction and Pigeon Forge's largest employer.

With a mix of top-flight roller coasters, authentic on-site craft demonstrations, musical performances, and games and activities for children of all ages, Dolly's theme park has captured the spirit of the Appalachian culture. Examples of the park's 10 environments include a huge fantasy **Treehouse** that toddlers and older children will have a ball exploring, **The Village** where you can board the *Dollywood Express* steam train or the carousel, and **The Wilderness** which features SkyZip, a zip line that gives harnessed guests a bird's-eye view of the park and mountains from 125 feet above the ground.

Plan ahead and the entire family can catch one of the four annual festivals, including the **Smoky Mountain Christmas.** Dollywood also celebrates the handcrafts heritage of America, particularly the Appalachian region. Visit **Craftsmen's Valley** to learn about the arts of blacksmithing, leather working, glass blowing, and other trades. Finished products are, of course, for sale.

Not even close to the scale of Disney World, what this park lacks in size and wonderment it gains in a lighthearted, manageable, and friendly experience. Adjacent to the theme park is **Dollywood's Splash Country,** a water adventure park full of fun summer activities; discounted admission to both is available with a two-park, three-day pass.

Dollywood
Pigeon Forge, TN 37863
1-800-365-5996
www.dollywood.com, www.mypigeonforge.com

SeaWorld Orlando and Discovery Cove

When you think of theme parks, spending a day with sharks and whales is probably not high on your mind. **SeaWorld Orlando** aims to change that mindset, and it does a great job. After being immersed in a Shamu show, touring the "hospital" where injured manatees are cared for and rehabilitated, or swimming with a dolphin at Discovery Cove, you'll not only be glad you spent a day (and we think you should spend at least two) here, but you'll also leave knowing a whole lot more about our neighbors below the sea.

FUN FACTS

SeaWorld Orlando is one of the first theme parks in the world to be fully viewable online. A specially outfitted Google bicycle went through SeaWorld and photographed nearly every inch of the park. You can visit SeaWorld from your computer by going to Google Maps in your browser and searching for SeaWorld, Discovery Cove, or Aquatica.

A world leader in animal conservation, SeaWorld helps all ages appreciate aquatic life with a fun yet educational approach. With more than 200 acres of exhibits hosted by friendly staff and naturalists, and numerous opportunities to get close to a variety of sharks, dolphins, manatees, and penguins, your family may feel as if you're living below the ocean's surface by lunchtime. If you crave more, look into their **Family Sleepovers** and summertime week-long sleep-away camps geared toward budding naturalists.

For vacationers, the renowned **Shamu Show** is a must. In a stadium setting, superbly trained Orca whales put on an Oscar-winning performance for a spellbound audience (people sitting in the first 10 rows should wear a raincoat). Don't stop there—**Pets Ahoy!** is a remarkable collection of funny skits put on by parakeets, dogs, and kittens. Kids taller than 48″ should line up for **Manta,** a new flying coaster that simulates riding on a sting ray, or enjoy the park's five other fun rides.

Braver families should check out **Sharks Deep Dive,** where you are submerged in a cage in a 120-foot-long pool teeming with more than 50 different species of shark. This experience will be a highlight of your trip, albeit an expensive one. A more budget-friendly alternative is to book a table at the **Sharks Underwater Grill,** where you see these denizens of the deep through a plate-glass wall right alongside your table. A huge grouper even comes over to see what you're eating.

Not remarkable enough? The unique **Beluga Interaction Program** takes up to 4 guests age 10 and older on a shallow-water encounter in the whales' habitat of the Wild Arctic section of the park. Another specialized program is the full-day **Marine Mammal Keeper Experience.** Kids ages 13 and older who are interested in being veterinarians or scientists will flip over a chance to work alongside professional trainers as they take care of manatees, turtles, whales, and a variety of other creatures. Again, there's a hefty fee in addition to the theme park entry, but these are truly one-of-a-kind vacation experiences.

A day at **Discovery Cove,** SeaWorld's nearby sister park, is like visiting the Caribbean. Your family will have to make advance reservations; only a limited number of people are admitted each day to this beautiful tropical landscape where you'll check your clothes, remove your shoes, and apply animal-safe sunscreen. Attractions within Discovery Cove include a dolphin training and swim session for ages six and older, a lagoon with rays and trainers ready to assist, and a lazy river that winds underneath an aviary where birds will sit on your shoulder. The all-inclusive price for this day-long adventure covers a continental breakfast, a full lunch at a thatched-roof grill, snacks, snorkel gear, towels, and sunscreen as well as general admission to SeaWorld Orlando or **Busch Gardens Tampa** (a great theme park for thrill riders) over seven consecutive days. It's our pick for best value if you have a week in Orlando.

If you are overcome by Orlando's humid summer heat and want to spend the day in a wave pool with state-of-the-art waterslides and lazy rivers, check out **Aquatica,** SeaWorld's water park. Aquatica offers great water play facilities in addition to the Dolphin Plunge, in which you slide through tunnels on inner tubes that pass through tanks filled with dolphins.

SeaWorld Orlando
Orlando, FL 32821
1-800-557-4268
www.seaworld.com, www.seaworldparksblog.com

Universal Orlando

Universal Orlando offers a special theme park experience by bringing the cinematic flair of major movies to its rides and live shows. We think it's the best destination for families who love cartoons, comics, and films, because you can learn how they're made at **Universal Studios Florida** and then dive into the storylines on the great rides at **Universal's Islands of Adventure.**

At Universal Studios Florida, we loved Jimmy Neutron's Nicktoon Blast, which rockets families through a journey featuring Nickelodeon's finest: not only Jimmy but also SpongeBob, the Rugrats, and characters from "The Fairly OddParents" and "Hey Arnold!". Even older kids who recall these classic TV cartoons will enjoy the ride. The best bet for the littlest tykes is **Woody Woodpecker's KidZone,** where Woody's Nuthouse Coaster offers a pint-sized thrill. Barney, Curious George, and Fievel each have a colorful and interactive playground, while Barney also performs a sing-along with Baby Bop and B. J.

FUN FACTS

The Egyptian hieroglyphics decorating the walls of **Revenge of the Mummy** spell out real words and warnings to the visitors.

Don't worry about restless teens, however, because many of the major rides are suited to older kids who want to "ride the movies." They'll have a blast on *Revenge of the Mummy*, which blasts riders through the mummy's tomb to create a psychological thrill with ghouls galore. The *Men in Black* Alien Attack allows you to play the MIB agent by zapping aliens. The *Terminator 2* show combines 3-D film, live action stunts, and special effects; and "Twister … Ride It Out" is a live-action tornado simulation.

The entire family will savor other movie-themed attractions even if they haven't seen the film. At Shrek 4-D, the story picks up where the first *Shrek* left off (on Shrek and Fiona's honeymoon). For a classic experience, try the "E.T." Adventure, which offers a journey to the mild-mannered alien's planet on flying bicycles. The "Blues Brothers" show offers multi-age appeal and fun entertainment.

Directly adjacent to Universal Studios Florida and sharing the admission ticket is Islands of Adventure. Although it's marketed for "serious" thrills, the park also contains plenty of rides, attractions, and interactive playgrounds for little ones. The entire "island" of **Seuss Landing** is a great place to meet some of the world's most beloved literary characters and includes the non-height-restricted Cat in the Hat ride and the Caro-Seuss-el with Seuss creatures instead of horses. On **Jurassic Park Island,** the Discovery Center offers games and educational displays while Camp Jurassic is yet another themed water playground to take the kids to while your teens brave facing T-Rex.

Send older children to the Amazing Adventures of Spider-Man, a 3-D Spidey's-eye view attraction. **Superhero Island** also offers the Incredible Hulk Coaster and Dr. Doom's Freefall. **The Lost Continent,** yet another themed island, features the popular racing coaster Dueling Dragons as well as Poseidon's Fury show.

Don't miss the new **Wizarding World of Harry Potter.** After entering Hogwarts Castle and exploring sets related to the books and films, board the wild ride and be part of a new "Harry Potter" adventure. There are three great attractions, plus stores and restaurants from the popular book series.

For nightlife, **CityWalk** offers 30 acres of restaurants, clubs, and entertainment, including a 20-screen movie theater, live music, and performances by Blue Man Group.

VACATION PLANNING TIPS

Families interested in parking the car and staying at one of the park's three themed, on-site **Loews Hotels** will pay more than elsewhere, but the first-in-line access your hotel room key card provides is worth its weight in gold.

Universal Orlando
Orlando, FL 32819
407-363-8000
www.universalorlando.com, www.universalstudios.com

Walt Disney World, Orlando

While Orlando is filled with dozens of themed attractions, the one theme park that nobody wants to miss is Walt Disney World. Disney urges you to "come and experience the magic," and we strongly encourage you to accept the invitation. Disney World is truly magical—it's the largest and most popular resort in the world and contains something for every member of the family among its 4 theme parks, 2 water parks, more than 20 themed hotels, and a plethora of restaurants, shops, and entertainment venues. Entire books have been written about it, so we'll just take a tour past some of our favorite attractions and remind you just how well Disney does everything.

Which Pirates of the Caribbean came first: the movie or the ride? Disney "old-timers" know the answer: the ride. At **Magic Kingdom,** where swashbuckling animatronics have been entertaining visitors for years, both young and old members of the family will find gentle and scary rides to enjoy. Our family favorites are blasting off at Space Mountain and Splash Mountain, the legendary indoor roller coaster and log flume ride. This is the park if you or the little ones are trying to collect autographs from favorite Disney characters, as many of them walk around here throughout the day.

FELLOW TRAVELERS SAY ...

"For the first time in a long time, we were all having fun together, taking time out of our busy schedules to experience a family vacation. The memories will never leave any of us; we often bring up the memories of Disney World. As soon as we returned home, my brother and I started begging our mom to take us back to Disney as soon as possible."

—L. L., www.travelBIGO.com

Older children and teens will find futuristic rides at **Epcot** that are sure to amaze them. The best attractions transcend our everyday experiences of speed and perspective. Mission: SPACE is a technologically awesome flight simulator that puts you in the driver's seat of a NASA spacecraft—a spinning and bouncing seat at that. Visitors can bypass the centrifuge and enjoy the ride's other effects by asking the Cast Member (Disney speak for employee) to direct you to the proper line. Test Track recreates another high-speed situation: automobile testing. You'll ride in a car with five other passengers as you climb hills, battle harsh road surfaces, recover from skids, and even crash into a barrier. (Don't worry, you won't come out looking like those crash-test dummies in the commercials!)

At **Disney's Hollywood Studios,** the Twilight Zone Tower of Terror has been terrifying everyone from older children to grandparents for years. After watching a short pre-show that evokes the old TV series, you'll board an "old" elevator to the top of the tower, only to have the elevator cables "snap" and cause a freefall of several stories. The Rock n' Roller Coaster features unexpected drops, sudden high speeds, and a blasting Aerosmith soundtrack. When you're ready for a rest, board "Toy Story" Mania! for an old-fashioned 3-D midway ride, or take in some of the movies here.

The entire family will love **Animal Kingdom,** where more than 1,500 animals reside on 500 acres of jungles, forests, and a grassy savannah. The world's largest animal-themed park boasts Kali River Rapids, a great way to cool down on a hot day. Just be sure to avoid the T-Rex on the loose! He's anything but fossilized.

Walt Disney World boasts two water parks: **Typhoon Lagoon,** a tropical island–style park that lets you snorkel with real sharks; and **Blizzard Beach,** a snow-themed collection of giant waterslides. Unfortunately, they are not worth the extra admission fee unless you have at least a half day and plenty of warm weather to enjoy them.

Sports-loving families should check out the **Wide World of Sports Complex.** It features 220 acres of sports fields, and if you're there at the right time, you can catch the Atlanta Braves or the Tampa Bay Buccaneers during their spring training.

Parents, grandparents, and adult kids will find plenty of entertainment suited to their tastes. On Expedition Everest in Animal Kingdom, visitors depart from a recreated Himalayan village on a roller coaster with many surprises. World Showcase at Epcot has 11 country-themed pavilions featuring shops, attractions, and ethnic restaurants (make reservations in advance if you have your heart set on a particular cuisine—we recommend the Moroccan!). This park's gentle Soarin' ride that floats over an IMAX vision of California is another treat for all ages.

VACATION PLANNING TIPS

Disney insiders have shared a few sanity- and money-saving tips with us:

- Get a **dining plan;** if you book a "Magic Your Way" package, you can buy a virtual coupon book that can cut up to 40 percent off the cost of meals. The Disney website frequently offers other deals.
- Book your meal reservations early, because Disney's character breakfasts and better restaurants book quickly.
- Use the **FastPass** system to reserve admission times to the most popular rides; it's free, and you'll have an hour's window in which to use it or book the next one.

Disney takes very good care of its families with young kids. The Rider Swap program allows guests to take turns waiting with youngsters too small to ride a certain attraction, then "swap" with another adult from their party to experience the ride without standing in line twice. You'll also find a number of baby care centers around the park, where you can change and feed your baby. Strollers are available for rental, and babysitters are available in the Disney hotels for children 6 months to 12 years.

Beyond the theme parks, you'll find five top-quality golf courses that reserve tee times and shuttle service for on-site Disney World hotel guests. Disney hotels rent a wide variety of water sports and sports equipment to guests.

Even if you're exhausted after a long day at the parks, we recommend getting out at night and seeing the huge variety of nightlife that Disney World offers. **Downtown Disney West Side** has restaurants serving everything from Cuban cuisine to seafood, with entertainment options including a 24-screen movie theater, a House of Blues music club, and the live Cirque du Soleil performance "La Nouba." **Downtown Disney Marketplace** offers the largest Disney character store in the world as well as a quiet lakeside restaurant. **Disney's Boardwalk** is home to more shops, restaurants, and nightclubs— most of which are adjacent to the water. Parents looking to get away from the kids should visit the Atlantic Dance Hall and the Jellyrolls piano bar, both 21-and-over venues. Transportation to and from these Disney areas is complimentary for guests of Disney hotels.

Lodging at Walt Disney World should be the least of your concerns. There are 24 official Disney Resort hotels near the parks in a variety of price ranges. All Walt Disney World resorts have swimming pools, food courts or themed restaurants, and arcades. In addition to well-landscaped grounds, original artwork, and a crowded shuttle system, there are a number of benefits that come from the on-site hotels: extended admission hours to beat the crowds (typically one hour earlier than the public and up to three hours' later); VIP privileges at Disney golf courses; advance dinner show and character breakfast reservations; a Walt Disney World I.D. card for charging all meals and purchases; and seasonal bonus shows or activities at the resorts.

Walt Disney World
407-939-6244
disneyworld.disney.go.com, www.disney.com

Outdoor Adventures

In This Chapter

- The scenic mountain drives and trails of Appalachia
- Exploring the natural beauty and fascinating history of the Great Smoky Mountains
- Swimming with Florida's majestic manatees

Although everyone associates the South with great beaches, other outdoor recreation options abound. You can take a scenic foliage drive, hike mountain trails in search of wildlife, or swim the blue ocean waters with mammoth mammals.

One of our favorite outdoor adventures is taking the family on a picturesque drive down the Blue Ridge Parkway when autumn leaves turn shades of orange and red; there's enough passing scenery to evoke silence even from children. Bordering the Parkway is Great Smoky Mountains National Park, full of well-marked hiking and biking trails and a myriad of eclectic family-friendly attractions. And if you've had enough of trails and the mountains, consider an animal encounter your kids will never forget.

No matter what you decide, pack your family's hiking boots, water bottles, sun block, and binoculars—and don't forget swimsuits!

Blue Ridge Parkway and Appalachian Mountains

Stretching 469 miles from the Shenandoah National Park south to the Great Smoky Mountains straddling the North Carolina-Tennessee border, the **Blue Ridge Parkway**—dubbed "America's Favorite Drive"—offers some of the best hiking and biking in the United States.

South of **Roanoke,** Virginia, start your hiking adventure at the **Mountain Industry Trail.** Here, you'll find **Mabry Mill,** a site harkening back to the old days with its whiskey still and other displays showing rural life in old Appalachia, an isolated mountain region whose inhabitants shunned outsiders for centuries. Easy-going **Round Meadow Creek Loop Trail** is home to the **Groundhog Mountain Observation Tower** and **Puckett Cabin. High Meadow Trail** leads to the **Blue Ridge Music Center,** whose outdoor amphitheater and indoor interpretive center are great places to relax and tap your feet to some locally produced bluegrass.

FUN FACTS

One curious roadside attraction is Puckett Cabin, where Aunt Orelena Hawks Puckett lived from 1874 until 1939, acting as midwife to more than 1,000 births. She began midwifery in her 50s, having given birth to 24 children herself, but none lived beyond infancy. Aunt Orelena charged new moms between $1 and $6 and was 102 when she delivered her last baby.

Upon driving into North Carolina, many of the trails offer prime sites for fishing, canoeing, and camping. Located at milepost 331 at **Gillespie Gap,** the **Museum of North Carolina Minerals** welcomes kids with its hands-on displays about gold, copper, kaolin, and other minerals found nearby. Heading south along the parkway, be sure to stop by the **Graveyard Fields Loop Trail.** (It's not as grim as it sounds.) It leads to a decayed spruce forest whose root stumps have the eerie appearance of graves. A similarly dark-named destination is **Devil's Courthouse**—a mountain cave said to be where the devil holds court, and for the Cherokee, the dwelling place of the slant-eyed giant Judaculla.

The southwestern end of the parkway leads to the **Cherokee Indian Reservation** at the edge of the Great Smoky Mountains. The reservation's museum, village, and outdoor dramas help visitors understand the 11,000-year-old culture, its fascinating legends, and the tragic tale of the Trail of Tears. Kids will like the decorative fiberglass bears designed by local Cherokee artists.

Swap trails for sidewalks in **Asheville,** North Carolina—a truly off-beat destination for those who want to kick off their shoes and jump right into hippie central. Roam the town's helter-skelter streets and enjoy local performers, unique galleries, shops, and perhaps a spontaneous drum circle in the central plaza. **The Folk Art Center** has craft demonstrations, the **Asheville Art Museum** displays contemporary American art, and the **Colburn Earth Science Museum** has hands-on geology exhibits. Asheville's historic sites include the **Biltmore,** a 125,000-acre estate featuring a Vanderbilt mansion with 250 rooms and 65 fireplaces, plus facilities for carriage and horseback rides, river float trips, hiking, and biking.

Blue Ridge Parkway Association
828-271-4779
www.blueridgeparkway.org, www.visitnc.com

Great Smoky Mountains National Park, Tennessee

Formed more than 200 million years ago, the **Great Smoky Mountains** are some of the oldest on Earth. In the bio-diverse national park that surrounds them, families can explore 800 miles of trails while trying to spot more than 10,000 documented species—and what some scientists believe may be an additional 90,000 undocumented species hidden in this unusual habitat. The park is home to some 1,500 Great American Bears, not counting the family-favorite Smokey.

Stretching across Tennessee and North Carolina, this land was once home to the Cherokee Indians. Ranger-led programs offered throughout the fall, spring, and summer focus on the natural wonders and history of the area. Aside from wildlife viewing, the park provides facilities for bicycling, auto tours, hiking, fishing, and especially horseback riding. If your family falls in love with the mountains, sign up for camp at the **Great Smoky Mountains Institute** at Tremont, a year-round residential environmental education center.

Beyond the majestic mountains, there is plenty to explore. In **Sevierville,** families with budding pilots can explore the **Tennessee Museum of Aviation's** kid-friendly interactive exhibits, historical aviation memorabilia, and authentic aircraft. On Route 441, racing fans will find a haven at the **NASCAR SpeedPark,** where kids and adults can burn rubber in a ⅝-scale NASCAR Cup vehicle and take a spin on the coasters in the Thrill Zone.

Not far off the track, one of the largest reptile zoos in the world, **Rainforest Adventures,** features more than 400 live animals. Kids can learn all about the fascinating animals of the rain forest—our favorites being the tree-dwelling kinkajou and the mischievous-looking ring-tailed lemur. For the spelunking-savvy, the **Forbidden Caverns**—once home to the Eastern Woodland Indians—have the largest wall of rare cave onyx known to exist. **Wilderness at the Smokies,** located minutes from Interstate 40, has grown into the Southeast's largest water play zone with two outdoor water parks, an indoor water park with a wave pool, a surf rider, and dozens more thrills.

Touristy **Gatlinburg** is the gateway for families who drive to the park each summer. Get on your Daisy Dukes and take a gander at **Cooter's Place,** a genuine "Dukes of Hazzard" museum with costumes and vehicles from the show. After that, ogle the **Ripley's Believe It or Not Museum and Aquarium of the Smokies.** Here, aquatic exhibits include a tropical rain forest, coral reef, shark lagoon, and children's Discovery Center. The Ripley's Odditorium is just what it implies, with unusual exhibits on display. There are plenty of restaurants and lodging in every price range in and around the town.

Great Smoky Mountains National Park
107 Park Headquarters Road
Gatlinburg, TN 37738
865-436-1200
www.nps.gov/grsm, www.tnvacation.com

Swimming with Manatees in Florida

Dive into the pristine, clear waters of Florida's **Homosassa** or **Crystal Rivers** and get up close and personal with these sociable aquatic animals, also known as "sea cows." Being in proximity of these gentle creatures is an unforgettable underwater adventure for any age. The region around **Homosassa Springs Wildlife State Park** in northwest Florida is home to the largest concentration of manatees in the world.

Local tours offering "swim with the manatees" experiences (appropriate for children ages three and older who can swim) are available at Homosassa Springs Wildlife State Park, which has been twice presented the National Recreation and Parks Association's Gold Medal Award.

Another local outfitter is **River Safaris and Gulf Charters,** the area's oldest boat tour company. If you're in the Crystal River area, you can contact **Crystal Lodge Dive,** a full-service manatee dive center, or the **Port Paradise Marina & Dive Center,** also a resort hotel situated on seven scenic acres.

November through February is prime viewing season for manatees in the wild. It's an incredible experience for school-age kids and a bargain as well, because many of the central Florida wildlife tours are given at little or no cost in state parks or on government-protected lands. The **Homosassa Springs Department of Environmental Protection Parks and Recreation** facility houses a captive manatee maintenance and research facility. The manatees in this program were either captive-born or recovered from the wild due to illness or injury. The public may view manatees in this program from an underwater viewing area or during one of the daily shows.

If you'd rather marvel at these massive, friendly creatures from afar, viewing facilities include **Blue Spring State Park** in Orange City, **The Manatee Observation and Education Center** in Fort Pierce, and **Lee County Manatee Park** in Fort Myers.

Homosassa Springs Wildlife State Park
4150 S. Suncoast Blvd.
Homosassa, FL 34446
352-628-5343
www.homosassasprings.org/Homosassa.cfm,
www.savethemanatee.org

The Midwest

The geographic center of the United States is a group of 12 states known collectively as the Midwest. Home to Dorothy, the Kansas girl who starred in the *Wizard of Oz*, and Huck Finn, whose creator Mark Twain came from Missouri, it is rightly considered the country's cultural heartland.

America's heartland is also multicultural. The Underground Railroad, a network for slaves escaping bondage, ran directly through the Midwest. Europeans from Ireland, Germany, Poland, Hungary, Sweden, and Finland immigrated to a new land whose rural topography and farm life were akin to their homelands. Each of these cultural and ethnic groups has added elements of their heritage to the Midwest potpourri.

Today, the states of Illinois, Indiana, Iowa, Kansas, Michigan, Minnesota, Missouri, Nebraska, North Dakota, Ohio, South Dakota, and Wisconsin comprise an enormous and diverse area. Part 3 looks at the many vacation possibilities: small-town pleasures and urban treasures; pockets of American, industrial, and arts history; the roots of popular culture; stunning national parks; and unexpected family attractions.

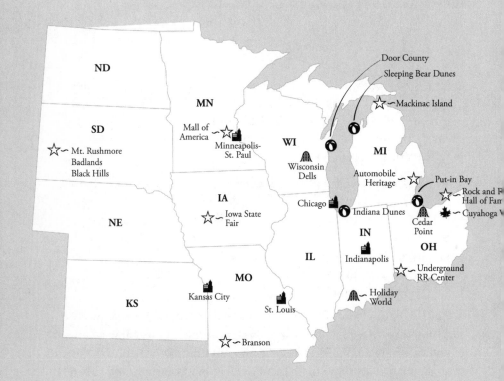

ND

MN

SD

NE

KS

Mt. Rushmore
Badlands
Black Hills

Mall of
America

Minneapolis-
St. Paul

IA

Iowa State
Fair

MO

Kansas City

St. Louis

Branson

Door County

Sleeping Bear Dunes

Mackinac Island

WI

Wisconsin
Dells

MI

Automobile
Heritage

Put-in Bay

Rock and R...
Hall of Fam...

Cuyahoga V...

Chicago

Indiana Dunes

Cedar
Point

OH

IN

Indianapolis

Underground
RR Center

IL

Holiday
World

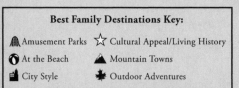

Best Family Destinations Key:

🎢 Amusement Parks ☆ Cultural Appeal/Living History

🏖 At the Beach ⛰ Mountain Towns

🏙 City Style 🍁 Outdoor Adventures

In This Chapter

- Chicago: the "most American" city
- Blues and barbeque in Kansas City
- Sports galore in Indy
- St. Louis' family-friendly culture
- Double the pleasures in the Twin Cities

The cities of the Midwest, while less glamorous than their coastal big siblings, have lots to offer travelers of any age and interest. Manageably sized and welcoming, each is surprisingly sophisticated with distinct world-class attractions, great food, reasonable prices, and good vibes. Because they are very different from one another, we urge you to read on and choose a destination that will most appeal to your family's interests.

Chicago, Illinois

The Windy City has been one of America's top urban centers since the first steel skyscraper was built here in the nineteenth century. It's full of great museums and culture, classic and modern architecture, expansive parks along the 18-mile-long lakefront, and fine restaurants—many of which welcome kids—just about everywhere you turn.

Park the car and head out on foot to sightsee along the famous **Magnificent Mile,** the Michigan Avenue shopping mecca that's home to the flagship American Girl Place. This is one neighborhood to try a burger made from Chicago's legendary Midwestern corn-fed beef, or stop for a slice of famous deep-dish pizza. Festivals for ice sculpting and snowplay are held all winter long and many Miracle Mile shops remain open past dinner to accommodate the crowds. Take a shopping break and ascend through the clouds to the **Skydeck,** 1,353 feet up in the former Sears Tower (now the **Willis Tower**). Step out onto The Ledge, where you actually stand four feet out from the building in a glass box looking straight down. It's scary fun—and an unforgettable photo op.

While the Obama family currently has the spotlight as Chicago's most notable denizens, legendary architect Frank Lloyd Wright is a historic favorite. Architecture buffs can see his work, as well as 1 South State Street, designed by Louis Henri Sullivan in 1899, considered the first modern skyscraper.

Chicago has some of the most entertaining museums in the United States. Starting nearest to downtown, the fantastic **Chicago Children's Museum** is adjacent to **Navy Pier,** a really fun destination packed with parks, teen-friendly shops (including some Chicago deep-dish pizza parlors), and a Ferris wheel. **The Art Institute of Chicago**'s favorite family exhibit is found in the Thorne Rooms, a collection of 68 fully decorated miniature rooms that will thrill anyone who has ever played in a dollhouse.

Museum Campus hosts the remarkable **Shedd Aquarium, The Field Museum of Natural History,** and the just-renovated **Adler Planetarium and Astronomy Museum.** Each is a major draw for families, so you'll want to return over a few days. The Shedd offers a wide array of aquatic exhibits and the new Fantasea, a live show starring resident beluga whales, dolphins, and penguins. Plan ahead and the entire family can book an overnight program to sleep with the fish; it's the cheapest hotel room in town—and what a view! The Field Museum hosts dinosaurs (Susie is the world's largest intact T. Rex skeleton), Egyptian mummies, extinct civilizations, and much more. A few miles west, the **Museum of Science and Industry** is a treasure trove of kid-friendly exhibits (don't miss the World War II

German U505 submarine, the coal mine, the Pioneer Zephyr train, the Chick Hatchery, the eco-perfect Smart House, and the museum's extraordinary multi-media exploration of the workings of the human body).

If you're short on time, get oriented on a guided **Lake Michigan** boat tour (that is, if it's not too cold or windy); you can see the city day or night from both the lake and the **Chicago River,** which meanders through downtown. Budget watchers can see the skyline from the L, Chicago's elevated train line, or hop on a free tour of **The Loop** (the L's inner circuit) every Saturday from spring through fall and led by the Chicago Architecture Foundation. Double-decker buses are also a popular way to get around.

Everyone in the family ages 12 and older (and between 100 and 240 pounds) can take a Segway tour exploring the lakefront, **Buckingham Fountain,** and Museum Campus by two-wheeled motorized magic. For a more traditional tour, bike rentals with helmets and tot trailers are available in **Millennium Park, Grant Park,** Navy Pier, and other locations in the central city. You and your kids can work off the pizza and cover a lot of ground while enjoying the ride on two wheels.

FELLOW TRAVELERS SAY ...

"The Segway is a magnificent invention—a machine so intuitive that it almost feels like an extension of your nervous system."

—R. B., www.FamilyTravelForum.com

City of Chicago Tourism
1-877-CHICAGO
www.explorechicago.org, www.enjoyillinois.com

Kansas City, Missouri

Kansas City, Missouri, is just over the state line from Kansas City, Kansas. Confusing? Yes—but once you've visited, you'll see that they don't have much in common besides their names. The rich tapestry of Missouri's Kansas City is woven from its varied contributions to American culture: Hallmark, Harleys, jazz, blues, baseball, and barbeque.

The city owes the revitalization of its downtown to the **Crown Center** complex, the international headquarters of Hallmark Cards. The **Hallmark Visitors Center**'s free tour tells the history of the greeting card company, and the center's **Kaleidoscope** is a must-see attraction for those with school-age kids. This free art workshop encourages kids to let their imaginations go wild while making use of mountains of materials recycled from Hallmark's card manufacturing process.

Another prize from the downtown renewal is **Union Station.** When the railroad station opened in 1914, President Wilson declared it "The Gateway to the West," but it closed in 1983. Now beautifully restored, trains once again roar through the second-largest train station in the nation, part of a complex that houses cinemas and live theaters, restaurants, and shops. The centerpiece of the revived landmark is **Science City,** where visitors can land a space shuttle, solve a crime, ride a bike 10 feet in the air, and watch a paleontologist prepare dinosaur fossils for exhibition.

VACATION PLANNING TIPS

History buffs can travel 20 minutes from Kansas City to Independence, Missouri, to visit the **Presidential Library and Museum of President Harry Truman.**

Another notable in American history, Jesse James' story is told at the **Jesse James Bank Museum** (site of the first successful daylight bank robbery) in Liberty, Missouri, and in Kearny, Missouri, at the **Jesse James Farm Museum,** where you can view the restored homestead of Frank and Jesse James.

Children ages 12 and older and their parents are welcome to enjoy the free tour of the **Harley Davidson Assembly Plant** to see how "hogs" are made. View an introductory film and then tour the production facility to see everything from robotic welding technology to final polishing. Distribute some allowance, and then leave time for the cool gift shop.

Located at the historic center of African American culture in Kansas City and collectively called the **Museums at 18th & Vine,** your first stop should be the **Horace M. Peterson III Visitors Center** for "A People's Journey"—an audiovisual presentation on African Americans' experience and heritage.

Other sights to enjoy here include the **Gem Theatre Cultural and Performing Arts Center** and the **American Jazz Museum,** the first devoted exclusively to this uniquely American musical art form. The informative interactive exhibits present sample recordings by legends such as Ella Fitzgerald, Louis Armstrong, and Duke Ellington (among others); artifacts include original musical instruments. The John Baker Film Collection Exhibit blends rare film clips with state-of-the-art audiovisual technology. In the evenings, families can enjoy performances at the Blue Room, an adjacent jazz club.

Across the building's lobby, **The Negro League Baseball Museum** recreates the look, sound, and feel of baseball during the height of the Negro Leagues, which were founded in 1920 at the former Paseo YMCA (a block from the museum) and saw their demise in the 1960s. Fans will appreciate the replica baseball field with life-size bronze statues of some early players. A photo and video gallery captures the earliest days of both segregated and integrated play.

FUN FACTS

With roots in the cattle industry, Kansas City has evolved into a barbeque-lover's heaven. There are more than 100 tantalizing barbeque restaurants to choose from, including those of legendary **Arthur Bryant,** who currently serves his slow-roasted meats at three restaurants in Kansas City. Also popular is **Gates BBQ,** originally located at 19th and Vine, operating six restaurants in the greater Kansas City area. Try them both, and have everyone in your family vote on their favorite.

In addition to the **Nelson-Atkins Museum,** considered the most distinguished art museum in the Midwest, Kansas City is home to several other interesting collections. Visitors can take a close look at a restored Lockheed L1049 "Super G" Constellation, a Martin 404, and a Douglas DC-3 at the **Airline History Museum,** which explores propeller-driven transport aircraft.

The entire family will love **Worlds of Fun** amusement park. Patterned after the Jules Verne novel *Around the World in Eighty Days*, it features five themed continent areas with more than 50 rides ranging in thrill levels from mild to wild. Adjacent is **Oceans of Fun,** the Midwest's largest tropical-themed water park featuring a million-gallon wave pool and several waterslides.

Kansas City Convention and Visitors Association
1-800-767-7700
www.visitkc.com, www.missouribeautiful.com/kansas-city-missouri-tourism

Indianapolis, Indiana

Indianapolis is probably best known for its sports triumphs, starting with the **Indianapolis Motor Speedway,** home of the **Indy 500,** the most famous auto race in America. It's home to Super Bowl winners the Colts, as well as its NBA team, the Pacers; and basketball was closely tied to the state long before the 1986 film *Hoosiers* dramatized a local high school's triumph in the sport.

Supporting those franchises is a vibrant and diverse city with much to offer visiting families. Whether you're looking for world-class museums or a nationally recognized historical restoration village, the capital of the Hoosier State is one of the Midwest's best cities for families.

Begin your exploration in the heart of downtown at **White River State Park,** which hosts several museums, an IMAX theater, Victory Field, NCAA Hall of Champions, and a zoo within its web of trails and waterways. You can explore it via multiple means of conveyance—on rental bikes, by Segway tours, aboard a gondola, via self-propelled pedal boats, and in kayaks. The Visitor's Center provides guidance, maps, and information.

The **Indianapolis Zoo** is much more than a collection of animals. An aquarium with a swim-with-dolphins experience and a botanical garden enhance its appeal to all ages. There are more than 2,000 animals in residence as well as special learning opportunities (with modest fees). Kids can watch an enormous elephant paint with a brush curled into his/her trunk, take a behind-the-scenes tour of the zoo, and ride with the engineer on the miniature train.

Of particular interest in White River State Park is the **Eiteljorg Museum of American Indians and Western Art,** which houses a major collection of both Western and Native American art. If little ones get restless in front of the stunning landscapes, take them to join the special activities for children in the museum's Discover Junction.

VACATION PLANNING TIPS

For easy and free around-town transportation daily, hop aboard the Blue Line with **IndyGo** and wind your way through downtown. You'll see major attractions including White River State Park, City Market, Victory Field, the Indiana Convention Center, and Circle Centre mall.

The Children's Museum of Indianapolis is the world's largest children's museum; if you're traveling with anyone younger than 12, this is a must-visit attraction. The "Take Me There: Egypt" is a clever, immersive virtual trip starting in the cabin of an airplane and leading to a set of Cairo streets, the interior of a typical apartment, and other simulations of daily life in Egypt. Budding paleontologists can explore the Dinosphere, a significant collection of real dinosaur fossils (including a full-size mastodon), a dinosaur dig, and a question lab with in-depth dinosaur information. We especially like the train exhibits in the basement, the full-size polar bear on the second floor, and the giant Water Clock. For pure fun, there's also a working antique carousel.

For the car guys and gals, a trip to the **Indianapolis Motor Speedway Hall of Fame Museum,** even on a non-race day, is an easy way to taste the experience of one of the most famous auto races in the world, the Indianapolis 500, which draws more than 400,000 people each Memorial Day weekend.

Every generation of the family will adore the **Conner Prairie Interactive History Park,** located about 10 miles north of the city in Fishers, Indiana. The park encompasses an original 1823 homestead of farmer William Conner and his Lenape Indian wife. The homestead was purchased by philanthropist Eli Lilly, heir to the family pharmaceutical business, as a testament to the state's place in American history. Within the park's 200 wooded acres are five themed historic areas that are just plain fun and a great way to illuminate life in another century. Participatory activities range from Native American dancing to tomahawk throwing, candle dipping to pie making, and pioneer kids' games to helping a carpenter. The Discovery Station has indoor activities as well. In summer, check to see if the Indianapolis Symphony Orchestra will be performing the outdoor Symphony on the Prairie series or any of their hour-long family concerts. The newest and most dramatic Conner Prairie experience is taking a helium-filled balloon ride 350 feet above the village (fair weather only). This replicates a famous 1859 hot-air balloon ride that caused a sensation in nearby Lafayette.

Indianapolis Convention and Visitors Association
1-800-323-INDY
www.visitindy.com, www.in.gov/visitindiana

St. Louis, Missouri

St. Louis is called the "Gateway to the West" in honor of its important role in the westward expansion of the United States. The city's towering icon, the **Gateway Arch,** is a monument to that spirit of exploration. Designed by the noted Finnish-American architect Eero Saarinen in 1963, the graceful stainless-steel arch changes color in different light.

FUN FACTS

McDonald's famous golden arches preceded Saarinen's design for the Gateway Arch by a decade.

The Gateway Arch measures 630 feet high and 630 feet from leg to leg. To reach the viewing area at its apex, board a "train" of tram capsules, which takes four minutes going up and only three to get back down. From the top, you can see for 30 miles all around, but beware—some people complain of claustrophobia in the tram. Located beneath what is officially called the **Jefferson National**

Expansion Memorial National Historic Site is the fascinating **Museum of Western Expansion.** Highlights include artifacts from pioneer and Native American communities, including an authentic tipi and an overview of the Lewis and Clark expedition.

With the city's location on the historic **Mississippi River,** we recommend sightseeing on "Ol' Man River" on a replica nineteenth-century Mississippi steamship. Dinner cruises and specialty cruises—including the Blues Cruise, complete with live music—are available.

Back on land, several attractions—most free—are located within **Forest Park,** one of the largest and loveliest parks in America. Be sure to visit the **St. Louis Zoo,** home to more than 6,000 animals, where you can ride the Zoo Train, check out the Butterfly Dome, and pet at the Children's Petting Zoo. The **St. Louis Art Museum,** America's first publicly funded museum, is housed in the beautiful Fine Arts Palace built for the 1904 World's Fair. Your family can explore all aspects of science—from aviation to ecology and dinosaurs to technology—at the **St. Louis Science Center,** an exciting hands-on playground-style museum. Visit a space station at the James S. McDonnell Planetarium, watch an Omnimax movie, and take a ride on a Segway.

VACATION PLANNING TIPS

St. Louis claims two "World's Largests"—a transportation museum and a brewery.

The **Museum of Transportation**'s collection includes planes, trains, automobiles, trolleys, buses, fire trucks, and boats—many of which your kids can climb on.

Anheuser-Busch Brewery tours show families the processes of mashing, fermenting, finishing, and packaging beer. Kids will love the stable of Clydesdale draft horses, and those 21 and older can enjoy free samples.

To explore other unique symbols of the city, put on a red shirt and cheer at **Busch Stadium,** home of the St. Louis Cardinals. If you miss a game, tours passing by the Official Team Store are available. **St. Louis Union Station,** dating to 1894, is no longer the busiest railroad station in the world, but it is a unique, very grand shopping, dining, and entertainment complex that evokes the past.

St. Louis Convention & Visitors Commission
1-800-916-0092
www.explorestlouis.com, www.visitmo.com

Twin Cities: Minneapolis and St. Paul, Minnesota

There's twice as much for families to do in the Twin Cities of Minneapolis and St. Paul, and their location along Minnesota's **Chain of Lakes** provides a myriad of outdoor pleasures. But what distinguishes Minneapolis and St. Paul is that residents take culture very seriously here and proudly present art and theater with gusto.

VACATION PLANNING TIPS

Drama, comedy, and music lovers of all ages will be thrilled by the region's two Tony award–winning theaters and other performance venues, but you'll have to order tickets in advance.

- The **Children's Theatre Company,** considered by many to be the pre-eminent children's theater in the United States, is a fabulous year-round resource.
- **The Guthrie Theater,** in its architecturally distinctive facility overlooking the Mississippi River, is a highly acclaimed regional theatre whose repertoire spans the classics to contemporary works.
- **Theatre de la Jeune Lune** presents innovative, visually spectacular performances.
- The **Fitzgerald Theater,** named in honor of F. Scott Fitzgerald (one of St. Paul's most famous native sons), is where the radio show *A Prairie Home Companion*, hosted by Garrison Keillor, is based.

Special-interest museums also run the gamut and are hugely inventive. The **Minnesota Children's Museum,** whose slogan is "Playing Is Learning," and the **Science Museum of Minnesota** are both renowned for their creative demonstrations and hands-on learning opportunities. Kids (and their parents) are never bored at these fun-filled spots. The fascinating **Mill City Museum** tells the story of Minneapolis as the "Flour Milling Capital of the World," the industry that put this city on the map. Adjacent to **St. Anthony's Falls,** which powered more than 20 mills along the Mississippi, the museum is housed in a restored mill where more than 12 million loaves of bread were once made daily from the wheat processed here. From the rooftop Observation Deck, you will have a great view of the river and the falls. History buffs will enjoy a visit to **Fort Snelling,** where costumed guides demonstrate crafts, military drills, and historical scenes of frontier life circa 1827.

Visitors to these cities can also enjoy the great outdoors. The Chain of Lakes are popular for boating, swimming, and fishing. Throughout the city, lakeside paths draw joggers, bicyclists, and inline skaters.

Lake Minnetonka in Wayzata offers swimming, boat rentals, cruises, and entertainment. The **Grand Rounds National Scenic Byway** is a 50-mile recreation loop for strolling, biking, and cross-country skiing within an urban environment. Other favorite amusement areas include the **Three Rivers Park** District with facilities for every season and **Minnehaha Falls.** When your feet get tired, hop on the **Minneapolis RiverCity Trolley** for transportation with entertaining commentary. Families with kids 13 and older can sign up for a guided Segway tour. Or you can board the paddle-wheeler *Minneapolis Queen* for a cruise on Ol' Man River.

FUN FACTS

According to Rollerblade.com (and who would know better?), when two hockey-playing Minnesota brothers discovered an old inline skate, they realized the design would be a good off-season hockey-training tool. They refined it and began assembling the first Rollerblades in the basement of their parents' Minneapolis home. It was that same year, 1980, when they founded the company that would become Rollerblade.

Today, you'll be sure to see inline skaters on the 10 miles of paved pathways surrounding downtown Minneapolis' chain of lakes. The paths offer bladers, bikers, and strollers city skyline views.

The fine arts scene is also very strong in the Twin Cities. The **Minneapolis Institute of Arts,** which is free to the public, houses a world-class collection and is rated among the top 10 art museums in the country. Check out the Family Center and special family programs on Sundays. Also free, **The Weisman Art Museum,** housed in an unforgettable building designed by Frank Gehry, presents an eclectic collection. The celebrated **Walker Art Center** explores contemporary art and presents work in all media—painting, sculpture, film, and live performances. Special family events occur on Free First Saturdays every month, and a WAC Pack with free family activities for both the museum and neighboring garden is available.

Fun awaits across the street at an extension of the museum, the fabulous **Minneapolis Sculpture Garden.** More than 40 sculptures, including Minneapolis' iconic "Spoonbridge and Cherry" by the husband-and-wife team of Claes Oldenburg and Coosje Van Bruggen, are on display in the largest outdoor urban sculpture park in the country. The huge lawn encircled by trees and flowers is perfect for running around. Kids really respond to the whimsical and curious forms by famous artists such as George Segal and Alexander Calder and to the special family activities. Even more child-friendly sculptures are on view in **Rice Park.** Here, you will find large bronze statues of the Peanuts gang as a tribute to Charles Schulz, a native of the city.

No trip to the Twin Cities is complete without a visit to the **Mall of America** in nearby Bloomington, covered in Chapter 12.

Minneapolis Convention and Visitors Association
1-888-676-MPLS
www.minneapolis.org

Saint Paul Convention and Visitors Authority
1-800-627-6101
www.stpaulcvb.org, www.exploreminnesota.com

Cultural Appeal

In This Chapter

- Learning about music and motor vehicles in Motown
- Enjoying Branson's endless entertainment options
- Shopping until you drop at the Mall of America
- Honoring our musical past and present at the Rock and Roll Hall of Fame

The heartland of the United States has lots of pop cultural appeal. Whether you're into cars or country-western music, shopping malls or aircraft, or some good old rock and roll, these best family destinations are sure to please every member of your traveling party.

Automobile Heritage Trail, Michigan

From the Supremes to the Chevrolet, exploring Michigan's Motor City with kids can be a real adventure. In many ways, what our family calls the **Automobile Heritage Trail** is the story of the American Dream.

One of our favorite museums in the United States, **The Henry Ford** in Dearborn, Michigan, was founded in 1929 to house inventor Henry Ford's immense collection of Americana. One example of every Ford Motor Company car sold since 1908 is on display. Some are "driven" by mannequins on virtual highways while other models are "parked" in idyllic countryside tableaux, suggesting the automobile's role in developing the American ideal of "vacation."

VACATION PLANNING TIPS

The Henry Ford has such a rich and diverse collection that we suggest you study the Visitor's Guide and pick out some of its unique treasures for a closer look. Be sure to allow at least two days for your visit—you won't regret it!

Among the astonishing highlights are the public bus from Birmingham, Alabama, on which Rosa Parks refused to give up her seat in 1955. You can sit in Ms. Parks' own seat and hear how the bus was bought on eBay. The presidential limousine in which the Kennedys rode on that fateful day in Dallas is respectfully parked behind a black velvet rope. Outside the museum café is a colorful Volkswagen Beetle–style "Oscar Meyer Weinermobile." Mr. Ford, fascinated by any kind of innovation, bought a chrome geodesic dome designed by R. Buckminster Fuller and several early airplanes (also on display).

Greenfield Village shares The Henry Ford grounds, and it's certainly worth dedicating a full day to visit. On 90 landscaped acres, costumed interpreters staff the restored buildings to bring 300 years of American history to life. For our family, the highlight was a five-minute ride in a Model T.

So where do cars come from? Alas, pre-TARP economic problems closed all Detroit assembly line tours long ago. However, families can take the **Ford Rouge Factory Tour** to see the assembly of Ford-150s and watch the streamlined, energy-efficient process from a mezzanine.

To impress on kids the merits of innovation, visit the **Edsel and Eleanor Ford House** in classy Grosse Point Shores. The house was commissioned by Henry Ford's only son, Edsel, who had earned the presidency of Ford Motor Company at age 25 with his streamlined designs and forward-thinking business strategy. The home was built in 1929 and is situated on almost 100 acres; a highlight for kids is the ¾-scale Tudor playhouse built for Ms. Josephine Ford's seventh birthday. In the garage are two fascinating Lincoln limousines that Mr. and Mrs. Ford designed for themselves.

Back in Motor City, the **Renaissance Center's** round black-glass towers line the Detroit River shoreline above the Randolph Detroit-Windsor Tunnel to Ontario, Canada. Home to the world headquarters for the **General Motors Company,** the RenCen's mezzanine level houses **GM World,** GM's display of new cars, technology, and products. It's open free to the public. The **Walter P. Chrysler Museum** has 65 of its own vehicles on display. Time-pressed families may have to choose between the **Cranbrook Art Museum** or a tour of **Fair Lane,** the 1,300-acre Henry Ford Estate and his 56-room mansion.

Michigan has played an important role in African American heritage, and attractions highlighting this history include the **Black Holocaust Museum,** the **Charles H. Wright Museum of African American History,** and the **Tuskegee Airmen National Museum,** among others. Best known is the **Motown Historical Museum— Hitsville USA,** where Berry Gordy Jr. started his record company. The tour includes a visit to The Echo Chamber, where that special Motown reverb sound was created with a hole cut in the ceiling. *American Idol* fans can try to capture the vocal stylings of Motown greats Marvin Gaye or Smokey Robinson by singing into the hole.

Metro Detroit Tourism
1-800-DETROIT
www.visitdetroit.com, www.michigan.org

Branson, Missouri

While Nashville holds the title of Country Music Capital, this Midwest city proudly labels itself the Live Entertainment Capital of the World—and boy, do they show it off.

With 50 operating theatres, there are many long-running shows. Among the most popular is the **Shoji Tabuchi Family Show,** which features '50s and '60s ballads and professional choreography performed by the multi-talented Tabuchi family. Prepare to be mystified at the **Kirby VanBurch Show,** where the "Prince of Magic" presents never-before-seen illusions and even live animals, including a rare Royal White Bengal tiger named Branson. Speaking of animals, **The Amazing Pet Show** features trained dogs, cats, and more in furry acts that will capture the hearts of young and old alike.

FELLOW TRAVELERS SAY ...

"You mainly see seniors, but many grandparents are in Branson over the summer with children, and it made me think that it would be good for a family reunion because there's a lot to do. We saw more than one show that kids would like, and in the summer there would be a lot of activities for them."

—D. B., www.FamilyTravelForum.com

Older generations will appreciate celebrity impersonators at **Legends in Concert.** Acts include Elvis Presley, Marilyn Monroe, The Blues Brothers, and Stevie Wonder. At **Yakov's Branson Show,** funny philosopher Yakov Smirnoff entertains audiences with his witty and off-kilter humor. Enjoy a fun-filled family dinner and show at **Dolly Parton's Dixie Stampede,** where you can indulge in hickory-smoked barbecued pork while watching performances by 32 magnificent horses, hilarious ostrich races, and live buffalo. For country western fans, the **Country Tonite Show** features music, comedy, dance, and even rope tricks.

Silver Dollar City theme park evolved around the entrance of Missouri's deepest cave, **Marvel Cave,** a tour of which is always included with your Silver Dollar City ticket. You travel 300 feet below the surface to the Cathedral Room entrance to view formations that are still alive and growing.

TRAVELERS BEWARE!

Marvel Cave tours usually last an hour, and because the tour requires a lot of stair climbing, it is not recommended for visitors with little kids, heart or lung conditions, or weak backs, knees, or ankles.

Table Rock, one of the largest lakes in the state, is located about six miles southwest of Branson, Missouri. Great for rafting, canoeing, jet skiing, and many other water activities, Table Rock Lake is also nationally known as a top bass-fishing lake. Many national and regional fishing tournaments are held here throughout the year. Be sure to visit **Mystic Caverns** to see the colorful formations, and check out the nature trails and wildlife exhibits at **Table Rock Dam.**

At the **Talking Rock Cavern,** take the 45-minute tour of the beautiful underground wonderland. As you explore the cave, you'll discover thousands of colorful crystal cave formations. Little ones will love the Speleo Box Crawl Maze, a simulated cave in which they crawl through 150 feet of winding and twisting passageways.

Branson/Lakes Area Convention and Visitors Bureau
1-800-296-0463
www.explorebranson.com, www.branson.com

Mall of America, Bloomington, Minnesota

The Mall of America (MOA) is a fantastically fun family venue offering enough shopping and recreation to keep your family busy for days. Located in the Minneapolis suburb of **Bloomington,** MOA is less than two miles from the Minneapolis–Saint Paul International Airport. If you fly in just to shop (and 40 percent of the 40 million annual shoppers are tourists), you won't need a car because the **Hiawatha Light Rail Transit** can whisk you directly from airport to mall.

FUN FACTS

Having a hard time imagining how big the Mall of America is? Consider that 258 Statues of Liberty could lie down inside the massive mall.

Fun features include Underwater Adventures, a 1.2-million-gallon walkthrough aquarium, and the four-story LEGO Imagination Center. Teens will especially appreciate NASCAR Silicon Motor Speedway, a virtual 195-mph ride; the A.C.E.S. Flight Simulator; and a 15-screen movie theater. There's even a Chapel of Love, where

more than 5,000 brides and grooms from around the world have said
"I do." New among the mall's many indoor attractions are a Barbie
Shop and the 12,000-square-foot MagiQuest adventure complex—
sure to please young wizards, warlocks, and witches.

The physical centerpiece of the mall, and perhaps the most exciting
element for families, is **Nickelodeon Universe.** At seven acres,
Nickelodeon's first such venture is the country's largest indoor theme
park. It has more than 25 fun-filled attractions ranging from gentle
kiddie rides to thrill-rated coasters. Kids can choose between a new
SpongeBob SquarePants Rock Bottom Plunge coaster, a Log Chute
(prepare to get wet), Jimmy Neutron's Atomic Collider, or a carousel. Character "meet and greets" are also sure to put smiles on kids'
faces.

The **Water Park of America,** the country's largest indoor water
park, is located across from the Mall of America at the Grand Lodge
Hotel. The park is open to hotel guests and day visitors. Bring a
towel and slide down the 10-story waterslide and or jump into the
massive wave pool.

Mall of America
952-883-8800
www.mallofamerica.com, www.minneapolis.org

Rock and Roll Hall of Fame, Cleveland, Ohio

Native son Alan Freed, the D.J. credited with coining the term "rock
and roll," inspired the Rock and Roll Hall of Fame Foundation to
build its Temple of Rock in **Cleveland,** where it has greeted more
than seven million visitors since 1995. The dramatic glass and
steel space designed by I. M. Pei cantilevers high above Lake Erie.
Anyone dancing into its soaring atrium to the music of The Rolling
Stones, Madonna, or Tupac is immediately taken with the coolness
of the place.

The museum's goal—to tell the story of rock and roll and its influence on our culture—is achieved through galleries featuring

permanent and rotating exhibits, movie theaters, and interactive listening stations including "500 Songs that Shaped Rock and Roll." In addition to special events, more than 100 musicians perform or participate in panel discussions at the museum every year.

Visitors older than 30 will recall most of the Hall of Famers (artists are not eligible for the Hall of Fame until 25 years after their first recording)—especially after seeing the entertaining review of past induction ceremonies. Depending on how many kids or grandkids they're toting, most parents are found in the displays designed to explain rock's rebellious spirit to today's audience. Explore the influence of gospel, blues, and folk on the genre, or relive pure Janis Joplin profanity and snippets of Woodstock nudity. The museum has many items you'd expect, such as Elvis Presley outfits—but what sets it apart are the details. You can't help being impressed by Jim Morrison's Boy Scout uniform (bad-boy Morrison, of all people!), mediocre report cards from John Lennon's days at his Liverpool grammar school, and memorabilia of Jimi Hendrix's days as a high school football star.

Teens will appreciate "The Beat Goes On," where they can select one tune and see the musical styles that influenced its creator, then hear the original artists. Once you've gotten the kids to listen to all your favorites, let them loose with big change in the superior memorabilia shop.

After touring the Rock and Roll Hall of Fame and Museum, check out the **Great Lakes Science Center** or the terrific family programs at the **Cleveland Museum of Natural History.** In season, try to catch the Cleveland Browns, Indians, or Cavaliers at play in this sports-crazy town.

You and your family may leave Cleveland snapping your fingers and swaying to the beat.

Rock and Roll Hall of Fame and Museum
1100 Rock and Roll Boulevard
Cleveland, OH 44114
1-888-764-ROCK
www.rockhall.com, www.positivelycleveland.com

In This Chapter

- Old-fashioned family fun at the Iowa State Fair
- Getting lost in time on Mackinac Island
- America's most visible icons: Mount Rushmore, The Badlands, and the Black Hills
- A poignant reminder of who we are at the National Underground Railroad Freedom Center

The history of the Midwest is wrapped up in immigrants and the homes they left behind, Native Americans and the demise of their culture, the slave trade and its legacy on African-American culture, and above all a respect for the new land that these people would all soon share. The celebration of American traditions and freedom ties this chapter together. We hope you'll be able to visit some of the best family destinations in the Midwest to experience and honor our common history.

Iowa State Fair

Held in Fairfield from October 25 to 27, 1854, before the great migration west, the first annual Iowa State Fair was the largest gathering to take place in the state up to that time, with nearly 8,000 people in attendance. The fair has been a staple of Americana ever since. Currently held in the state's capital, **Des Moines,** the internationally acclaimed fair attracts more than a million visitors during its two-week run each August.

With a great emphasis on 4-H, livestock, and agriculture, you'll see many animals—sheep, cattle, goats, llamas, and even dogs and cats—on display and/or for sale. We love the contest for the biggest animals, the oddest of which is the "Heaviest Pigeon." The butter cow, a sculpture made of butter, has been a staple of the fair since 1911. Past creations include not just the six breeds of dairy cows but also famous icons such as Garth Brooks, Elvis Presley, Iowa native John Wayne, and even a butter recreation of Leonardo da Vinci's "The Last Supper."

VACATION PLANNING TIPS

You can easily make the Iowa State Fair a multi-day affair. If your family is interested in getting into the fair's true spirit and staying for the full 15 days, look into the adjacent 160-acre campground, which is available for both tent and RV campers.

Every year, the fair kicks off with a parade through downtown Des Moines and into the fairgrounds. Entertaining musical performances by popular artists are free with admission. To see the best of the best in young Iowan talent, stop by the Bill Riley Talent Search, where the brightest budding stars perform for fairgoers.

If anyone in your family has a competitive spirit, consider entering one or more of the contests and championships at the fair. There is a contest for every interest, including bench pressing, checkers, and spelling bees; for the littlest tots, there's the decorated diaper contest and diaper derby. The Blue Ribbons Kids club gives youngsters under 10 a hands-on experience of the fair.

Families who can't make an appearance in Iowa during the Fair's two-week run in August need not fret. Des Moines will keep the family active with a beautiful **Botanical Garden,** lots of public pools, hiking trails, and parks. Activities run the gamut from recreation at the **Adventureland** amusement park to education at many museums and theaters. One of the city's most unusual attractions is the **National Balloon Museum and U.S. National Ballooning Hall of Fame,** a volunteer-run museum dedicated to 200 years of ballooning history. Families can tour changing exhibits, learn about zeppelins and weather, or hoist kids into the hot air balloon gondolas that serve as seating in the museum library.

The Iowa State Fair
East 30th Street and East University Avenue
Des Moines, IA 50317
515-262-3111
www.iowastatefair.org, www.seedesmoines.com

Mackinac Island, Michigan

Frozen *Somewhere in Time* like the popular Christopher Reeve
romance filmed there, Mackinac Island has been cherished by
Midwesterners in the know for more than 150 years.

> **FELLOW TRAVELERS SAY ...**
>
> "I live in a typical Michigan family. The kind that still has their windows
> rolled down in forty-degree weather, stops for deer [crossing the road]
> at least once a week, and lives in a town that has as many bars as it does
> churches. We're known as Michiganders, and every year we join the Yoop-
> ers by making our pilgrimage to Mackinaw. That is our summer vacation."
>
> —C. T., www.travelBIGO.com

Named for the Indian word for "turtle" because of its shape and pronounced MAK-in-naw, the 1,800-acre island situated in the **Straits
of Mackinac** between Lakes Huron and Michigan has a long and
storied history. It was a cherished fishing site for Native Americans,
served as a center of fur trading by early trappers, and was a fish pro-
cessing port for the British.

The British-built **Fort Mackinac** crowning the island's cedar
forests was built for the War of 1812. It might seem like a very
long way to climb for a bit of history, but don't miss it. Enthusiastic
re-enactors populate the 14 original buildings and demonstrate the
lives of American soldiers living in the 1880s, and kids can play
dress-up in the Kids Quarters. Scheduled military music concerts
and parades take place frequently in summer. Several other historic
buildings—all within a few minutes' walk of each other in the tiny
town—are also well worth a visit.

FUN FACTS

In 1875, Mackinac Island became America's second national park (after Yellowstone) and was transferred to the state of Michigan 20 years later. When the first automobile (known as "horseless carriages" back then) rolled off a ferry onto Mackinac Island in 1898, residents were stunned. It is said that within two weeks, the Mackinac City Council and State Parks Department agreed to outlaw the dangerous new invention. The ban on motorized vehicles is still in effect, with horse-drawn sanitation carts, steam-powered street sweepers, and lots of pedal power keeping the busy island spotlessly maintained.

Automobiles are banned on the island, but you can rent a bicycle from one of the many vendors clustering around the ferry pier or from your Victorian B&B. Circling the flat, 8-mile (12.8-km) perimeter road on two wheels is a must for active families. You can also hire a horse-drawn taxi for a more leisurely tour around the island. With so much water, you'd think boating is a big activity, but the safety issues posed by strong currents, swells of passing freighters, and the very cold temperature of Lake Huron make vendors hesitant to even rent canoes. Steady breezes and the grand view make for great kite flying, especially at waterfront **Windermere Park.**

The historic **Grand Hotel,** which opened in 1887, is known for having the world's longest porch. The Grand has hosted presidents, film stars, and wealthy guests; in the high summer season, visitors can't even get all the way up the driveway to see it unless they're registered or have a reservation for High Tea.

Many people make Mackinac Island a day trip by taking one of the frequent ferries from **Mackinac City** (this one's pronounced MACK-in-nak; go figure!), a cute beachfront town with ice cream parlors, T-shirt shops, and the ubiquitous fudge vendors. It's a good base for sightseeing along **Michigan's Upper Peninsula.**

Mackinac Island Tourism Bureau
Mackinac Island, MI 49757
800-454-5227
www.mackinacisland.org, www.michigan.org

Mount Rushmore, The Badlands, and the Black Hills

Located on the outskirts of the Black Hills National Forest, **Rapid City** is the starting point for a classic family road trip through a region that has drawn generations of tourists. Attractions range from the high tech to the silly: Journey Museum whizzes through 2.5 billion years of history, geology, and Native American traditions while the Reptile Gardens' crocodiles and snakes scare the heck out of preschoolers. Families also come for Storybook Island in Rapid City, Flintstones Village in Custer, and Bear Country USA in Keystone. Active families prefer the hundreds of miles of hiking and biking trails throughout the scenic Black Hills.

FUN FACTS

Wall Drug, east of Rapid City, has been delighting carloads for nearly eight decades, since it began advertising "Free Ice Water" on road signs. Today, it spends $400,000 each year on billboard ads. This 76,000-square-foot destination is a wonderland of animated singing cowboys, stuffed bison, mechanical bucking horses, a giant T. Rex, fudge shops, postcard shops, and yes—a drugstore. It makes for a fun place to stop, shop, and dine.

Mount Rushmore National Memorial, located about 25 miles southwest of Rapid City, is the most recognized landmark of this region. Danish American sculptor Gutzon Borglum began the project in 1927 at age 60, and when he died in 1941, he hadn't finished. The "Shrine of Democracy" is an awesome site with a walking trail, 2,500-seat amphitheater, visitor's center, and museum. Hear how nearly 400 men helped carve the heads of Presidents George Washington, Thomas Jefferson, Theodore Roosevelt, and Abraham Lincoln at an average salary of $1 per hour. The evening lighting ceremony, performed during the summer, is a particularly impressive sight.

About 17 miles southwest of Mount Rushmore is another incomplete sculptural marvel, the **Crazy Horse Memorial.** It was started in 1948 at the request of Lakota elders to symbolize Native Americans' spirit, pride, and courage. The educational complex also includes an

Indian Museum, Native American cultural center, and a sculptor's studio and workshop. If you're planning to stay overnight in the area, check into the beautiful Custer State Park, where herds of bison roam freely. Overnight accommodations include camping sites, cabins, and a lodge.

Wind Cave National Park is home to native wildlife such as bison, elk, and mule deer. The underground limestone cave complex, where you can see rare crystal formations and learn about the "windy" sound that accounts for its name, is fun to tour.

Even before carving on Mount Rushmore began, families were flocking to **Hot Springs** to the warm, healing waters of spring-fed Evans Plunge. Today, families still splash in the springs, although the waterslides are by far more popular. You can tour the fascinating Mammoth Site, an ongoing archeological dig, to see the 26,000-year-old bones of woolly mammoths that lived here; kids ages 4 to 13 are welcome to spend the day with the Junior Paleontologist Excavation team.

Although somewhat out of the way, the stark Badlands National Park makes for an extraordinary side trip. Located about 80 miles southeast of Rapid City, the desolate 244,000-acre park was named by nineteenth-century fur traders, who referred to it as "bad lands to cross." The geological formations—steep canyons, jagged spires, fossils, and a moon-like landscape—can be seen from eight hiking trails ranging from easy to very challenging.

Black Hills Visitor Information Center
1851 Discovery Circle
Rapid City, SD 57701
605-355-3700
www.blackhillsbadlands.com, www.travelsd.com

National Underground Railroad Freedom Center, Ohio

In the time of American slavery, crossing the Ohio River from the southern state of Kentucky into the northern city of Cincinnati,

Ohio, meant freedom for the escaped slaves. In honor of that treacherous journey to freedom, the National Underground Railroad Freedom Center was built along the banks of the Ohio River.

The Freedom Center museum explains that the Underground Railroad was a secret network of escape routes that existed in the years leading up to the Civil War. Along the way, citizens who opposed slavery gave runaway slaves food, shelter, and guidance.

In 3 pavilions, the 158,000-square-foot museum illustrates the horrors of slavery and the fight for freedom. Although intense at times, this living history experience is also inspiring and serves as a lesson in courage and human rights for the entire family.

The centerpiece and main exhibit is the "Slave Pen," an authentic nineteenth-century wooden structure recovered from Kentucky, less than 60 miles away from its current home, that was once used to hold more than 75 slaves in "storage." Other educational displays include "Brothers of the Borderland" and "The Struggle Continues," which show visitors how the fight for freedom—even in contemporary times—is not over. The Visitor Information Desk will alert you to the exhibits and displays that may be inappropriate for younger children.

Cincinnati has a less-serious side as well. During the warmer months, take in a **Cincinnati Reds** baseball game at the Great American Ball Park, which has a special family seating area. Also enjoyable is the **Cincinnati Zoo,** the second oldest in the nation, which features more than 500 animals and 3,000 plant species. This zoo even has a breeding program and introduces its newest offspring in the popular Zoo Babies exhibit. On the Kentucky side of the Ohio River, the **Newport Aquarium** features 7,000 aquatic creatures, including king penguins, American alligators, otters, and pythons.

National Underground Railroad Freedom Center
50 East Freedom Way
Cincinnati, OH 45202
513-333-7500
www.freedomcenter.org, www.cincinnatiusa.com

Amusement Parks and Outdoor Fun

In This Chapter

- The world's largest, fastest, and scariest coasters at Cedar Point
- Cuyahoga Valley National Park highlights the historic Erie Canal
- Great Lakes beach destinations
- Holiday World's themed rides and attractions
- Wild and wet Wisconsin Dells

The Midwest's theme parks, beaches, and parklands number among America's very best—so good, in fact, that many are destinations that lure families from afar to enjoy a one-of-a-kind experience.

Cedar Point, Sandusky, Ohio

An intense knot will form in your throat when approaching the looming metal structures just off of the **Sandusky,** Ohio, shoreline. After winning *Amusement Today* magazine's award for the Best Amusement Park in America more than a dozen years in a row, it's no wonder that the colorful twisted monsters of Cedar Point Amusement Park send chills down visitors' spines.

Opened in 1870 on the 364-acre peninsula in **Lake Erie,** Cedar Point has a collection of rides ranging from toddler-friendly favorites to terrifyingly fast rides that'll make your hair stand on end. The park is open from mid-May to late October, with limited shoulder season hours.

One of the most distinctive aspects of this amusement park is the juxtaposition of old and new. The classic wooden coasters may not look like much, but they make for rickety and rousing rides.

Kiddy Kingdom is the place to be for the wee ones who might not measure up to the height requirement for some of the park's larger and faster rides. The Gemini Children's Area attracts junior thrill seekers while Planet Snoopy and Camp Snoopy playland give kids and nostalgic adults the chance to meet the lovable characters from the Peanuts cartoons. After spending time with Snoopy and Woodstock, head over to take a paddlewheel excursion (perfect for older generations in the family). For movie buffs, the Good Time Theatre holds live performances at its indoor ice rink. The Frontier Trail Zone is packed with kid-friendly Wild West–themed rides, crafts demonstrations, and a high-dive show. For a more tranquil attraction the entire family can enjoy, stop by the park's small petting zoo. For a separate fee, all ages can enjoy the water rides at **Soak City.** Teen and older adventurers should check out nearby **Challenge Park,** where some ride-goers plummet to within 6 feet of the ground and then soar through the air on the RipCord Skycoaster while others play a tough round of mini-golf below.

TRAVELERS BEWARE!

Don't try to "jump the queue" at this theme park or you'll be sent to the end of the line.

For a break from all the squeals and shrieks, visit the nearby lake town of Sandusky, Ohio. Learn about the history and art of carousels at the truly unique **Merry-Go-Round Museum,** where you can take a spin on the oom-pa-pa-ing 1939 Allan Herschell carousel. If the family isn't too waterlogged from Soak City, the indoor water park at **Great Wolf Lodge** offers five pools and nine waterslides. Venturing across the Sandusky Bay, you can meet camels, zebras, giraffes, and more at the **African Safari Wildlife Park,** where kids have the chance to feed the not-so-camera-shy animals.

Cedar Point
One Cedar Point Drive
Sandusky, OH 44870
419-627-2350
www.cedarpoint.com, www.shoresandislands.com

Cuyahoga Valley, Ohio

Families following Ohio's winding **Cuyahoga River** south will encounter the **Ohio and Erie Canal,** a 308-mile waterway connecting Lake Erie to the Ohio River. This transportation route, which influenced local and national prosperity, was hand-dug by mostly German and Irish immigrants who earned about 30 cents a day plus a jigger of whiskey, food, and shelter.

To begin a historic journey down the 100-mile Cuyahoga or "crooked river" (aptly named by the area's original Native American inhabitants), explorers have the option of parking their vehicle at various trailheads to hike along the **Ohio and Erie Canal Towpath Trail** or riding the **Cuyahoga Valley Scenic Railroad.** The Valley Railway, in operation since 1880 and originally used for transporting coal, allows riders to tour the length of the canal or board at multiple locations along the trail. Bicyclists can even jump aboard for an inexpensive fare. Younger kids will enjoy the special themed railroad events—recent features have included Thomas the Tank Engine and Polar Express—that take place throughout the year.

If you're weary from hiking or locomotives aren't your preferred mode of transportation, horseback riding services are offered in the **Brecksville Reservation** area in the northern part of the park.

FUN FACTS

In 1969, the badly polluted Cuyahoga River caught on fire for 24 minutes. For years afterward, "the burning river" was a symbol of the United States' failure as a steward of the environment.

The event led to the establishment of the 1972 Clean Water Act and other anti-pollution regulations, and today fishing and swimming are popular pastimes in the Cuyhoga.

Along the Towpath Trail, named for the mules and horses that walked alongside the canal pulling boats, visitors can see remnants of old locks and other canal structures. At the far north of the park, the **Canal Visitor Center** focuses on life along the canal and human history in the valley. Roughly midway through the park, The **Boston Store Visitor Center** features exhibits that tell the story of canal-boat building in the valley. From here, follow Route 271 east to Brandywine Village and get a look at the 60-foot **Brandywine Falls,** the underlying layers of which formed some 400 million years ago. To the west of the visitor center lies the much smaller, but peaceful and scenic, Buttermilk and Blue Hen Falls.

In the village of **Peninsula,** farmer's markets are held from winter to early spring at **Happy Days Lodge,** located on Route 303 just after the Pine Lane trailhead. Early September is the time to watch monarchs feed in the fields rich with goldenrod and New England asters. These places serve as important refueling sites for long-distance travelers on their way to oyamel forests near Mexico City, more than 2,000 miles away.

Due south of the lodge is **The Ledges,** an area known for its cliffs, rock formations, and caves. Continuing south on the trail, Lock 27 is also known as **Johnnycake Lock.** After several boats had run aground due to flooding, the stranded canal passengers were reduced to a diet of corn meal pancakes known as "johnnycakes."

The best wildlife viewing is at **Beaver Marsh,** located south of the **Hunt Farm Visitor Center** and just north of the Ira trailhead. Once an automobile junkyard, the marsh is now home to herons, turtles, amphibians, and of course beavers. **Junior Ranger programs** are available for nature-loving youth at the park's visitor centers, where they can complete a series of fun activities to earn a Junior Ranger Badge. Inquire about EarthCaching, an offshoot of geocaching that makes for fun family discovery of interesting geological features; it's offered at specific sites throughout the trail.

Cuyahoga Valley National Park
Peninsula, Ohio 44264
330-657-2796
www.cvnpa.org, www.positivelycleveland.com

Favorite Great Lakes Beaches

The Great Lakes, from west to east, are **Lake Superior, Lake Michigan, Lake Huron, Lake Erie,** and **Lake Ontario.** They make up one-fifth of the world's fresh surface water. Together, they comprise almost 11,000 miles of shoreline, making attractive recreation areas for families in the Midwest and south central Canada. Unfortunately, the combination of populous cities, industrial activity, and overdevelopment has had an adverse affect on the lakes' cleanliness—especially on the warmest lakes used for swimming.

Despite the effects of pollution, the lakes are so large that they continue to support an unusual diversity of flora and fauna. Anglers come to catch the bass, trout, and pike among the estimated 180 species of fish. In dense evergreen forests and cultivated plains, along rocky shorelines, and in thousands of small lakes, the region hosts more than 130 rare species and ecosystems. Wildlife includes white-tailed deer, black bears, bobcats, beavers, and moose. Yet it's the shoreline, waterfront, and sand dunes that attract most families. This section outlines some favorite family-friendly Great Lakes beach get-aways in Ohio, Michigan, Indiana, and Wisconsin.

Geologically, the Great Lakes region was created by glaciers, and the **Seaway Trail,** a National Scenic Byway along the coast of Lake Erie, is a prime example of a glacial landscape. Generations of Ohio families have spent their summers on **Put-in-Bay,** a charming island of Victorian homes and B&Bs in Lake Erie east of Toledo. Visitors hop on a high-speed ferry for the day, rent a bike, and explore. Put-in-Bay has a pretty town square with some restaurants; small, dark sand beach coves for swimming; and excellent fishing, hiking, and biking. Neighboring **Kelleys Island,** more distant, is much less developed.

FELLOW TRAVELERS SAY ...

"One of my most memorable vacations was a trip to a campground called Association Island, situated on a large island in the middle of Lake Ontario. Prior to the trip, I had never seen any of the Great Lakes and was awed by how picturesque our vacation site was; driving across a bridge and onto the island for the first time, with the strong breeze blowing off the lake and swaying the trees, was memorable."

—K. K., www.travelBIGO.com

Michiganders head to **Sleeping Bear Dunes National Lakeshore,** a beautiful stretch of quiet beach on Lake Michigan's eastern shore where the water is so calm and shallow that it's relatively warm. Lake Michigan is home to the world's largest freshwater sand dunes, rising high above the lake. Newcomers should start at the **Hart Visitor Center** in Empire for maps, information, and guidance on where to climb these giants. After marching up and down the dunes, pile into the car for a seven-mile drive along the **Pierce Stocking Scenic Trail** and admire the views of Lake Michigan and Big and Little Glen Lakes. Families with teens looking for action may end up at nearby **Traverse City,** a much more developed resort town offering a charming downtown lined with boutiques, restaurants, and a classic movie theater. The area's many vineyards and cherry and apple orchards make for awe-inspiring views, and several local wineries offer free tastings (with non-alcoholic offerings for youngsters).

On the southern coast of Lake Michigan, notched between Michigan and Illinois, look for the **Indiana Dunes National Lakeshore**, where 15,000 acres of beach, sand dunes, bogs, and wetlands have been protected for recreational use. In Porter County around Chesterton, families flock to **Indiana Dunes State Park,** a three-mile stretch along Lake Michigan's south shore where unusual drifting sand hills make for a beautiful day at the beach. You'll find a beach pavilion with bathhouses and a snack bar, and lifeguards are on duty from Memorial Day to Labor Day. This state park has campsites open for three seasons, because many visitors come for the fall birding.

Lake Michigan is also the source of much fun on the east side of **Wisconsin's Door County Peninsula.** Protected by 10 lighthouses, **Door County** has a myriad of tourist activities to satisfy all ages and interests—boating, beaching, biking, camping, and antiquing, to name a few. Cherries and apricots are found at farm stands in summer and are celebrated at seasonal festivals. Thanks to Belgian immigrants, northeastern Wisconsin is the only place to try Chicken Booyah, a rich, hearty chicken and beef stew.

Our beach pick is in the relatively small (865 acres) **Whitefish Dunes State Park** in Sturgeon Bay, the busiest in the state and the focus of many summer activities. Rimmed with a forest of beech trees, the dunes have a fine white sand ideal for castle building. The park has a boardwalk where power walkers and those pushing strollers can circle **Clark Lake** and watch the ducks, or search for wildlife at Old Baldy or Whitefish Creek. Year-round family programs include a tour of the remains of eight Native American villages within the park and naturalist-led walks along the many trails.

Great Lakes Information Network
734-971-9135
www.great-lakes.net

Holiday World, Santa Claus, Indiana

If you and your family prefer a kinder, gentler theme park, Holiday World may be just what you're looking for. Located south of Indianapolis, it began as Santa Claus Land in 1946, laying claim to the title of the world's first theme park. In 1984, the park expanded the holiday theme to include Christmas, Halloween, and the Fourth of July; a water park was added in 1993. Aside from a few roller coasters, you won't find the thrill rides here that attract hordes of teenagers, which makes it perfect for families with children ages 10 and younger or for adults who simply don't care for super-scary roller coasters. Family amenities include unlimited free soft drinks, a new mom nursing area, and wristbands so toddlers don't get lost.

Don't be fooled by the park's soothing themes—there is still plenty of fun and excitement for those old enough to enjoy it. The park's award-winning, wooden roller coasters are extremely popular rides. If your kids are taller than 4', we suggest you visit in the afternoon when lines are shortest. Ride the coasters in order of terror: The Raven first, then The Legend, and finally The Voyage. Sit in the back car to catch the most air, and stay until nightfall to ride them again in the dark.

Holiday World makes a noticeable effort to maintain a natural land-scape, and roller coasters thread through heavily forested sections. Even the water park is nicely landscaped. And speaking of the water park, be sure to clamber up ZOOMbabwe for a ride down the world's largest enclosed waterslide. Zinga riders race through an enclosed tunnel on rafts, then shoot out into an enormous funnel that pro-pels them from side to side—so high it appears they will flip. Try the Jungle Racer, a 10-lane, 5-story racing slide, the new Wildebeest, or let the calm waters of the Congo River float you downstream on an inner tube. Holiday World's season runs May to mid-October; if you anticipate returning, save money by purchasing a two-day pass.

Holiday World
452 East Christmas Boulevard
Santa Claus, IN 47579
812-937-4401
www.holidayworld.com, www.in.gov/visitindiana

Wisconsin Dells, Wisconsin

Anything but dull, the Dells area is flooded with year-round activities for everyone. Kids can slide, splash, and frolic in huge indoor and outdoor facilities with areas earmarked for tots to teens. Who can resist lazy river rides, play/spray areas, bubbling geysers, curling waterslides, and flumes? Themed areas include Kiddie City at **The Treasure Island Resort** and the **Kalahari Water Park,** which brings Tanzania to Wisconsin!

Four major water parks are located within resorts, and several smaller indoor and outdoor facilities are located at other hotels, where non-guests can pay a day-use fee. Additionally, freestanding water parks such as **Noah's Ark** provide even more opportunities for fun. Bring several bathing suits, water shoes, towels, and a disposable underwater camera, because the only reason to visit the Dells is if you plan to get wet.

The dramatic topography of hidden valleys and deep canyons or gorges, known as *dalles* to the French settlers who moved to this area in the late 1600s, is now a favorite vacation destination welcoming more than two and a half million visitors each year. Located 188 miles northwest of Chicago and 230 miles southeast of Minneapolis, most visitors arrive by car from other Midwest locales to enjoy the Dells' natural splendor and water-logged fun.

Eco-conscious travelers should check out **Yogi Bear Jellystone Park;** for more than 20 years, they've been recycling garbage and invite guests to join the green movement as well. Upon arrival, guests are presented with a "green bag" complete with instructions about sorting requirements for garbage. The budget-minded campground also has three water play areas for kids—one of the many activities they offer along with miniature golf, boat rentals, birthday packages, and three playgrounds.

After you've dried off and the wrinkles have disappeared from your fingertips, make time to explore the spectacular scenery of the region. You can take in the towering sandstone cliffs and hidden canyons on the 55-foot *Mark Twain* or in a **DUKW**, a unique World War II amphibious half truck/half boat vehicle that originated in the Dells and is now used for sightseeing throughout the country. The Duck tour, as it's known, covers eight and a half miles of land and the waters of **Lake Delton.** Additionally, you can take a half-hour guided horse-drawn wagon tour through the narrow passages of Lost Canyon.

FUN FACTS

In the summer of 2008, Lake Delton, due to sustained rains, breached its shoreline and drained into the nearby Wisconsin River. Within the following year, the lake was refilled and literally back in business.

The water parks have grown alongside many other popular family attractions, including **Tommy Bartlett's Ski, Sky, and Stage Show,** where you can watch incredible feats performed by daredevil skiers, contortionists, and skyfliers as well as a laser light show. Check out **It's Magic** for internationally recognized grand illusionist acts. Many families prefer to spend rainy days visiting **Robot World and Exploratory,** the **Ripley's Believe It Or Not Museum,** or the **Circus World Museum.** In winter, try out your skiing, snowboarding, or tubing skills at one of the area's resorts. For the animal lovers in your family, stop by **Nachas Elk Ranch** for a wagon tour of a working elk ranch.

The Wisconsin Dells Visitor and Convention Bureau
1-800-223-3557
www.wisdells.com, www.travelwisconsin.com

The Southwest

America's great Southwest has fostered myths of pioneers battling with Native Americans; songs of cowboys and dude ranches; images of the wide-open plains, barren mountains, and arid canyons preserved in some of America's most famous national parks; and the reality of booming Sun Belt cities growing at a faster pace than the rest of the country. The states we cover in this part—Arizona, New Mexico, Oklahoma, and Texas—give proof to those myths about the Wild West and offer much, much more to family travelers.

To see it all, we recommend you plan a Southwest vacation that combines sophisticated urban attractions with a leisurely road trip to visit the world-famous national parks and monuments—a great strategy with restless teens and school-age kids who aren't accustomed to being cooped up on long drives.

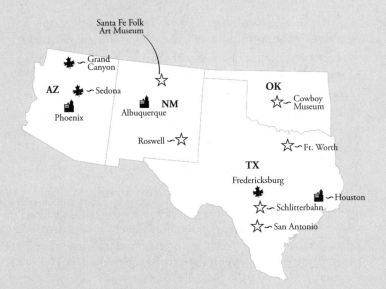

Santa Fe Folk
Art Museum

Grand
Canyon

AZ

Sedona

Phoenix

Albuquerque

NM

Roswell

OK

Cowboy
Museum

Ft. Worth

TX

Fredericksburg

Schlitterbahn

Houston

San Antonio

Best Family Destinations Key:

🏛 Amusement Parks   ☆ Cultural Appeal/Living History

◐ At the Beach   ▲ Mountain Towns

🏢 City Style   ❋ Outdoor Adventures

City Style

In This Chapter

- Albuquerque's stunning pueblos, atomic sites, and New Age culture
- Houston's diverse arts and cultural scene
- Wild West fun in the desert or on the golf course in Phoenix and Scottsdale

The Southwest's cities have a lot to offer families. Albuquerque is New Mexico's overgrown university town and the place to discover the indigenous cuisine, cultures, and Native American heritage of the state. The oil industry has made Houston rich, turning it into Texas' capital of fine arts, performing arts, and cultural diversity. And the greater Phoenix area is more than a retirement destination—it's where cowboys, Indians, and those interested in the best of the Southwest's rich heritage come to play.

Albuquerque, New Mexico

The small city of Albuquerque, New Mexico's capital in the heart of the Southwest, is an ideal place to begin exploring this fascinating region. Families will encounter the mystical history of the local Native American tribes, drive through breathtaking landscapes, witness the birth of the atomic age, enjoy homemade Southwest and Mexican cuisine at the many eateries catering to the University of New Mexico students, be enveloped by inspiring art, and begin to the feel the region's unique cultural vibe. The following five Albuquerque highlights are not to be missed.

For first-time visitors to the Southwest, the **Indian Pueblo Cultural Center** offers a wonderful overview of the region's history and is free of charge. A nonprofit organization owned and operated by the 19 pueblos (villages) of New Mexico, it provides information on the history, art, and culture of each group; displays Native American arts; and offers traditional dances and art demonstrations in an outdoor performance space. The extensive gift shop sells a huge array of authentic work by native artisans at fair prices.

Located just west of Albuquerque, the **Petroglyph National Monument** preserves more than 15,000 petroglyphs and is considered a very sacred place by Native Americans. Archeologists believe that ancestors of today's Pueblans used stone tools to scratch, peck, or carve most of the images in basaltic rock between 1300 and 1680 A.D. After the Spanish conquered the area and instilled the Catholic religion, the Pueblans stopped many of their ceremonial and artistic practices. Ironically, a few eighteenth-century petroglyphs thought to be carved by Spanish settlers have been discovered. Stop at the Visitor Center for orientation and information; ranger-guided hikes and talks are often available. The most popular spot for viewing petroglyphs is **Boca Negra Canyon,** where you can take any of three self-guided trails (5 to 40 minutes long) ranging from easy to moderately strenuous.

TRAVELERS BEWARE!

Only those with stronger legs and lungs should attempt to hike the more strenuous one and a half miles through **Piedras Marcadas Canyon** or **Rinconada Canyon,** a more difficult two-and-a-half–mile trek.

Our favorite site is 65 miles west of Albuquerque at the **Pueblo of Acoma,** also know as "Sky City" because it's located 7,000 feet above sea level on a sandstone mesa. The drive from Albuquerque is punctuated by breathtaking scenery and unforgettable views of geologic formations. As you approach the actual village, you'll understand how its location provided defense against the Acoma tribe's enemies. Archeologists date the pueblo to 1150 C.E., making it one of the oldest continuously inhabited communities in the United States. Groups are taken by bus to the top of the mesa, where they take a one-hour walking tour led by an Indian guide (you cannot roam around independently). You and your family will see many interesting sights, including adobe dwellings with mica windows, wood ladders leading into ceremonial areas called kivas, cisterns for collecting rainwater (there is no running water or electricity), and the Spanish Colonial San Esteban del Rey Mission. If you have time to visit only one pueblo, we recommend Acoma.

If there's a budding scientist or American history scholar in your family, he or she will enjoy a visit to the **National Museum of Nuclear Science and History.** New Mexico was considered the perfect place to develop this secret science during World War II, and the state has other sites from the atomic age including the nuclear testing ground at Los Alamos and the laboratory at Alamagordo. Geared toward older children and adults, the museum exhibits include explanations of the principles of atomic energy, full-scale models of "Fat Man" and "Little Boy" (the bombs dropped on Hiroshima and Nagasaki), and information on peaceful applications of the technology. Many military aircraft, including a B-52 bomber, missiles, and a 280-mm atomic cannon, are on display. Their size will evoke cries of "awesome" from the kids!

For the best views of Albuquerque, Santa Fe, and New Mexico's high desert environs, ride the **Sandia Peak Tramway.** The longest tramway in the United States travels 2.7-miles from the lower terminal, with a vertical rise of 3,819 feet. The 15-minute ride swoops your family from the desert to the mountainous terrain of the **Cibola National Forest** past sightings of deer, bears, eagles, changing plant life, and dramatic granite formations. At the summit, the observation deck provides an 11,000-square-mile panoramic view—and in this city's progressive, environmentally conscious culture, you should have clear views every day.

TRAVELERS BEWARE!

Be prepared for a 20-degree drop in temperature as you ride the Sandia Peak Tramway to the top of the summit.

Albuquerque Convention & Visitors Bureau
1-800-284-2282
www.itsatrip.org, www.cabq.gov/fun/

Houston, Texas

What we love about this southern city for families is the cultural appeal of fine and funky arts, modern architecture, and the fascinating Space Center Houston.

About an hour's drive from downtown, **Space Center Houston** is the Official Visitors Center of NASA's **Johnson Space Center,** home to astronaut training and NASA Mission Control (remember: "Houston, we've had a problem"). While you wait for a guided tour, you can peer into actual space capsules, play with multimedia displays about the Space Shuttle program, talk with NASA staff, and listen to broadcasts from the International Space Station. Younger kids will love the dozens of interactive exhibits in Kids Space Place.

The right stuff is in the 1,600-acre federal Johnson Space Center, open only to high-security, guided tram tours. Despite the limited access, the tours are informative; depending on what project is in-house, you may be able to enter a few buildings and watch a bit of space shuttle work or weightlessness training going on. It's a thrilling experience.

VACATION PLANNING TIPS

At Houston's NASA facility, visitors age 14 and older can book a "Level Nine Tour" and spend five intense hours in the space boots of a real astronaut. Twelve spots are available, weekdays only, for this comprehensive experience, priced at $85 including lunch in the actual astronauts' cafeteria. Book ahead at www.spacecenter.org, and bring a photo ID to clear security for any of the guided tours.

In Houston's Museum District, stop by the small and surprisingly cool **Art Car Museum,** a funky scrap metal shed opposite a huge chrome-armored "Carmadillo." Fondly known as the Garage Mahal, the museum showcases the Art Car Movement: decorated trucks, low riders, and mobile artworks that will amuse everyone. Other cultural highlights in the Museum District include **The Menil Collection,** a Philip Johnson landmark that houses a priceless selection of antiquities, world masters, rare books, Surrealist art, and other twentieth-century works from the heirs of the Schlumberger oil fortune.

Young children will find art to their liking at the bright and lively **Children's Museum of Houston,** a well-stocked learning space in a fanciful pagoda designed by Robert Venturi. Free to all on Thursday evenings, it has 14 interactive galleries for babies to age 12. The **Houston Museum of Natural Science** is just as well endowed, with exhibits on natural science, a planetarium, and an IMAX theater.

All ages will enjoy the **Beer Can House,** with its glistening façade of you know what, as well as the **Project Row Houses.** This set of 22 tiny, wood-sided "shotgun" houses (shoot a bullet in the front door and it comes out the back …) has been restored as galleries celebrating art and African American culture.

VACATION PLANNING TIPS

You wouldn't be in Texas if you didn't try Tex-Mex food or barbecue, so be sure to order kid-pleasing specialties such as enchiladas, nachos, jalapeno pork sausage, sweet water duck, brisket, barbecue turkey breast, or ribs served with cheese bread and Austin baked beans. Goode Company Texas BBQ is a popular local chain.

For outdoor recreation, drive south to the **Kemah Boardwalk,** a 35-acre carnival of sorts that offers restaurants (including the Aquarium restaurant with a 50,000-gallon tank), shopping, an arcade, and pay-per-ride treats such as a carousel and a Ferris wheel. The **Armand Bayou Nature Center,** about 28 miles away in Pasadena, is the largest urban wildlife refuge in the United States. Families can walk along the boardwalk through swamps and marshes looking for birds and other wild animals. There's also a butterfly garden, an 1800s farm site, and touch tables that are perfect for curious little ones. If the humidity is overwhelming, you can head to the beach at **Galveston,** about three hours south by highway. If you can look beyond the myriad souvenir shops and oil wells pumping offshore in the Gulf, you may enjoy this historic city by the sea.

Greater Houston Convention & Visitors Bureau
1-800-4-HOUSTON
www.VisitHoustonTexas.com, www.traveltex.com

Phoenix and Scottsdale, Arizona

Like the mythical bird, America's sixth-largest city rose from the Arizona desert in the 1870s, when a gold prospector found ancient irrigation canals and established the Phoenix mining town. These days, the Valley of the Sun offers activities for the entire family.

FELLOW TRAVELERS SAY ...

"It was the nights I loved most, out in Arizona. The temperature was cool enough to make you forget about that nasty sunburn you received that day, and there were never any clouds to block the stars or moon."

—C. N., www.travelBIGO.com

Start your visit by exploring the "old" city at the **Pueblo Grande Museum and Archeological Park,** where you can walk through the ruins of a 1,500-year-old Hohokam village with its ancient irrigation canals and tour full-size replicas of the original houses. Another way to appreciate how the city has evolved is on a four-hour **Desert Storm Hummer Tour.** We love the power of the giant 4×4 Hummers as they climb boulders to explore the scenic canyons and unusual wildlife of the Sonoran desert. Tours run day or night.

The renowned **Heard Museum** showcases more than 35,000 artifacts from the region plus a stunning collection of Kachina Dolls. The Phoenix branch has many multimedia galleries and performances geared to children.

Phoenix is a great foodie city for nouveau Southwestern cuisine, but families will want to mix up the serious with the corny. Chow down at **Chandler's Rawhide Western Town** with its Wild West play land, shows, games, rides, and Sundown BBQ Cookouts; or grab a table at **Scottsdale's Pinnacle Peak Patio Steakhouse,** where Southern fare is served with music and dancing—and anyone wearing a necktie gets it cut off and nailed to the rafters!

Serious cowfolk head to **Cave Creek Trailrides** and select from guided horseback rides, open to ages 6 and older. More of the real thing can be found at the **McCormick-Stillman Railroad Park,** where toddlers 3 and younger ride free on the restored Paradise and Pacific Railroad train. **Goldfield Ghost Town,** once a prosperous mining town, is now a fun attraction where families can join an Apache Trail tour, pan for gold, and watch scheduled "gunfights" along Main Street. Phoenix's cultural medley includes the highly regarded **Phoenix Art Museum,** which caters to kids with loaner hands-on activity packs and audio guides designed with families in mind. **Heritage Square** features several restored houses from the city's Victorian era and the **Arizona Doll and Toy Museum.**

In 1937, internationally renowned architect Frank Lloyd Wright came here to build his winter camp, **Taliesin West,** and the influence of his new form of desert architecture can be seen throughout the region. On summer evenings, you can join a guided tour of Taliesin West—a masterpiece of style illuminated in its desert environs. Kids can appreciate the importance of architecture at Wright's classic **Phoenix Biltmore Hotel,** whose lobby is decorated with reproduction furniture and his signature terracotta tiles incised with Native American patterns. A folksy architectural gem is the **Mystery Castle,** a private home built by Boyce Luther Gulley in the 1930s from recycled materials as a gift for his daughter, who leads tours of the curiosity today. More local indoor attractions include the **Hall of Flame Museum,** an interesting look at the work of firefighters, and the **Arizona Science Center,** one of the better hands-on science learning museums with a planetarium and IMAX theater.

Among the region's outdoor adventures is the **Phoenix Zoo,** with native mountain lions, bighorn sheep, and a Leapin' Lagoon water play area that provides welcome relief on sizzling summer days. The **Desert Botanical Garden** is the world's largest collection of desert plants. Walk the Desert Discovery Trail through red buttes, join a tour or workshop, or take an early-morning hike on the Urban Wildlife Nature Trail in the 1,200-acre **Papago Park.** For a very different outdoor adventure, try tubing down the Lower Salt River rapids in **Tonto National Forest.** Salt River Tubing in Mesa welcomes all explorers age seven and older and at least 48 inches tall.

VACATION PLANNING TIPS

Driving is the only practical way to get around the Valley of the Sun. At Heritage Square and around town, ask the orange-shirted Copper Square Ambassadors for information or helpful advice on local attractions.

There are thousands of urban hotel rooms in Phoenix and family-oriented golf resorts in Scottsdale. The best values are in summer, when temperatures can be brutal; on the upside, there's little humidity and lots of air-conditioning. The Grand Canyon, four hours away, is covered separately in Chapter 17.

Greater Phoenix Convention & Visitors Bureau
1-877-CALL-PHX
www.visitphoenix.com, www.arizonaguide.com

Cultural Appeal

In This Chapter

- Oklahoma's National Cowboy & Western Heritage Museum
- Roswell's celebration of aliens
- High culture meets folk art in Santa Fe
- Schlitterbahn Waterpark's world-renowned water rides

The cultural diversity of the Southwest provides family attractions to suit all tastes. Among the most engaging museums are the galleries devoted to Western and Native American art in Oklahoma, and the remarkable collection of folk art in Santa Fe. For a 360-degree, 3-D cultural experience, families can blast off into the alien world of Roswell or dive into a Bavarian-themed waterpark in New Braunfels.

National Cowboy & Western Heritage Museum, Oklahoma

The fascination with the American West and its cowboys has spawned museums across the vast lands west of the Mississippi, and one of the best is found in Oklahoma City. Formerly known as the Cowboy Hall of Fame, the National Cowboy & Western Heritage Museum (NCWHM) offers a wide range of exhibits featuring Western art, including works by Charles Russell, Frederic Remington, and Albert Bierstadt.

Theme galleries worth your time include The American Cowboy Gallery, The American Rodeo Gallery, and The Western Performers Gallery. Firearms get their own gallery, as does Native American Art. James Earle Fraser's four-ton sculpture, titled "The End of the Trail," is housed in the Monumental Sculpture Gallery.

Kids will love Prosperity Junction, a replica of a turn-of-the-century cattle town. The large hall encompasses a railroad depot, blacksmith shop, school, church, and homes. The children's building is home to ongoing programs and exhibits to delight and educate young ones.

VACATION PLANNING TIPS

If you are still in the cowboy mood after touring the National Cowboy & Western Heritage Museum, head south about 60 miles to the **Gene Autry Museum** in—where else—Gene Autry, Oklahoma. This small but interesting museum honors one of America's most beloved movie cowboys.

The **Chisholm Trail Museum,** about 40 miles northwest of Oklahoma City, presents the history of the famous cattle drive trail that ran between Texas and the railheads of Kansas. You'll find a small historical village as well as the original Governor Seay Mansion, home of Oklahoma's governor in the early 1890s.

If you're traveling with older children, consider making time for a more somber visit to the **National Memorial to the Lost,** dedicated to those who lost their lives—and to their rescuers—in the 1995 bombing of the Federal Building in Oklahoma City. At the end of your day, head to **Bricktown,** Oklahoma City's most happening nightlife and dining district.

National Cowboy & Western Heritage Museum
1700 NE 63rd Street
Oklahoma City, OK 73111
405-478-2250
www.nationalcowboymuseum.org, www.okisbeautiful.com

UFOs and Roswell, New Mexico

On July 8, 1947, an unidentified flying object careening through the New Mexico sky crashed in Roswell, forever changing this once-quiet town. The U.S. military initially issued a press release stating that a "flying saucer" had been recovered at the crash site but then quickly retracted it. The military, in a harried and clandestine frenzy, then announced the object had simply been a stray weather balloon, only to change the story once again in 1997, stating that the UFO had actually been a secret spy satellite. Whether or not the telling—and retelling—of events at Roswell is accurate, the town has become one of our favorite offbeat Americana destinations in the Southwest.

Conspiracy theorists, extraterrestrial skeptics, and curious tourists all gather at the **International UFO Museum and Research Center** to learn about the history of the Roswell incident and the chaos that ensued from the mysterious object's impact. Peruse the yellowing newspapers with sensational titles splashed on the front page, and read all about "The Great Cover-Up" and concurrent recorded UFO sightings. Also in the facility is a gift shop for all kinds of alien memorabilia and a small research center full of resources to start your own E.T. conspiracy theories.

On nearly every street corner of Roswell, pairs of giant almond-shaped eyes on oblong light posts fix their blank, creepy gaze on the tourists milling about. In early July, the annual **UFO Festival** attracts alien-costumed visitors from all over the world, sparking Martian madness and featuring guest speakers and appearances from sci-fi celebrities. Along with an elaborate and fun UFO Festival Parade, the four-day event also includes alien costume contests, live music, UFO plays, and rocketry classes for the kids.

When the family tires of little green men, head over to the **Roswell Museum and Art Center.** The permanent collection is comprised of beautifully rendered watercolors and historical materials. Several miles east lies **Bottomless Lakes State Park,** designated New Mexico's first state park in 1933. The lakes were formed when the area's underground caverns collapsed; the deepest, Lea Lake, reaches a depth of 90 feet. Year-round there's trail hiking, camping, picnicking, fishing, boating, and wildlife viewing. Farther north, the **Bitterlake National Wildlife Refuge** provides a protective wetland for birds, mammals, reptiles, and amphibians. Throw in 70 natural sinkholes of different shapes and sizes and a few of the area's recreational activities—and you have a perfect family adventure.

City of Roswell Visitor Center
1-888-ROSWELL
www.roswellmysteries.com, www.newmexico.org

Santa Fe, New Mexico, Museum of International Folk Art

For families who find most art museums inaccessible, dull, or overwhelming, have we got a museum for you: Santa Fe's Museum of International Folk Art (MOIFA). The basic philosophy of this unique institution is that folk art is the art of the everyday and comes from the traditions of community and culture. Home to the world's largest collection of folk art, the 135,000 artifacts originate from more than 100 countries and 6 continents.

A family favorite that will enthrall all ages is the museum's permanent exhibition titled "Multiple Visions: A Common Bond." The works on display include toys, dolls, costumes, and masks. Also in the collections are textiles of all kinds, religious folk art, as well as paintings, beadwork, and more to dazzle the eye.

Located in the basement, Lloyd's Treasure Chest provides a behind-the-scenes look into museum activities and gives visitors the opportunity to glimpse the actual art storage area and admire the pieces not generally seen by the public. Families can interact with select folk art works up close and personal by pulling out drawers storing the works.

Kids of all ages will enjoy the book and toy lounge, which features books, hand puppets, and trains as well as other fun and interactive games related to current museum exhibits. Although the kids won't

notice, the toys are carefully selected to be educational and empha-
size multicultural themes.

Art-loving families will adore Santa Fe's **Georgia O'Keefe
Museum,** which features more than 1,000 pieces by its namesake
artist—a visionary painter who was famous for her flowers. Visitors
can participate in a hands-on learning experience with free monthly
programs from the education staff.

About an hour away, the inhabited adobe dwellings at **Taos Pueblo,**
some of which are open to curious explorers, showcase Anasazi history. Be sure to stroll around downtown Sante Fe, where stucco
shops and galleries are clustered around Spanish-style squares and
you'll find the fun **Sante Fe Children's Museum.**

Museum of International Folk Art
Museum Hill
706 Camino Lejo
Santa Fe, New Mexico 87505
505-476-1200
www.moifa.org, www.santafe.org

Schlitterbahn Waterpark Resort, Texas

Schlitterbahn Waterpark Resort in New Braunfels—both an amusement park and a 238-room hotel—has been voted "World's Best
Water Park" for more than a dozen years running. The German
name "slippery highway" refers to the lazy rivers that keep guests
wet no matter where they go.

FUN FACTS

Schlitterbahn Waterpark has its own iPhone application that uses the
phone's GPS capability to allow you to track family members' where-
abouts and find the nearest locker room!

The New Braunfels location is the original and largest of the company's four parks. Within its 65 acres, you'll find more than 40 water

rides. At the Wolfpack Raftslide, four-person rafts can take the entire family on a spiraling 700-foot run.

Other favorite rides include Torrent, which propels you with powerful blasts of pressured water, and Master Blaster, which transports your raft uphill almost six stories on fast-moving currents. Perhaps the most popular, Dragon's Revenge, is described in park literature as "spinning tunnels, theatrical lighting, fiber optics, riveting original music, aromatic atmosphere, fog, faux fire, and an encounter with an angry dragon." All that excitement takes place in 1 minute 45 seconds.

The recently debuted Congo River Expedition is a multi-sensory experience in which the bravest cross a rope bridge to a Congo Outpost underneath a volcano, board a mysterious Congo River float trip, then get tossed over the edge of a plummeting waterfall.

VACATION PLANNING TIPS

The park is comprised of three distinct zones called Blastenhoff, Surfenburg, and Shlitterbahn West, and though the latter was designed for preschoolers, many parents find the original Blastenhoff rides to be more toddler-friendly. Keep these tips in mind as you prepare to get wet:

- Some rides have two-hour waits; it's much less crowded on weekdays.
- Many rides have a minimum height of 42 inches and scary special effects.
- Lifeguards occasionally close the lake-fed rides due to low water levels or storms.
- Buy a two-day pass so kids don't wear out, or consider booking a room on-site.

New Braunfels is a cute alpine-themed town with oompah bands, bierhausen, and an autumn **WurstFest**. Several local companies rent inner "toobs" for a float down the authentic **Comal** or **Guadeloupe Rivers**.

Since 2000, three other parks have opened. The smaller **Schlitterbahn Beach Waterpark** on South Padre Island has 12 water rides and is a popular alternative to swimming in the Gulf of Mexico. The

Galveston Island Waterpark is climate-controlled, with a unique convertible roof and heated pools. More than 30 family attractions, including three interconnected rivers and two uphill water coasters, make it a good bet year-round in this touristy beach town.

If you're closer to Kansas City, Missouri, than New Braunfels, Texas, you might want to consider a trip to **Schlitterbahn Vacation Village** instead—it's a hotel, water park, and mall complex connected by manmade rivers.

Schlitterbahn Waterpark Resort
New Braunfels, Texas
830-/625-2351
www.schlitterbahn.com, www.newbraunfels.com

Amusement Parks and Outdoor Fun

Chapter

17

In This Chapter

- The Grand Canyon's natural splendor
- Explore San Antonio's famous fort at the crossroads of Native and Hispanic culture
- Sedona's mystical family attractions
- Pack your cowboy hats and lassos to enjoy Fort Worth's Americana

The southwestern part of the United States, with its cowboy and Indian legends firmly rooted in this arid soil, is one of the most fun places for kids to explore American history.

While there are hundreds of sites and monuments that commemorate the settlement of this region and the takeover of Native American lands by pioneers from the East, we like the following sites for the fun way they bring American history and the region's remarkable natural beauty to life for all ages.

Grand Canyon National Park

At 277 miles long and up to 6,000 feet deep, the Grand Canyon—cut by the Colorado River through Arizona, Nevada, and Utah—is enormous and truly spectacular. America's second most popular national park (after the Great Smoky Mountains; see Chapter 10) welcomes more than 5 million visitors per year—more than

90 percent of whom head to the **South Rim Visitor Center** and nearby hotels, motels, and restaurants. Try to spend at least one night; whether you're sightseeing from the rim or a trail, the changing sunlight presents an amazing array of colors and vistas.

Most families drive around the rim and stop at the many scenic overviews to observe the canyon and the Colorado River from different perspectives.

TRAVELERS BEWARE!

The Grand Canyon's size, while awe-inspiring, can make hiking dangerous. Keep the following in mind:

- Steep sides and slippery paths require parents packing infants to go slowly.
- After age three, kids can walk one mile each day per year of age.
- Allow about twice as much time to ascend as to descend.
- All but the most athletic will tire easily from the lack of oxygen and high temperatures.

The most popular trails are the South Kaibab, near Yaki Point on the East Rim Drive; Bright Angel, leading down from the village into the canyon; and Hopi Point, the gathering spot for a legendary sunset view. Not far from the South Rim visitor center is the Yavapai Observation Station, whose canyon views and exhibits on the region's fascinating geology should engage school-age kids. From here, take the easy-going, approximately three-mile-long Maricopa Point Nature Trail. Stop for lunch at **El Tovar,** a classic National Park lodge perched right on the rim in Grand Canyon Village with a good restaurant that welcomes children.

Serious hikers hoping to get away from the crowds should drive to the **North Rim.** Experienced camping families and hikers ages 12 and older with their own gear will enjoy the North Kaibab Trail, not far from the ranger station. Families with kids age 8 and older should look into the half-day mule rides down the rim to Roaring Springs or the easy-going 5-mile Widforss Trail. The best of the nearby lookouts is at Point Imperial, about 11 miles from the **Grand**

Canyon Lodge. At the **Grand Canyon West entertainment complex,** the famous Skywalk—a 4,000-foot-high glass bridge—extends out over the Colorado River and the canyon rim. See who in your family is brave enough to walk onto the amazingly engineered bridge and look down. To learn about four different tribes in the area or see the cowboy shows, stop by the Hualapai Indian Village.

Grand Canyon Village is the place to go for horseback riding, flight-seeing, museums, and shopping. An IMAX theater offers virtual tours of the canyon for those too weary or laden with little ones to descend from the overlooks. Ranger lectures are often given about the park's natural history; even preschoolers can earn a Junior Ranger badge by studying the canyon.

"Reserve ahead!" should be your mantra for any Grand Canyon trip, and try to avoid the July–August high season, when the park is flooded with visitors. Xanterra Parks & Resorts manage Grand Canyon–area hotels, and the National Park Service handles campgrounds. For the best experience, always wear protection from the sun and cold, carry plenty of drinking water, check trail conditions, and follow the map.

Grand Canyon National Park
928-638-7888
www.nps.gov/grca, www.grandcanyon.com

San Antonio, Texas

San Antonio is defined largely by its river and famous *Paseo del Rio,* or **River Walk,** along the San Antonio River. Fed by numerous springs, the water of the San Antonio River was pure and abundant, and it was this river that originally drew both Native Americans and their Spanish intruders to the area. Concerned about the potential for French expansion into what would be Texas, the Spanish *conquistadores* and Franciscan priests expanded north from Mexico and in the early 1700s built five missions along the San Antonio River. The first mission, and the one destined for lasting fame, was San Antonio de Valero. The Mexican soldiers posted there soon renamed it after their hometown, Alamo de Parras—*alamo* being the Spanish word for cottonwood.

FUN FACTS

The states comprising the Southwest joined the Union fairly late in the game:

- Texas: state #28 in 1845
- Oklahoma: state #46 in 1907
- New Mexico: state #47 in 1912
- Arizona: state #48 in 1912

The Alamo took on mythic proportions during the Texas Revolution of 1835–1836. After attacking and occupying the small town of San Antonio and the Alamo, Texas troops were surrounded by Mexican troops in late February 1886. A 13-day siege ended with the complete defeat and demise of the Texans.

Both myth and movies have shaped perceptions about that battle, but the central story—of Lt. Col. William Travis drawing a line in the sand and asking those willing to die to cross it—is now considered fiction by most historians. Successive expansions of the heroic Texas mythology demonized the Mexican troops and further clouded the history. However, there is no doubt that, in what would be the final and victorious battle for Texas Independence at **San Jacinto,** Texan troops rallied around the cry "Remember the Alamo" and extracted bloody vengeance in the process.

In downtown **San Antonio,** the Alamo survives today as a pale version of its original form in the shadow of skyscrapers and parking garages. (To make the history more entertaining for kids, **Alamo Plaza Attractions** has a Ripley's Haunted Adventure, Guinness World Records Museum, and a Tomb Rider 3D arcade across the street.) It's worthy of a visit, but don't expect the full mission experience or pure history. The other four original Spanish missions (San Jose, Concepción, San Juan, and Espada) survive in various states of their original layout, with the restored **Mission San Jose** being the most beautiful and most fully intact—best conveying the feeling of the village that was the mission.

But you'll probably head first to where it all started—along the San Antonio River. You can stroll or boat along the two and a half–mile stretch, with restaurants, shops, hotels, and some gardens lining both sides. It's lovely, relaxed, crowded, and commercial. A three-mile extension of River Walk called the Museum Reach passes the **San Antonio Museum of Art** on its way to the Pearl Brewery.

One of the delights of River Walk is **La Villita,** San Antonio's original neighborhood, which has been transformed from decay into a charming village of shops, galleries, artists' studios, and restaurants. Other notable and walkable sites include the **Hemisfair Plaza,** which was the site of the 1968 World's Fair, and **King William Street,** an area of restored nineteenth-century homes—one of which, **The Steves Homestead,** is open to the public.

For pure fun, head to **Sea World** or **Six Flags Fiesta Texas,** which includes the **White Water Bay** water park. On a rainy day, visit the **San Antonio Children's Museum, Institute of Texan Cultures, McNay Art Institute,** or the San Antonio Museum of Art, built in a beautifully restored brewery. For shoppers, stroll down Dolorosa Street to Market Square and **El Mercado,** which offers a full range of items—including clothing, leather goods, and decorative items— made in Mexico. **Mi Tierra** restaurant offers some interesting Mexican artisanal pieces like tiles, dresses, fabrics, and T-shirts in addition to its authentic Tex-Mex cuisine. A meal here is a good way to begin or end your visit. For day trips out of the city, explore **Bandera, Fredericksburg,** and **New Braunfels.**

The Alamo Historic Site
300 Alamo Plaza
San Antonio, Texas 78205
210-225-1391
www.thealamo.org, www.visitsanantonio.com

Sedona, Arizona

The word "Sedona" may sound Native American, but it was named for the wife of the city's first postmaster—a woman known for her hospitality and industriousness. Located in the very heart of Arizona, the city is famous not only for its Western-style hospitality but also for its breathtaking red sandstone formations and their place in Native American culture.

To get the full experience of the area's awesome geological landscapes, take the family for a drive along the stunning **Oak Creek
Canyon.** Midway through the canyon, **Slide Rock State Park** is one
of Arizona's most fun places to slide down a natural rock chute into
the shallow creek waters below.

Sedona's scenic beauty and rugged terrain provide many opportunities for outdoor adventures. Biking, hiking, camping, climbing,
swimming, water sliding, ballooning, Jeep tours (guided or
unguided), golf, horseback riding, birding, star-gazing, and picnics
on the banks of gurgling Oak Creek or in Sedona's city and state
parks are just some of the options for all ages.

FUN FACTS

Which is correct: vortices or vortexes? Although most dictionaries list
both words as acceptable, you probably won't hear the former uttered
in Sedona. There, the residents prefer to use "vortexes" to refer to the
purported Indian power spots.

Next, check out Sedona's famous **vortexes,** where ancient Indians
were believed to have drawn their power from Earth's natural energy
fields. No matter what your beliefs, your family will appreciate the
beauty of these natural rock formations. Be sure to visit the gracefully spired Cathedral Rock, Sedona's most famous vortex and one
of the most photographed rock formations in the valley. The bell-
shaped Bell Rock Vortex is one of the most bizarre formations,
and its strong energy field (measured by the amount of twist in the
branches of nearby juniper trees) makes it a favorite spot for UFO
watchers.

The Airport Mesa Vortex offers a gorgeous view of the valley spread
below, particularly at sunset when the light sparkles off the distant
red rocks. Reputedly the most powerful vortex in the Red Rock
Valley, the Boynton Canyon Vortex is also one of the best for hiking.
Several ancient Sinagua Indian cliff dwellings can be observed along
the canyon trails; their small size makes them perfect for young children to explore.

Native American ruins and monuments such as the **Montezuma Castle National Monument** offer many historical and cultural insights. The 800-year-old cliff dwellings of Montezuma were mistakenly named by explorers who thought that the Aztecs had fled to this area after the conquest of Mexico. In truth, this five-story, castle-like ruin set high on a cliff was built by Sinagua Indians, who were ancestors of the Hopi. Adjoining Montezuma's Castle is the **Yavapai-Apache Visitor Activity Center,** offering information on all of the different American Indian tribes that lived in the region. A few miles north is **Montezuma's Well,** with more of these mysterious ancient Indian cliff dwellings gathered around a pool of water.

Are you ready for more action? Spend a day at the new 104-acre **Out of Africa Wildlife Park** or enjoy a ride on the **Verde Canyon Railroad,** a 4-hour, round-trip excursion through Sycamore Canyon.

Sedona Chamber of Commerce
928-282-7722
www.sedonachamber.com, www.arizonaguide.com

The Wild West in Fort Worth, Texas

Fort Worth owes its nickname of "Cowtown" to the **Fort Worth Stockyards,** which for more than 140 years has drawn cattle from all over the state. Around the turn of the century, when the railroad arrived, the cattle, the slaughterhouses, and the meat packers did, too.

> **FUN FACTS**
>
> Depending on the wind, there was a distinctive odor three miles south of the stockyards in downtown, which led Dallas citizens to look down their noses at their neighboring city (not to mention hold their noses while visiting the town). While the odor is long gone, the stockyards—now mainly inactive—remain as part of the legacy of the West.

Your family can start your tour of Cowtown at **Stockyard Station** with a walking tour of the **Stockyard Historic District.** It's on the way to the world's only twice-daily **cattle drive,** where the resident longhorns of the Fort Worth Herd are driven by the Herd's cowboys and cowgirls through the stockyards. On Friday and Saturday afternoons, volunteers hold a **Cow Camp** where they demonstrate the tools and techniques used to work cattle in the 1800s.

Families will enjoy the **Cowtown Cattlepen Maze,** where kids race to navigate the labyrinth of pens while parents can watch from an elevated viewing platform. At the **Stockyards Museum,** photos and artifacts trace the history of the stockyards from the trail drives of the 1870s, through the peak years of the 1940s, to the declining years of the 1980s.

Housed in the old horse and mule building, the **Texas Cowboy Hall of Fame** pays tribute to more than 70 outstanding cowboys and cowgirls with individual booths devoted to each (George Strait and Willie Nelson are included). There's also a major collection of period wagons, an exhibit devoted to the history of the local Justin boots company, and a children's interactive Exploratorium. Don't leave the building without a stop at the **Jersey Lilly Old Time Photo Parlor,** where you can dress in period Western costumes for a classic family photo.

If you're in town on a Friday or Saturday night, don't miss the **Stockyards Championship Rodeo** in the Cowtown Coliseum. It's the real rodeo deal, with bull riding, roping, barrel racing, rodeo clowns, and more. If you're visiting in the summer or on many major holiday weekends, **Pawnee Bill's Wild West Show** is a re-enactment of the original 1909 show, still offering trick roping, trick shooting, trick riding, and cowboy songs.

VACATION PLANNING TIPS

Don't miss dinner at **Billy Bob's Texas,** celebrating more than 25 years as the self-proclaimed "world's largest honky-tonk." In addition to serving legendary barbecue meals, this Texas-sized entertainment complex offers a PG-style three-acre nightclub and a fun game arcade. Professional cowboys perform nightly in the indoor bull-riding arena.

Lunch is also served at Billy Bob's, but it's more subdued because bulls are resting for the evening.

For families wanting to broaden their cultural palette, the nearby Fort Worth Cultural District encompasses six museums, including the well-regarded **Kimbell Art Museum.** The **Amon Carter Museum** has a major collection of noted Western artists Frederic Remington and Charles M. Russell among its more modern art. And if you're still hungry for things Western, visit the **National Cowgirl Museum and Hall of Fame.**

When the kids are ready for a theme park fix, take a break from the West and head east 20 minutes to the twin Western-themed amusement parks of **Six Flags Over Texas** and the **Six Flags Hurricane Island** water park, located in nearby Arlington.

For more Western immersion, you can drive to and through Dallas for an evening at the **Mesquite Championship Rodeo.** Fans come from far and wide to watch cowboys and cowgirls practice the rodeo arts. Other Dallas attractions include the **Children's Museum at the Museum of Nature & Science** in the historic Texas State Fairgrounds. The **Nasher Sculpture Museum** and **Dallas Museum of Art** are both located downtown, not far from the **Sixth Floor Museum,** a private museum devoted to different outlaws. This fascinating small museum is housed in the Texas Book Depository Building, from whose window Lee Harvey Oswald is alleged to have shot President John F. Kennedy in 1963. For a different behind-the-scenes look, grab the family and book a tour of **Cowboys Stadium,** home of the legendary Dallas Cowboys football team.

Fort Worth Convention & Visitors Bureau
1-800-433-5747
www.fortworth.com/visitors, www.visitdallas-fortworth.com

Mountain States

The Mountain states of Colorado, Idaho, Montana, Utah, and Wyoming are home to hundreds of peaks that inspire many family vacation planners.

If you're traveling in winter, it's probably for the region's incredible skiing and snowboarding conditions—which you will find at many famous mountain resorts such as Aspen or Vail in Colorado; Park City, Utah; or Jackson Hole, Wyoming.

If you're visiting in summer, a road trip is the classic way to explore the cultural sites, historical monuments, Wild West towns, and stunning natural attractions that define the rugged land just west of the Continental Divide.

Chart a course along as many of the two-lane blacktops as the kids have patience for, because therein lie some of the United States' greatest treasures.

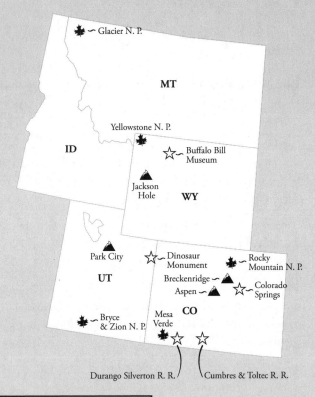

Glacier N. P.

MT

Yellowstone N. P.

ID

Buffalo Bill
Museum

Jackson
Hole

WY

Park City

Dinosaur
Monument

Rocky
Mountain N. P.

Breckenridge

Colorado
Springs

Aspen

UT

Mesa
Verde

CO

Bryce
& Zion N. P.

Durango Silverton R. R.

Cumbres & Toltec R. R.

Best Family Destinations Key:

Amusement Parks   Cultural Appeal/Living History

At the Beach   Mountain Towns

City Style   Outdoor Adventures

Mountain Towns

18

In This Chapter

- Hobnobbing on the slopes with Aspen's glamorous jetsetters
- Action-packed adventures and a family-friendly welcome in Breckenridge
- Exploring the untamed West year-round in Jackson Hole
- Movies and snow in Park City

In any introduction to our favorite mountain towns of the Mountain States (Colorado, Idaho, Montana, Utah, and Wyoming), it's all too easy to take the mountains—and gorgeous mountain views—for granted. What sets the "best" mountain towns apart from all the other ski resorts, base villages, and more densely populated cities of this region is their residents' devotion to their lifestyle. By and large, these towns thrive on a communal love of the outdoors, preservation of local history, sophisticated cuisine and culture, and an independent Western spirit. They also love to welcome visitors who appreciate them for what they are.

Aspen and Snowmass, Colorado

As mountain towns go, **Aspen** is truly one of the crown jewels, legendary for the wealthy and star-studded clientele whose private jets clog the tiny airport during holidays. Families will quickly understand the appeal of this charming and friendly former mining town, now a sophisticated high-end destination with shops, restaurants, bars, and galleries on par with many major cities.

Sited in the Roaring Fork Valley of west-central Colorado, Aspen was one of the richest mining towns of the late nineteenth century. The demise of silver prices was devastating to the economy, and by 1935 only 705 of the 12,000 inhabitants remained. Aspen's transformation into a ski resort began in the 1940s and since then has blossomed into a world-renowned, year-round center of outdoor activities and indoor culture.

The skiing universe circling Aspen has grown from the original **Aspen Mountain** to include the independent mountain resorts of **Aspen Highlands, Buttermilk,** and **Snowmass.** All share a free shuttle bus system and one lift ticket. Aspen Mountain is ground zero: its rugged peaks rise dramatically above the town. Aspen, which hosts the annual X-Games, offers solid intermediate and expert skiing but has no beginner runs or children's programs.

FUN FACTS

Aspen High School has its own chairlift that leads straight up to Aspen Highlands, the resort that hardcore skiers and riders prefer. It's used by students as well as members of the Aspen Valley Ski and Snowboard Club, whose alumni include Gretchen Bleiler and many U.S. Ski Team competitors.

Buttermilk has a good children's program, smooth and easy slopes, and a terrain park with many whimsical snow features beloved by kids. About 12 miles northwest, Snowmass has become a special family destination of its own, with runs for every level of skier or boarder, several excellent terrain parks, an excellent children's ski school, and daycare for ages 8 weeks and older. At Snowmass, slopeside condos are a good base from which to explore the area in any season.

Off slope, both the Wild West–style Aspen and the purpose-built Snowmass host many winter activities for families. Within its car-free base camp village, Snowmass organizes campfire sing-alongs, storytelling complete with roasted s'mores and hot chocolate, Snowcat dinner rides, and arts and crafts activities. Free concerts are held in the adjoining **Snowmass Village Mall.** Many local tour operators run snowshoe and cross-country outings or day trips for whitewater rafting, fly fishing, cycling, and hiking—gear and lessons included.

At any time of year, the **Snowmass Village Recreation Center** is a great family destination, with climbing and bouldering walls, outdoor heated pools, fitness rooms, and a gym. The **Aspen Recreation Center** has the same facilities, plus indoor and outdoor ice skating rinks, classes, and tennis in season. The sister **Red Brick Recreation Center** also has a climbing wall, a kids' playhouse and bounce house, and fitness classes. After a day on the slopes, there's nothing like a dip in the pool or hot tub, so day passes are well worthwhile.

On both Aspen Mountain and Snowmass, naturalists from the **Aspen Center for Environmental Studies** (ACES) lead kids ages seven and older on **snowshoe nature tours.** Only at Snowmass, ACES naturalists lead free **nature ski tours** for skiers and boarders ages seven and older (intermediate skills required) and comparable daily programs in the summer.

Summers in Aspen/Snowmass are ideal for active families, with options including mountain biking, mountain boarding, hiking, disc golf, paintball, and trout fishing, plus storytelling, sing-a-longs, and craft activities. Music has always been a big part of the cultural life here. The **Aspen Music Festival** has an active performance and teaching program in summer, and there are several other musical events elsewhere in the region. The **Anderson Ranch Arts Center** offers free slide lectures plus art classes for kids of all ages.

When you need a break from relentless recreation, head to Aspen for some serious shopping or just casual wandering around the compact, walkable village with its beautifully preserved historic buildings. Stop at a sidewalk café and enjoy the view of the glorious mountains.

Aspen/Snowmass
1-800-525-6200
www.aspensnowmass.com, www.colorado.com/Aspen.aspx

Breckenridge and the I-70 Ski Corridor

Route I-70 stretches more than 2,100 miles from Maryland to Utah, but it's the scenic last several hundred miles snaking through the Rocky Mountains that lead to the ultimate mountain getaway for ski bums or active families. Whether you choose a tunnel cut under the **Front Range** or the sky-high **Loveland Pass,** you'll reach the authentic mountain town of **Breckenridge,** Colorado—the place where we begin our action-packed adventure.

This woodsy Western town of Victorian and historical structures is home to the **Breckenridge Ski Resort,** where you can feel the rush of cold air skiing or snowboarding down steep mountainsides or enjoy a bumpy ride behind a sled pulled by beautiful Siberian huskies. **Kinderhut** is a nursery with a fully trained staff ready to make your toddler into a snow sports pro. Breckenridge was the first public mountain to permit Vermonter **Jake Burton** to test out his "snowboard" invention back in 1985, and whatever your winter fancy, this area still welcomes it. In fact, excellent snow sports instruction is available along I-70, where **Vail Resorts** manages many of the top programs.

For those who haven't developed their snow legs yet, "Breck"—as locals like to call their former mining town—is known for mountain biking, hiking, and river sports in summer. No matter the season, many visitors choose the moderately priced townhouses, B&Bs, or condos over on-mountain lodging in this "Wild West" town because it's a fun, safe place for 'tweens, teens, and college kids to hang out.

In town, the **Breckenridge Recreation Center** allows guests to escape the cold or enjoy the brilliant summer skies in its sauna, steam room, huge pool with waterslide, and indoor and outdoor Jacuzzis; the center also offers daycare for children ages two months through six years. A few of Breckenridge's many festivals are January's **Ullr Fest,** celebrating the Norse God of Snow, and the **Budweiser International Snow Sculpture Championships,** where you can watch performances, parades, and 20-ton blocks of snow being turned into works of art.

VACATION PLANNING TIPS

Breckenridge and Summit County, Colorado, rely on extensive public transportation to achieve their green goals of reducing carbon dioxide emissions and keeping snow on their peaks all winter. Families can bypass the rental car line and catch a shuttle from the Denver Airport to any of these resort areas, then have the following free transport options:

- The **Summit Stage** is a bus offering transportation around the county.
- The **Main Street Shuttle, Circulator Route, Peak 8 Evening Route,** and **Breckenridge Ski Resort Shuttle** transport guests and locals from the residential areas to downtown or to the ski resort.
- The **Ski KAB Express** runs between the mountain resorts of Breckenridge, Keystone, and A-Basin.

The **Edwin Carter Museum** displays the wildlife conservation achievements of the "log cabin naturalist" Edwin Carter, whose natural specimens played a significant role in the development of the Denver Museum of Nature and Science. The **Country Boy Mine** offers guided underground tours, mining exhibits, and gold panning. The **Mountain Top Children's Museum** provides water play, a dress-up area, and the Kidstruction Zone.

East toward **Denver,** south of I-70, **Arapahoe Basin** (also called A-Basin) boasts the highest snowfall of any Colorado mountain and usually has the longest ski season of them all, often closing after Independence Day.

The three mountains of **Keystone Resort** tower above other mountain resorts at 11,000 feet. Their three base villages of condo clusters are each packed with support services, pedestrian shopping, ice skating (or boating in summer), and dining. Families can warm up with a cup of hot cocoa at the **Rocky Mountain Chocolate Factory** while feasting on fudge and watching the ice skaters glide around on Keystone Lake.

The upscale **Vail Resort,** located west of Breckenridge, is a mecca for skiers and snowboarders from around the world. It, too, has three base villages; families with school-age kids usually prefer bustling Lionshead with its skating rink, shops, cafés, condos, and a gondola that rises straight up to **Adventure Ridge.** This snow play park has eight lanes of lift-served tubing, a mini-snowmobile course, snow bikes, and all kinds of other day and nighttime fun. Posh **Vail Village** is a charming Bavarian-style, pedestrian-only area filled with hotels, shops, bistros, and nightlife that is also popular with families. When the snow has melted, whitewater rafting trips on the gentle-flowing **Lakota River** are available for family fun; keep an eye out for beavers, foxes, coyotes, and deer along the banks.

Vail was developed in the 1950s by World War II veterans of the 10th Mountain Brigade; to see films about the area's snowboarding and skiing history and memorabilia from past Winter Olympics, be sure to schedule a visit to the **Ski and Snowboard Museum and Hall of Fame** in Vail Village. Nearby at the **Betty Ford Alpine Gardens,** there's a rock garden with more than 150 plant varieties and even a children's garden, as well as hiking trails and a school-house museum. The best time to visit the garden is from "mud season" (when the snow melts) until late September.

The upscale **Beaver Creek Resort** is a family resort with ski-in, ski-out suites and concierges who will bundle up your kids in the mornings for you. The area's location allows for fly-fishing, horse-back riding, kayaking, mountain biking, rock climbing, whitewater rafting, and hiking in summer, when the alpine-style base village becomes the cultural hub for outdoor concerts.

Town of Breckenridge
Breckenridge, CO 80424
970-453-2251
www.townofbreckenridge.com, www.snow.com

Jackson Hole, Wyoming

The first people to cross the tall, steep mountain passes into the high-altitude valley of **Jackson Hole** most likely arrived while the last massive glaciers were still receding. Ancient Clovis stone arrow-heads and artifacts from the Shoshone, Bannock, Blackfeet, Crow, and Gros Ventre Indian tribes have been found in the region. The early trappers settled the mountain town of **Jackson** as a commercial center; today the town is a destination for jet-setting celebrities such as Sandra Bullock and Harrison Ford.

Jackson is a year-round playground—the ultimate vacation destination for those who love the untamed West. No one who visits forgets the four arches made of elk antlers that grace the corners of Jackson's town square. Regardless of the time of year you visit, there's an array of activities the entire family can dig into as well as sophisticated galleries, shops, and fine restaurants for those who prefer to admire the mountains from a distance.

FUN FACTS

In late May, the local Boy Scouts help support the **National Elk Refuge** with their annual **Jackson Boy Scout Antler Auction.** Each spring between March and May, the scouts collect antlers the bulls have shed. It's said that the auction sells almost 10,000 pounds of elk antlers.

Several mountain resorts cater to kids ranging in age from 6 months to 18 years. The best known, **Jackson Hole Mountain Resort,** features an award-winning Kid's Ranch that teaches your miniature cowboy or cowgirl skiing and snowboarding essentials. If your teens are stellar skiers, JHMR's Team Extreme teaches the rudiments of back-country equipment, safety, and travel while major athletes such as Tommy Moe, Micah Black, Travis Rice, and Jamie Sundberg drop by classes to say hello.

Winter sees more than 500 inches of fluffy falling powder, and winter fun includes wilderness snowmobiling, horse-drawn sleigh rides, and dog sledding. Other mountains, including **Snow King** and **Grand Targhee,** offer tubing to those taller than 42" as well as skiing. If it's cold outside, mosey into the historic Silver Dollar Bar at the **Wort Hotel** before Happy Hour, when kids can get a snack at a bar decorated with 2,032 inlaid silver dollars.

During the warmer seasons, shutterbugs and outdoor enthusiasts delight in numerous activities. Team up with **Teton Science Schools Wildlife Expeditions** guides who have a reputation for locating all kinds of wildlife; families may see elk, moose, bison, pronghorn antelope, bighorn sheep, mule deer, and of course a bear every now and then. Families with younger children will appreciate the new visitor's center open at the **Grand Teton National Park** Laurence S. Rockefeller Preserve, accessed by car or bike from the scenic Moose-Wilson Road. The visitor center is a good starting point for easy hikes to see deer and moose, go on a photo safari, explore Phelps Lake, or find out about horseback riding.

FELLOW TRAVELERS SAY ...

"As I drifted down the lazy Snake River, I listened intently to the guide's instructions and practiced the different paddle commands with great ease ... At the sight of the next rapid, I eagerly paddled forward without fear. The raft gained speed, the scenery became a blur, and the calm foundation became unstable and choppy. With one foot, I held on to the bucking bronco and had the time of my life."

—J. D., www.travelBIGO.com

Summer sports enthusiasts will find many activities within an hour's drive of town: they can mountain bike the National Elk Refuge, try a rafting or whitewater excursion on the **Snake River,** enjoy stunning hikes in **Yellowstone** (covered in detail in Chapter 20) and Grand Teton National Parks, and go fly fishing on the Snake or Shoshone Rivers.

Although the Jackson Hole region provides lots of rustic fun, there is also culture to complement an active getaway. Guests can enjoy a family-friendly dance or theater performance and explore the hands-on Children's Discovery Gallery at the **National Museum of Wildlife Art.**

Jackson Hole Chamber of Commerce
307-733-3316
www.jacksonholechamber.com, www.wyomingtourism.org

Park City, Utah

Once a major gold and silver mining town, Park City has experienced a boom by mining the year-round appeal of both town and mountains. Many visitors fly into Salt Lake City and drive directly to this charming, sophisticated, and lively mountain town. In the winter, most come for the skiing at **Park City Mountain Resort, Deer Valley Resort,** and **The Canyons.** In January, the town is packed with big names for the **Sundance Film Festival.** In the summer, the wide array of adventure options is sure to please any active family.

The 2002 Winter Olympics put Park City on the world map. In preparation for the games, the **Utah Olympic Park** was built as both a training and competition facility. It hosted the ski jumping, Nordic, bobsled, and luge events during the Olympics and today serves as a training facility for U.S. and international athletes. The Olympic Park Visitors Center offers tours of the training facility— and in non-winter months, several extreme speed-thrill experiences.

At the Olympic Park, adults and kids ages 3 and older can take a ride down the Quicksilver Alpine Slide, a sled on a steel track that weaves down a narrow course. It's the next best thing to the real bobsled run—a 5G, 80-mph ride driven by a professional —that allows kids ages 16 and older to ride in winter, and ages 14 and older to ride in summer. For a mellow pursuit, stroll through the **Alf Eigen Ski Museum,** whose interactive displays simulate skiing and snowboarding. Our favorite is the virtual ski machine that lets you experience the Olympic downhill, slalom runs, and a powder run from the nearby Alta Ski area.

FUN FACTS

Park City boasts the world's steepest zip line, called XTREME. They guarantee to send you down the K 120 ski jump hill at 50 mph. If you prefer something tamer, go for the ULTRA Zipline. (Note that each zip line has weight thresholds, requiring participants to weigh at least 50 pounds for the ULTRA and 100 pounds for the XTREME, with a maximum weight on both rides of 275 pounds.)

The Park City Mountain Resort offers a diverse menu of summer fun. The Alpine Slide is a luge-like bobsled-on-wheels where you can race your siblings in parallel tracks to the bottom. At 48" tall, you get to solo; below that, it's a ride with Mom or Dad. You'll get a slightly more controlled ride on the Alpine Coaster; the Zip Rider drops 550 feet over a 2,300-foot run. Calmer activities include miniature golf, horseback riding, guided mountain sled tours, a human maze, a few small amusement park rides, and a trampoline bungee experience.

All three ski areas offer extensive lift-served mountain bike and hiking trails, thereby eliminating the leg-burning climb uphill. Both The Canyons and Deer Valley Resort offer regular outdoor musical events, with acts ranging from the Utah Symphony to bluegrass and jazz festivals.

Most resorts offer great children's programs in both winter and summer. They book up well in advance, so you need to plan ahead. And if you've had enough of the great outdoors, the great indoors will welcome you for a wide range of shopping options in the stylish boutiques of downtown Park City.

Park City Chamber of Commerce and Visitors Bureau
1-800-453-1360
www.parkcityinfo.com, www.utah.com

Cultural Appeal

Chapter

19

In This Chapter

- Cody: a town built by—and starring—Buffalo Bill
- A wealth of natural and manmade sights in Colorado Springs
- Dinosaur National Monument's awe-inspiring fossils
- Colorado's steam-powered trains

Sometimes on a long road trip our family just needs a break: a stop at a town where we won't have to unpack and repack each night, where the car stays parked, and where there's enough to do and see that everyone is satisfied. We think that Cody, Wyoming; Colorado Springs, Colorado; Vernal, Utah; and Durango, Colorado—each with a variety of manmade and natural attractions in a relatively small area—will fit the bill for your family.

Buffalo Bill Museum and Cody, Wyoming

After a visit to the **Buffalo Bill Historical Center** in Cody, your family will know who the real king of the Wild West was. Inside the historical center complex, the **Buffalo Bill Museum** offers entertaining exhibits about "Wild West Show" legend William Frederick Cody's personal life as well as works devoted to the appreciation of the American West.

You can mosey past beautiful watercolors of cowboys, horses, and stagecoaches at the **Whitney Gallery of Western Art** or peer into a full-size teepee on display at the **Plains Indian Museum,** where you can learn the history of native tribes such as the Lakota, Crow, and Cheyenne. The **Cody Firearms Museum** houses an impressive collection of Winchesters.

The **Draper Museum of Natural History** is a real kid-pleaser. Upon arriving, kids can pick up an Explorer's Guide full of activities and a passport for gathering various animal stamps. The museum's spiral design simulates a descent in elevation as visitors walk from the alpine environment of bighorn sheep and mountain goats, through forest and meadows, and down to the plains and basins. Along the way, you'll learn about the geology, wildlife, and peoples of the Greater Yellowstone region.

VACATION PLANNING TIPS

The Buffalo Bill Historical Center hosts two major annual happenings: a celebration of **Cowboy Songs and Range Ballads** in April and the **Plains Indian Museum Pow Wow** in June. Plan your vacation to take in a performance or two at one of these events.

Founded in 1896, **Cody** is a wonderful town for walking and soaking up the history. Be sure to stop by the **Irma Hotel;** built by Buffalo Bill in 1902 and named after his youngest daughter, it's still a working hotel and restaurant. In the summer, you may catch a free evening gunfight re-enactment out front. Reconstructed on the site of Old Cody City, the **Old Trail Town** comprises a collection of historic relics and buildings built between 1879 and 1901 as well as the **Museum of the Old West.** The museum displays Plains Indians artifacts, guns of the frontier, carriages, and period clothing as well as Butch Cassidy and the Sundance Kid's "Hole-in-the-Wall" cabin. **Cody Trolley Tours** provide another way to see and learn about the city while giving your feet a rest.

Don't miss out on the summertime **Cody Nite Rodeo,** which includes special children's activities such as face painting and trick roping nightly. The **Cody Stampede** is a championship rodeo and celebration with parades and fireworks held each July.

Both **Yellowstone National Park** (see Chapter 20) and **Shoshone National Forest** are nearby. Buffalo Bill himself helped create the first road between Cody and Yellowstone, and his hunting lodge just outside the park is still standing and open to visitors.

Buffalo Bill Historical Center
720 Sheridan Avenue
Cody, WY 82414
307-587-4771
www.bbhc.org, www.yellowstonecountry.org

Colorado Springs, Pikes Peak, and Garden of the Gods

It's hard to hold a candle to **Colorado Springs,** home to a diverse range of peoples and cultures from Native Americans to gold miners to subsequent gold rush millionaires—and, more recently, professional athletes. **Pikes Peak,** the area's star attraction, was sighted by Zebulon Pike back in 1806, but it wasn't until the late 1850s that the peak reached its pinnacle of fame.

FUN FACTS

Katherine Lee Bates, enraptured by the "purple mountains' majesty" seen in and around Colorado Springs, penned a poem titled "Pikes Peak" in 1895. Put to music composed by Samuel A. Ward, the poem became the song "America the Beautiful," which school children across the country still sing today.

The slogan "Pikes Peak or Bust" became a rallying cry during the gold mining boom, when the landmark was used as a beacon for prospectors. Today, the awe-inspiring Pikes Peak is the crown jewel of the **Pike National Forest.** From the gateway at 7,400 feet to the 14,110-foot summit, it is accessible via a 12-mile hike up the Barr Trail, a 19-mile scenic journey by car, or on the 8.9-mile-long **Pikes Peak Cog Railway,** a three-hour ride that has been thrilling families since 1891. Climb aboard and you'll hear the conductor's tale of the mountain's aged bristlecone pines, daunting male bighorn sheep, and common yellow-bellied marmots.

Another must-see is the **Garden of the Gods,** a 1,300-acre park at the foot of Pikes Peak that's surrounded by 20 spectacular towering red sandstone formations. The park has 15 miles of scenic trails, from easy to moderate, for hiking, biking, or horseback riding. On one of the free daily guided walks, you can spot rattlesnakes and wildflowers, hear the raspy scream of the red-tailed hawk, or catch a glimpse of the egg-robbing black-billed magpie. Guests can embark on summer bus tours, rappel off sandstone cliffs, or even grill at one of the garden's two picnic sites.

FUN FACTS

Rich Buzzelli, best known for his photography of the garden's spectacular landscape, was struck by lightning on Pikes Peak in July 1995 and died at age 37. Many of his works are now on display at the Visitor Center.

Manitou Springs, a National Historic District, is a charming Victorian town located four miles west of Colorado Springs. Be sure to visit the **Manitou Cliff Dwellings,** Anasazi Indian homes that were built by Native American tribes who roamed the **Four Corners** area of the Southwest from 1200 B.C.E. to 1300 C.E. Stop by the Pueblo-style **Anasazi Museum** to view the dioramas depicting the former inhabitants' daily life and exhibits of tools, pottery and weapons.

Just outside Pike National Forest lies **Seven Falls.** Located in a natural box canyon and flanked by the towering **Pillars of Hercules** rock formations, these awesome falls gush in seven distinct cascades down the granite head of the canyon. There are two hiking trails at the top of the falls, which are best viewed from the **Eagle's Nest Observation platform.** Not far away, the **Cave of the Winds** at the foothills of Colorado's Rocky Mountains is, according to Apache lore, where the Great Spirit of the Wind resided. Exploring the caves by handheld lanterns, guests will see spiky stalactites and flowstone curtains that appear as waterfalls frozen in time.

In the town of Colorado Springs, Olympic hopefuls and future gold medalists in the family will enjoy the **U.S. Olympic Training Center Complex.** Take a free guided tour of the center, which includes the facility's 45,000-square-foot aquatic center, its even larger sports center, and the Olympic Shooting Center, the largest indoor shooting facility in the Western Hemisphere.

Colorado Springs Visitor Information Center
1-800-368-4748
www.visitcos.com, www.colorado.com

Dinosaur National Monument, Colorado and Utah

Dinosaur National Monument Park, a result of Earl Douglass' discovery of dinosaur fossils in 1913, will make your family's Jurassic dreams come true.

Before entering the park, which spans the Colorado-Utah border at an elevation ranging from 5,000 to 9,000 feet, pause at the **Utah Field House of Natural History State Park Museum** in **Vernal.** The museum's outdoor Dinosaur Garden has on display a prehistoric collection of full-size dinosaur replicas—including a menacing 20-foot Tyrannosaurus—from the Pennsylvanian through the Pleistocene ages. Inside, after being greeted by a 90-foot-long Diplodocus skeleton, visitors can view short films on fossil digs, chisel and prepare a dinosaur bone, and travel back in time to explore the Cenozoic, Mesozoic, Paleozoic, and Precambrian periods.

Just minutes away along Route 40 East lies the town of **Jensen,** where you can head north to enter Dinosaur National Monument Park. Although the Quarry Visitor Center is indefinitely closed due to structural damage, nearby is a **Temporary Visitor Center** where you can view real dinosaur fossils and other exhibits. There is even a **Fossil Discovery Hike** to see all types of bone fossils and fragments still embedded in the rock. It's well worthwhile for your little Indiana Jones.

There are plenty of other ways to discover the area, including the 11-mile scenic drive **Tour of the Tilted Rocks,** along which you can see many petroglyph and pictograph panels and impressive views of the area's geological formations. Keep a sharp eye for mule deer, prairie dogs, and birds unique to the area. **Harpers Corner Scenic**

Drive is a 31-mile autoroute beginning at the **Canyon Area Visitor Center.** Along with striking views from high-elevation roadside stops, you can get a good look at the Plug Hat Butte—and, toward the end of the route, a 300-degree vista with views into the beautiful Whirlpool, Lodore, and Yampa Canyons.

Within the park, whitewater rafting is a very popular way to explore the jagged canyons, folded geological features, and ancient rivers. Many of Dinosaur National Monument's rivers feature hazardous waters and are not for inexperienced paddlers. Rafters wanting a challenge can ride the Class III and Class IV rapids at sections of the **Green** and **Yampa Rivers.** Those with younger children can join tours on the gentler, family-friendly waters at **Split Mountain Gorge.**

VACATION PLANNING TIPS

A population of peregrine falcons has been established in the park's rugged canyons—an ideal habitat for the once-endangered raptor. To see them and some dinosaur fossils from the banks of the park's rivers, plan a family rafting trip. Fees and river permits are required for private boating trips within the park. For more information and a list of authorized tour companies that offer float trips, visit www.nps.gov/dino/planyourvisit/ riverrafting.htm or call the park's river office at 970-374-2468 (open 8 A.M.– noon weekdays only).

Dinosaur National Monument also provides great opportunities for school-age kids through the Junior Ranger and Junior Paleontology programs offered at the visitor center. Young explorers receive a booklet of fun activities to complete, upon which they receive a badge for their achievements. The park has a wealth of other recreational activities year-round, including horseback riding, bicycling, back-country camping, fishing, snowshoeing, cross-country skiing, and snowmobiling. In this semiarid climate, temperatures can range from 0 to 30°F in January and 50 to 100°F in July, so dress in layers and bring plenty of water.

Dinosaur National Monument Visitor Center
4545 E. Highway 40
Dinosaur, CO 81610-9724
435-781-7700
www.nps.gov/dino, www.utah.gov

Historic Steam Railways of the Rockies

A ride on a steam train is one of the most family-friendly adventures in the West and a tribute to the industry that transformed the region. While you'll read about many other tourist railroads and rail-related cultural sights, the most spectacular rides are on two remnants of the vast **Denver and Rio Grande Western Railroad** narrow-gauge empire. Narrow-gauge track, in this case 3-feet wide, is about 1¾ feet narrower than the track used elsewhere throughout the United States. Use of this gauge enabled the railroad to build quickly and cheaply and maneuver the tight curves of the mountainous terrain, although it limited the train's speed and length.

The Denver and Rio Grande began laying track in 1870 and by 1881 had completed a 3-foot-wide empire all over Southwest Colorado. Much of it disappeared after the introduction of paved highways in that part of the state, but the routes from **Durango** to **Silverton** and from **Chama** to **Antonito** were spared. Little has changed in 130 years for these southwestern Colorado lines; the trains that you ride today are almost exactly what you would have been riding more than 60 years ago and should thrill kids of any age.

The Durango and Silverton Narrow Gauge Railroad between the namesake cities is a 90-mile, full-day trip with a few hours' stop in Silverton for sightseeing and lunch. The train starts at 6,000 feet in altitude and climbs more than 3,000 feet to Silverton, crossing the Animas River five times. The route has been featured in almost 20 movies, adding a slice of Hollywood to this unique trip. The train averages 18 mph, and since the temperature may decrease by 10 degrees in just 45 miles, some families will prefer sitting in the enclosed parlor cars. If you think this sounds like too long a day for your little ones, choose the train going up to Silverton and bus returning, so you'll have time to explore the new **Durango Discovery Museum** in the former railroad powerhouse.

FELLOW TRAVELERS SAY ...

"Just like the early settlers, we headed westward, passing through old mining towns and across the Continental Divide. John Wayne filmed *The Searchers* and *True Grit* around here. Scary, precipitous mountain roads led to Silverton, the northern end of the steam-powered Durango & Silverton Railroad. We'd have loved the eight-hour trip in nineteenth-century parlor cars, but time wasn't on our side. *Ticket to Tomahawk* had been filmed here, and the railroad was used for the hilarious safe-dynamiting scene in *Butch Cassidy,* as well as in the movies *Viva Zapata!* and *Support Your Local Gunfighter.* Butch and Sundance did their jump into the raging river at Durango, where both *City Slickers* and *Around the World in 80 Days* were filmed."

—A. B., www.FamilyTravelForum.com

East of Durango, the **Cumbres & Toltec Scenic Railroad** travels over Cumbres Pass at more than 10,000 feet above sea level—the highest mountain pass reached by rail in the United States. With 431 turns along the 64 miles from Chama to Antonito, along with lots of animal life almost everywhere, this is no high-speed train trip. On this National Historic Landmark, history will ride along as you see northern New Mexico and southwestern Colorado as few can. There are two routes—either leaving from Chama, New Mexico, less than 10 miles from the border and heading to **Osier,** Colorado (52-miles round trip, 6 hours); or from Antonito, Colorado, to Osier and back (75 miles, 6 hours and 20 minutes); the difference being that the route from Chama is slower and steeper. At Osier, really more of a point on the railroad instead of a town, lunch is served in a large dining hall. What makes both of these lines unique is that the steam locomotives used are original to the D&RGW and date from the 1920s, along with most of the equipment. An extra bonus is the scenery—towering mountains and vast valleys with river beds far below your window.

The symphony of the sounds of the train struggling up and down the mountains, heightened by the sometimes staccato noise of the steam locomotive on its mountain assault, is unforgettable.

TRAVELERS BEWARE!

Keep in mind that on the trains of yesteryear, many modern-day conveniences do not exist. There are restrooms on the trains, but food opportunities are somewhat limited—and air conditioning is not part of the ride. These minor inconveniences should not dissuade you from this historical family getaway, however.

Durango and Silverton Narrow Gauge Railroad
1-877-872-4607
www.durangotrain.com

Cumbres & Toltec Scenic Railroad
Antonito, CO 81120 or Chama, NM 87520
1-888-CUMBRES
www.cumbrestoltec.com, www.colorado.com

Outdoor Adventures

In This Chapter

- Bryce and Zion's colorful canyons
- Glacier National Park's summertime snow-capped peaks
- Mesa Verde National Park's amazing cliff dwellings
- Rocky Mountain National Park's extensive trails
- Yellowstone's many natural wonders

Striking scenery and geological wonders draw many families to the American West. In the mountain region, the national parks that protect these wonders offer amazing sightseeing opportunities as well as numerous outdoor adventures for more active families. From the many parks located in these states, we chose those whose distinctive geological features can be appreciated by any age. Before you jump into the car to explore, here's a quick glossary to share with the folks in the backseat.

Geological features are created in stages; a *plateau* is a level expanse of elevated land; in other words, a flat-topped mountain that's easy to see. When a *canyon*, which is a narrow gorge with steep sides, is carved into a plateau by moving water, the softer rock underneath weathers until the canyon walls become *cliffs*, or vertical rock faces, and the remaining plateau stands above the surrounding land like a table, or *mesa*. Continuous uneven erosion creates *buttes*, or small hills. A *geyser* is a natural hot spring that ejects steam and water; they are so rare that after explorers named one in Iceland Geysir (after *geysa,* the Norse word for "rush"), geologists adopted the name for every one.

Bryce and Zion Canyons, Utah

Along the far western edge of the Colorado Plateau are a series of colorful cliffs with two distinctive canyons known as the **Grand Staircase,** so called because the bottom layer of rock at Bryce Canyon is actually the top layer at Zion Canyon, and the bottom step at Zion is the top step down into the Grand Canyon.

For families, the first canyon to visit is the one named after Mormon pioneer Ebenezer Bryce. Bryce Canyon is famous for the many oddly shaped rock formations, such as spires that resemble stalagmites or people, and natural stone amphitheatres in a myriad of hues. The multicolored stone shapes, formed by ice and rainwater erosion, are studied by geologists for their ties to the Grand Staircase and volcanic Cedar and Black Mountains nearby.

FUN FACTS

The unique limestone formations called "hoodoos" are what earned Bryce Canyon its national park designation. Canadian linguist Bill Casselman cites the word's origin in the Hausa language is the term *hu'du'ba,* which means to "produce retribution" or spook someone.

Begin touring at the **Bryce Canyon Visitor Center** to watch the short educational film and find out about scheduled events in this small but unique park. During the summer there are frequent family programs, wrangler-guided horseback tours, or muleback rides. Winter brings snowshoeing and cross-country skiing. Have the kids look out for the threatened Utah prairie dog, whose white tail and black eyebrows are unique to the region.

Geologically related but nearly a hundred miles away, the 10,000-foot canyon walls within the much larger **Zion National Park** were built by a process of sedimentation on a relatively flat basin more than 240 million years old. Families based in the outdoors retreat of **St. George, Utah,** can hitch a ride on the free **Springdale shuttle bus** heading to the south entrance of the canyon. Make a quick stop at the Visitor Center and the **Zion Human History Museum** to get better acquainted with the area's rich history and environment.

Along the Zion Canyon Scenic Drive, visitors can choose to bicycle (or hike) their way down the paved Pa'rus Trail. From late May to early September, parents can even drop off their kids at the **Zion Nature Center's Junior Ranger Program** and enjoy the trails on their own for a few hours. Pa'rus Trail is easy; Riverside Walk to the Temple of Sinawava, Lower Emerald Pools, and Weeping Rock are also relatively easy trails that offer brilliant views of waterfalls and the surrounding sandstone features of buttes, mesas, and arches. The aptly named Angel's Landing, at an elevation of 1,488 feet, may be too strenuous for inexperienced hikers—but the two-mile paved trail leading to it can be reached by taking the **Grotto shuttle bus.**

Walter's Wiggles is also a fun sight to see, although it requires considerable effort to reach. The workers who slaved to build this winding vertical trail were paid a meager $3.50 per day. During construction, the pioneer of this project, Walter Ruesch, purportedly was quoted as saying, "Zion is God's country; don't make it look like hell." Look out for a white-throated swift or a California condor—just 2 of the 207 species of birds in the canyon—as well as the Great Basin rattler and the common California fence lizard.

St. George, Utah, is a good place to base the family. The town is home to lots of good restaurants, day spas, outdoor outfitters, and surprisingly interesting shops as well as hotels and motels from all the major U.S. chains. Kids will especially enjoy the downtown Historic District.

Bryce Canyon National Park
Bryce, UT 84764
435-834-5322
www.nps.gov/brca

Zion National Park
Springdale, UT 84767
435-772-3256
www.nps.gov/zion, www.utah.com

Glacier National Park, Montana

Before the influx of French, British, and Spanish expeditions to Montana (which is the Spanish word for *mountain*), and long before the mining craze of the late seventeenth century, the lands of Glacier National Park belonged to the Blackfeet, Salish, and Kootenai tribes, who called the region "Shining Mountains."

Begin your visit outside the park's boundary on the 50-mile-long **Going-to-the-Sun Road.** An impressive undertaking that took a little more than a decade to complete, the winding road introduces the region's majestic mountains, valleys, prairies, and incredible wilderness. For those who are wary of driving it, the park's shuttle provides two-way service between the **Apgar Transit Center** and **St. Mary Visitor Center.** Adrenaline junkies have the option of bicycling the road in the summer but should inquire about possible road closures ahead of time.

FUN FACTS

A 1933 press release issued by the Department of the Interior stated that Going-to-the-Sun Road received its name from the Blackfeet deity, Sour Spirit, who journeyed down from his place in the sun to teach the tribes the art of hunting. On his return, Sour Spirit had his image reproduced on Shining Mountain for all to see. Alternate histories hold that a white explorer in the 1880s entirely made up this legend and name.

In the park, join a guided hike or go it on your own to explore the diverse landscape filled with junipers, Ponderosas, Douglas firs, and indigenous scrub being chewed on by white bighorn sheep. Among the most prominent geological features resulting from the shifting of the Earth's crust is **Mt. Cleveland,** the park's tallest peak at 10,466 feet.

Set yourself a goal to reach the **Granite Park Chalet** or the **Sperry Chalet,** stone lodges built around World War I by the Great Northern Railway. They still offer lodging, although Granite Park is a self-service place where you will have to bring in your own food and water. It overlooks spectacular **Bear Valley** and is a good location to spot wildlife, including grizzly bears. At **Haystack Bend,** just above the **Weeping Wall** and on **Haystack Butte,** you may see mountain goats and bighorn sheep.

> **FUN FACTS**
>
> How high are you climbing? Gnarled, bent trees known as krummholz (German for "twisted wood") appear in a line around the park's peaks. When you see them at Glacier, you can tell everyone you've reached 6,000 feet!

The real stars of the park are the glaciers—including the notably receding **Sperry Glacier**—which have contributed to the scoured look of the landscape. Today, 26 of the 150 glaciers noted in 1850 remain. The park's lakes—131 of which are named—are remnants of long glacial valleys dammed at their outlets by *moraines*, or deposits of rock and debris left by moving glaciers. The water left from glaciers is surprisingly clear, and you can often easily see detail of the bottom of lakes 30 feet below.

To really get the lowdown on Glacier's ever-changing environment and have fun while doing so, take the kids to the **Discovery Cabin** in Apgar. Open from the third week in June through Labor Day, the cabin offers kid-friendly activities such as puppet shows, a mystery touch box, rock sorting, and animal habitat identification games. Those unafraid of heights should test their courage at the bridge over **Avalanche Gorge,** a real kid pleaser located on the **Trails of the Cedars Nature Trail.** Park visitor centers located in Apgar, **Logan Pass,** and St. Mary's also offer the Glacier Junior Ranger program in which kids can receive a special badge after completing a list of fun and educational activities.

Boating is another popular way of seeing the park, particularly on **Bowman** and **McDonald** Lakes on the west side or **St. Mary** and **Two Medicine** Lakes on the east side. Rentals are available at several locations, including **Agpar, Rising Sun,** and **Many Glacier.** For more adventure, try canoeing, kayaking, or rafting on the **Flathead River** with tours based in **West Glacier.** You can enjoy fishing without a permit at Lake McDonald, where families can also clip-clop their way around on horseback. Winter visitors will find great skiing or snowshoeing on trails around areas such as **Marias Pass, North Fork,** and **Two Medicine.**

Outside the park in the town of Browning, the **Blackfoot Nation Reservation** welcomes visitors to learn about the tribe's history and cultural practices; the Blackfeet are one of the 6 tribes out of 564 in the United States who still live on their ancestral lands.

Glacier National Park
West Glacier, Montana 59936
406-888-7800
www.nps.gov/glac, www.visitmt.com

Mesa Verde National Park, Colorado

There should be no whats, ifs, or buttes when deciding whether to visit this southwestern destination with its geological splendors. Mesa Verde stands out among the many national parks in the region because, in addition to its beautiful geological features, it was inhabited for centuries by Native Americans who carved homes out of the fascinating terrain.

FUN FACTS

Mesa Verde means "green table" in Spanish. The region was given this name by early explorers because erosion of the earth's top surface left only small plateaus of rock standing—like tables—above everything around them. During the Spanish era, the mesas were covered with loess, a rich, claylike soil that enabled the Pueblo Indians to farm corn and beans, giving the land its rich green color.

Scientists say Mesa Verde should technically be called *Cuesta Verde*. Mesas and cuestas are similar except that the cuestas gently dip in one direction, just as Mesa Verde does—a 7° incline to the south. Mesa Verde National Park is actually made up of smaller, separate mesas between canyons eroded by wind and water.

Nearly a millennium and a half has passed since the first people appeared in the region, settling there for more than 700 years until abandoning their cliff dwellings in the late 1200s C.E. Today, the region of more than 52,000 acres atop the northeast section of the Colorado Plateau offers more than 4,000 archeological sites showcasing the homes and artifacts left behind by the Mesa Verde ancestral Pueblo Indians.

Inhabited in the thirteenth century by ancestors of Arizona and New Mexico Pueblo Indians, the medium-size cliff dwelling, **Balcony House,** depicts an elaborate adobe maze of passageways and tunnels. Here, kids will enjoy climbing the 32-foot ladder at the entrance of the dwelling. The **Cliff Palace** is exceptional for its 150 rooms and 23 kivas (rooms often used for ceremonies) constructed with sandstone, mortar, and wooden beams. Excavated between 1959 and 1961, the **Long House** is considered the second largest cliff dwelling in the park, while **Spruce Tree House** is slightly smaller. These sites, along with the **Step House,** are worth the trip on the winding and scenic road that leads to them. The majority of Mesa Verde's other cliff dwellings contain very few rooms.

Tours for each dwelling can be arranged at the **Far View Visitor Center,** which also has exhibits on historic Native American jewelry, pottery, and baskets. Located 15 miles from the park entrance, it's a good place to begin your historic trip through the area. Open year-round and offering guided tours of the Spruce Tree House, the **Chapin Mesa Archeological Museum's** dioramas illustrate Pueblo Indian life; prehistoric artifacts are also on display.

The park has a number of trails begging to be explored—each giving hikers the chance to spot indigenous yucca plants and plateau lizards, feel the formations of sandstone and shale dating back 90 million to 78 million years, and take in far-as-the-eye-can-see views. One must-see vista is **Park Point,** on the **Point Lookout Trail.** Here, at the highest elevation in the park at 8,427 feet, you can gaze out over the Montezuma and Mancos Valleys and the surrounding countryside. Be sure your kids join the Junior Ranger program so they can get a little more out of each dwelling tour and trail hike.

On the final leg of your trip, head an hour east along Route 160 to the town of **Durango,** where you can experience the cowboy culture set in the early days of Western settlement. To explore the area and the nearby **San Juan National Forest,** catch a scenic ride on the Durango and Silverton Narrow Gauge Railroad, which has transported passengers and precious metals through the canyons for more than a century (see Chapter 19 for details). In addition to a number of outdoor activities, the humble town of Durango plays host to many annual festivals, from bluegrass shows to local food tastings.

Mesa Verde National Park
Mesa Verde, Colorado 81330
970-529-4465
www.nps.gov/meve, www.durangogov.org

Rocky Mountain National Park, Colorado

Visited by more than 3 million people each year, **Rocky Mountain National Park** is 415 square miles of rock-ribbed wilderness. At least 60 mountains rising more than 12,000 feet shape its boundaries, and the landscape inspires visitors with snow-clad peaks, verdant meadows, alpine flowers, and pristine lakes. Although the scenery should be enough to hold any child's attention, if the striking vista fails, the names of the peaks will certainly entertain: Chief's Head, Isolation, Mummy, and Storm, to name a few.

The park is also home to an array of wildlife, most of which are big and furry. There are more than 3,000 elk in the meadows, and bighorn sheep are commonly spotted by **Sheep Lakes** in the summer months. Mule deer are mostly found at lower elevations of around 7,000 feet; moose frequent the western edge of the park's boundaries where there are plenty of willow thickets along the **Colorado River.** In total, within the park there are more than 60 species of mammals, 280 bird species, and 6 types of amphibians (including the endangered boreal toad), as well as countless insects, fish, and beautiful wildflowers.

Designated the tenth U.S. National Park in 1915, the park has 355 miles of hiking trails that range from flat lakeside paths easy for all ages to more intense and steep mountainous climbs. Biking, scenic drives, and horseback riding are other ways for a family to explore the varied terrain. There are also opportunities to fish and camp within the park. The myriad of ranger-led programs offered by the park year-round are fun for kids. To acclimate your children and prepare them for the majestic beauty they are about to experience, stop by the **Beaver Meadows Visitor Center** to watch the 23-minute movie *Spirit of the Mountains.*

FELLOW TRAVELERS SAY ...

"The mountains ... were indescribably enchanting. As I climbed up into Pikes Peak, I felt like I was on top of the world, which was actually partly true. The scenery of snow-capped mountains and quaint cabins exhilarated and thrilled me. My senses were overflowing with the sights, smells, sounds, tastes, and feelings of ... [the] park."

—D. X. www.travelBIGO.com

The eastern gateway to the park is **Estes Park,** a small mountain village and resort community that archeologists say drew Ute, Shoshone, and Comanche Indian families for summer vacations more than 10,000 years ago. Now, modern families enjoy the town's dry and mild climate throughout the year. In addition to many seasonal outdoor and recreational activities, there are plenty of other attractions. Visit the **Estes Park Museum,** which includes hands-on areas for children and displays of local memorabilia, including the car made by local entrepreneur F.O. Stanley.

Families can also take in the many horse shows all summer long at **Stanley Park Fairgrounds.** A wide variety of breeds are represented, and most shows have no admission charge. Another popular activity is nightly cowboy sing-alongs around a campfire in downtown Bond Park. Or check out the **Enos Mills Cabin,** an 1885 museum with memorabilia of the famous naturalist. The **MacGregor Ranch Museum,** a working ranch, is one of the area's earliest homesteads with equipment, household belongings, and clothing dating back to 1860.

Rocky Mountain National Park
Estes Park, CO 80517
970-586-1206
www.nps.gov/romo, www.estesparkcvb.com

Yellowstone National Park

Theodore Roosevelt saw it as a gift for all humans to enjoy. Nearly three decades later, his fifth cousin and 32nd President of the United States, Franklin D. Roosevelt, described it as the ultimate icon of America. Today, more than two million acres of undisturbed nature at **Yellowstone National Park** provide an invaluable family experience at little to no cost. The catch? If you're lucky, maybe a giant rainbow trout from the Big Horn River.

VACATION PLANNING TIPS

From Montana's Little Big Horn, it is approximately 130 miles (2½ hours) to the park, which you could enter from its north, northeast, or east entrances. Note that the north entrance at **Gardiner, Montana,** a fun mountain town with lots of family attractions, is the only one open to cars year-round. During the winter months, the west, south, and east entrances are open only to officially permitted, tracked-over-snow vehicles such as snowcoaches and snowmobiles. Tours to visit the park in these vehicles can be arranged in nearby tourist towns in Idaho and Wyoming. If your family would benefit from the expert guidance of park naturalists, go straight to the **Yellowstone Institute,** the park's educational arm that provides family programs year-round including meals, guides, activities, and lodging at modest prices.

In their native tongue, the Blackfoot Indian tribes knew this territory in Montana as the "big sky." True to their name, Yellowstone's vast fields, forests, and lakes stretch farther than the eye can see, reaching from Montana in the north deep into Wyoming to the south. To best navigate the park, we suggest starting out at **Yellowstone Lake,** easily reached from the park's east or south entrances. Known to be the continent's largest mountain lake and covering more than 80,000 acres, Yellowstone Lake is ideal for fishing. Thousands of trout populate these waters, and impressively, all the fish are wild. For the more thrill-seeking types, canoeing and kayaking give the family a close-up view of nearby geysers, hot springs, and mud pots.

Trekking westward from the lake, the west side of the park is overflowing with activities for kids during the summer and early fall seasons. Before visiting the most famous attractions—the **Old Faithful** geyser and **Grand Canyon** area—take a self-guided tour of the other kinds of thermal features the park offers so you can build up the excitement. The **Biscuit, Midway,** and **Black Sand Basin tours** will awe and amaze the entire family with fascinating geysers, smelly bubbling pools, and *fumaroles* (an opening in the Earth's surface that emits steam and gases released from boiling groundwater).

At the nearby **Canyon Visitor Education Center,** you can learn more about these geological features, enjoy interactive exhibits and fun educational films, and find out what the center's 9,000-pound rotating kugel ball is all about. After completing a list of fun and easy requirements within the park, kids will receive an official Yellowstone Junior Ranger patch.

Most of the visitor centers are open from late spring to early fall. During the later fall months, camping and lodging within the park become scarce and the crowds depart. In winter (our family's very favorite season), only the north entrance remains open to private vehicles, and the Albright Visitors Center there is the only one that is open year-round. For winter lodging and park excursions, **Flagg Ranch Resort** is a good bet for icy expeditions, offering multiple-itinerary snowmobile tours stopping at popular park attractions.

On the north side, the **Roosevelt Arch** looms impressively over the park entrance, which was once meant for coach trains to pass through. Beyond the northern park portal, the entire family can spend the day trotting along the rim of the Cascade Canyon at **Mammoth Hot Springs.** If you haven't had your fill of geological features, **Wraith Falls** are worth a small trek up the hillside. Named by a team of geological surveyors for its eerie specter-like shape, the falls offer more than just scenery; there's diverse wildlife in the area. During winter visits, travelers can spend their time on the slopes at any of the area's popular skiing trails. **The Indian Creek Loop Trail** in particular is perfect for beginners and families with small children.

FELLOW TRAVELERS SAY ...

"When we decided to leave the park, it was dark already, and we had passed by an elk and a brown bear, both alone and eating in the brush. Not long afterward, we had to stop for a couple of bison on the road, one larger and more defined than the other. Dad had stopped the car and was slowly inching forward, flickering the bright lights on and off in efforts to make them move. My mother and sister both gave exclamations of "Ooh!" and "Wow!" For there were not just two bison but also a whole herd, settled on both sides of the road. To our left, there were about 30 bison, all lounging on the slope of the hill. To our right, there were about 20 of them—some of them babies—unaware of the purple Mazda and the traffic behind it."

—Z., www.travelBIGO.com

While the trip certainly doesn't have to end here, the **Canyon Village** area is an ideal location to settle down and rest from a long and exhausting journey. Entering the park through the Northeast entrance, travelers will pass by the **Slough Creek Campground,** a good place to hunker down for a few nights and enjoy some fly-fishing on the side—although the campground has limited amenities.

Before leaving the wild paradise of Yellowstone National Park, one last look is in order. You won't regret one last, short hike from the Canyon Visitor Center to take in the 308-foot drop of the **Lower Falls** of the Yellowstone. The brilliant view may inspire a few words worthy of Roosevelt or may just leave everyone in your family speechless.

Yellowstone National Park
Yellowstone National Park, WY 82190
307-344-7381
www.nps.gov/yell, www.wyomingtourism.org

The West

So how did we group California, Nevada, and Hawaii into the American West? As you can see from the previous parts of this guide, we clustered a number of states into broad geographic regions that fortunately often had a historical kinship. Not so here.

Alta California, steeped in the language and culture of Mexico, was the 30th U.S. state and became part of the union after the land was seized during the Mexican-American War in 1850. Nevada, tied to Arizona and other desert states by the coming railroad, was in 1864 the 36th state to join. And Hawaii was the last of the 50 states, joining in 1959.

What these states do have in common is a very vibrant tourism industry. From the golden shores of San Diego to the stars of Hollywood and the bridges of San Francisco, California dreamin' is a common pastime among family vacation planners. Nevada is known for the gambling mecca of Las Vegas, a surprisingly family-friendly city. Hawaii is, simply, a paradise. Whether you picture your teens sunbathing on Maui, yearn to hike the volcanoes of the Big Island, or long to chase wildlife in the jungles of Kauai, you and your family can do it in this state.

Best Family Destinations Key:

🏔 Amusement Parks   ☆ Cultural Appeal/Living History

🏖 At the Beach   🔺 Mountain Towns

🏙 City Style   🍁 Outdoor Adventures

Lake Tahoe

Virginia City

NV

Napa Valley

San Franscisco

Yosemite N. P.

CA

Hollywood

Universal Studios

California Beaches

Disneyland

Los Angeles

Las Vegas

Lake Mead

Hoover Dam

Kauai

North Shore

Oahu

Maui

HI

Legoland

San Diego

Hawaii Big Island

City Style

In This Chapter

- The family-friendly side of Vegas
- Los Angeles' movie stars and sunny beaches
- A spectacular zoo and Mexican flair distinguish San Diego
- San Francisco: for the young and young at heart

Selecting our favorite-for-families cities in the big tourism states of California, Nevada, and Hawaii wasn't easy because there are so many great destinations to consider.

However, Family Travel Forum's motto, "Have Kids, Still Travel!", inspired us to show parents and grandparents what we love about these famous cities, then offer you ideas on how to make your visit there rewarding, engaging, and most of all fun for young family members.

In a chapter that outlines the pleasures of Las Vegas, Los Angeles, San Diego, and San Francisco, we know you'll find enough to see and do to fill a lifetime of school holidays—no matter how many kids you have, their interests, or their ages.

Las Vegas, Nevada

Many families don't associate any activity that "stays in Vegas" with kid-pleasing fun, and the city's tourist office doesn't promote the destination to guests younger than 21 (who can't gamble). But that doesn't mean that there aren't a lot of surprisingly fun and unusual attractions—many of them free—to entertain families interested in an urban adventure. Las Vegas has it all: style, culture, history (if you count the **Liberace Museum**), beaches (at the Cancun Resort & Casino), and outdoor adventures in the Nevada desert. If you keep your eyes open, stay prepared to shield your tot's eyes, and keep your wallet shut, you'll be surprised at what this legendary city founded by mobsters, for mobsters, has to offer families.

FELLOW TRAVELERS SAY ...

"I still get goose bumps when I think of my first sight of Sin City all lit up from the airplane."

—C. S., travelBIGO.com

Nothing compares to Las Vegas in terms of pop culture appeal. Even from a distance, there's no ignoring the giant pyramid, outdoor roller coaster, illuminated fountains, the "Eiffel Tower," and other iconic designs that mark the city's eclectic hotel architecture. Vegas would not be Vegas without the stunning array of marquee lights, digital billboards, and after-hours culture along the central casino hotel zone known as The Strip.

VACATION PLANNING TIPS

Learn how to plan the Vegas vacation that suits your family and style. Check out *The Complete Idiot's Guide to Las Vegas* (Alpha, 2009) for insider tips on where to stay, where to play, and what shows are a must see!

A good place to start your family tour is the **Stratosphere Tower,** where you can get a good view of the city. Like many attractions, an admission ticket can be packaged with a meal and a show—often a good value for an evening out.

Free attractions abound in Vegas. Make **M&M World,** where the candy is celebrated in film and museum, one of the first free stops. The **Fremont Street Experience** is a five-block-long pedestrian mall in Vegas' nostalgic downtown where, in addition to old-fashioned casinos, shops, and restaurants, there are free nightly concerts and

"Sky Parades," a popular light and sound show. It's not the best neighborhood, so plan to take a taxi. Many of our favorite free attractions are inside the themed casino hotels.

At the Italian-styled **Venetian casino,** you can roam the cobblestone lanes of the shopping arcade and listen as gondoliers serenade honeymooners who drift by along indoor canals. **Caesar's Palace** shopping arcade has an hourly Talking Statues show in which the Roman gods Bacchus, Venus, and Apollo come to life. Kids will love the **Lion Habitat at the MGM Grand Hotel,** where they can watch the majestic cats through protective glass.

The new **CityCenter** complex has an ice-based Glacia fountain and glass tubes of water sculpture throughout its shopping arcade. At **New York, New York,** families who have never been to the Big Apple can enjoy the sidewalk cafés and fire escapes that give the food court a real city feel. The **Circus Circus** hotel calls itself the World's Largest Permanent Circus and has live shows every half hour. You might catch trapeze artists, tightrope walkers, or jugglers in one show, then clowns and animal acts in the next show. While you hang around waiting for the shows, let the kids explore the very fun (albeit *not* free) **Circus Circus Adventuredome,** an indoor amusement park with rides designed for all ages and all thrill levels.

Fronting the casino hotels is another slew of free attractions. The notorious "The Sirens of TI" has evolved from a popular, swashbuckling pirate battle held in the **Treasure Island Casino** fountain into a show of bikini-clad vixens wrapped in pyrotechnics, music, acrobatics, and dance. Five 20-minute shows take place nightly, and if the kids are too young to ask questions or old enough to be amused, this may become your favorite. Las Vegas' volcano erupts hourly in a peaceful lagoon outside the **Mirage Hotel.** Expect the earth to shake as flames shoot into the sky 60 feet above the water, accompanied by the music of Grateful Dead drummer Mickey Hart and tabla player Zakir Hussain. The **Bellagio Fountains,** another fantastic water show set to music, takes place outside the Bellagio, one of the city's most upscale casino hotels.

To get away from casinos altogether, visit **Mystic Park Falls,** where "Sunset Stampede"—a free 10-minute show including detailed audio effects, geysers, and laser-light animals that stampede across the prairie—is a big hit with younger kids; it shows four times daily.

For outdoor recreation, escape to **Red Rock Canyon** off scenic Highway 159 in the heart of the Spring Mountains. It's popular with hikers and mountain climbers; ask for trail advice at the **Bureau of Land Management Visitor Center.** At the **Ethel M. Chocolate Factory & Botanical Cactus Garden** in Henderson, you can learn something about the 300 cactus plants outside, enjoy a video tour of the candy-making process, and pause for free samples.

 FELLOW TRAVELERS SAY ...

"Read up on the different buffets and their specialties and hit a couple while you're there. Save money and your waistline by eating smaller meals at either lunch or dinner and have one big buffet a day. Ask about coupons at your hotel or the casinos, or check out all the free magazines you'll find around town; there are savings on dozens of shows, buffets, and attractions."

—B. K., FamilyTravelForum.com

Las Vegas is also the testing ground for many new entertainment creations, providing an ever-changing variety of paid attractions that will dazzle your family. They range from the staid **Imperial Palace Auto Showcase,** a must-see for anyone who loves celebrity cars, to **CSI: The Experience,** an interactive game and performance for young forensic investigators that takes place at the MGM Grand. A few theaters present live performances by the famous **Cirque du Soleil,** an acclaimed circus troupe whose acrobatics, dance, music, and visual effects are mind-boggling. The **Las Vegas Cyber Speedway** at the Sahara Hotel has a 3-D motion theater where kids 48 inches and taller can choose to be a passenger in an out-of-control Indy 500, NASCAR, or off-road race or drive their own

Grand Prix race car. More than 20 years ago, the noted magicians Siegfried and Roy established a conservation and educational foundation at the MGM Mirage Hotel called **Secret Garden and Dolphin Habitat.** There are daily guided tours of this small zoo garden, the tropical home of royal white tigers, white lions, golden tigers, black panthers, and white leopards. Adjacent is a dolphin habitat where you can book educational and trainer-for-the-day programs in advance.

To escape Nevada's heat, you'll want to turn your schedule around and plan naps and/or pool time during the day and sightseeing at night. You'll need comfortable shoes, although walking isn't always practical in this sprawling city; traffic backs up and taxis are expensive. Good news—an elevated monorail runs back and forth along The Strip, and many hotels offer free shuttles to partner casinos.

Las Vegas Convention & Visitors Authority
1-877-VISIT-LV
www.visitlasvegas.com, www.travelnevada.com

Los Angeles, California

From *Baywatch* beaches to movie star footprints, there's a lot for families to enjoy in the vast Greater Los Angeles region. We cover **Hollywood** in Chapter 22, review the beaches in more depth in Chapter 23, and make suggestions for touring the famous theme parks in Chapter 24.

Through fossils embedded in the **La Brea Tar Pits,** the city of Los Angeles can trace its history back to 38,000 B.C.E., when dinosaurs (*not* the stars of *Jurassic Park*) called the region home. More contemporary history dates to 1769, when Spanish explorers discovered the area and decided to found a settlement next to the river, which they named Rio de Nuestra Señora la Reina de los Angeles de Porciuncula (River Porciuncula of our Lady the Queen of Angels). Within 20 years, the first of millions of Mexican immigrants arrived and shortened the town's name to "Los Angeles" (or, as we like to call it, the City of Angels). Within a generation, the Gold Rush had begun and Los Angeles' population of American fortune seekers and European immigrants swelled enormously.

FUN FACTS

Hancock Park, location of more than 100 black and oozing, smelly "pits" known as the La Brea Tar Pits, was donated to the city by G. Allan Hancock, who inherited Rancho La Brea and its asphalt mine from his father in the nineteenth century. Asphalt is the lowest grade of crude oil (*la brea*, or "tar" in Spanish, is a byproduct) and its stickiness when warm made it useful in building. The Page Museum has some very neat prehistoric skeletons and fossils of saber-toothed cats and mammoths that were trapped in the warm goo since the last great Ice Age. The Tar Pits still ooze between 8 and 12 gallons of asphalt per day and continue to trap insects, worms, lizards, birds, small rodents, and the occasional curious dog. The bubbles on the surface are caused by escaping methane gas.

Just as in any big city, L.A. has many cultural venues catering to a wide variety of interests. You can't go wrong with the **L.A. County Museum of Art** for visual arts and **MOCA** for modern art, but our favorite is the **Getty Museum.** It's up on a hill, and after leaving your car in its pre-reserved lot, your family will ride in a silver tram three quarters of a mile up Getty Center Drive to the arrival plaza, catching glimpses of Century City, downtown Los Angeles, Westwood, and UCLA en route. The galleries are filled with an enormous variety of European fine arts, illuminated manuscripts, decorative arts, and European and American photographs. The museum's entertaining audio guides and family-oriented lectures and events makes the Getty our one must-see museum in L.A. for families.

If your kids are young, steer them to the **Children's Museum of Los Angeles,** which is well regarded for its hands-on learning areas. The **California Science Center** is another good choice for young children because of its hands-on presentations and IMAX theater.

The **Petersen Automotive Museum** is in the **Miracle Mile** area of Wilshire Boulevard, right in the middle of town. If you have a mini motor head in your family, this collection of rare, antique, flashy, and otherwise famous cars—we mean *The Beverly Hillbillies'* old jalopy and the flying DeLorean from *Back to the Future*—is for them. Note that from here, it can be an hour drive in traffic to either the beach or downtown, so you'll want to plan your visit around different neighborhoods. You might combine Petersen's with a visit to the classic **Farmer's Market** for an outdoor lunch, followed by shopping among the market's classic stalls or **The Grove,** a leading-edge life-style mall.

Downtown Los Angeles, the old and funky eastern side of the city where post-Apocalyptic films such as *Bladerunner* were filmed, has become a fashionable place to live, and you can make a no-cost day out of touring its architectural sights. **El Pueblo de Los Angeles Historic Park** is the site of some restored historic buildings including Avila Adobe; the Old Plaza Church; the Old Plaza Firehouse; and **Olvera Street,** a colorful tourist market with little Mexican restaurants, shops, and bodegas decked out in Old World Spanish architecture. **City Hall,** built in 1926 and a favorite of TV and movie directors, once starred as police headquarters in the *Dragnet* series.

Also downtown are several theaters for Broadway-style shows; the stunning **Walt Disney Concert Hall** designed by noted architect Frank Gehry; and the **Biltmore Hotel,** a restored Spanish Renaissance gem whose ornately gilded and coffered lobby was the setting for *Ghostbusters* and *The Nutty Professor,* among other films. If you stop by the Biltmore for tea in winter, lace up some free loaner ice skates and dance across the ice under the palms on a public rink across the street from the hotel. Not every city has a destination library, so kids are sure to be inspired by the **Los Angeles Central Library,** with its awesome reading rooms. The restored 1925 landmark has a multicolored tile pyramid on its roof and some good restaurants nearby. Another nearby landmark is **Union Station,** built in 1939 and a treat for train and architecture buffs. Also downtown, the **Staples Center** is a state-of-the-art sports and entertainment complex for the Los Angeles Clippers, Lakers, Kings, Sparks, and Avengers sports teams—but tickets are expensive and hard to come by.

There's lots of space for outdoor fun, from large parks within each neighborhood to the glorious beaches along the Pacific Coast. Dating from 1896, when Colonel J. Griffith donated land to the city, **Griffith Park** comprises more than 4,000 acres of varied terrain between Hollywood and the San Fernando Valley. Facilities include 28 tennis courts, hiking trails, the Los Angeles Equestrian Center, Fern Dell Park, a merry-go-round, pony rides, and train rides. The **Griffith Observatory,** on the southern slope of Mount Hollywood, holds the largest astronomical image ever created: a 3,040-square-foot porcelain enamel wall that captures 1.7 million galaxies, stars, and asteroids—all compiled from actual observation.

Within the park and dating from 1913—the same year that Cecil B. DeMille shot the first Hollywood movie, *Squaw Man*—is the West's largest collection of natural history artifacts in the **Natural History Museum of L.A. County.** A good place to start with little kids is the Parsons Discovery Center, where children can investigate giant stuffed polar bear teeth and snake X-rays, among other natural curiosities.

On your Griffith Park day, or if your teens are touring **U.S.C.,** make it a point to see the whimsical **Watts Towers,** a collection of 17 tile- and glitter-covered wire sculptures that rise 100 feet above the neighborhood. Revealed by Simon Rodia in 1955 after more than 30 years of labor, they are one of L.A.'s few National Historic Landmarks and have spawned a neighboring arts center, with tours, lectures, changing exhibits, and an annual September Jazz Festival.

The **Los Angeles Zoo**—home to more than 1,500 exotic animals and the city's botanical gardens—is always fun. Kids will especially like the Campo Gorilla Reserve, a West African–style habitat for six African lowland gorillas. At any time of year, Los Angeles offers amazing outdoor adventures close by, from offshore beaches such as pretty **Catalina Island** to snow sports havens such as **Big Bear** or **Mt. Baldy.**

"Catalina was no far-flung destination, but as our ship drifted toward the fog-bathed island, I felt just like the Spaniards of old approaching the dreamlike New World. Here, I had expected surfboards and sandcastles. Imagine my shock when I stood before a frontier of mountains and sweeping brush valleys; meditative Descanso Beach, Two Harbors campground, Lover's Cove, and immense orange schools of garibaldi fish."

—I. D., www.travelBIGO.com

Books could be written (and updated weekly) about the restaurant and shopping scene in high-style Los Angeles. It seems that just as the locals proclaim the latest in food or fashion, the SoCal (or "Surfer Dude," "Valley Girl," "O.C.," or "PacRim") style spreads throughout the country then loses its trendiness. The great neighborhoods for eating include **Little Tokyo** for sushi, **Koreatown** for noodle restaurants and bubble tea, and **Fairfax** for Middle Eastern fare. Low-budget and high-end Mexican cuisine is available everywhere; the outdoor cafés of the Westside—**Beverly Hills, Westwood, Brentwood,** and **Santa Monica**—are hot spots for celebrity chef cuisine and celebrity sightings.

Shoppers can find everything from the hippest fashions to hand-crafted, one-of-a-kind pieces to used costumes once sported by the cast of your favorite films. The three-block area in Beverly Hills known by its main street, **Rodeo Drive** (pronounced ro-DAY-oh), is packed with high-end gilded shops; and the Hollywood section of **Melrose Avenue** has ever-changing boutiques, funky collectible stores, galleries, and furniture showrooms.

Los Angeles Convention and Visitors Bureau
1-800-228-2452
www.discoverlosangeles.com, www.visitcalifornia.com

San Diego, California

Year-round, people return from San Diego exclaiming, "The weather was perfect!" Located 120 miles south of Los Angeles, between grand mountains and a sparkling 70-mile stretch of Pacific beach,

San Diego has all the ingredients for an unforgettable urban family vacation with a beach twist: watch dolphins at **SeaWorld,** surf with them in **Mission Bay,** or learn more about them at the world-famous zoo. In between all the activities, you'll be able to wiggle your toes in the pristine white sand and bask beneath the warm sun.

Your first stop should be the incomparable **Balboa Park.** It's home to the **San Diego Zoo,** which houses more than 4,000 animals. In the "Elephant Odyssey" exhibit, visitors have a chance to mingle with replicas of prehistoric elephants and meet their living relatives. Kids will love the hands-on fossil digs that reveal life-size ancient elephant remains.

Spend at least one day at the Smithsonian of the West, Balboa Park's 1,400-acre wonder world. You can take a half-mile miniature train ride, climb onto the hand-carved carousel dating from 1910, or attend the puppet theater. On day two, come back to the park to visit the kid-friendly **Natural History Museum, Aerospace Museum,** or **Fleet Science Center.** Picnic and playground areas with special sections for tiny tots are also on site. Families with Lego maniacs in tow can drive a half hour north to the **Legoland California** theme park (read more about Legoland in Chapter 24).

For fun in the sun, head to **Mission Bay Park** for swimming, sailing, and kayaking, plus lots of play areas and space for picnicking. Allow a day for nearby **SeaWorld San Diego,** the home of Shamu. Kids can pet dolphins, feed bat rays, and meet penguins and marine life from around the world in an entertaining and educational setting. The shimmering coastline between **Mission Beach** and **Pacific Beach** is connected by a popular paved boardwalk that's perfect for biking and blading. The Pacific beaches offer more water play, such as surfing, boogie boarding, snorkeling, and sand castle building. For the older kids, **Belmont Amusement Park** on Mission Beach is great fun, featuring one of only two remaining oceanfront roller coasters still operating on the West Coast.

Sir, yes Sir! Nicknamed "America's Finest City," it is no surprise that San Diego is a major military hub. The Navy, Marines, and Coast Guard all have bases here, and four Navy vessels have been named the USS *San Diego* in honor of the city. San Diego has the largest naval concentration in the world, with ships, submarines, destroyers, and more docked in this sunny SoCal city. Families can tour the **USS Midway Museum,** a retired World War II aircraft carrier that rests in San Diego Harbor.

Plan a stop at **Seaport Village** on the waterfront for a delicious meal or snack, a fun shopping experience, and a spin on the 1890s Looff Carousel. Other intriguing neighborhoods for a bite to eat include the Victorian-era **Gaslamp Quarter** and the lively **Bazaar del Mundo** in Old Town. Here, historic buildings have become colorful Mexican shops and restaurants where children can sample treats from south of the border.

The **San Diego Zoo's Wild Animal Park,** about 30 miles north of downtown, is a huge wildlife sanctuary and botanical garden where 3,500 animals representing more than 400 species roam freely. A day here is more like a safari experience. If your family is as interested in the environment and conservation as ours is, plan ahead to catch a free lecture at the amazing Conservation Research Institute and learn more about their work.

"The Wild Animal Park was amazing. There was a watering hole where we could observe the animals drinking and playing. It was like a scene from *The Lion King.* I recommend that if you go, take the Journey into Africa tour that gets you even closer to the animals. But what I recommend most of all would be their large and unusual petting zoo, the Nairobi Village. This petting zoo is not the normal pig and goat kind you find at fairs. This one had different kinds of deer and other animals that did not mind you coming up and petting them since they are very tame. Also, they have the Balloon Safari, which is a 15-minute hot-air balloon ride that looks over the entire park. It is a little pricey, but the view is breathtaking and something you will never forget!"

—M. P., www.travelBIGO.com

San Diego Convention & Visitors Bureau
619-232-3101
www.sandiego.org, www.visitcalifornia.com

San Francisco, California

A rich cultural haven for the arts and high-tech, a chilly break from the hot and humid summers that most U.S. cities endure, an eclectic mix of modern and Victorian-era architecture along winding streets, and a free-wheeling attitude and variety of lifestyles—it all adds up to a delightful family escape in San Francisco.

FUN FACTS

The quotation, "The coldest winter I ever spent was a summer in San Francisco," which acknowledges the cool breezes and constant summer fog from the surrounding San Francisco Bay, is wrongly attributed to literary genius Mark Twain—although the true origins of the saying are unknown.

Begin your tour of San Fran by strolling along the storied streets and bumpy hills that encourage each family member to explore their own interests. Whether it's shopping or stopping for high tea at a fancy hotel on **Union Square** or taking an exciting ride on the unique **cable cars** (the free and amazing how-it-works **Cable Car Museum** is a must for travelers with budding mechanics), all roads eventually lead to **Fisherman's Wharf.** The eight blocks that make up this waterfront district include historic ships, museums, and wax figures at **Ripley's Believe It or Not**—all worth checking out. We recommend skipping the souvenir stands and overpriced, mediocre seafood restaurants. The area is colorful, noisy, and filled with street performers, jugglers, mimes, and bands.

Aquatic life is plentiful in this picturesque city, and **Aquarium of the Bay** allows you to walk through a 300-foot transparent tunnel and peer out at approximately 20,000 aquatic animals actually living in San Francisco Bay. An hour south, the world-famous **Monterey Bay Aquarium,** allows kids to touch various animals (all safe to be handled) at the Touch Pool. On this day trip from San Francisco, make sure to visit the aquarium's 28-foot-tall Kelp Forest, which requires weekly gardening by scuba divers to maintain the sea life, which can grow up to 4 inches per day.

After your under-the-sea experience, visit the **Cartoon Art Museum**—perfect for art enthusiasts. This creative hot spot offers guests a trip down memory lane with animated art from famous comics, movies, and advertisements. While you're in the creative mood, stop by the **Museum of Children's Art,** where the little ones can make their own masterpieces and view the work of other talented kids from around the world. The city oozes inspiration from the contemporary works on display at the **San Francisco Museum of Modern Art** to the shops of the gay and lesbian **Castro** area or the **Haight-Ashbury** hippie haven of the '60s, where parents and grand-parents can relive their youth and introduce younger generations to The Grateful Dead, lava lamps, and hemp jewelry.

Next on your list of stops should be the **Exploratorium** at the **Palace of Fine Arts** in **Golden Gate Park,** the city's favorite pub-lic green space. The Exploratorium's hands-on learning experiences invite visitors to explore every inch of their environment, from view-ing specimens under the scope at the Microscope Imaging Station to the Tactile Dome, where you have to find your way out of a darkened dome by using your sense of touch. Kids will love this unique experi-mental museum, and parents will embrace the opportunity for kids to expand their minds in a uniquely fun way.

The **Rooftop at Yerba Buena Gardens,** a family entertainment complex located in the **Moscone Convention Center,** invites families for a day of fun. The 11-acre complex features bowling, an indoor ice-skating rink, a children's play area, and a carousel. The futuristic **Métreon,** Sony's 350,000-square-foot entertainment area, includes shops, restaurants, and the largest IMAX theater on the West Coast. Both complexes have paid attractions but are free to wander around in and are great places to spend a rainy day.

FELLOW TRAVELERS SAY ...

"I hadn't been to Fisherman's Wharf in a while but I must say we thoroughly enjoyed the new sites, the talent, the food, and the great atmosphere. Oh, and if you go, don't forget to check out the barking Sea-lions lounging about off Pier 39. Very entertaining and totally free. There's a great arcade on Pier 39 that I literally had to drag [my family] away from. In addition, I discovered this very cool museum on Pier 45 called the Musee Mechanique. It's an old penny arcade with many antique games that you can still play. Very cool I must say."

—SG, www.FamilyTravelBoards.com

Guided cruise tours of the Golden Gate City—perhaps most beautiful when seen from the water—are a thrill for all ages. Kids love visiting the eerie former home of the nation's most notorious criminals at **Alcatraz Island,** the world-famous penitentiary in San Francisco Bay. Book ahead, however, because the cruise/land tours sell out quickly. If you're sightseeing with children younger than 6, instead take the narrated **San Francisco Bay** tour, which cruises under the stunning **Golden Gate Bridge,** sails by the prison, and focuses on the coastline, where kite boarders and kite surfers practice their sports.

The great family-friendly dining options in this city are seemingly endless, and they don't stop at **Ghirardelli Square** (chocolate) or the **Boudin Bakery** (San Francisco sourdough bread)—although both are signature eats. **Chinatown,** right in the heart of downtown, is a state of mind as well as the largest Chinatown outside Asia. After dim sum, do a little shopping and explore Chinese culture at the **Golden Gate Fortune Cookie Factory.**

San Francisco Convention & Visitors Bureau
415-391-2000
www.onlyinsanfrancisco.com, www.visitcalifornia.com

Cultural Appeal

- The Big Island's Aloha spirit
- Hoover Dam's awe-inspiring engineering
- The kid-friendly side of California's wine country
- Hollywood's family-friendly, star-studded fun
- A taste of the Wild West in Virginia City

It's hard to define cultural appeal in the American West, where dynamic pop culture dominates the arts scene and whatever's new is quickly disseminated around the world. Therefore, our choices in this chapter lean toward the classics—the best destinations to explore with your family that are unique to this region.

We look for those differences whenever we travel because it helps us appreciate how unique our own home is. We want to reaffirm that even if we go to Hawaii for the beach, there is a valuable local culture; if we go to Las Vegas for the lights and the glitz, we can learn something historical about engineering, conservation, and mining; and if we go anywhere in California, two wonderful industries—wine and the movies—distinguish this state from the 49 others.

Big Island of Hawaii

Bigger than all the other Hawaiian Islands combined, Hawaii's "Big Island" certainly fits its name. The Big Island has so much to offer that it is impossible to run out of things to do and see. Home to almost every kind of climate found on earth, the Big Island boasts a huge range of natural spectacles: lush rain forests, sunny beaches, grassy cattle ranches, and even snow-capped mountains.

But it is not simply the natural wonders that make the Big Island so fascinating. Known as the most culturally rich of all the Hawaiian Islands, the Big Island is alive with the traditions of kama'aina, the native-born. Locals say this is because Pele, the Hawaiian volcano goddess, is alive and active here—manifesting herself through the constant eruptions of the Kilauea Volcano.

VACATION PLANNING TIPS

Dreaming of a trip to Hawaii? Check out *The Complete Idiot's Guide to Hawaii* (Alpha Books) for a list of places to stay, must-see locations, and restaurants that will fit your style and budget.

To get a sense of the ancient Hawaiian culture, pay a visit to **Puuhonua o Honaunau National Historical Park** in South Kona, on the western coast. This 180-acre park is one of Hawaii's most sacred places. Centuries ago, it was a "City of Refuge" where defeated warriors and those who had broken tapu (sacred laws) could be purified by priests. It was said that if lawbreakers could make it to the city before being caught by their pursuers, they would be absolved of their sins and allowed to return home.

While in the park, take a walking tour around the Great Wall, a 10-foot-high, 17-foot-thick stone barrier that posed a final challenge for those trying to enter the city. Then, explore the back country surrounding the city on a hike that takes you past temples, ancient sled courses, and scenic cliffs. Or make your way down to the beach, where you may spot one of the green sea turtles sunbathing. In the park, kids can try their hands at lei making, basket weaving, and traditional Hawaiian games. You can also watch cultural demonstrators perform Hawaiian dances and make dugout canoes.

For another traditional experience, check out **Puukohola Heiau** in North Kohala, a huge stone heiau (temple) built in the eighteenth century by King Kamehameha the Great. If you want to get a feel for today's Big Island culture, be sure to make a trip to the **Hilo Farmer's Market** in Hilo, on the lush east coast. Open every Wednesday and Saturday, its 200 vendors offer a plethora of Hawaiian food, clothing, and art.

A trip to the Big Island would not be complete without a visit to **Volcanoes National Park,** home to the Kilauea Volcano, the world's most active. There, you can walk through the 400-foot Thurston Lava Tube, explore the craters, and watch the volcano's frequent eruptions. You can even take a helicopter tour and look into the volcano's crater from above. Follow the marked trail to the East Rift Zone, where you can watch steam explode into the sky as the molten lava meets the ocean. Visiting at night allows you to see the bright red lava even more clearly.

TRAVELERS BEWARE!

Be sure to come to Volcanoes National Park prepared. Wear shoes that are comfortable enough for the rocky hike. You should also pack snacks and drinks, because there are no food vendors near the viewing sites. If you're visiting at night, don't forget your flashlight—the trail is unlit. Binoculars may also be useful to see the eruptions better, because visitors are required to stay a safe distance away from the shore for safety.

For even more breathtaking natural sights, visit the **Mauna Kea** mountain. At 33,000 feet from the ocean floor to the top, it is the tallest sea mountain in the world. You can visit the summit, which is considered one of the best stargazing spots in the world; if you visit in winter, it is the only place on the island with snow. Other must-sees are **Parker Ranch,** where you can find real cowboys; and **Waipio Valley,** a gorge with beautiful waterfall and beach views that are well worth the hike.

Hawaii Visitors and Convention Bureau
1-800-648-2441
www.bigisland.org, www.gohawaii.com

Hoover Dam

The Hoover Dam, the nation's largest reservoir, is an engineering marvel that draws more than a million spectators annually. When full, it contains the equivalent of a two-year flow from the **Colorado River** (about 9.3 trillion gallons). Due to low water levels caused by a dry spell throughout the region, the dam currently operates at about two-thirds capacity.

The dam has assured residents of Arizona, Nevada, California, and northern Mexico a steady water supply since 1936, when it first tamed the Colorado River.

FUN FACTS

A daily crew of 3,500 to 5,200 men and women spent five years constructing Hoover Dam. The dam is composed of stacked concrete blocks that are connected with steel and waterproofed with a cement grout. By the numbers, it is 726.4 feet high, 1,244 feet wide, 660 feet thick at the base, and 45 feet thick at the top and cost $165 million dollars to build. An estimated five million barrels of cement were used in its construction.

To enjoy the majesty of this manmade feat, several million visitors drive across it in an endless traffic jam. We think kids will enjoy a more up-close look, so plan ahead to buy tickets to the **Visitors Center, Dam Tour,** or **Powerplant Tour.** The Visitors Center displays the artwork adorning this Art Deco–era civic project and has displays on the history of its construction. The Dam Tour is a mile-long, two-hour guided exploration of how it works, including a chance to see the largest water pipes ever built. The Powerplant Tour offers film, audio, and an on-site overview of the dam's operations, including a look at the 17 massive turbines that provide electricity for the entire Southwestern United States.

Tickets are sold on a first-come, first-served basis. This area can get really crowded on summer holiday weekends, so it's best to arrive by 2 P.M. The Hoover Dam is just 30 miles southeast of Las Vegas on U.S. Highway 93.

Hoover Dam Visitors Center
U.S. Bureau of Reclamation
702-494-2517
www.usbr.gov/lc/hooverdam, www.lasvegastourism.com

Napa Valley and California Wine Country

Just northeast of San Francisco and comprised of the towns of Napa, Sonoma, Yountville, and Santa Rosa (among others), the 30-mile-long **Napa Valley** is home to more than 300 California wineries. Although visiting them is primarily an activity for adults, several wineries, such as **Robert Mondavi, Beringer,** and **Sterling Wineries,** are particularly kid-friendly. If Bacchus calls, plan a family vacation where children can enjoy tours geared for them, watch the bottling and labeling of fancy grape juice or—at the magic age—imbibe and develop an oenophile's palate for themselves.

FUN FACTS

The California Wine Country is the second most visited region in the state, behind only Disneyland in Anaheim (see Chapter 24).

To plan your Napa road trip, call ahead to one or more of the wineries for a schedule of operations and to book a family tour.

Besides wine, the region boasts two natural wonders. In **The Petrified Forest,** well-marked trails meander past trees that have fossilized as a result of an eruption of Mount St. Helens more than six million years ago. An explanation of the geological process is presented in the adjoining museum, and there is a gift shop of mineral specimens. **Old Faithful Geyser** erupts at regular intervals—one of the three such phenomena in the world. When you arrive, you will see a bubbling pond that turns into a huge spout of water reaching heights of 60 feet before calming down until the next eruption, approximately 40 minutes later. Don't miss the adjoining exhibit area.

In nearby **Sonoma Valley,** children will enjoy visiting the many you-pick berry, fruit, and vegetable farms. The town of Sonoma also has the adorable, kid-friendly **Train Town,** a 1½-mile-long miniature train ride with a goat-feeding stop. From here, walk to **Sonoma Cheese Factory,** where you can learn about "curds and whey" and sample many varieties of Sonoma Jack cheese. Pick up some lunch at the deli to enjoy in the town's plaza, where picnic tables, swings, and a duck pond make for a perfect toddler stop.

For outdoor fun, head to **Sonoma Coast State Beach,** a 17-mile stretch of the Pacific with dramatic bluffs. Approaching from Highway 1, you can watch the harbor seals and picnic at **Goat Rock Beach** near the mouth of the **Russian River.** Although swimming is prohibited, the beach is great for frolicking and sunbathing. **Lake Sonoma** is another popular destination for a quiet afternoon picnic.

Guided touring options include **bike tours** along gently rolling hills or the **Napa Valley Wine Train,** a trip through time in a 1947 Pullman Vista Dome dining car or fully restored railcars dating from the early 1900s. On Family Fun Nights, parents can relax with a gourmet dinner while kids ages 3 to 12 play games, watch movies, and enjoy a meal with a professional caregiver in a separate railcar. In Yountville, families can watch **hot-air balloon** launches, and while the rides may be too pricey for families on a budget, it is fun just to watch them inflate and take off.

Children who love Snoopy and all the other Peanuts characters will want to visit the **Charles M. Schulz Museum** in Santa Rosa. While there, stop by the **Pacific Coast Air Museum** if anyone in your family is an airplane buff. **Safari West** is Santa Rosa's wildlife preserve created to protect endangered animals. This is ideal for older children; guided tours are quite lengthy yet offer a chance to encounter giraffes, gazelles, wildebeests, and zebras on a safari adventure.

Napa Valley Conference & Visitor Bureau
707-226-7459
www.napavalley.org, www.legendarynapavalley.com

The Real Hollywood, California

While Los Angeles has many tourist attractions, it is the cinematic myth of Hollywood that most intrigues traveling families. Although the neighborhood of **Hollywood** is no longer the epicenter of the motion picture business, **Paramount Pictures** still maintains its classic lot with soundstages there, and many support companies (labs, smaller stages, equipment rental houses, and so on) call it home.

VACATION PLANNING TIPS

Movie pilgrims will want to tour Hollywood, located east of Beverly Hills and northwest of downtown. The key streets are loosely bounded on the south by Melrose Avenue, on the west by La Brea, on the east by Vermont Avenue, and on the north by the Hollywood Hills. Parking is scarce and expensive, and pedestrian traffic is dense; put the car away and take the public Metro to the stops at Hollywood and Highland or Hollywood and Vine. Don't forget to wear your most stylish walking shoes.

The famous **Hollywood Sign** with its 50-foot illuminated letters read "Hollywoodland" back in 1924 when it advertised a real estate development of the same name in Beachwood Canyon (now a prosperous neighborhood). In 1949, the sign was renovated and the "land" dropped from the name.

The movie business landed in Hollywood around 1911, with the construction of Nestor Studios, followed by the Lasky-DeMille Barn (as in Cecil), which survives today as the **Hollywood Heritage Museum.** After that start, the business just kept growing with Paramount, Warner Brothers, RKO, and Columbia Pictures eventually building there. Since the 1950s, some companies have migrated over the hills to Burbank or to other parts of Los Angeles.

Hollywood Boulevard was always the Main Street of Hollywood, anchored by its classic icons—**Grauman's Chinese Theatre** and the **Walk of Fame**—now joined by the **Kodak Theatre** in the **Hollywood & Highland Center,** the new venue of the yearly Oscar show. Grauman's opened in May 1927 in the most spectacular theater opening ever. Thousands of people lined the boulevards with riots breaking out as the stars of *King of Kings* arrived for the film's premiere. It remains one of the favored theaters for movie premieres today. Beneath Grauman's Chinese pagoda-like entry, the dramatic forecourt is imprinted with a number of handprints and footprints of the stars and leads on to the Walk of Fame, celebrating its 50th anniversary in 2010. This famous walk runs both directions on Hollywood Boulevard from La Brea Avenue to Gower Street and beyond, as stars are still awarded to outstanding artists in film, television, music, radio, and theater.

TRAVELERS BEWARE!

Numerous hustlers and homeless have set up residence in Hollywood. We recommend you do your sightseeing by day.

The Kodak Theatre is within a shopping mall and can be toured daily. Families should drop by the very stylish **Hollywood Roosevelt Hotel** across the street and tour its small lobby museum of movie history. The great collection of photographs and memorabilia celebrate the very first Academy Awards ceremony, held here in 1929. The rooftop pool and Teddy's Bar are long-time hangouts for Hollywood celebs.

Studio tours are available weekdays at **Paramount Studios,** and although the tour can't compare with the entertainment extravaganza of the Universal Studio Tour (see Chapter 24), the authentic lot is classic early '20s Hollywood. Don't expect to see much of the inside of the buildings, however.

While we respect the privacy of actors, it's hard not to recommend **The Starline Movie Stars' Homes Tour,** leaving frequently from many stops. Don't expect to be invited in for coffee with Brad and Angelina, but the tours provide an interesting journey through the wealthier residential areas, with lots of gossip about the stars and the occasional drive-by of a real star's home or former home. Our family prefers this to peeking through bushes on our own with a map (usually out of date) of the stars' homes.

For more touring fun, the **"Behind-the-Scenes" Tour** will take you by bus to some sites seen in Hollywood's biggest hits.

Want to be a star in Hollywood? Arrange to be in a TV audience by ordering tickets in advance through www.tvtix.com or www.hollywoodtickets. com, which feature sitcoms and talk shows. On Camera Audiences (www. ocatv.com) specializes in reality TV shows. Peak production season runs August through March. If you can't find tickets for your favorite shows online, check the websites of the individual shows, which may offer them for free; minimum age restrictions may apply.

Hollywood Chamber of Commerce
323-469-8311
www.hollywoodchamber.net, www.hollywoodandhighland.com

Virginia City, Nevada

Take a step back in time in Virginia City, a mining town that was the biggest settlement between Denver and San Francisco during its glory days. With gold in nearly every hill in the vicinity, Virginia City was a rich town where women in fingerless gloves and feathered hats walked around with lace parasols. The choice of attire for men was frock coats, cowboy hats, and of course pistols. Although the $400 million dollars worth of gold extracted from the ground before 1900 is long gone, Virginia City still boasts that boomtown feeling.

FELLOW TRAVELERS SAY ...

"The city was my high school history textbook brought to life ... I watched a 150-year-old gold mill wake from its slumber, followed the footsteps of former miners, and rode the same tracks that used to move the city's riches to another town."

—P.L., www.travelBIGO.com

Families should begin their visit at the **Chollar Mine** to learn where gold and silver come from. A 30-minute tour takes visitors 400 feet into the main haulage tunnel where they experience for themselves how difficult mining is. Old equipment is still scattered around the tunnel, and a guide even demonstrates how miners removed ore from mine walls. Note that the tour isn't for everyone—the tunnel is narrow and dark, not suitable for young kids, claustrophobics, or people with back problems. At the **Comstock Gold Mill,** families can see how gold was processed. The restored gold mill still works, and if you look carefully, you can still spot tiny flecks of gold that were too difficult to salvage.

After exploring the mines, check out some more Comstock relics by visiting **The Way It Was Museum.** It features the most complete collection of mining artifacts from the area as well as rare photographs, lithographs, and maps of the booming bonanza period. Also visit the 1860 home of the "King of Comstock," John Mackay, at the **Mackay Mansion Museum,** where all the original furnishings are intact. A family favorite is the children's bedroom and playroom, which feature kid-size furniture, dolls from the 1900s, and a Civil War–era rocking horse.

Train fans must see the **Virginia & Truckee (V&T) Railroad.** At its peak during the nineteenth century, as many as 45 trains hauled millions of dollars of gold and silver from Virginia City in a single day. Now, the railroad is a popular attraction with visitors who want stunning views of the mountains and a quick glimpse of the city's most famous landmarks. The 35-minute excursion gives riders a comprehensive history lesson but is short and interesting enough to keep restless kids entertained. Another way to explore the town is with the **Virginia City Trolley,** a hop-on 20-minute narrated tour. Learn about the famous men and women who once lived in the city, including George Hearst, founder of the publishing giant, and *Huckleberry Finn* author Mark Twain.

Virginia City Convention and Tourism Authority
1-800-718-7587
www.visitvirginiacitynv.com, www.travelnevada.com

At the Beach

In This Chapter

- The blondes, the boardwalk, and The Beach Boys at California beaches
- Maui's family-friendly gems
- Oahu's world-class surfing beaches

The states of California and Hawaii have thousands of miles of Pacific Ocean coastline with countless beaches. We have done a round-up of the most popular beaches for families, using criteria such as cleanliness; shallow, warm surf; gentle waves; and lots of nearby activities. Then, for a bit of fun, we included a beach that's not very relaxing or appropriate for novice swimmers, but it's one of the most famous Pacific beaches in the world. And it's a blast!

California Beaches

The state that gave us The Beach Boys boasts a number of famous beaches tucked into the 1,100-mile Pacific coastline. No matter your interest, take time to visit one of our favorite California beach destinations. We think these are worth waiting for a parking space.

Working your way south to north, from the warmest water to the coldest, begin at **Doheny State Beach Park** in **Dana Point,** north of San Diego. At this broad sand beach with lifeguards, the water is just right for beginners eager to hang 10—so go ahead and rent a surfboard!

Along the **Orange County** coast north of San Diego and south of Los Angeles, **Newport Beach,** where large rental homes hug the sand and surf, is the star. This affluent community has everything from fish shacks on the **Newport Pier** to designer boutiques at **Fashion Island,** and the surf's up just enough to thrill beginners. There's extra family fun offshore on **Balboa Island,** where parents enjoy the quaint shops and restaurants and kids are eager to hop the car-ferry to Balboa Peninsula's **Fun Zone.** This small and cozy midway has an old-fashioned carousel, Ferris wheel, bumper cars, and a kid's climbing area.

FELLOW TRAVELERS SAY ...

"Five generations of our family, 21 members ranging from 20-months to 93-years-old, chose beautiful Newport Beach for our reunion .... We had lots of fun at Knott's Berry Farm in nearby Buena Park. What was once an actual berry farm is now a 160-acres theme park offering world-class rides, unique family shows and one-of-a-kind attractions."

—R.G.M.G., www.FamilyTravelForum.com

North in **Huntington Beach,** the community that calls itself "Surf City," families will find a broad sand beach, a Navy S.E.A.L. installation, and lots of breakers for more advanced surfers. You can stroll among the surf rats and buy SoCal-style gear on Sixth Street or check into one of the many resort hotels and sign up for surfing lessons. A must-stop along the Huntington Beach Pier is the **Surf City Store.**

Only 22 miles off the coast of **Long Beach** and a ferry ride away lies **Santa Catalina Island,** a retro resort town surrounded by an unspoiled nature preserve. You can rent kayaks and paddle through the crystal-clear waters, explore the underwater world aboard a glass-bottom boat, or lap ice cream cones in the adorable—if touristy—pedestrian village. Catalina's small sand beach leads to calm, shallow water that is protected by the harbor, so it's safe for younger children to swim and play. B&Bs and rental cottages must be booked weeks in advance for summer weekends.

Santa Monica has the public beach closest to the Los Angeles tourist sites. The section of the 27-mile-long concrete boardwalk that runs between hippie **Venice** and star-struck **Malibu** is a haven for dog walkers, strollers and those pushing strollers, and all matter of vehicular and pedestrian traffic. Several concessions along the boardwalk rent bikes and inline skates, and many outdoor cafés offer a spot to take a break from the bright sunshine and strong ocean breezes. The **Venice Beach Boardwalk** is especially colorful. The **Pacific Ocean Park** amusement park on the famous Santa Monica Pier is a great place for lounging in the sun, fishing, snacking, riding a carousel, and taking in the Southern California scene.

FUN FACTS

If you're visiting between March and August, you may catch a "grunion run." These silver-bellied, oversized minnows like to lay their eggs on the sand. For six to eight nights per month following high tide, thousands of them swim onto shore to lay eggs, where they are either caught or return to the sea.

Families who prefer boating to sand castles should drop by **Marina del Rey,** site of the largest manmade yacht harbor in North America. Bordered by Los Angeles on three sides, it boasts dockside restaurants, waterfront hotels, golden sands, shoreline parks, and every boating, cruising, and water sport imaginable.

Driving **Highway 1,** also called the **Pacific Coast Highway,** between Los Angeles and San Francisco is one of America's most beloved road trips. Many great stops dot this 10-hour journey, but one of the most famous beaches you'll pass is **Big Sur,** whose beauty was extensively chronicled by photographer Edward Weston. If you drive slowly along the winding coastal blacktop, you'll catch spectacular sights of the churning Pacific, sheer cliffs, and almost lunar landscapes. (Don't even consider swimming, though, because the currents here are treacherous.) Just north at **Pfeiffer Big Sur State Park,** you can hike and picnic amid the southernmost stand of the famed coastal redwoods.

About 90 minutes south of San Francisco is Santa Cruz, whose **Santa Cruz Beach Boardwalk,** dating back to 1907, is the oldest of America's great beachfront amusement parks. You'll find old and new rides, games, arcades, a bowling alley, and a 1911 Looff carousel. Santa Cruz' beautiful Pacific beaches are a bit too cold for most swimmers, but your kids may dive in or decide to take surfing lessons at **Cowell Beach** at the Santa Cruz Wharf.

California Tourism Industry Site
1-877-225-4367
www.visitcalifornia.com, www.beachcalifornia.com

Maui, Hawaii

Named "Best Island in the World" 15 times by *Condé Nast Traveler* magazine—largely for its gorgeous beaches—Maui is an excellent choice for a family beach getaway. With 120 miles of shoreline, thousands of waterfalls and pools, and a variety of marine activities, this island paradise with more than 80 sun-dappled, sandy beaches is a perfect spot for all ages to relax.

One of the best family beaches is **Hana Beach,** lauded as the safest beach in east Maui. **Kapalua Beach** is a beautiful golden stretch along the west coast of the Keanae Peninsula, with a spectacular view of Molokai. Another family favorite is **Palauea Beach** in **Wailea,** which is ideal for families with young children because it is sheltered from the winds and the water is shallow. Be sure to check out four-mile-long **Kaanapali Beach,** one of Maui's best locations for swimming and snorkeling at **Black Rock.** Nearby, historic **Lahaina Town,** an old whaling village, is now a lively tourist area where you can stroll among shops and restaurants while you enjoy beautiful ocean views.

VACATION PLANNING TIPS

If you're looking for the real aloha spirit, stay at the **Kaanapali Beach Hotel,** known as Hawaii's "Most Hawaiian Hotel." From check-in to checkout, the entire staff shares authentic native traditions with guests, from a welcome ceremony to classes in lei making and other crafts for parents and kids alike. Evening entertainment includes Hawaiian singing, nightly hula shows, and weekly performances by local *halau* (hula schools), where children learn the sacred chants and movements of their ancestors. The KBH Sunday brunch has been rated the best on Maui and offers an extensive selection of food, champagne, and Hawaiian entertainment served by proud and friendly staff.

At the beach, you and your older children can try your hand at surfing. We recommend **Goofy Foot Surf School** in Lahaina, where teachers back their classes with the guarantee that they'll get you up on a board and surfing or your lesson is free. These beaches are also great for snorkeling, with lots of coral reefs to explore and tropical fish to admire. You might even see turtles or an occasional octopus.

For families with younger children, Maui offers a countless number of activities. Marine lovers will enjoy the **Maui Ocean Center,** a state-of-the-art aquarium and marine park that fascinates young children with more than 60 exhibits on the beauty and delicacy of Hawaii's marine life. Or explore beneath the surface of the ocean in a real submarine at **Atlantis Adventures.** Among the shallow coastal waters, you'll see multitudes of fish. Young kids will love **The Sugar Cane Train,** which takes riders on a 30-minute, 12-mile ride through fields of sugar cane while the conductor points out landmarks. If you're lucky, the conductor may even favor you with a song.

VACATION PLANNING TIPS

Active families should consider the **Maui Explorer Pass,** which enables you to save 15 percent on regular admission prices to the top attractions.

Families with older children and teens should be sure to visit **The Hawaii Nature Center,** which offers guided tours of the **Iao Valley** and its beautiful rain forest environment as well as some of the most spectacular hiking on the island. The eco-adventure **Piiholo Ranch Zipline** is sure to entertain kids and thrill parents as well. Hawaii's longest, the zip line reaches heights of 600 feet, and riders can go as fast as 40 mph between the trees. All riders must be at least 10 years old and should weigh between 75 and 275 pounds.

Another must-see is **Haleakala National Park,** home to Haleakala, the world's largest dormant volcano. The elevated view of the island chain is spectacular, but leave early in the day to avoid the clouds that frequently fill the crater in the afternoon and obstruct the view. And don't forget to drive **The Road to Hana,** Maui's most famous drive. A curvy, narrow road carries you on a three- to four-hour drive through a rain forest with hundreds of waterfalls and beautiful views.

Maui Visitors Bureau
1-800-525-6284
www.visitmaui.com, www.gohawaii.com/maui

North Shore's Banzai Pipeline, Oahu

There are very few beaches where surfers wait for the waves to be *small* enough to surf. But in winter months, waves can reach deadly heights—up to 30 feet—at the **Banzai Pipeline.** Located in **Ehukai Beach Park** on the **North Shore** of Oahu, the waves of "The Pipe" attract professional surfers from around the world.

Surf season typically takes place between November and February. During this time, you can watch some of the world's best ride several massive pipelines—tubular waves caused by the Pacific crashing over a shallow reef break. Every winter, the North Shore hosts the **Vans Triple Crown of Surfing** competition, considered "the Super Bowl of surfing." While at the North Shore, be sure to check out the nearby **Sunset Beach** and **Waimea Bay,** the birthplace of big-wave surfing.

But less-experienced surfers need not despair—the Banzai Pipeline's waves are not this rough the entire year. During summer months (May–September), it's a favorite locals beach. The waves calm to a gentle one to two feet in height, so the beach is safe for even your youngest to enjoy the water. Although the North Shore is more than an hour away from **Honolulu,** it's worth the drive: secluded beaches are a refreshing break from Oahu's crowded resorts. Once you've soaked up enough sun, make the short drive to **Haleiwa,** a laid-back surf town with several great restaurants and shops.

> **FUN FACTS**
>
> The Banzai Pipeline got its name in 1961 when surfing movie producer Bruce Brown was exploring Oahu's North Shore with professional surfers Phil Edwards and Mike Diffenderfer. They found this perfect wave, filmed there, and wanted to name the new beach. While brainstorming names, they drove by a pipeline construction site. Diffenderfer suggested they call the beach "The Pipeline," and the name stuck. As legend has it, Bruce Brown yelled "Banzai!"—Japanese for "Long life!" or "Hurrah!"—as Phil Edwards caught one of the huge waves. A surfing legend was born.

During your stay on Oahu, you'll probably visit **Waikiki Beach,** the resort section of Honolulu. In town, kids can get up close and personal with sea life at the **Waikiki Aquarium** or on an **Atlantis Submarine** ride. You should also pay a visit to the **Honolulu Zoo,** a small but entertaining zoo lush with tropical plants.

Of course, you need not stick to the usual resort activities every day, because the rest of Oahu has much to offer. A popular attraction is the *Arizona* memorial at **Pearl Harbor;** try to get there early to avoid crowds. Just outside Waikiki is the **Diamond Head Trail,** a great hike with gorgeous views of the island. The trail is somewhat strenuous, so be sure to bring plenty of water and head out early before it gets too hot. A slightly easier hike is at the **Nuuanu Pali Lookout,** where you will find stunning views of the surrounding landscape.

North Shore Chamber of Commerce
Haleiwa, HI 96712
808-637-4558
www.gonorthshore.org/visitor_info.htm, www.visit-oahu.com

Amusement Parks

In This Chapter

- Taking part in the magic of Disneyland
- Toying around with Legoland's many amusements
- Riding the movies at Universal Studios Hollywood

Amusement parks, theme parks, and water parks—a travel guide that selectively covers the best family destinations in the states of California, Nevada, and Hawaii has lots to choose from. If you haven't read the Las Vegas section of Chapter 23, you'll find that the city itself, from a child's point of view, is one huge amusement park. Likewise, Hawaii can be considered a giant outdoor Polynesian-themed park focused on sun, sand, volcanoes, and jungle adventures.

That's why we chose to focus on three unique parks in California that take thrill rides and coasters, add fun themes, and deliver an experience unlike any other. And given that there are 26 amusement parks and 21 water parks just in California, we're confident that any family traveling with children will be able to break up a long road trip with a kid-fun stop along almost any route.

Disneyland and Anaheim, California

When your kids wish upon a star, they may dream of opening their eyes to the magic of Disneyland in southern California. Here, kids and adults alike wander through fantasy after fantasy, discovering traditional Disney characters such as Mickey Mouse—from the original park opened by Walt Disney himself in 1955—fused with modern Disney classics such as *High School Musical.*

The magic begins at **Disneyland Park,** where favorite classic Disney themes and rides such as It's a Small World—albeit "modernized" recently to much outcry from fans and foes alike—await. Don't miss the state-of-the-art audio-animatronics on display at the Main Street U.S.A. Opera House, where a revitalized "Abraham Lincoln" shares his most famous speeches. Thrill seekers can take a ride on the Indiana Jones Adventure, following Indy on his journey through the iconic Temple of the Forbidden Eye. Cool down afterward at Pixie Hollow in Fantasyland and meet the delightfully sunny Tinker Bell. Next, make your way to Tomorrowland for your Jedi training, where fans will learn light saber tricks and more on the path to becoming Jedi knights.

VACATION PLANNING TIPS

We know a family road trip without a day at an amusement park can seem like a beach vacation without sunshine. Here are a few money-saving tips for what's always a surprisingly expensive day out:

- Buy a Southern California CityPass and get 30 percent off tickets to several of the parks.
- Check with your AAA or AARP office for member discounts.
- Check the park websites for military and union discounts.
- Ask every family member to carry daypacks with his or her own water bottle, snacks, towel, and rain or water-ride poncho.
- Be proactive! Offer kids a souvenir allowance and help them learn to live within a budget like you do.

On day two of your vacation, head over to **California Adventure Park** (included in your Disneyland ticket price), the place to be if you love live entertainment and are a true fan of Hollywood. Part of the Disney family since 2001, California Adventure offers something for the entire gang. Your littlest travelers will adore Mickey's Playhouse, while 'tweens will flock to High School Musical. The very clever Soarin' Over California, a simulated ride over California where your toes touch the top of the Golden Gate Bridge and brush the evergreens at Yosemite, is a favorite virtual reality ride for all ages.

Three on-site Disney hotels offer fun family benefits, such as easy park re-entry and monorail access, but are more costly than others nearby in Anaheim; check their website for seasonal savings when you combine hotel stays with admission tickets. At the upscale **Disney's Grand Californian Hotel,** parents can send the kids to Pinocchio's Workshop (open from 5 P.M. to midnight) for games, arts and crafts, and other kid-friendly fun while Mom and Dad have a romantic dinner alone or head to the spa for a massage. At the original **Disneyland Hotel,** home of the high-priced but extraordinary Mickey Penthouse, you'll find inventive character-packed swimming pools, and at **Disney's Paradise Pier Hotel** the guest-only movie theater complements the children's playroom.

After maxing out on all things Disney, take some time to enjoy the city of Anaheim, known for its sports teams and family-fun atmosphere. Just steps away from Disneyland, take a stroll through the **Anaheim Garden Walk** in the **Downtown Disney** entertainment and nightlife district. The retail shops, movie theaters, dining, bowling alley, and clubs are sure to be a hit with everyone. Leave time to check out the **House of Blues** and **ESPN Zone.**

FUN FACTS

Anaheim is the biggest star of all! In honor of the city's 150th anniversary in 2007, the city of Anaheim inaugurated its very own **Anaheim Walk of Fame,** with the legendary Walt Disney receiving the first star. Find it near the Harbor Boulevard entrance to Disneyland.

If your vacation falls during the hockey or baseball seasons, be sure to check out championship hometown teams the **Anaheim Ducks** (named for the 1992 Disney film *The Mighty Ducks)* and the **Los Angeles Angels of Anaheim.** The 2007 Stanley Cup winners play at the **Honda Center,** just a short ride from Disneyland, and their baseball neighbors, the Angels, are just across the Orange Freeway at **Angel Stadium.**

Looking to add some culture and education to your trip? Head to the **Muzeo,** a museum filled with interactive exhibits that will keep kids enthralled for hours.

Other spots to see in Anaheim are the **Pearson Park Amphitheater,** where live performances will entertain the entire family from May to September each year. **Adventure City** is also great, particularly for little kids, because it's a smaller, cheaper, and more manageable park with pint-size roller coasters.

In nearby Buena Park, **Knott's Berry Farm** welcomes tots to **Camp Snoopy** while 'tweens and teens can enjoy more adventurous rides and shows. For a really unusual treat, you can tour—or even rent a room on—the *Queen Mary,* an historic Art Deco ocean liner in Long Beach that has been converted into a hotel.

Disneyland
Anaheim, CA 92803
714-781-4565
disneyland.disney.go.com, www.anaheimoc.org

Legoland and Carlsbad, California

For any child—or adult, for that matter—who has ever spent time building Lego models on their living room floor, the Legoland amusement park in southern California is a must-see. Spread across 128 acres, the park features 15,000 Lego models built with more than 35 million building blocks. The smallest model, a pigeon located on a building in the Washington, D.C., portion of **Miniland U.S.A.,** consists of a mere four Legos. And the mammoth "Bronty," a giant dinosaur, is the largest model in the park, featuring more than two million bricks. No matter their size, all of the 50-plus attractions and shows in the park are interactive, family-friendly, and especially geared for children.

> **FUN FACTS**
>
> Ole Kirk Christiansen, a carpenter from Billund, Denmark, founded the Lego Group in 1932 when he began producing wooden toys. In 1940, the business began to manufacture plastic toys. Nearly a decade later, Lego came out with the interlocking plastic Automatic Binding Bricks the company is famous for today. The Lego name itself derives from the Danish phrase *leg godt*, meaning "play well."

Legoland has nine different themed areas for the family to explore. We love the **Land of Adventure,** which transports the gang back to 1920s Egypt with 75 Lego models and nearly half a million bricks. Explore the Pharaoh's empire or even take a dark ride through Lost Kingdom Adventure while trying to excavate ancient treasures of the Egyptian world. For more insight into the past, visit Dino Island to see life-size dinosaur models.

Little adventurers can ride the junior coaster, Coasteraurus, which reaches the tame speed of 20 miles per hour, or become a Lego-tologist by digging up Lego dinosaur bones and fossils buried in a giant pit. Families who love knights in shining armor should pay a visit to Castle Hill and watch a medieval jousting tournament.

Younger kids will enjoy **Explore Village,** where they can take a charming boat ride through a variety of Lego recreations of their favorite fairy tales or even go on a safari trek through a Lego Africa. And in **Fun Town,** youngsters can use their imagination to become Lego-lovin' firefighters, pilots, and factory workers. Kids ages 6 to 13 can even attend **Volvo Driving School;** if they pass the test, they can receive their very own official Legoland driver's license. The newest Fun Town fun is at the **Legoland Waterpark,** a water play zone with a five-story Lego tower from which kids can hurtle down through tubes or in six-person rafts; a separate admission fee is required.

Finally, a family favorite that brings the most famous landmarks of the United States right into the heart of Legoland is Miniland U.S.A. Featuring more than 24 million bricks, this area recreates the Las Vegas Strip, the Daytona International Speedway in Florida, San Francisco's Golden Gate Bridge, and even a Mardi Gras parade in New Orleans. The tallest structure in the park is the Freedom Tower in New York City. Although the actual structure has not yet been built, the Legoland version of the tower soars 28 feet and took four months to construct. Also on display are the Capitol Building and the White House in Washington, D.C.; look for the First Family to change, if need be, every four years.

Beyond Legoland in Carlsbad, families can visit **SeaLife Carlsbad,** a branch of Europe's most popular aquarium and marine life attraction, and play golf and tennis in a town known for its recreation resorts.

Legoland
Carlsbad, CA 92008
760-918-5346
www.Legoland.com, www.visitcarlsbad.com

Universal Studios Hollywood

If you could choose only one thing to see in Los Angeles, opt to experience the wonders of **Universal Studios Hollywood.** Aptly billed as the Entertainment Capital of L.A., this movie- and TV-themed park sits adjacent to the real working film studios of Universal Pictures. This allows Universal to include a unique **Studio Tour** as a bonus, providing a fun taste of the Hollywood that has shaped Los Angeles and fascinated the world.

The Studio Tour is a tram ride on the Universal **backlot,** through movie history, past soundstages, original sets, thematic façades, and recreated streets. With Whoopi Goldberg as your virtual Studio Tour Guide, you'll drive into and through some remarkable movie situations. (For a big fee, you can order a VIP Studio Tour and catch a glimpse of current productions.)

Along the route is the *War of the Worlds* set of a small town devastated by a cleverly choreographed 747 jetliner crash, with special effects providing smoking wreckage and shattered debris. Next door you may even see a dinosaur. You'll drive into a spectacular chase scene from *Fast and Furious: Tokyo Drift*, survive a flash flood, and have a near miss with a giant shark. The latest thrill is King Kong 360 3-D, designed by director Peter Jackson to plunge ride-goers into the middle of a pitched battle between a dinosaur and King Kong seen in 3-D.

VACATION PLANNING TIPS

One admission pass includes both the Studio Tour and the Universal Themepark. We think the Studio Tour is best while you're fresh. The tour takes 45 minutes, so count on an early snack stop.

Plan ahead with detailed information from the website. Universal sells a two-day admission pass online for the price of one, so you won't have to miss anything or feel compelled to pay extra for the Front of the Line Pass because you have too little time.

Jurassic Park—The Ride floats through the lush Jurassic era, with hidden thrills and chills and a big wet finish. Shrek 4-D features amazing "OgreVision" animation and sensory immersion in a comic saga. The Adventures of Curious George is a giant play zone where the fun-loving chimp takes kids on a voyage through space, a wild romp in the jungle, and a trip to the zoo.

On The Simpsons Ride, you join that wacky family on a hysterical adventure. The Revenge of the Mummy—The Ride, billed as "the world's first psychological thrill ride," provides a scary, multisensory trip through the dark side.

If you're ready to ramp it down a bit, check out Universal's Animal Actors, where very real furry creatures show how four-legged pros do it in the movies. Some of the animals have had real starring roles, in films including *Evan Almighty*, *Night at the Museum*, *Ace Ventura Pet Detective*, and *Dr. Doolittle*. (No pawographs, please.)

In the "showing how it's done" vein, do not miss Waterworld—A Live Sea War Spectacular, where special effects experts put on a major thrill-packed show full of spray and surprises.

At the end of the day, head uphill on foot (10 minutes) or grab a shuttle bus (5 minutes) to **Universal Studios Citywalk,** a stylish promenade featuring entertainment-themed restaurants, clubs, specialty shops, and movie theaters. There's a Gospel Brunch at **B. B. King's,** concerts at the **Gibson Ampitheater,** and good food all around. Then, stagger back to the hotel for some serious sleep at the end of a fun-packed day. You've earned it.

Universal Studios Hollywood
Universal City, CA 91608
1-800-UNIVERSAL
www.universalstudioshollywood.com, www.discoverlosangeles.com

Outdoor Adventures

Chapter

25

In This Chapter

- Kauai's mountainous jungles and eco-friendly fun
- Exploring Lake Mead in your own houseboat
- Digging into Lake Tahoe's snow sports paradise
- Discovering Yosemite National Park's endless adventures

Although California, Nevada, and Hawaii all boast amazing natural landscapes, each state's opportunities for outdoor adventures are quite distinct.

The famously strong waves of the Pacific Ocean and the towering Sierra Madres, the blistering Nevada desert, and the volcanic origins of the Hawaiian Islands create fantastic possibilities for extreme sports. But when it comes to family-friendly adventures and beautiful natural environments to inspire a lifelong love of nature, we think the following destinations are among the best in the region.

Kauai, Hawaii

Nicknamed "The Island of Discovery" and "The Garden Island," Kauai is the oldest and northernmost of the Hawaiian Islands. In comparison with Oahu and Maui, it has a laid-back character and unspoiled environment; a volcanic isle covered with lush mountains, grottos, hidden beaches, and waterfalls, it is an especially eco-friendly choice for a family vacation.

Kauai offers adventures on both land and water—from hiking along dramatic canyons to rafting the only navigable rivers in the state of Hawaii. And Kauai's beauty is not limited to experienced naturalists; hikers and non-hikers of all ages can enjoy the varied terrain. If your kids are not already outdoor enthusiasts, don't push too hard—and we guarantee they will be by the end of your visit.

FUN FACTS

Recognize the scenery? That's because more than 50 movies—including *South Pacific, Honeymoon in Vegas, Jurassic Park, and Raiders of the Lost Ark*—have used Kauai's lush jungles and tropical foliage for scenic location shoots.

Even the youngest travelers in your family will be able to experience the Hawaiian rain forest at **Koke'e State Park**'s 20-minute self-guided nature walk. Older children and fit outdoor enthusiasts can explore the 19 trails of varying lengths through the park's 4,345 acres of rain forest. At nearby **Waimea Canyon,** which Mark Twain nicknamed "The Grand Canyon of the Pacific," you will be amazed by the 10-mile-long gorge whose reddish-orange hues change throughout the day. The canyon can be reached on foot or by guided horseback and helicopter tours. Families with older adventurers will also enjoy Zodiac raft trips and kayaking treks on the **Wailua River,** which weaves through jungles and waterfalls.

Because it's only 33 miles wide and 25 miles long, you can pack the family into a rental car to experience many of Kauai's striking natural attractions. Most activity is along the 90 miles of dramatic coastline, because the island's mountainous interior is largely forest preserves. In those regions that are difficult to reach by car—such as the world-famous **Napali Coast,** now a state park—helicopter, boat, and raft tours allow you to experience Kauai's untouched nature. Additional guided tours visit the **Huleia National Wildlife Refuge** and other unusual spots, such as taro fields and sand dunes—leaving few places completely inaccessible. While these tours are expensive, keep in mind that this is one remote destination you may never get to again.

Of course, a trip to Kauai would not be complete without a few days at the beach. Here, the beaches are varied and among Hawaii's most beautiful. Famous spots include **Hanalei Beach Park** and **Ke'e Beach** on the North Shore; **Lydgate State Park** on the eastern Coconut Coast; and **Mahaulepu Beach** and **Poipu Beach Park** on the South Shore. **Poipu,** with its sparkling soft-sand beach and gentle surf, has what's considered the island's best beach for kids and novice swimmers; it is also Kauai's most densely developed region with the widest range of hotels and resorts.

For a taste of Kauai's culture, watch a luau show and eat traditional Hawaiian food in the Poipu or Koloa areas at the **Coconut Beach Resort** or at **Smith's Tropical Paradise.**

Kauai Visitors Bureau
Kauai, HI 96766
1-800-262-1400
www.kauaidiscovery.com, www.kauai-hawaii.com

Lake Mead National Recreation Area, Nevada

Lake Mead National Recreation Area (LMNRA) is a fascinating region on the Nevada-Arizona border that offers a variety of year-round outdoor adventures. Its massive lakes (**Lake Mead** and **Lake Mohave**) annually attract nearly nine million boaters, swimmers, and fishermen while the blistering desert caters to hikers, photographers, and anybody seeking a rugged outdoor experience. Families can observe deep majestic canyons, expansive mountain ranges, unique colored soils, and intricate rock formations.

If you've seen the **Hoover Dam** that contains it, you can appreciate the size of Lake Mead. At an elevation of 1,221 feet, it extends approximately 110 miles upstream toward the **Grand Canyon** and about 35 miles up the **Virgin River.** The width varies from several hundred feet in the canyons to a maximum of eight miles, making it one of the largest water reservoirs in the world. The lake is presently low, but because its volume is determined in part by snowmelt that comes from the Rockies through Arizona's Lake Powell, fluctuation in the lake's level is natural.

While some families choose to camp in this area (and there are many RV and tent campgrounds), the LMNRA also offers an alternative mode of shelter for those who want to take their outdoor exploration a bit further. At several marinas, families can rent a **houseboat** with homelike amenities and spend several days exploring picturesque canyons and natural stone bridges. To alleviate the inconveniences caused by low water and the shifting shoreline, the National Park Service has moved marinas to make them more accessible, and rangers regularly alert boaters to exciting new sightseeing opportunities.

Rental companies feature an impressive selection of boats, water toys (small power boats, inner tubes, floats, and more), and thorough instructions on how to operate them. Larger, more deluxe boats can accommodate a reunion group, and even the cheapest watercraft sleep up to six people. Costs are reasonable year-round, but be warned: crowds can really be daunting during July and August, when the desert really heats up.

LMNRA Visitor Center
702-293-8990
www.nps.gov/lame, www.travelnevada.com

Lake Tahoe, California-Nevada

With the most snowfall in the United States, frequent blue skies, and a long, temperate season, Lake Tahoe is the perfect winter destination—which explains why it's home to six big mountain resorts: **Alpine Meadows, Northstar,** and **Squaw Valley USA** on the lake's **North Shore;** and **Heavenly, Kirkwood,** and **Sierra-at-Tahoe** on the lake's **South Shore.** The Nevada-California state line runs right through the middle of this premier snow sports region, but you won't care what state you're in once you arrive. At an altitude of 4,580 feet and a surface area of 191 square miles, scenic Lake Tahoe is the highest and second-deepest lake in the United States. As Mark Twain—an observant and loquacious naturalist—once said of the area, "I thought it must be the fairest picture the whole earth affords."

Less than an hour from Reno, a few hours from Sacramento, and within a four-hour drive of San Francisco, Tahoe attracts active families who come for the laid-back California vibe, plentiful recreation facilities, and extensive eco-initiatives (water conservation, food service, carpooling, and more). In winter, in addition to the world-class skiing and snowboarding, families can enjoy ice skating, snowshoeing, and sledding.

Squaw Valley USA, site of the 1960 Olympics, maintains an enclosed cable car between its lively base village up to **High Camp,** where energetic teens and kids can chill at the amazing sky-high skating rink, bungee jump course, scenic vista restaurants, and night-lit snow tubing and ski trails. Squaw stays open for skiing until late May most years, but High Camp's lagoon pool stay opens summers, too, for mountain bikers and hikers who come to sunbathe.

Snow haters and couch potatoes have day spas, periodic culinary events, and wine festivals throughout the year as well as hip boutiques in downtown **Tahoe City,** shops and restaurants in **Truckee,** and a manmade kayak course and casinos in **Reno.** Summertime offers indoor rock climbing, golf, tennis, fishing, boating, biking, and hiking—with or without professional instruction or guides. Summer is also the season when the snow-capped mountains are best appreciated from the deck of a sightseeing vessel. We especially like the **M.S. Dixie II,** a classic paddle wheeler in service since 1949 that makes several guided trips daily.

VACATION PLANNING TIPS

Tahoe has a winter high season and a summer high season. The ski-in, ski-out lodging at the major mountain resorts gets pricey in winter, but if you choose the **Ski Tahoe North's Interchangeable Lift Ticket** (valid at seven mountains) and get equipment rentals and lodging near the small, novice-friendly **Diamond Peak, Homewood, Mount Rose,** or **Sugar Bowl** ski areas, it's much more affordable. In summer, the on-mountain lodging is cheaper than the many lakefront resorts. You won't need to rent a car, because most of the region's resorts offer a free mountain shuttle in winter and there's a cheap summertime trolley system.

Lake Tahoe Area Ski Information
1-800-588-SNOW
www.SkiLakeTahoe.com, www.visitinglaketahoe.com

Yosemite National Park, California

"All other travel is mere dust and hotels and baggage and chatter." It's difficult to say that this destination is better than other national parks, but we can certainly understand what inspired the Scottish-born writer John Muir to call **Yosemite National Park** nature's finest creation. Yosemite owes its splendorous stone formations and diverse, rugged landscape to continuous geological changes throughout Earth's history. Northern California's **Sierra Nevada** mountain range extends in altitude from near sea level to more than 13,000 feet along its crest in the Yosemite area.

Among many attractions, Yosemite is well known for the **Pacific Crest National Scenic Trail,** which crosses Donohue Pass at a dizzying 11,056 feet and continues to the park's north entrance at Dorothy Lake. (The remainder of the 2,650-mile trail—for those who like really long trips—begins in Mexico, winds all the way up the Cascades and Sierras, and ends in Canada.) Perhaps even more famous, the 211-mile-long **John Muir Trail** overlaps part of it and is a great way to see many of Yosemite's sensational sights.

Near the south entrance of the park in Wawona is the 2,200-foot **Chilnualna Falls,** which you can see more closely after a brief, steep hike. The nearby **Mariposa Grove** is filled with nearly 500 mature **giant sequoias,** some of which exceed 3,000 years in age.

FUN FACTS

The bark of a giant sequoia—which can sometimes be up to 24 inches thick—is fire resistant. In the event of a natural forest fire, these hardy trees remain standing. At the same time, fire helps new sequoia growth by opening the sequoia cones and scattering the tiny seeds, clearing forest debris from the mineral soil, providing a nutrient-rich seed bed, and clearing competing species.

Arguably the most popular portion of the park, **Yosemite Valley** is home to **Yosemite Falls,** made up of three separate falls totaling 2,425 feet in height. The falls flow November through July and can best be seen from the areas around **Sentinel Meadow** and the **Yosemite Chapel.** The first attraction visitors see, however, is the **Bridalveil Fall,** standing 620 feet tall and at its heaviest flow in the spring. Watch rock climbers test their mettle on the 3,000-foot granite face of **El Capitan,** the largest monolith in the world and the location of the 1,000-foot **Horsetail Fall.** These glowing-orange waterfalls flow from December to April and are best seen in mid- to late February at sunset.

From **El Capitan Meadow,** take in impressive views of the **Cathedral Rocks** and **Spires.** Atop the 8,122-foot **Sentinel Dome,** the famous wind-blown Jeffrey pine rewards adventurous hikers with a short rest. From the pristine **Mirror Lake,** guests can see the remarkable landmark **Half Dome,** which stands at nearly 5,000 feet above a valley floor covered in talus shards and is a popular spot for hikers and rock climbers. Among other popular features are **Nevada, Vernal,** and **Glacier Falls;** the last is famous for the view from **Glacier Point.**

VACATION PLANNING TIPS

Curry Village and **The Ahwahnee Village** are the park's commercial areas, with hotels and educational facilities where kids can learn the art of basket weaving, bead working, and acorn grinding. Book ahead if you want to stay at one of the national park lodges; if you're trying to save money by staying outside the park, select a hotel as close as possible to the western entrance.

While summers in the Sierra mountain region can bring sudden and intense downpours and thunderstorms, Yosemite actually receives less than 5 percent of its annual precipitation in the summer months—often making for a warm and dry season. Don't forget to take along water bottles, bandanas, and sun block to combat the heat.

In Ahwahnee, the **Yosemite Museum** is a perfect place for kids to observe displays on the Miwok and Paiute people who have inhabited the park since 1850. Nearby, the **Yosemite Valley Visitor Center** offers insights into how Yosemite's spectacular landscape was formed; it also features a replica of a giant sequoia base, a bear cave, and a glacier. Since 1902, the **Ansel Adams Gallery** has preserved Native American history and featured the famous photographer's work. The **Pioneer Yosemite History Center** transports kids to the park's early days. In winter, the **Yosemite Ski School** by the south entrance offers programs for kids and ski novices. In the west, **Badger Pass Ski Area** is equipped with five lifts and classes for the little ones. Summer is the time for rafting along the **Merced** and **South Fork Rivers** or kayaking on the calmer waters of the **Tenaya Lake.**

Yosemite National Park
Yosemite National Park, CA 95389
209-372-0200
www.nps.gov/Yose, www.yosemitethisyear.com

The Northwest

In this part, we turn to the Northwest to share some of the best family destinations in Alaska, Oregon, and Washington. Scientists believe the rich culture of the region began about 14,000 years before the first Europeans reached the Northwest, when tribes from northern Asia migrated to southern Alaska and British Columbia. The social structure, agricultural skills, and communities established by these immigrants were very sophisticated, and their rich culture was strong enough to withstand the onslaught of later European settlers.

In time, the Pacific Northwest's vast natural resources made it attractive to the world. Jonathan Swift wrote about the Northwest in *Gulliver's Travels* (1726) even before Russian explorer Vitus Bering discovered the Bering Strait. Englishman James Cook moored on Vancouver Island in 1778 for a month of scientific discovery, and one of his sailors, George Vancouver, later returned on his own. Lewis and Clark wrote about reaching the Columbia River in 1805 with details of Native American life, natural history, and geography. In the nineteenth century, greenhorns came to settle the land and crowd out the Native Americans, forever changing the region.

Vacationers can expect a region in which exciting cities and distinctive multicultural attractions are within an hour or two drive of a major national park, a fantastic ski mountain, incredible waterfalls and rivers, and the beauty of a rugged Pacific Ocean coastline.

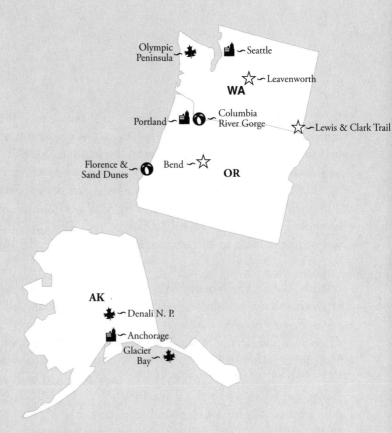

Olympic
Peninsula ⟶ 🍁

🏭 ⟶ Seattle

☆ ⟶ Leavenworth

WA

Portland ⟶ 🏭 🔴 ⟶ Columbia
River Gorge

☆ ⟶ Lewis & Clark Trail

Florence &
Sand Dunes ⟶ 🔴

Bend ⟶ ☆

OR

AK ·

🍁 ⟶ Denali N. P.

🏭 ⟶ Anchorage

Glacier
Bay ⟶ 🍁

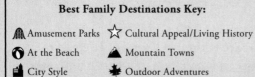

┌───┐
│   **Best Family Destinations Key:**   │
│   │
│ 🎡 Amusement Parks   ☆ Cultural Appeal/Living History │
│   │
│ 🔴 At the Beach   ⛰ Mountain Towns   │
│   │
│ 🏭 City Style   🍁 Outdoor Adventures   │
└───┘

City Style

In This Chapter

- Anchorage's civilized outpost in the Last Frontier
- Hip Portland's clean, green ethos
- Seattle's richly satisfying urban experience

A chapter devoted to the best cities of three of the most far-flung states might raise some eyebrows, especially when compared to more cosmopolitan cities such as New York City or Miami. Yet it's the differences wrought by geography and a western spirit that make Anchorage, Seattle, and Portland special.

Here, an urban escape means finding culture in the history of indigenous people, the tales of survival, and the arts that flourish in harmony with the landscape. We think this contrast makes them among the best family destinations in the country, and we urge you to plan a Pacific Northwest getaway.

Anchorage, Alaska

The first thing you learn about Anchorage is that its motto, "Big Wild Life," is no idle boast. Just driving along the **Seward Highway** to the popular cruise ship port at **Seward** will reward you with views of white whales cavorting in the cold water at **Beluga Point.**

Anchorage is Alaska's largest city and constitutes more than 40 percent of the state's total population. It lies slightly farther north of the equator than the Scandinavian capitals of Oslo or Stockholm—even farther north than Helsinki, Finland, or St. Petersburg, Russia—yet is situated at the southern side of the state rightfully considered America's Last Frontier.

Anchorage grew from humble beginnings in 1914 as the site of a railroad construction port for the **Alaska Railroad.** Fifty years later, it was humbled by the magnitude 9.2 **Good Friday Earthquake,** the second largest temblor ever recorded anywhere. Anchorage rallied, and four years later in the midst of rebuilding, oil was discovered in **Prudhoe Bay.** The city has been growing ever since.

It has a rich, well-documented history that comes alive at its wonderful museums and sites. The **Anchorage Museum at Rasmuson Center** starts with the region's indigenous people and early explorers, then continues to chronicle Alaska's statehood (1949) and the Alaska Pipeline project.

The **Alaska Native Heritage Center** contains traditional village settings and cultural artifacts of the Eskimo, Aleut, and Indian peoples who pioneered the techniques necessary for living on this inhospitable land.

> **FUN FACTS**
>
> At 570,374 square miles, Alaska is the largest state in the union—one fifth the size of the entire Lower 48. With a population nearing 700,000, there is nearly 1 square mile of land for *each resident.*
>
> Alaska is called Land of the Midnight Sun because in summer, there is no true night—only a short period of twilight after 11 P.M. At the summer solstice, June 21, Anchorage receives 19.5 hours of sunlight. Just try getting to sleep!

Like all of Alaska, Anchorage features a variety of scenic adventures for all ages—most just outside the city. About 40 miles north in **Wasilla** is the **Iditarod Trail Headquarters.** This small museum celebrates the dogs and their mushers (masters) who race annually all the way from Anchorage to **Nome** on the coast of the Bering Sea.

Since 1973, mushers with teams of 12 to 16 dogs have participated in the **Iditarod Trail Sled Dog Race** along a 1,150-mile-long frozen route once used to haul mail, supplies, and people during the 1920s Gold Rush era. As told in the museum's film, the advent of small planes and snowmobiles caused the trail to be abandoned until the first race, when 22 brave dog teams crossed the finish line in 10 to 17 days. Dog sledding is the state's official sport, and here kids will have a chance to talk with a musher or take a short dog sled ride (available May to September). For animal lovers, there are also a **Musk Ox Farm** and a **Reindeer Farm** in nearby Palmer.

You shouldn't leave Wasilla without a stop at the **Museum of Alaska Transportation and Industry** to poke around trains, planes, and automobiles. Train buffs will be jazzed by the HO-scale train set. There really is something for the entire family here.

Check out a **Kenai Fjords** tour that combines a journey on the **Alaska Railroad** with a sightseeing vessel to tour the picturesque fjords and **Resurrection Bay.** Cruising past glaciers among fjords, inlets, and islands provides a great opportunity to see frolicking sea otters, puffins, eagles, sea lions, humpback and Minke whales, and other wildlife.

Just 40 miles south of Anchorage, the **Alyeska Ski Resort** offers year-round adventures such as paragliding, river rafting, kayaking, horseback riding, flightseeing, dog sledding, glacier hiking, and fishing. Many families come in winter for the alpine and cross-country skiing, snowboarding, snowshoeing, and ice skating or the more extreme pursuits of heli or snowcat skiing.

Freezing from touring glaciers and snow-covered mountains? Feel like taking off your mukluks and putting on a bathing suit? Take the entire family to **H2Oasis** in Anchorage, where it's always 86° and you will find an indoor wave pool, lazy river, children's lagoon, and an uphill water coaster!

Anchorage Convention and Visitors Bureau
907-276-4118
www.anchorage.net

Portland, Oregon

The most populous city in Oregon, **Portland** has a reputation for being a laid-back yet sophisticated town where outdoor recreation and culture are given equal billing. For its young, prosperous, and environmentally friendly residents, the heart of the old city is the **Saturday-Sunday Market.** Weekends from March to December, this functioning food and dry goods market is a fun place to dine at ethnic food stalls (excellent Philippine noodles!); see the work of more than 350 craft vendors; listen to world music; and shop for friendship bracelets, batik scarves, antique teapots, and fine art.

When you leave the market, stroll around **Old Town,** a fun neighborhood to explore any day because of its **Chinatown,** entered through a ceremonial gate donated by Portland's sister city of Kaohsium, Taiwan. The neighborhood has dozens of old cast-iron buildings that have been converted into lofts and entertainment venues. Allow time for a visit to the **Classical Chinese Garden,** a lovely Ming Dynasty–style garden.

Active families will enjoy a full-day bicycle ride on rental mountain bikes from one of the shops in the **RiverPlace Marina** development. This is a safe activity for all ages thanks to a scenic mile-long, car-free zone in **Portland's Waterfront Park** along the Willamette River. From late April to early October, speed demons can park their bikes and strap themselves in for a guided **Willamette Jetboat Excursion.** Seeing Portland from its river provides the perfect opportunity to enjoy the view of some of the many notable bridges.

Washington Park, the city's crowning gem, has enough hills to provide a thorough workout for hikers and bikers. The park is home to a pretty Japanese garden and an arboretum as well as **The Portland Children's Museum,** featuring water play, art studios, and moving toys; and the **World Forestry Center,** where families can learn about smokejumpers and loggers as well as sustainable forestry practices. The noted **Oregon Zoo** fosters many conservation and public education programs and entertains families with a summer concert series, a winter Zoolights Festival, and a fun Zoo Railway.

VACATION PLANNING TIPS

Think twice before renting a car on your trip to Portland. An inexpensive train will whisk you right from the airport to the city. Once you're in the city, Portland's great public transit system makes cars unnecessary. Public transit is totally free within certain core areas of the city, and you can rent a bike or catch a hybrid bus to go longer distances.

For our family, indoor culture begins at **Powell's City of Books,** the self-proclaimed largest bookstore in the world whose welcoming atmosphere and kaleidoscope of displays makes it a real treat for all ages. Another child-friendly stop is the hands-on **Oregon Museum of Science and Industry,** which boasts an earthquake simulator, a planetarium, a real submarine, and a Science Playground for kids younger than eight that includes a water play area and puppet theater.

The **Portland Art Museum** houses a great contemporary art collection as well as exhibits on Native American art. Families will enjoy a stroll through the fun and hip **Pearl District,** which is full of galleries in renovated warehouses. **Nob Hill**—a teen magnet—is where more than 250 classic Victorian and Georgian mansions have been restored and turned into boutiques, galleries, and restaurants.

Portland truly has something for all ages and interests. Snow sports fans flock to **Mount Hood,** a year-round skiing and snowboarding mountain resort offering teen snowboarding clinics such as **Windells Camp** and a zip line adventure park all summer long. But the region is also known for its rock climbing, and beginners can hone their skills at the **Portland Rock Gym.** Armchair athletes may appreciate the **Oregon Sports Hall of Fame and Museum,** which exhibits Terry Baker's Heisman Trophy and other awards among several interactive sports challenges.

Travel Portland
1-800-962-3700
www.travelportland.com, www.traveloregon.com

Seattle, Washington

Seattle, the birthplace of Starbucks Coffee, Boeing, Amazon.com, Expedia, and other household brands, is a vibrant city surrounded by (and frequently misted with) water. One of the West Coast's urban jewels, it's a fun and family-welcoming place that is constantly evolving, so we like to return again and again. We suggest you begin with a stop at the **Seattle Center,** a 74-acre cultural center built on the site of the 1962 World's Fair that contains many of the best-known attractions.

Jump start the fun on the way to Seattle Center by hopping aboard the **Seattle Monorail,** linking the downtown area's shops and restaurants to the Seattle Center for a short but exciting ride. This unique form of eco-friendly transportation runs every 15 minutes in both directions.

Once you reach the center, you will be blown away by all it has to offer—the huge complex is home to theaters, museums, concert venues, and much more. The **Space Needle**'s glass-encased elevator will lift you 520 feet above ground, presenting a fabulous 360-degree panorama of downtown, **Puget Sound, Lake Union,** and **Mt. Rainier,** the snow-capped peak that crowns almost every Seattle vista. It's a great place to observe all the boat and seaplane activity that connects the commercial center with outer islands and to figure out the lay of the land.

> **FUN FACTS**
>
> **SkyCity,** the restaurant on top of the Space Needle, was the first revolving restaurant in the country when it was built in 1961. It makes a complete rotation every 47 minutes—fast enough for great views of the entire city but slow enough to not cause motion sickness.

Another must-see for toddlers and younger kids is the **Children's Museum.** Kids can shop in the child-size Neighborhood or visit the Artists' Studio, a wonderful drop-in workshop with a professional artist on staff. In the Technology Studio, older kids can record a song or become part of a video game. While you're at the Seattle Center, don't miss the **Pacific Science Center,** a huge science museum that features a planetarium, an IMAX theater, and many unique interactive exhibits. Teens may want to visit the nearby Experience Music Project (EMP), an interactive museum exploring the roots of American popular music and Seattle's local heroes, the Jimi Hendrix Experience.

If you have a family of outdoor enthusiasts, don't miss the **REI Flagship Store.** In addition to browsing all kinds of outdoor gear, shoppers can actually try on harnesses and shoes and climb an indoor, 65-foot-tall mountain. You can also test drive bikes on a dirt trail, climbing boots on a root-and-rock trail, and wet weather gear in a rain forest room. From there, pay a visit to **Lake Union,** where you can rent kayaks and canoes for guided or independent tours of the lake. Or board **Ride the Ducks of Seattle,** a 90-minute narrated tour by land and sea in an authentic World War II amphibious landing craft.

Across Lake Union, you will find **Gas Works Park,** built around a former gas-processing plant that once supplied Seattle's power. The park is a perfect spot for flying a kite or picnicking; some of the machinery in the plant has been cleaned up and painted, providing great climbing adventures for the little ones. A short drive away from the park is the **Woodland Park Zoo,** an award-winning botanical garden where you and your family can come face to face with Komodo dragons and more than 300 other animal species.

For a taste of old Seattle, visit the **National Historic District** on the waterfront; **Pike Place Market** is a charming shopping center where you can buy produce and fish from among 100 farmers and fishmongers or crafts created by 200 local artists. Look for the 14 painted musical notes scattered around on the sidewalks. These are the spots where street performers entertain on a rotating basis with music, puppetry, and theater in addition to scheduled live jazz, Dixieland, and opera performances. You can also visit the **Original Starbucks.**

FELLOW TRAVELERS SAY ...

"One can enjoy everything from Seattle's famous Space Needle to regional food, fun, and fantastic sightseeing opportunities. Don't leave Seattle without getting out on the water at least once. We had a blast kayaking for the first time on **Lake Washington.** Each of the members in the family [also] picked one excursion they wanted to do. My sister's was a doll museum. Needless to say I was appalled at the idea of visiting a doll museum. **Rosalie Whyel Museum of Doll Art** was a fascinating spot, even for a 16-year-old boy who normally would not be caught dead around dolls. There are more than 1,200 items featured ranging from old to new dolls, teddy bears, toys, dollhouses, miniatures, and other childhood paraphernalia. They are artfully displayed, making them easy to look at and enjoy."

—N. K., www.travelBIGO.com

Before you leave this lively city by the Pacific, don't forget to take the family to the **Seattle Aquarium,** home to more than 400 species of marine life, where you can take in underwater views through The Dome and touch sea creatures in the Discovery Lab. For other unique maritime experiences, visit the **Hiram M. Chittenden Locks,** where you can watch an impressive parade of sailboats, motorboats, tugs, barges, and yachts as they navigate through the locks; or take a ride on the **Washington State Ferry System,** which carries commuters to Bainbridge Island, Bremerton, and the Kitsap Peninsula.

Seattle's Convention and Visitors Bureau
206-461-5800
www.visitseattle.org, www.experiencewa.com

Cultural Appeal

In This Chapter

- Celebrating Oregon's fascinating ecology at Bend's High Desert Museum
- Taking in Alpine culture at Leavenworth's little Bavaria
- Following in the footsteps of America's greatest explorers on the Lewis & Clark Trail

When our family thinks of the Northwest, we envision gray cliffs overlooking a churning sea, forests of dark evergreens, towering totem poles, vibrant Chinatowns, and a holistic, eco-friendly approach to life among the laid-back citizens of the region.

With a wide and multicultural array of attractions in Oregon, Washington, and Alaska to choose from, we have selected three destinations that are among the best at communicating their culture with visitors of all ages.

High Desert Museum and Bend, Oregon

Bend is a high desert mountain town that claims to receive more sunshine than the rest of Oregon and welcomes active families to explore its diverse recreational offerings. Considered a good base camp by mountain bikers, hikers, and rock climbers venturing into the **Cascade Mountains,** it is also home to young families who relish an eco-friendly lifestyle and the fine windsurfing on the lakes that surround it.

Visitors can gain a thorough understanding of the local culture— and meet animals they could never approach in the wild—in an afternoon spent at the fascinating **High Desert Museum.** This unusual learning complex offers a replica of a mining camp and several living history displays about the **Oregon Trail.** This major migration route through central Oregon was used in the mid-nineteenth century by miners seeking riches, ranchers looking for land, and settlers hoping for a new life in the Pacific Northwest. The trail defined a generation of American history.

The museum is also home to rescued animals native to the North-west, including bobcats, lynx, horned owls, river otters, falcons, and other birds of prey. Thrills (and possibly chills) await in the Desertarium, an exhibit of indigenous reptiles—such as Gila monsters and rattlesnakes—which kids can study up close.

FUN FACTS

Want to adopt a rattlesnake? For as little as $20 per year, your family can adopt one of the rescue animals at the High Desert Museum. You'll receive periodic reports on the animal's welfare and the knowledge that you're helping save a wild animal's life.

A pathway takes visitors through 100 years of life in Bend with a chance to talk to costumed interpreters. We loved visiting a mining camp, watching the Wells Fargo Express, and learning about mending clothes from a local seamstress. Kids get a chance to help out with the daily chores (something they may have no interest in at home!) of the Blair family cabin and can learn how to churn butter, split wood, and dip candles—chores the pioneers of the High Desert did to survive. There's also a working sawmill from the 1800s and a ranch house typical of the region long ago. The High Desert Museum also has fine arts galleries and more traditional exhibits that illustrate the lives of early fur traders and the difficulties of life on the Oregon Trail. The By Hand Through Memory exhibit focuses on Plateau Native Americans during the Reservation Era, the changes that have affected them, and how they've retained their identities. The Whose Home? Exhibit is an ideal place for kids to let off some steam in a nature-themed playground.

Once you've learned about the region's history and culture, spend a day or two exploring the town. Life in Bend certainly benefits from its proximity to beautiful **Mt. Bachelor,** with a peak that reaches just over 9,000 feet into the sky, a vertical drop of nearly 3,500 feet for skiing and snowboarding, and an average annual snowfall of 370 inches. The mountain's 3,683 acres of trails and back country are accessible by lift.

The **Lava Lands Visitor Center,** located in **Deschutes National Forest,** showcases the local geology and ecology of Bend with a cool exhibit on the volcanic activity of the Cascade Mountains. Younger family members enjoy visits to nearby **Paulina Lake,** where they are able to test the weight and buoyancy of rocks and experience the sights and sounds of an active volcano. **Wanderlust Tours** is one local company that offers canoe, cave, and volcano tours in the summer—both during the day and under moonlight—and snowshoe outings in winter.

When the family is ready to relax, they'll enjoy this foodie haven with its strong emphasis on micro-breweries, wine bars, and organic restaurants featuring locally grown seasonal produce. A wonderful civic reuse project, **The Old Mill** is a 270-acre development filled with cafés and good restaurants surrounding what was once a lumber mill on the **Deschutes River.** The original three-chimney powerhouse is home to the outdoor clothing and gear mecca, **REI.** Remnants of another mill up the river have been incorporated into a park with a riverfront beach and a great kids' **logging mill–themed playground.** Just watch them play on the water wheel, buzz saws, and logs.

High Desert Museum
59800 South Highway 97
Bend, OR 97702
541-382-4754
highdesertmuseum.org, www.visitbend.com

Leavenworth, Washington's Bavarian Village

A small town in Washington State located at the base of the 8,000-foot Cascade Mountains, Leavenworth is a slice of Bavarian culture in the middle of America. More than 100 unique shops and restaurants invite families to explore the town that boasts the appearance and ambiance of the Alpine mountains of Germany. Leavenworth is a four-season destination that attracts more than two million visitors a year with colorful festivals and outdoor recreational activities.

The German heritage is taken very seriously in Leavenworth. Imagine "Heidi"-style white stucco homes with little ornate wood balconies, horse-drawn carriages, and guys wearing *lederhosen* marching with an oompah band. Yes, you can eat *wiener schnitzel* and buy cuckoo clocks. Year-round, the village hosts a variety of family-friendly Bavarian-themed festivals. Celebrating the winter months, Leavenworth puts on a popular **Bavarian Ice Festival** each January. A hearty **Kinderfest** takes place on July 4th, and fall events include **Oktoberfest** and an annual **Autumn Leaf Festival.**

FUN FACTS

Although widely visited for its recreation of Bavarian culture, Leavenworth was not originally a German town. The land, initially home to the Yakima, Chinook, and Wenatchi Native American tribes, was settled in the 1890s by pioneers seeking riches through gold and fur. Leavenworth blossomed when the Great Northern Railway was constructed through town, but when trains were rerouted in the 1960s, the village nearly collapsed into extinction. The idea to rebuild the town with a German theme was meant to promote tourism to the region. It worked!

Located near the **Wenatchee National Forest,** Leavenworth offers outdoor fun aplenty. Summer days can be spent mountain biking, whitewater rafting, or kayaking on the **Wenatchee River** adjacent to the town. Consider rock climbing or backpacking in the **Alpine Lakes Wilderness;** horseback riding and hiking are other popular activities. And under a blanket of snow each winter, the village of Leavenworth also hosts a cross-country ski course at its golf course, a small downhill ski area, snowmobiling trails, and horse-drawn sleigh rides through town.

Nearby **Wenatchee** is the self-proclaimed Apple Capital of the World. Visit some of the town's 3,500 growers and watch the sorting and packing of apples for distribution all over the world. **The Washington State Apple Commission Visitors Center** offers a souvenir shop and free samples of fruit and juice.

To commemorate the area's agricultural roots, the **Chelan County Fair** takes place each September. The first weekend of October brings **Cashmere's** famous **Apple Days Celebration.** In the springtime, when all the orchards are abloom, there is the **Washington State Apple Blossom Festival,** an 11-day carnival that occurs in late April and early May.

Leavenworth Chamber of Commerce
509-548-5807
www.leavenworth.org, www.experiencewa.com

Lewis & Clark Trail, Washington-Idaho-Oregon

In 1803, Virginian and frontiersman Meriwether Lewis prepared to embark on a long and arduous journey with his former Army captain and friend William Clark that would forever place the pair on the map of American history. Imagine the zeal their **Corps of Discovery** must have felt when they arrived at the final leg of their three-year, 4,600-mile journey across an uncharted land. Today, you can simulate their wilderness experience by more comfortable means.

The town of Spalding is home of the **Nez Perce Cultural Museum,** which details relations between the corps and the Nez Perce (pronounced *"nayz piers"*) Indian tribe. For a more outdoorsy experience, head to **The Sacajawea Interpretive, Cultural, and Education Center** in Salmon, Idaho, where visitors can get some insight on one of the most significant players in the history of westward expansion: Sacajawea, the teenage Shoshone mother and the Corps' guide.

From the tri-cities—composed of Kennewick, Pasco, and
Richland—in southeast Washington, amateur explorers can create
their own expedition at Pasco's **Sacajawea State Park,** where Lewis
and Clark camped and traded with local tribes in October 1805.
Learn more at the interesting **Interpretive Center,** then head outdoors for a picnic or encourage the kids to expend some energy at
Columbia Park in Kennewick, site of the **Family Fishing Pond**
converted from a stagnant lagoon, the **J&S Dreamland Express**
train constructed from donated airline baggage cars, and a splashy
children's water feature.

During the drive west along the **Columbia River** (explored in more
depth in Chapter 28), the vegetation turns greener, hills rise more
dramatically above, and Oregon's Mt. Hood begins to peek across
the water. Windsurfers and kite boarders skate across the river in
swarms.

Lewis and Clark reached the Pacific Ocean at Washington's
southwestern-most tip of Long Beach in November 1805 and
ended the westbound portion of their expedition in the land
of the Chinook Indians. Travelers today enjoy the quirky beach
town atmosphere, especially in summer.

Cape Disappointment State Park features a number of hiking trails
as well as the **Lewis and Clark Interpretive Center.** Built back in
1975, this museum effectively juxtaposes journal entries with Corps
of Discovery memorabilia, making for a fascinating visit. Nearby
North Head Lighthouse, one of two operating lighthouses on
the peninsula, conducts tours daily during the summer. It helps
guide ships through the especially rough and shipwreck-prone Cape
Disappointment, nicknamed the "Graveyard of the Pacific." Look up

in the sky in Long Beach and you might see a kite or two or twenty. Kiting is a popular hobby in this area, as reflected by the presence of the **World Kite Museum.** Here, kids can make their own kites and learn about the kites of different cultures.

The proper end to a Lewis and Clark journey through southern Washington requires crossing the Columbia River to Astoria, Oregon. This is where the Corps of Discovery encamped during the winter of 1805–1806 before their return journey. **Fort Clatsop National Memorial** replicates their experience, with costumed interpreters giving programs in the summer and a year-round visitor center. On the way there, you may spot some elk—an important source of food for Lewis and Clark.

Lewis & Clark National Historic Trail NPS Office
Omaha, NB 68102
402-661-1805
www.nps.gov/lecl, www.lewisandclarktrail.com

At the Coast

In This Chapter

- Playing in and around the Columbia River Gorge
- Visiting North America's highest peak in Denali National Park
- Having a blast at Florence's Sand Dunes National Recreation Area
- Taking in Glacier Bay National Park's stunning scenery
- Road-tripping along the Olympic Peninsula

The stunning Pacific Ocean coastline of the Northwest invites families to picnic, fly kites, play in the sand, cruise by and admire the beauty, and do almost anything *but* get into the water or sunbathe. Cold and dangerous, we can only recommend swimming, boating, and other water sports to families who know these waters well. For the rest of you, we detail three quite wonderful attractions located on the various coastlines of a region surrounded by water.

Columbia River Gorge, Oregon-Washington

The Columbia River begins in southeastern British Columbia, flowing for more than 12,000 miles before reaching the Pacific Ocean. In the very last stretch, erosion from the river cut the beautiful **Columbia River Gorge,** a 4,000 foot-deep, 80-mile-wide canyon whose scenic beauty surprised even the explorers Lewis and Clark.

VACATION PLANNING TIPS

If you are coming from the Oregon side, try taking the **Historic Columbia River Highway**—the first planned scenic highway in the United States. The 75-mile stretch offers breathtaking views of the area, helping you sidestep that nagging question, "Are we there yet?"

Perhaps the most famous sight along the highway is **Multnomah Falls,** a series of nine waterfalls that can be easily seen by taking a short hike from a roadside parking lot; a beautiful stone and wood lodge dating from 1925 at the site makes a good rest stop.

With 77 cascading waterfalls on the Oregon side alone, the gorge region is perfect for water lovers, with both guided and DIY opportunities for fishing, boating, waterskiing, and whitewater rafting. Those with smaller kids might want to do a cruise on the historic sternwheelers with **Portland Spirit River Cruises.** Tracing the steps of Lewis and Clark's **Corps of Discovery** along the Columbia River, you and your kids can take in the scenic views of the nearby **Cascade Mountain Range,** home to 14 major peaks including **Mt. Hood, Mt. Adams,** and **Mt. St. Helens.** Follow the footsteps of these two historic explorers and make your own unique discoveries (detailed in Chapter 27).

Another great option for families with little kids is the **Mt. Hood Railroad.** From April through December, you can take in the scenic views while on a two or four-hour excursion. If you are looking for more adult activities, this area supports 30 wineries and 50 vineyards, and a winery tour is a fun option for a relaxing break from the rigors of active exploration.

The Gorge offers exciting museums and visitor centers to help your family understand the area's history. As a popular summer destination, the Columbia River Gorge can get very busy, so we recommend making reservations well in advance—especially if you're interested in camping at the nearby **Memaloose State Park** or **Viento State Park.** If you prefer topause at Mt. Hood, the **Timberline Lodge,** a great base for summer skiing and snowboarding, was built in the late 1930s as a W.P.A. project from huge timbers with incredible carved details. It is a symbol of the Pacific Northwest and can be seen in several movies, including *The Shining.*

Columbia River Gorge Visitor's Association
1-800-98-GORGE
www.crgva.org, www.experiencewa.com

Denali National Park and Preserve, Alaska

Since its discovery more than a century ago, this Alaskan wilderness has been a symbol of hope. Be it the determined miners digging through rock and weathering the elements in search of a small nugget of gold or mountaineers looking to score a personal triumph on **Mount McKinley,** Denali National Park has continued to attract thrill seekers from around the world.

> **FUN FACTS**
>
> It is said that on a disastrous expedition to find a suitable route to Denali's goldfields, the 8th Cavalry was rescued from starvation by the Indians of Telida village. Their chief discovered the lost and tired Army contingent when he cut open a bear that had just robbed the white men's food cache; the bacon he found inside the bear's stomach indicated that the Cavalry party was near.

To really comprehend the area's remarkable history, head to the **Denali Visitor Center** to see the 20-minute film *Heartbeats of Denali.* Next door at the **Alaska Railroad** train depot, your family can board one of five sightseeing trains. The most popular, the **Denali Star,** runs two trains south from Fairbanks to Anchorage and back, and all trains generally operate daily in summer and weekends during winter months.

The 92-mile-long **Denali Park Road**—the only road in the park—whips through steep valleys and over high mountain passes. During summer, private vehicles are permitted to drive the first 15 miles to **Savage River** but may not proceed beyond this point. To venture deeper into Denali, guests can arrange a bus trip at the **Wilderness**

Access Center, located at mile 1 on the Park Road. Sightseeing options range from hop-on/hop-off park shuttles to guided tour buses and courtesy shuttles that travel between various facilities, campgrounds, and day-use areas.

Visible everywhere is the looming giant, Mount McKinley (called Denali or "the great one" by the Athabaska Indians), whose lofty snow-clad summit reaches 20,320 feet. The highest mountain on the North American continent, Mt. McKinley is still growing at a rate of about one millimeter per year thanks to ever-active plate tectonics. The park has hundreds of glaciers as well; the largest, **Kahiltna Glacier,** spans 44 miles. Other notable glaciers include the **Muldrow, Ruth,** and **Peters glaciers.**

The National Park Service has plenty of activities in store, ranging from early summer programs at several of the area's campgrounds to sled dog demonstrations with the park kennel's fierce and beautiful Alaskan huskies. Daily guided walks are also offered from both the Denali and **Eielson** visitor centers. On these short, moderate treks, hikers might get the chance to spot grizzly bears, caribou, moose, Dall's sheep, or golden eagles. Trails are mostly centered around the Denali Visitor Center, which makes going-it-alone hikes easier for novice map readers.

Nearby, the **Murie Science & Learning Center** serves as the park's winter visitor center and offers similar exhibits inside.

 FELLOW TRAVELERS SAY ...

"My family enjoyed our wonderful stay at the Kantishna Roadhouse in Denali Park, Alaska. My children, ages 11 and 13 at the time, were thrilled by hiking to see a glorious view of Mt. McKinley. Some other memorable places we visited were Haines, the Raptor Center, Barrow, and the Kenai Peninsula. Our knowledge of eagles, whales, and glaciers grew from our Alaskan vacation, and the kids began a real love for the environment there ...."

—C. G., www.FamilyTravelForum.com

Winter in the park opens up endless snow sport activities, including snowshoeing and cross-country skiing. Denali National Park even celebrates an annual **Winterfest,** generally taking place in February and featuring festive events such as snow sculpting competitions.

Denali National Park & Preserve
Denali Park, AK 99755
907-683-2294
www.nps.gov/dena, www.travelalaska.com

Florence, Oregon, and Sand Dunes National Recreation Area

Sandland Adventures is the place to begin any visit to **Florence,** gateway to the spectacular 32,000-acre **Sand Dunes National Recreation Area.** Sandland has led guided dune buggy tours through the park since 1978, revealing the beauty of fine white sand dunes—some as high as 80 feet—rolling between clusters of Douglas fir and Ponderosa pine that have survived the region's geological fluctuations for more than 6,000 years.

Your family will love flying across the ridges of dunes and skidding around turns, all at 50 mph. Every few minutes, guides stop to explain how the region had been under the ocean thousands of years before or how the continuous wind and shifting sand created this natural playground that seems immune to man's intrusion.

The much slower classic group tour covers the area in a one-hour guided tour aboard a slow and steady dune bus holding up to 24 passengers. Much taller than the buggies, these provide a bird's-eye view of the amazing scenery and views past the dunes to the often-foggy beach and Pacific Ocean beyond. After your ride, stick around to take a spin on Sandland's go-kart track, or try the bumper boats, railroad, or miniature golf.

Sand Dunes Frontier rents ATVs to those brave enough to ride the dunes on their own. Frontier offers ATVs to licensed drivers and mini dune buggies to kids ages 10 to 15. They even offer two-seater MiniRails for parents with small children (who get strapped into the passenger seat; helmets mandatory). The company has a mile-and-a-half-wide play area within the dunes, where visitors can test drive their ATVs and practice climbing up and running down the dunes and digging out vehicles when they get stuck (a frequent occurrence).

For a more unique dune adventure, give sand boarding a try. **Sand Master Park** rents sand boards and encourages customers to ride their boards down its 40 acres of dunes.

Florence Area Chamber of Commerce
Florence, OR 97439
541-997-3128
www.florencechamber.com, www.traveloregon.com

Glacier Bay National Park, Alaska

Welcoming more than 300,000 visitors each year, **Glacier Bay National Park** is the most unique of our family destinations, with no roads leading to the park. To reach this UNESCO World Heritage site, you have to travel by air or sea.

Vast numbers of visitors arrive by cruise ship, because many cruise lines pass by on the way to the famous **Inside Passage.** Other options for intrepid families trying to reach this stunningly beautiful destination include tour, charter, and private vessels.

The only lodging option within the park is Glacier Bay Lodge near Bartlett Cove. The best aspects of the lodge are waking up to the beautiful view of the **Fairweather Mountain** range and being able to take their Glacier Bay Tour, which brings you face to face with the **Margerie** and **Grand Pacific Glaciers,** 2 of the 16 tidewater glaciers. On-the-ground excursions include whale watching, hiking, kayaking, and fishing.

From glaciers to snow-capped mountains, the park offers breathtaking views of fjords and ocean coastlines, with activities for true adrenaline junkies. **Alaska Mountain Guides** will take you on their one-day kayaking trip to Point Adolphus, a popular area for whales. Or step aboard the 45-foot-long, 23-passenger *Taz* for a day cruise to see humpback whales do their acrobatics and listen to them harmonize. You'll welcome the boat's heated interior on chilly days.

FUN FACTS

In September 1899, an earthquake with a magnitude of 8.4 rocked through Glacier Bay National Park. According to studies done by the U.S. Geological Survey, it struck in Yakutat Bay, uplifting some beaches by as much as 45 feet and causing avalanches and a 48-foot tsunami. The few prospectors and settlers who lived within a 300-mile radius reported being knocked over by the shock. The quake shattered Muir Glacier, a popular sightseeing attraction, and destroyed the wooden passenger walkway installed there by steamship companies. It took a decade for tourists to return, and they haven't stopped coming since.

If you're planning to camp or kayak on your own amid the natural splendor, you must attend a training session at the **Bartlett Cove Visitor Center.** A free orientation will net you a permit for camping or kayaking, plus a bear-resistant food container. Permits are free and are required between May 1 and September 30.

Traveling with little kids means taming the extreme adventure, of course. A fun activity for the young at heart is the National Park Service **Junior Park Ranger** program, run from the NPS office on the second floor of Glacier Bay Lodge. NPS Rangers also board regularly scheduled vessels to hand out kids' workbooks, give lectures, and encourage safe wildlife viewing. In this park, kids between the ages of 2 and 6 can get their own coloring book (or download it from the NPS.gov site) and become a **Glacier Bay Pee Wee Ranger!**

Alaska Airlines offers daily jet service from nearby Juneau to **Gustavus** (about a half-hour flight) during the summertime. A 10-mile-long road stretches from the airport in Gustavus to Bartlett Cove in the park and onto Rink Creek Road. All the businesses and B&Bs in town are along these roads, and families are invited to stop for a map and tourist information. Summer temperatures in the area fall between 50 and 60 degrees, so be sure to bring your warm clothes and raingear, because it rains frequently in southeast Alaska.

Glacier Bay National Park, Alaska
Gustavus, AK 99826
907-697-2230
www.nps.gov/glba, www.travelalaska.com

Olympic Peninsula, Washington

Surrounded by virgin coastline and carved by more than 60 glaciers, the Olympic Peninsula celebrates the natural wonders of ancient rain forests, rough-hewn ocean beaches, and pristine lakes. Rising majestically in the center of this awesome natural paradise are the snow-capped, saw-toothed peaks of the **Olympic Mountains.**

FUN FACTS

Any *Twilight* fans out there? If so, be sure to visit the town of Forks, the setting for the popular vampire book series. Author Stephanie Meyer said she selected Washington's Olympic Peninsula because she was looking for "someplace ridiculously rainy." Due to logistics and production costs, however, many scenes from the movie were filmed in coastal Oregon and other parts of Washington.

With nearly 1 million acres of wilderness and more than 600 miles of hiking trails, the **Olympic National Park** is the region's main attraction. Explore giant forests of fir, hemlock, and cedar; sandy beaches; fields of wildflowers; bubbling springs; and more than 60 miles of coastline. At **Hurricane Ridge** in the Port Angeles area of the park, nature hikes deliver nearly 360-degree views of the Olympic Mountain Range, the **Strait of Juan de Fuca,** and the southern tip of **Vancouver Island.** On the ridge, you can find snow in summer and experience the 75-mph winds that give the ridge its name.

Another gem of the park is **Lake Crescent,** a 12-mile-long glacial lake that plunges more than 600 feet at its deepest point. This picturesque lake offers swimming, boating, and fishing as well as several diverse hiking trails. Some popular trail options for those hiking with kids include the Marymere Falls (a spectacular 90-foot waterfall just a mile from Lake Crescent), Mount Storm King Trail, and the Pyramid Peak Trail.

The park has so much to offer that it's difficult to decide what to do; fortunately, you can't go wrong with most of the hikes. Be sure not to miss the **Hoh Rainforest,** one of the few rain forests in the Northern hemisphere; **Mount Walker,** with panoramic views of

Puget Sound, Mt. Rainier, Mt. Baker, and the Cascades; and the **ocean beaches,** with more than 60 miles of sand and tide pools. If you're tired from your day of hiking, unwind in the **Sol Duc Hotsprings,** where you can take a soothing soak in any of the three mineral pools whose water temperatures range from 90°F to 105°F.

FUN FACTS

Legend has it that dragons once fought each other to the death in Sol Duc Valley, and their hot tears created Sol Duc Hotsprings.

Outside the park are another half-million acres of natural beauty. Kids of all ages will love the **Dungeness National Wildlife Refuge,** a magnet for marine life and water fowl boasting more than 250 species of birds, 41 species of land mammals, and 8 species of marine mammals. Or spend a day on the water in **Port Townsend,** where you can rent kayaks, rowboats, and sailboats or go scuba diving and snorkeling. At the **Port Townsend Marine Science Center,** kids can touch marine wildlife and get an up-close look at the animals that live in the waters around the peninsula.

While the Olympic Peninsula is known for its outdoor activities, that's not all it has to offer. Every Saturday, you can visit **Sequim's Open Aire Market,** where you can find vendors selling fresh produce and handmade art—a beautiful souvenir of the region's unique culture. Kids will enjoy picking their own strawberries and lavender in the fields nearby.

FELLOW TRAVELERS SAY ...

"My eyes opened wider as I tried to take it all in: the blinding snow fields, the tree trunks so large I could not wrap my arms around them, the meadows of wildflowers rolling over the landscape so endlessly that I was reminded of Oz. The timing of our vacation could not have been better, as we managed to come at the peak of the wildflower season and during an unheard-of sunny week near Seattle, the city of rain. We even had the rare opportunity to see Mount St. Helens from a crest on Mount Rainier when it was not enshrouded with fog. What impressed me the most was that in the relatively small radius of the park there is a snapshot of almost every major ecosystem in the world."

—L. N., www.travelBIGO.com

Olympic Peninsula Tourism Commission
Port Angeles, WA 98362
1-800-942-4042
www.olympicpeninsula.org, www.visitolympicpeninsula.com

Mexico, one of the richest tourist destinations in the world, is easily accessible to North Americans and offers an unforgettable, top-value family vacation. The country's natural beauty encompasses high mountains and exquisite sandy beaches in both the Atlantic and Pacific regions. Sophisticated cities have impressive historical centers, excellent museums, and friendly citizens who speak some English. World-class resorts here are generally a better value than comparable ones in the Caribbean or Hawaii.

The heritage of Mexico's ancient Olmec, Aztec, Teotihuacan, and Mayan civilizations has left countless archeological sites that provide a remarkable window into the past and a bounty of treasures for Mexico's museums. The cuisine is complex, delightful, and differs dramatically from American Tex-Mex. And unlike a generation ago, the assimilation of the Spanish language and arts by popular culture has made this foreign country seem familiar to all ages.

In this part, we focus on destinations that most traveling families will find interesting and comfortable. Many are found on the highly developed Yucatan Peninsula, famous for its sunbathing beaches, Mayan culture, and historic cities. The Pacific beaches have a stronger eco-appeal to adventuring families and naturalists. The country's interior has many fascinating cities and mountain towns with a variety of cultural attractions and activities.

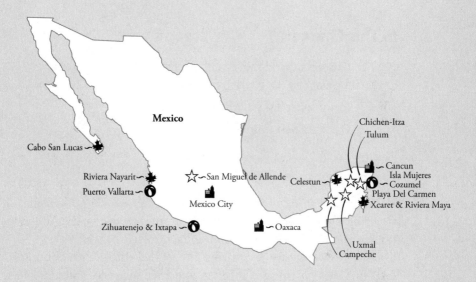

Mexico

Cabo San Lucas

Riviera Nayarit
Puerto Vallarta

San Miguel de Allende

Mexico City

Zihuatenejo & Ixtapa

Oaxaca

Celestun

Chichen-Itza
Tulum

Cancun
Isla Mujeres
Cozumel
Playa Del Carmen
Xcaret & Riviera Maya

Uxmal
Campeche

Best Family Destinations Key:

Amusement Parks   ☆ Cultural Appeal/Living History

At the Beach   ▲ Mountain Towns

City Style   Outdoor Adventures

City Style

In This Chapter

- Cancun's world-famous beach resort wrapped around a great city
- Mexico City's sky-high family fun
- Oaxaca's rich cultural heritage

When people think of Mexico, their thoughts usually go straight to the idyllic beaches of Quintana Roo on the Atlantic or the Acapulco-Ixtapa-Puerto Vallarta coast on the Pacific Ocean. Situated in between, however, are fascinating cities filled with rich traditions, long histories, distinctive cuisines, and friendly, welcoming people. Your kids will be able to practice their Spanish while being immersed in one of North America's most vital and fascinating cultures.

Safety issues—food, water, health, and personal safety—are the biggest concern for most families traveling to foreign countries. If you decide to go, be sure to take appropriate precautions and heed the safety advice of locals you meet. Some tips:

- The U.S.-Mexico border towns have been plagued by drug violence. Tourists should be very careful in these areas and avoid them if possible. Check the U.S. Department of State website at travel.state.gov for the latest alerts.

- In Mexico City, only use radio cabs or "sitio" cabs called by your hotel or restaurant. Do not hail a passing Volkswagen taxi or "libre" (free) taxi, which are implicated in many robberies and kidnappings. At the airport, use only the "official" authorized airport taxis after prepaying the fare at ticket booths inside the airport.

- Pick-pocketing and robbery are occasional issues in Mexico City. Watch your things; leave passports and valuables in the hotel safe; do not wear expensive jewelry or watches; and be careful where you walk at night. The concierge of your hotel will have up-to-date advice.

- Alcohol abuse is responsible for the majority of tourist arrests, violent crimes, accidents, and deaths in Mexico. Speak to your teens, especially those traveling without you on spring break. The legal drinking age is 18, but it is rarely enforced.

- Motor vehicle accidents are a leading cause of death of U.S. citizens in Mexico. Do not rent a moped without a helmet for every family member, and be alert for unexpected charges for damages or other fees.

- With regard to food safety: drink only bottled water and do not eat raw vegetables or fruits, except in well-established restaurants. Beware of spoilage at outdoor buffets in hot weather. Only fully cooked street food should be sampled.

Given the negative press in recent years about crime and safety in Mexico, we would be derelict if these problems were not addressed. Keep in mind that they affect only a tiny fraction of visitors to Mexico, and if travelers are aware and take appropriate caution, their trips can be trouble-free.

Cancun, Quintana Roo

Cancun has taken on a certain mythical status after three decades as one of the major resorts in the Western Hemisphere. Though its neighbor to the south on the **Yucatan Peninsula**, the **Riviera Maya,** has stolen some of this thunder, Cancun is still a major beach destination—now more upscale than ever after renovations following the hurricanes of 2005. Yet Cancun is also a city of more than 600,000 people with a rich local culture—albeit one that's seldom seen by tourists. It offers both beach and city pleasures and an excellent base from which to explore the rest of **Quintana Roo.**

Most families will go straight from the airport to their beachfront hotel, which will probably be in the **Zona Hotelera** where the parade of hotels goes on for miles. Many families will never leave the grounds of the hotel (for good reason). Clean, beautiful, crushed-coral sand beaches and warm, crystal-blue water line the number 7–shaped strip known as the **Cancun Peninsula.**

> **VACATION PLANNING TIPS**
>
> The Yucatan's naturally mild climate hovers in the mid-80°s F, with strong sun and brief daily showers in summer, some boisterous winds during the June to November hurricane season, and the occasional cold rain and wind between December and March. Breezes off the Gulf of Mexico keep the sea a perfect-for-kids 82°F to 86°F year round.
>
> When booking your resort, keep in mind that the hotels on the north side of the Cancun Peninsula (the top part of the 7) front the calmest seas. Most hotels sit on the peninsula's east coast, facing an Atlantic that can be deceptively gentle or stirred up by strong breezes, with an ever-present riptide. Many resorts have lifeguards stationed by color-coded warning flags, and even skilled swimmers are urged to swim within their jurisdiction. For weak swimmers, the hotel pool is your best bet.

When you venture beyond your resort, many recreational pursuits await. The Cancun Peninsula creates the large, protected **Laguna Nichupte,** a lagoon full of mangrove swamps with channels as well as open water. A number of small budget hotels face the calm, gentle lagoon, and this is also where tour operators launch kayaking, jet skiing, snorkeling, scuba, and parasailing tours as well as submarine cruises and dinner cruises. Also on the lagoon, a **Wet 'n Wild** water park has fun waterslides as well as an ever-popular swimming with dolphins program (more on that in Chapter 32).

For a bird's-eye view of the nearby Yucatan jungle, an excursion to **Selvatica** clips you onto the longest zip line (2 miles) in Mexico. Several ecotours also offer a day-long Mayan cultural experience mixing a zip line and swimming in a cenote (pronounced sen-NO-tay; a water-filled sinkhole) with Mayan food, music, and traditions, so you can learn about the region's indigenous Indians. A day trip to the world-class Mayan archeological site of **Chichen-Itza** (see Chapter 30) is another popular tour option.

Don't miss **La Casa del Arte Popular Mexicano,** a wonderfully small and dense folk art collection that will especially delight children. It's found at **El Embarcadero,** at the **Isla Mujeres** ferry pier (see Chapter 31), and the fun gift shop can take care of your entire souvenir shopping list. Next door is a gently swirling **Scenic Tower** ride that your little ones will enjoy.

You'll find great shopping and good prices in Cancun, especially in the locals' part of the city known as **El Centro.** At several mercados downtown, you'll find huarache sandals, *huipiles* (embroidered Mayan dresses), wood carvings, weavings, very stylish silver and pewter ware, talavera ceramics, pottery, and baskets. Along the main road of the hotel strip are modern air-conditioned shopping malls tucked into stucco façades.

FELLOW TRAVELERS SAY ...

"Swimming with [dolphins], these gorgeous, gentle creatures, and watching them perform numerous back flips and twists from such a close distance was enthralling. My favorite part was when the dolphins propelled us across the water by simply nudging our feet with their noses."

—J. S. www.travelBIGO.com

Kukulcan Boulevard is lined on the lagoon side with restaurants and clubs that provide a healthy and active nightlife. **The City** is the club of clubs, a giant of a disco known to American teens via *MTV Spring Breaks,* which tapes here. Leash your teens before they see the schedule of live nightly shows plus occasional major musical acts such as 50 Cent, Beyoncé, and Deep Dish. Kukulcan also hosts a variety of international shops, many of them high-end, plus the **Cancun Aquarium,** which has well-designed displays of local aquatic life.

For more local dining, don't miss the lively downtown restaurant row on **Calle Yaxchilan,** where a fine authentic meal can be had for a reasonable price and you won't be able to find a single chain restaurant. Also downtown, families can enjoy a stroll around the **Parque de las Palapas,** the city center's main public park. In this very cool quarter, several cafés serve both local and international cuisine, and small galleries showcase their art.

You can get around town via the excellent and inexpensive local bus system or by taxi. There are set rates, which you should confirm with your hotel concierge before setting out.

Cancun Tourism
Cancun, Q. Roo, Mexico
+52 (998) 881-27-45
cancun.travel

Mexico City, Distrito Federal

Situated between both coasts and the hub for many international flights, Mexico City offers an urban family experience rich with cultural gems, archeological treasures, and kid-friendly diversions. This is a huge, sprawling, bustling city, the center of which is almost European in look and feel. Careful planning is the key to enjoying it, because your plate will be full—both literally and figuratively—while becoming acclimated to an altitude of more than 7,000 feet. We like to start our visits at the **Zocalo,** a great initiation for families interested in history, culture, and Old World Mexico City.

 FUN FACTS

Mexico City's town square is called Zocalo (pronounced ZOH-ka-loe, and it's the third largest public square in the world after Beijing's Tiananmen Square and Moscow's Red Square.

The Zocalo is the heart of the architecturally preserved **Centro Histórico,** a designated UNESCO World Heritage Site. Along its perimeter, you'll find the **Catedral Metropolitana,** dating from 1567 and the largest cathedral in Latin America. The **Museo del Templo Mayor,** originally the center of Aztec religious life for

300,000 people, is both an archeological site and a museum on the square. In winter, the square hosts a huge ice-skating rink and one of the largest Christmas trees in the world. Along one side, the **Palacio Nacional** is a guarded building with government offices and priceless murals depicting Mexico's history by Mexican artist Diego Rivera. Entry is free.

Get out and create your own walking tour; don't worry about getting lost, because most residents speak English or welcome your Spanish student's efforts and will happily escort you to your desired location.

Top sights near the historic city center include the **Museo Interactivo de Economia (M.I.D.E),** or Museum of the Economy, dedicated to exploring the meaning of money in state-of-the-art, multimedia, bilingual ways that kids respond to regardless of their age. The imposingly beautiful **Museo del Palacio de Bellas Artes** houses one of the country's most significant fine arts collections and is well worth even a brief visit. In the downstairs theater, don't miss the twice-weekly performances of **Ballet Folklorico,** which features the traditional folk dances of each region performed in authentic costumes and set to wonderful music.

Surrounding the lovely **Plaza Alameda,** a public garden with vendors offering food and crafts on weekends, are other family-friendly attractions. The **Museo de Arte Popular** presents both contemporary and traditional folk arts from throughout the country and its store offers one of the richest troves of handicrafts in the city.

On the west side of the gardens is another treasure, the **Diego Rivera Mural Museum,** built to house the 60-foot-long mural by Rivera titled "Dream of a Sunday Afternoon in Alameda Park," which was rescued from the lobby of the Hotel del Prado after it collapsed during the huge 1985 earthquake. Walk the kids through the details of this autobiographical mural and the fascinating characters portrayed. It is an experience not to be missed. For an authentic shopping experience, head east to the **Mercado de la Merced,** one of the largest, most vibrant markets in the city.

VACATION PLANNING TIPS

One of the best ways to see and traverse the city is atop the **Turibus,** the best of breed among double-decker, guide-narrated, hop-on/hop-off sightseeing buses. It will drive past almost any sight you'll want to visit on one of its two routes (free transfer allowed between them). Plot your stops carefully, and opt for their two-day pass; it's a bargain. Chauffeured cars are available from every hotel, and although more expensive, they offer families more flexibility while sightseeing.

Plan to spend another day venturing out to **Paseo de la Reforma,** a boulevard leading through the **Zona Rosa,** one of the major upscale business and shopping areas, and on to **Chapultepec Park.** This park, once a hunting reserve for Aztec nobles, is one of the largest urban parks in the world and home to some major museums.

The **Museo Nacional de Antropologia** is considered by many to be Mexico City's premier attraction and one of the world's most important museums. Outside, the 18-foot monolith of Tlaloc fore-tells the extensive collection of priceless historical finds and cultural artifacts inside. The highlight is the massive Aztec Calendar Stone, which displays a dramatic vision of the cosmos; allow plenty of time to discover more riches. The nearby **Museo de Arte Moderno** has a large, permanent collection of Mexican painters including Frida Kahlo and Diego Rivera and foreign artists influenced by their work.

Also in the park, **Papalote Museo del Nino** is a superb modern children's museum housing interactive educational exhibits. There's also a Megapantalla, or IMAX, theater showing four different mov-ies daily. Everyone, from infants to teens to adults supervising them, will find something of interest here.

Be sure to ask your hotel concierge for a schedule of free performances in the park (it could be Aztec pole dancers, "Swan Lake" ballet, or cos-tumed acrobats) and current opening hours of attractions. If traveling with teens, consider booking a Segway Tour of the park.

Most visitors will want to explore the world of the famous Mexican artistic duo, Diego Rivera and Frida Kahlo. In the charming neigh-borhood of **Cocoyan,** filled with colonial homes and little shops, you can see **Casa Azul,** now the **Frida Kahlo Museum,** where she lived from 1929 to 1954—often with Diego in an intense and incendiary relationship. Her blue house is full of intriguing artifacts of their life and makes for a memorable tour, even for kids who can follow along with a free audio guide.

For a day trip out of the city and into the past, take a bus tour to **Teotihuacan,** the remarkable site of an ancient city first occupied around 500 B.C.E. and which peaked in 500 C.E. You'll see remnants of the Temple of Quetzalcoatl, Avenue of the Dead, and the celebrated Pyramids of the Sun and Moon, plus three museums full of artifacts.

And if your kids have had it with culture, you can throw in the towel and head to **Six Flags Mexico,** located on the southern edge of town. In addition to the usual array of American rides and coasters, you'll find the **Dolphinarium,** offering swims with the creatures.

Tourism Secretary of Mexico City
01-800-008-90-90
www.mexicocity.gob.mx

Oaxaca, Oaxaca State

With churches, museums, archeological sites, traditional fine art, and frequent festivals, **Oaxaca**—capital of the state of the same name—is a haven for families interested in authentic Mexican culture. While the legacy of pre-Hispanic civilizations makes this UNESCO World Heritage Site appealing to adults, all ages will enjoy the historic town center's colorful cobblestone streets, colonial architecture, wonderful shops and restaurants, nearby artisan villages, and the strong sense of history present in today's society.

Oaxaca and neighboring villages are at their best (and most crowded) during the major fiestas: **Guelaguetza,** a month-long summer celebration of dance, music, and a beauty pageant for the indigenous women of Oaxaca; **Dia de los Muertos,** a late-October ceremony for the dead that coincides with Halloween (and which may be frightening for little children); **Noche de Rabano,** followed by other Christmas parades, that show off the work of local artisans; and **Carnaval** and **Semana Santa,** which track the Catholic Easter season. Try to plan your visit around these or other recurring events, such as mariachi and state band performances or home games of the **Guerreros** baseball team.

Begin your tour in Oaxaca's **zocalo** (main square) lined with many historic churches and craft shops. **Santo Domingo de Guzman,** a former church and convent, is home to both the **Museo de las Culturas,** filled with art and religious treasures, and the **Museo Regional de Oaxaca,** with archeological treasures. The church is surrounded by the **Ethnobotanical Garden,** and across the street is **EL IAGO,** the graphic arts institute, where kids will enjoy a stop at their cafe for an ice cream break. A quick walk away is the **Rufino Tamayo Museum,** a typical courtyard home that houses the artist's personal collection of pre-Columbian and early Mexican ceramics and folk art.

At the **Plaza de la Constitucion,** stop by the **Mercado Benito Juarez,** where you can buy flowers, fruits, crafts, and various hand-made goods. This market is commonly referred to as "Mercado de la comida," due to the delicious foods that are offered. Kids will love the empanadas (pastry stuffed with meat or cheese), and their eyes will pop when they see the crunchy chapulines—fried grasshoppers in chili sauce, considered a delicacy. The plaza is the center of the action, surrounded by museums and government buildings such as the **Federal Palace.**

The Saturday bilingual hour at the **Oaxaca Lending Library** gives kids a chance to learn Spanish, while many Spanish language schools offer a kids' curriculum as well. The library can provide information about volunteer opportunities helping disadvantaged local children, another way to give back to this community.

If you or your children have an interest in the arts, the **Museum of Contemporary Art** has some intriguing sculpture and art objects sure to spark discussion; it's housed in Casa Cortez, one of the oldest buildings in the city. For local folk art, an eight-mile journey will take you to the **Museo Estatal de Arte Popular Oaxaca (MEAPO)** in the village of San Bartolo, Coyotepec. Those interested in eco-tourism can head to the rustic area of Sierra Norte for hiking and biking. **Tierra Ventura** arranges tours for eco-conscious travelers, educating visitors on the efforts of local crafts workshops to become greener.

TRAVELERS BEWARE!

Budget travelers staying in the many small B&Bs—typically cozy, welcoming, and well-maintained family homes—will find that laundry facilities are few and far between. Be prepared to hand wash your clothes. Paper products are scarce in public restrooms and restaurants, so bring your own packets of tissues, premoistened towelettes, and hand sanitizer.

If you're heading to one of the regional **Market Days,** where kids will enjoy seeing donkeys auctioned off and fresh tortillas being baked, you may pass **El Arbol del Tule,** a 2,000-year-old cypress tree. Here, local children dressed in Robin Hood attire will point out carved images in the trunk. At **Hierve el Agua,** a natural hot spring, you can heat up or cool off after a day of exploring the ruins. Of the many Oaxacan artisan villages—many of them quite impoverished—**Arrazola** is where local craftspeople create beautiful wood carvings of animals, and **Teotitlan del Valle** is where rug weavers show off their work and kids get to try the looms. Spanish speakers will find using public transportation such as buses and taxis easy and cheap; otherwise, ask your hotel to arrange for a reasonably priced driver/guide to help you explore the environs. It's well worth the cost.

This region has several archeological sites, but if you have an appetite for only one, let it be **Monte Alban,** just 30 minutes from Oaxaca. Set on top of a 6,400-foot-high plateau, this ancient city—one of the earliest in Mesoamerica—was home to the Zapotec people (who still live in the area today) and was a major power in southern Mexico from 500 B.C.E. to 750 C.E. In addition to several pyramids and an expansive ball court, there is a small museum whose glass floor protects a collection of bones excavated from the site, so make sure your kids watch where they're walking! Yagul and Mitla are two other sites featuring burial caverns worthy of a visit. Mitla is more grandiose, but Yagul has tombs that you can actually enter, creating a labyrinth-like atmosphere for young adventurers.

If your family has had enough of the hot and arid interior and craves some serious beach time, both **Puerto Escondido** and **Huatulco** are 150 miles west on the Pacific coast. A new four-lane road is scheduled to open in 2011, which will reduce the current painfully slow travel time to three hours. Puerto Escondido is a classic Mexican fishing village with great beaches and a more hippie crowd. Huatulco is a fully planned resort area not unlike Ixtapa or the original Cancun, with gorgeous beaches, newer condominiums, and resort hotels.

Oaxaca, Mexico Tourism
Oaxaca, Oaxaca, Mexico
1-800-44-MEXICO
www.visitmexico.com, www.oaxaca-travel.com/guide

Living History

Chapter

30

In This Chapter

- Fortified Campeche preserves elements of sixteenth-century life
- Glorious Chichen-Itza and other Mayan sites help visitors appreciate indigenous culture
- The tranquil, artsy mountain town of San Miguel de Allende

It is a testament to the vitality and depth of Mexico's culture that every one of the destinations we have chosen as best for bringing history to life is also a UNESCO World Heritage Site. This designation comes from the World Heritage Convention, a United Nations–sponsored group established in 1959 to select outstanding monuments of universal value—regardless of origin—to be preserved for the world's patrimony. To quote UNESCO, "By regarding heritage as both cultural and natural, the convention reminds us of the ways in which people interact with nature and of the fundamental need to preserve the balance between the two."

At these very different historical sites, you will learn how Mexico's indigenous peoples respected the connections between man and nature and see how this tradition continues today. We hope you'll find time during your vacation to visit at least one of these remarkable attractions and introduce the entire family to one small aspect of Mexican culture.

Campeche, Yucatan

Mexico's State of **Campeche** lies along the Gulf of Mexico on the western coast of the **Yucatan Peninsula.** With a history dating back to ancient times, this land was home to many sophisticated Mayan settlements built on the principles of advanced mathematics, engineering, and astronomy. The region's beachfront location, friendly people, and Mayan treasures make it an excellent destination for exploring Mexican history and culture with school-age children.

In Campeche City, you can stroll along quiet streets lined with brightly painted stucco houses, colonial mansions, and stone walls—all part of the UNESCO World Heritage–designated region. A principal port and valuable gateway in the Spaniards' quest to conquer the entire peninsula, Campeche was fortified in the sixteenth century after repeated assaults by Dutch and English pirates. Many of the fortifications have been repurposed; a stop at the **San Pedro Bulwark** will reveal handicraft vendors and a visitor's center with all the maps and information you need. The **Fort of San Miguel** houses the **Campeche Regional Museum,** featuring artifacts from the pre-Hispanic era and displays of colonial memorabilia such as cannons, a moat, and a drawbridge. At the **Fort of San Jose Alto,** the San Carlos Bulwark is now home to the **City Museum** and displays a scale model of the walled enclosure, with the prison and other rooms.

Between the **Puerta de Tierra** and the **San Juan Bulwark,** visitors can walk atop the only intact section of the old wall or attend a nightly multi-lingual **Sound and Light Show**—fun in a nerdy sort of way—recounting the struggle between natives and pirates, followed by a folkloric dance.

FUN FACTS

The woven straw Panama hat, worn by the men who built the Panama Canal, actually comes from **Becal,** the center of this indigenous craft. Created from the *jipi* palm and dyed with pigments from native plants, these distinctive sombreros are a labor-intensive endeavor requiring artistry and patience. You will certainly see many hats for sale throughout Mexico, but in Becal you'll get a real appreciation for this art form.

A tourist tram is available to cart you around, but if you're looking to explore on your own, walk to the **Zocalo**—a park dating from 1540— in the center of the city. Nearby is **House 6,** whose façade is typical of the lavish architecture of the seventeenth century. Now a cultural center, it provides a glimpse into the lives of wealthy European business owners and serves as an information center for tourists. The **Cathedral Church of Nuestra Senora de Concepcion** is also close by, as well as the state-run **Casa de Artesanias Tukulna Hand Crafts Shop,** where you can learn about and buy the best Mayan ceramics, hammocks, hats made from palm fronds, colorfully embroidered dresses and blouses, and woven items.

Kids will enjoy a stop at the **World Patrimony Plaza** for a 20-minute show of interactive musical fountains. The reconstructed waterfront, called the **malecon,** is great for taking a stroll, bicycling, or just relaxing beneath the rose-colored sunsets reflected on the calm Gulf of Mexico. South of the city are some natural beaches, not groomed like in resort areas but wilder: **Playa Bonita** is where the calm surf welcomes infants and toddlers to play; **Seyba Playa,** about 20 miles from the city, is known for its rock formations and clear water; and at **Siho Playa,** you can enjoy the waves of the gulf or try a delicious meal at **Tucan Siho-Playa,** a seaside resort on the beach just 30 minutes from Campeche.

Any aspiring Indiana Jones in the family should know that the archeological sites in Campeche are much less crowded than the more famous sites in the Yucatan and Quintana Roo. You can test your stamina by climbing pyramids at the former Mayan capital of **Edzna.** At this once-important economic, political, and religious center, buildings are linked to a series of canals, reservoirs, and cisterns that collected and circulated the community's most precious commodity. Near the Guatemalan border is another World Heritage site, **Calakmul,** located in the **Biosphere Reserve.** Surrounded by Mexico's largest rain forest jungle, this is one of the biggest Mayan sites ever discovered, with more than 7,000 structures. The stars of this stunning site—very hard to reach by land—are two enormous pyramids, each standing at about 174-feet tall. A sound and light show is presented here on weekends. Other noteworthy archeological sites include **Dzibilnocac, Tabasqueno, Dzibalchen, Nohcacab,** and **Toh-Cok.**

During the late nineteenth and early twentieth centuries, due to an increased demand for rope, many local ranches switched from cattle to the cultivation of the henequen or sisal plant, which can be made into rope fiber. Sprawling haciendas sprang up to house the prosperous European growers. When sisal was replaced with synthetic fiber, many of the haciendas became hotels in which you and your family can stay.

Secretary of Tourism for State of Campeche
Campeche, Campeche, Mexico
1-800-226-7324
campeche.travel, www.visitmexico.com

Chichen-Itza and the Mayan World of Yucatan

Many travelers are so dazzled by the sea and sand of Cancun and the Riviera Maya on Mexico's northeastern coast that they don't realize how close they are to some great archeological sites. The **Yucatan Peninsula** was a major center of the vast Mayan empire that developed and evolved between 2000 B.C.E. and 1500 C.E., and at its heart is **Chichen-Itza**, a UNESCO World Heritage site that was recently voted one of the "Seven Manmade Wonders of the World."

The golden age of the Mayan civilization from 250 to 900 C.E. produced sophisticated art, architecture, mathematics, and astronomy. In addition, the Mayans had the only fully developed written language in the pre-Hispanic Americas. When the Spanish conquistadores arrived in the early 1500s, they first targeted the highly developed and gold-rich Aztec cities in central Mexico. Although the Mayans lacked such riches and fought tenaciously, by the end of the century the Spanish had finally conquered them. Fortunately, families will find that many elements of the Mayan culture still flourish, whether in the artwork on display at all-inclusive beach resorts or the cuisine featured at trendy restaurants.

FUN FACTS

The Mayans thought pyramids held great power and favored high, back-sloping foreheads—resembling the sloping wall of a pyramid—in their royalty. To achieve this look, persons of aristocratic birth practiced cranial deformation—they shaped their infants' heads by applying boards held in place under pressure to gradually flatten their foreheads. Talk about blockheads!

Of the many Mayan centers in the Yucatan, Chichen-Itza, which means "at the mouth of the well of the Itza tribe," is among the largest, best excavated, and best preserved. Although the region seems hot and arid, underground rivers that feed natural sinkholes, or cenotes, caused the Mayans to build here. One of these, the **Cenote Sagrado** or Sacred Well, was the stage for several centuries of human sacrifice (kids love these stories!)—often an attempt to please the demanding rain god. Particularly impressive is the pyramidal **Temple of Kukulkan** (*El Castillo* in Spanish), which can no longer be climbed by visitors. The 6-square-mile site has about 30 buildings, many ornately adorned with intricate carvings of animals, plants, and figures (many now simply mounds).

Like all Mayan settlements, Chichen-Itza was organized around the temples and palaces of the rulers and supporting nobles. Because the Mayans were highly attuned to astronomy, buildings were carefully oriented to line up with stars and constellations. The Temple of Kulkukan is so precisely aligned and constructed that every year, on the day of the spring and autumn equinoxes, at about 3 P.M. local time, the sunlight moves across one side of the pyramid—throwing shadows in the shape of a serpent's body that moves down the structure's side to join a carved serpent's head at the bottom. Thousands of visitors come every year to observe this remarkable sight.

Every major Mayan city had **ball courts** where the game pok tap pok was played, and Chichen-Itza's was the largest in ancient Mexico. The goal of the game was to get the ball through the rings mounted in the wall without using your hands, although a racquet could be used. Some theories say that the captain of the first team to score a goal would later be decapitated; it was considered an honor to die this way with a guaranteed pass to heaven.

A small **museum** is on site, and in the evenings, the **Son et Lumière** (sound and light) show dramatizes the history of the Mayans at Chichen-Itza.

If you can pry the kids away from the beach, Chichen-Itza is fascinating to explore. However, you'll need to allow a long, full day for the experience, because it's 128 miles west of Cancun—about a two-hour ride—by comfortable tourist bus.

> **FELLOW TRAVELERS SAY ...**
>
> "Last winter, I traveled to the Yucatan with my parents. It was a very relaxing trip, and we got to explore quite a bit. My favorite part was definitely the Mayan ruins. It's best to not limit yourself to Chichen-Itza, because while it is very interesting, it's also quite overcrowded and you are not allowed to climb the famous pyramid (because of a "careless tourist"). We went to two other places and were permitted to climb to the top of some very tall structures, which was fascinating and exhilarating. I would also recommend visiting a cenote or two."
>
> —Neagan, www.FamilyTravelBoards.com

Consider staying the night and exploring more of the Yucatan state, which has a few small beaches on the northern and western sides. The colonial architecture and culture of the city of **Merida** makes it a good base, and it's near **Uxmal,** another extraordinary Mayan archeological site that is also a World Heritage site. The nearby **Flamingo Preserve at Celestun** is a special family experience, as well (see Chapter 32). Throughout this agricultural region are charming **haciendas,** former nineteenth-century plantation homes renovated and adapted as rural resorts—some of which are quite luxurious bases for a great family adventure.

Families based at a beach resort in the state of **Quintana Roo** who want to pursue Mayan culture will find two well-known but smaller archeological sites: **Tulum,** on the seaside within the town of funky thatch-roof cabanas and beach bars; and **Coba,** a large complex about 45 minutes inland from Tulum that's entangled in dense jungle. Smaller sites are dotted throughout the region and at **Xel-Ha** and **Muyil** on the Riviera Maya (covered in Chapter 32).

Chichen-Itza
Yucatan CP 97751 Mexico
1-800-44-MEXICO
www.chichenitza.com

San Miguel de Allende, Guanajuato

It's a beautifully preserved, sixteenth-century city filled with fine restaurants, art galleries, and Spanish-language schools that draw foreigners who love it so much they never leave. Welcome to **San Miguel de Allende.** This gorgeous cobblestone colonial town, recently named a UNESCO World Heritage Site, is in the eastern part of the mountainous province of Guanajuato, about 120 miles northeast of Mexico City.

> **VACATION PLANNING TIP**
>
> Check the local calendar before going to San Miguel de Allende to see whether there are any festivals during your visit. Some of the larger ones include **Sanmiguelada,** a religious festival each September, and the **Fiesta de San Antonio** in June, which celebrates the saint's day with fireworks, live music, and bullfights. There's always something going on in busy little San Miguel and for certain events, accommodation prices go up, so plan ahead.

Start your love affair with San Miguel by walking around the historic downtown. At the main square, **El Jardin,** you'll find families picnicking and using the free WiFi during the day or listening to mariachi bands at night. You can browse some of the great handcraft and antique shops filled with items made of hand-blown glass, gold, and silver. Art galleries and daily markets also abound in this neighborhood. A once weekly **flea market** takes place on the hilltop overlooking the city; it's a good place to see the view as well as search for local pottery, woven and embroidered articles, jewelry, clothing, and the stylish rope-soled espadrilles for which San Miguel is famous.

The city's temperate climate and low-cost, highbrow lifestyle have made it the choice of expats from around the world, and the local **Library** is their focal point. Here, you can find out what is going on by checking the English-language weekly for concerts, lectures, theater, and educational excursions to nearby towns. A highlight of any visit to San Miguel is the weekly house tour, usually on Sundays, organized by the library. Families who sign up will board a bus and see four of the most wonderful private homes around town. It's a fun way to get behind the façades of the city's most exclusive residential buildings, and even kids seem to enjoy the adventure. A nominal per-person charge pays for transportation and a small contribution to the library.

Pause your walking at the **Parque Juarez,** another public garden where you can join other families relaxing by the fountains. Some hotels have day spas where you can spoil yourself and your adult family members, but locals head to the nearby hot springs at **La Gruta.**

Architecture buffs should seek out the city's low-key colonial edifices, some of which exemplify the eclectic mix of architectural styles. **Parroquia de San Miguel Arcangel,** a parish church, has a beautiful neo-gothic pink stone façade while the interior features neoclassical influences. The eighteenth-century **Templo de la Concepcion,** a neoclassical church, was inspired by the Church of the Disabled in Paris.

FELLOW TRAVELERS SAY ...

"Suddenly, there was no world outside of where I was; there was only San Miguel. There were only cobblestone streets, burros walking the sidewalks, fresh mountain air, the smell of tortillas and *pan dulce* wafting from the bakeries, colorful colonial houses, and a serene stillness unmatched by any other place I have ever been. It was like we had gone back into another time—so much that I was surprised to see an old TV set playing idly in the corner of a restaurant ..."

—J. P. B., www.travelBIGO.com

San Miguel also has official museums: the **Oratorio de San Felipe Neri** displays more than 30 oil paintings, and **Templo de Nuestra Señora de la Salud** has the oldest bell in the city as well as a painting collection. The old residence of General Ignacio Allende, a leader of the Mexican independence movement, is now the **Museo Historico Casa de Allende.** Inside the house is a collection of weapons, documents, and other objects that belonged to the war hero.

San Miguel Tourist Office
Guanajuato, Mexico
1-800-44-MEXICO
www.visitmexico.com, www.internetsanmiguel.com

At the Beach

In This Chapter

- The Caribbean islands of Cozumel and Isla Mujeres
- Nightlife and shopping in Playa del Carmen
- Puerto Vallarta's romantic Pacific setting
- The twin west coast resorts of Zihuatanejo and Ixtapa

With nearly 5,600 miles of coastline and 150 rivers, Mexico offers families a wide variety of beach experiences. Whether you're interested in a gold-sand tropical paradise on the shores of the Caribbean or a rocky patch at the foot of a jungle-clad cliff overlooking the Pacific, you'll find it here.

Because most North American families come to Mexico for its beaches—and you're unlikely to get to more than one during your vacation—we encourage you to read the other chapters in this part to learn about the vibrant cities, rich cultural activities, historical sites, and unparalleled outdoor and eco-adventures that await nearby.

Cozumel and Isla Mujeres, Quintana Roo

Just a short trip by car and ferry from the Cancun airport, Cozumel and Isla Mujeres are where all those photographs of a lone palm tree on a white sand beach are taken. From world-class diving and snorkeling in Cozumel to the beautiful private beaches, gentle surf, and sea turtle sanctuaries of quieter Isla Mujeres, these two islands rich in Mayan history offer families a delightful escape to paradise off the Caribbean coast.

VACATION PLANNING TIPS

If P.A. systems by the pool and huge buffets aren't your family's thing, book a stay at one of the small beachfront hotels or B&Bs, which are especially nice on Isla Mujeres. Keep in mind that both islands are popular ports of call for huge cruise ships as well as for Cancun day trippers. Select a resort away from the port, and you'll see that after everyone else has headed home to party, the port towns quiet down, restaurants fill with local families, and that authentic Mexican culture you're seeking returns.

The more-developed Cozumel is the largest island in the Mexican Caribbean and a major stop for cruise ships. Beyond the port town of **San Miguel,** which is filled with tourists intent on bargain hunting, the island has culture and adventure activities the entire family will enjoy. Just a few blocks from the pier is the **Museo de la Isla de Cozumel,** where kids can dive right into exhibits about the local environment and Mayan culture and learn about the Spanish invasions in 1518. On Sunday evenings, stroll through **Village Plaza,** where the music and aroma of delicious foods makes for a lively atmosphere.

You may want to rent a car for one day to search for deserted beaches along the eastern coast. The **Punta Sur Park and Nature Preserve** is a 247-acre jungle of white-sand beaches, reef formations, and wildlife around the Columbia Lagoon. Pause for the 20-minute video at the visitor's center and learn about the park's diverse ecosystems and habitats, home to rare birds and the picturesque Faro Celarain Lighthouse.

Because of its pristine reef system and underwater caves, Cozumel is a popular base for families interested in diving. With classes for all ages and abilities, scuba diving and snorkeling are easily accessible and inexpensive—and many of the large, all-inclusive resorts on Cozumel's coastline teach elementary resort diving courses. Experienced divers should check with their hotel or the tourist office before going out with a local tour operator.

All ages can enjoy the **Chankanaab Lagoon Water Park.** This open-air, largely natural park has white-sand beaches, seaside restaurants, jet ski rentals, and an interesting botanical garden. The park's **Dolphin Discovery Center** has swim with dolphin programs and a sea lion show.

In contrast, the artsy and sleepy **Isla Mujeres,** or Island of Women (named for the Mayan goddess Ixchel), just 25 minutes by ferry from Cancun, is small enough to walk around, although golf carts are a popular mode of transportation as well. Life centers on the small mercado, where a variety of stalls sell food made by local families, are perfect for stocking up on picnic supplies. The island's main cultural site is the Ixchel Sculptural Walkway, a sea-view path leading visitors past statues of the goddess. The road to Ixchel is engulfed by intense vegetation, almost jungle-like, with vendors selling handwoven hammocks, food shacks, and young men pulling stubborn bulls. Just as in Chichen-Itza (see Chapter 30), the shadows from Mayan-built arches align perfectly with the sun on the spring and autumnal equinox—a configuration that allowed Mayan priests to predict the weather.

FELLOW TRAVELERS SAY ...

"Families who enjoy picnics may want to bring along their own takeout containers, as the Mexicans typically eat their meals outdoors at tables near the [mercado] stalls, rather than taking food away with them. Our favorite midday meal on Isla [Mujeres] was at **Playa Lancheros,** a pretty beach located on the island's Caribbean side. The house specialty is a Mayan-style grilled fish ... rubbed with a mixture of Mayan spices that give it an orange tinge and a delicious mild flavor. Nearly everyone was eating this house specialty, but the accommodating staff indulged my fish-adverse daughter with a plate of rice, beans, and chicken. While we waited for our meal, we took a refreshing dip in the ocean."

—A. T., www.FamilyTravelForum.com

Isla Mujeres has worked hard to protect its environment from overdevelopment, and its natural assets provide the only other distraction for families who need a break from the beach. The small **Garrafon Nature Park** (also operated by Xcaret and described in Chapter 32) is a fun eco-outing where you can see the part of the Great Maya

Reef, snorkel, and zip line. Local companies have guided tours to the **Sleeping Sharks Caves,** made famous by Jacques Cousteau and Ramon Bravo, or to **Dolphin Aquatic Park** for dolphin swim programs. Sea turtles call the island home, too, and the **Sea Turtle Sanctuary,** open to the public, works to preserve them in nesting season.

Cozumel Tourist Office
Isla Cozumel, Cozumel, Q. Roo 77600
+52 (987) 872-75-85
www.islacozumel.com.mx

Tourism Office of Isla Mujeres
Isla Mujeres, Q. Roo 77400
+52 (998) 877-03-07
www.isla-mujeres.net/tourism/home.htm

Playa del Carmen, Quintana Roo

Playa del Carmen, located just off the main highway about an hour south of Cancun, is a hip, funky, and almost Euro-chic beach town. What used to be a disagreeable little port for the **Cozumel ferry** has blossomed into a lively area with its own eclectic personality. Set in the middle of the Riviera Maya, it's the go-to place for families suffering from resort fever who need to get away from their getaway for some manmade diversions. But let's be very clear: quiet it's not.

FELLOW TRAVELERS SAY ...

"In Mexico, there are beautiful beaches and lots of history. In the state of Quintana Roo, there are many places to visit Mayan Ruins. Quintana Roo also has a system of underground rivers and caves that you can explore by snorkeling with a guide—this is fairly inexpensive. All-inclusive resorts are the best way to go; all the food, drink, airfare, and transportation to/from the airport are paid for in one flat rate, and everything (separate activities, going out, souvenirs) is inexpensive. The cities I would recommend are Cancun, Cozumel (slightly more expensive), and my favorite, Playa Del Carmen. If you go to Playa Del Carmen, you should check out the neat fire show at The Blue Parrot—it is amazing!"

—sarita92, www.FamilyTravelBoards.com

Anyone visiting the highly walkable Playa del Carmen (or Playa, for short) Beach must spend time on **La Quinta Avenida (Fifth Avenue or 5ta Avenida)**, the pedestrian-only main street running parallel to the scruffy beach. The more recently built north end near the fanciest condos has businesses ranging from Lacoste and Tommy Hilfiger stores to stylish wine bars, Italian ristorantes, and fajita joints. You'll also find boutiques and galleries offering huipiles (Mexican blouses with handmade trim), silver earrings, gold Aztec-inspired jewelry, wooden sculptures, and other work by local artisans. After a 15-minute stroll south past discos, ATM machines, and more T-shirt and Cuban cigar shops than we could count, you'll arrive at **Avenida Juarez,** which leads to the ferry pier—and next to it, the main square or **zocalo.**

Not all of the shopping is on Quinta Avenida; families will find terracotta-tiled cul de sacs off this lane lined with tiny boutiques selling European swimwear, Indonesian sarongs, and more. For local wares, try the cheaper craft shops a few blocks inland from the zocalo, which sell all kinds of goods made from wood and conch shells. You'll also find straw sombreros, imitation pre-Hispanic figurines, and herbal medicine pharmacies with Mayan-inspired remedies and aloe sun-relief products. For more local flavor, take the excellent and cheap public bus to **South Playa del Carmen,** where an outdoor market and playground have opened.

The outdoor adventures in the surrounding **Riviera Maya** are covered in Chapter 32, and the nearest archeological sites (reviewed in Chapter 30) include **Tulum,** a small but striking Mayan site sitting high above the sea, and **Coba,** an impressive archeological site in the jungle about an hour west of Playa del Carmen.

If ancient ruins don't get your family's adrenaline pumping, check out the water sports offered by local adventure tour operators. You can try snorkeling, scuba diving, cave diving (scuba diving in underground caves), and kite surfing. **The Great Mayan Reef** (or Great Mesoamerican Reef) runs parallel to the shoreline, and your family will love swimming among hundreds of colorful tropical fish. The same adventure tour operators offer explorations of the region's underground river system and cenotes (sinkholes) located in the

Zona de Cenotes, just west of Playa. With proper guidance and support, you can explore caverns full of stalactite and stalagmite formations—a sight that few visitors ever take time to see.

FUN FACTS

If you have long hair, get it braided the first night you're in town! Braids make it easier to manage wind-blown, salt-sprayed hair. Many artisans located along the beach and around the ferry pier charge a few pesos per braid. You can add a washable henna tattoo to complete the tropical look.

Playa del Carmen Tourist Office
Playa del Carmen, Q. Roo 77710
+52 (984) 206-31-50
www.rivieramaya.com, www.visitmexico.com/playadelcarmen

Puerto Vallarta, Jalisco

Cooled by the trade winds, picturesque Puerto Vallarta wraps around the shore of **Bahia de Banderas,** one of the largest natural bays in Mexico. Once just a remote Pacific coast paradise in the state of **Jalisco,** it matured from a romantic beach cove to an international jetsetter getaway in the 1960s and has since evolved into a full-scale resort city with cultural attractions and eco-adventures in addition to beach-going fun.

FELLOW TRAVELERS SAY ...

"Just got back from Puerto Vallarta. We spent a wonderful week there. Beach is great, sandy, absolutely no rocks. You can walk the beach for miles ... We [went to] to PV only once, by choice. It is a busy city, and we come to relax not to fight traffic ... We have 2 teenagers—17 and 15, and the whole family had good time. Just a side note, we went on a tour—horseback ride to a waterfall—well worth the money, not for the physically challenged though."

—Margie, www.FamilyTravelBoards.com

Set in the heart of what used to be known as the **Mexican Riviera**—classy **Mazatlan** is to the north, and the cliff divers of **Acapulco** are to the south—Puerto Vallarta is tucked into 100 miles of coastline enhanced by the blue skies and lush tropical greenery of the Sierra Madre mountains.

The mystique of this admittedly charming village began in 1963, during the location filming of *Night of the Iguana,* a John Huston film of the Tennessee Williams play (not something for kids to watch). The Academy Award–winning film starring Ava Gardner and Richard Burton (traveling with his secret girlfriend Elizabeth Taylor) put the photogenic beach town on the international tourist map.

The Hollywood connection is fun, and a multi-generational beach vacation would not be complete without a visit to **Las Caletas,** the secluded beach cove below John Huston's former vacation home. Now, it's a full-day sightseeing attraction; kids of all ages will love the petting zoo, snorkel and kayak facilities, restaurants, and a small Aztec pyramid where folkloric shows are held. Despite all the development, it's still a very nice beach-going experience.

You'll have a choice of excursions to nearby beaches that are, by virtue of being off the beaten path, much less crowded and developed. To the north and reached by public bus is the lively town of **Bucerias,** where expats enjoy the mild climate and inexpensive condo accommodations. It still has a very Mexican feel, however, and its broad, gold-sand beach slopes gently into the bay, creating a calm and shallow swimming spot for novice swimmers and little ones.

Families will also enjoy nearby **Mismaloya,** a beautiful beachfront town whose crumbling stucco buildings have a certain Old World charm. A dense jungle coast frames the white sand, and from the water you can look up at the Sierra Madres in the distance. About three miles south, the Tomatlan River meets the sea and forms a pretty cove where the rushing water adds a very exotic feel. Local tour operators can also arrange a boat trip to **Yelapa,** another fishing village whose pristine beach sits below a hillside of palm and frangipani trees where the kids can see many waterfalls. This beach fronts a calm and protected cove off Banderas Bay, making it a very safe splashing area for your youngest.

The more recently developed **Marina Vallarta** and **Nuevo Vallarta** in the neighboring state of Nayarit (see Chapter 32) are lined with high-rise hotels, all-inclusive resorts, and a well-groomed broad sand beach that is favored by sea turtles during the summer nesting season.

If you tire of beachcombing, there's boating, water skiing, and snorkeling in Banderas Bay. Deep-sea fishing for sailfish, bonito, yellowfish, billfish, marlin, and dorado is popular, too. At the **Dolphin Center,** you can pet and swim with bottlenose dolphins. In the foothills, there's hiking, mountain biking, horseback riding, and Jeep safari tours that let visitors explore the rugged coastline.

Downtown in **El Centro,** whitewashed houses splashed with fuschia and bougainvillea as well as nightclubs catering to the vibrant same-sex couple scene, line cobblestone streets that wind up the hills. Everyone's social center is the waterfront **Malécon,** a broad tree-lined promenade replete with bronze sculptures, restaurants, chic boutiques, souvenir shops, and the lively **Plaza de Armas** at the southern end. Just off the square, the crown and bell tower of **Nuestra Senora de Guadalupe** church form a distinct landmark. And in the so-called **Gringo Gulch** neighborhood, the star-studded **Casa Kimberly**—the former Elizabeth Taylor-Richard Burton house—can be toured for a nominal fee.

VACATION PLANNING TIPS

The locals spend Sunday at the beach with their own families, and the favorite thatch-roof seafood places fill up for the big midday meal. Use Sundays for sightseeing or shopping in town, and at sunset, head to the **Sunday Night Festival.** Throughout the year, PV's Malécon comes alive with locals and tourists alike participating in festivities, including markets, street performers, food, music, and more.

FIDETUR de Puerto Vallarta
Puerto Vallarta, Jalisco 48310
1-888-384-6822
www.visitpuertovallarta.com, www.visitmexico.com

Zihuatanejo and Ixtapa

Mexico's Pacific coast is a favorite sun 'n' sand getaway for West Coast families because of its proximity and good values. Two neighboring beach areas—the fishing village of **Zihuatanejo** and the high-rise, international resort of **Ixtapa**—are a good pair to consider depending on your family's needs and interests.

Let's start with **Zihua** (ZEE-wah, as the locals call it), which—despite its proximity to a purpose-built resort brought to you by the folks who designed Cancun—has retained a funky charm and a few traditional Mexican ways.

FELLOW TRAVELERS SAY ...

"Have just returned from Mexico with the family (me, the husband, the 2 kids ages 12 and 13) and we saved so much money! We stayed in a condo that was a pretty good deal. It meant we got to go to the local markets and buy food, so we got to practice our Spanish. We did go out for a few meals, but it was really fun shopping for food and cooking together. We didn't rent a car but walked everywhere (we were in Zihuatanejo) or took the bus. We brought our own snorkel gear, and I brought some cheap inflatable air mattresses—they were $2.99 at home as opposed to $10. My husband and I bought tequila and made our own drinks ... I also did all my Christmas shopping in the local markets because the crafts are so beautiful."

—Linda, www.FamilyTravelBoards.com

Most of Zihua's condos and small hotels are located outside the port along the densely wooded hill above **Playa La Ropa,** the town's prettiest beach. It's a mile-long, half-moon cove of glistening white sand lapped by the gentle waves of the Pacific, although during the winter rainy season, the surf gets rougher.

It's an ideal family destination where you'll find vendors offering photo ops with leashed iguanas; guys renting out parasails, windsurfers, and sea kayaks; small restaurants with sand floors where you can dine barefoot; sunset booze cruises; and ecotour leaders looking for clients. If you want to be left alone, there's plenty of room for that, too. Tucked behind the lush palm groves are many small, family-run bungalows where you can rent inexpensive rooms or private cabins. The beach across the broad bay is Las Gatas, and the underwater reef offshore makes it the most ideal for snorkeling or scuba diving.

Closer to the downtown are **Playa Madera,** the "Wood Beach" that's really a small, secluded cove with some snack-food shacks; and **Main Beach,** the sandy strip near the cruise ship port where tiny ferries leave for Zihua's other beaches. Lifeguards are stationed at all area beaches, so be sure to heed them. When you tire of the beach, head into the authentic downtown where you can shop in surprisingly fine craft shops or dine at one of the many restaurants favored by locals. The kids don't have to love Mexican food; these resorts have drawn foreigners for two generations, and many have opened up international restaurants.

If you're staying in an all-inclusive resort such as the **Club Med Ixtapa**, chances are you're staying in the modern Ixtapa development, about 20-minutes away by public bus. **Playa Linda,** or beautiful beach, is just north and has an adjoining fenced-in swamp with alligators. From here, you can take a ferry to tiny **Las Brisas;** this islet serves as a breakwater so the waves at **Quieta Beach** are gentler for swimming. From either town, you can enjoy family fun off the beach. Bike equipment shops and tour operators are located in central Zihua or at the main mall in Ixtapa. Venturing slightly north of Ixtapa leads you to **Parque Aventura,** a place for zip-lining and hiking through the nearby jungle.

FELLOW TRAVELERS SAY ...

"I found the beach at Club Med Ixtapa to be really nice—wide enough for plenty of people. Comfortable beach chairs and lounges. The water can be a little rough, which makes it fun for adults and older kids for body surfing, but you need to keep an eye on younger ones who aren't strong swimmers. My children didn't spend much time on the beach, though, because there was so much else for them to do."

—S. M., www.FamilyTravelBoards.com

Less than 20 miles north of the Ixtapa is **Playa Troncones,** a 3-mile stretch of beach with a few small hotels, cafés, and—most importantly—enough surf to support a burgeoning learn-to-surf industry. The high waves come between June and late October, around the same time the Ridley sea turtles lay their eggs. Since a spate of shark attacks in 2008, the Mexican government has run boats and specially manned towers to watch over the surrounding 9-mile stretch from **Playa Saladita** to **Playa Linda.**

Ixtapa-Zihuatanejo Tourist Information
Zihuatenejo, Guerrero 40880
+52 (755) 553-12-70
www.ixtapa-zihuatanejo.com, www.visitmexico.com

Outdoor Adventures

32

In This Chapter

- Enjoying the marine life of the arid, mountainous Baja peninsula
- Birding at Celestun Flamingo Preserve in Yucatan
- Ecotouring and beaching in Riviera Nayarit
- Playing at the eco-theme parks of Xcaret and Riviera Maya

The country of Mexico—surrounded by the Atlantic Ocean and Caribbean Sea to the east, the Gulf of Mexico to the north, and the Sea of Cortez and Pacific Ocean on the west—offers families an unparalleled variety of water sports and opportunities for interacting with marine life. An estimated 26 percent of the country's land mass is devoted to forest and woodland, and the varied terrain—ranging from desert at sea level to hundreds of mountains more than 3,000 meters in elevation—guarantees that most visitors interested in an ecotour or mountain adventure will find one nearby.

Add in a climate that ranges from temperate to tropical, and it's no wonder that Mexico is a popular destination year-round for outdoor adventurers. Here are four of the best destinations that accommodate travelers of any age whose taste in adventure ranges from mild to extreme.

Cabo San Lucas, Baja California

Mexico's **Baja Peninsula** is a dramatic study in contrasts. A desert surrounded by water, this extremely arid land is covered with cacti and barren mountain ranges. The sky is alive with cormorants, boobies, petrels, and terns; the inhospitable land is home to black jackrabbits and fish-eating bats; and the rough seas support California gray and humpback whales, harbor porpoises, and southern sea otters, along with more than 800 species of fish. Situated at the tip of the peninsula, where the raging Pacific Ocean meets the tranquil Sea of Cortez, is **Los Cabos,** comprised of **Cabo San Lucas** and **San Jose del Cabo.**

In a region that enjoys 350 days of humidity-free sunshine each year and is just a quick, cheap flight from Los Angeles, it's no wonder that lively Cabo San Lucas is overrun with touristy shops, nightlife, and massive resorts and condo overdevelopment.

Picture charming streets lined with colonial architecture and small, less-expensive hotels and uncrowded beaches, and you see San Jose del Cabo. Art lovers will enjoy browsing through the **Centro del Arte** (Art District) galleries presenting paintings, sculpture, and pottery as well as beadwork and embroidery created by artists of the Huichol Indian tribe. Outdoorsy families should visit **Estero de San Jose,** a sanctuary that's home to 200 bird species.

Whether you're in a big Cabo San Lucas all-inclusive resort or a tiny San Jose B&B, you'll see families playing together everywhere. Golfers will be thrilled by the challenging **Cabo Real** course designed by Robert Trent Jones Jr. and **Cabo Del Sol** designed by Jack Nicklaus. Here in the "Marlin Capital of the World," sport fishing is also extremely popular, but the early-morning, open-sea boat trips rarely accept young kids. Instead, plan a diving trip to see giant manta rays and sea turtles or a snorkeling excursion. Other options for teens are exploring the region on all-terrain vehicle tours or on horseback. Due to the strong undertow, the area beaches are best for sand castle building, sea kayaking, and surfing (and surfer watching). For the adventurous and strong swimmers, jet ski tours are available.

In Cabo San Lucas, visit **The Glass Factory** and watch artisans create beautiful glassware and ornaments from recycled bottles.

An unforgettable day with Pacific bottlenose dolphins awaits your family at **Cabo Dolphins.** Dolphin encounters (for ages 4 and older) are small-group experiences accompanied by a trainer who provides you with an introduction to these majestic creatures and a chance to get into the tank and touch them. After learning some training techniques, depending on the child's age, he or she may have the opportunity to interact further by dancing with them or riding on their back or tummy across the pool.

One of our family's favorite activities is the short cruise from the harbor in Cabo San Lucas to **El Arco,** or "Land's End," the arched rock formation where the Pacific Ocean and the Sea of Cortez meet. Not only is it a stunning sight, but you can also see a colony of sea lions at home lounging among the rocks. Some boats make a stop at nearby **Playa del Amor,** or Lover's Beach, where you can swim and snorkel next to El Arco on the calmer Sea of Cortez side in a protected national park. **Playa del Divorcio** (Beach of Divorce) is opposite on the churning Pacific. While the beach is peaceful, swimming is extremely unsafe due to strong currents and fierce undertow. If you don't plan to stop for a swim, take the cruise at sunset for even more astounding views. Older kids will appreciate the Jazz & Wine Sunset Cruise where you'll all enjoy wine, hors d'oeuvres, and contemporary jazz while taking in the incredible sights.

Los Cabos Tourism Board
1-866-LOSCABOS
www.visitloscabos.travel, www.visitmexico.com

Celestun Flamingo Preserve, Yucatan

Celestun is a friendly little fishing village about 60 miles southwest of Merida in the state of Yucatan on the Gulf of Mexico. Don't expect dozens of luxury hotels, however; there's not much here except a few condos on the fringes of town. Many of the few tourists who make it this far are on road trips across the Yucatan or on day excursions from Merida. While the region's infrastructure is pretty basic, there are a few hotels, some great seafood restaurants, a couple small shops, a harbor, and a long stretch of undeveloped beach.

What brings most visitors to this far-flung locale is the unique **Celustun Biosphere Reserve,** which in its simplicity personifies the term "ecotourism." The Celestun estuary is an enclosed body of water with an outlet to the sea, and its combination of fresh and salt water has spawned a mangrove forest that supports a variety of undersea wildlife. There are many beautiful birds here, too, with warblers and sandpipers frequenting this area.

The most famous bird that lives off this brackish water ecosystem, and the bird that brings most tourists here, is the flamingo. These pink- to scarlet-feathered wading birds with impossibly long legs gather at Celestun by the thousands.

FUN FACTS

The flamingo (*el flamenco* in Spanish, like the dance) is found along the Yucatan coast from Holbox off the coast of Cancun as far west as the biosphere. Flamingoes favor Ria Celestun because it has brackish water, a shallow muddy bottom, and it's an easy place to catch artemia, a tiny, bright-pink shrimp that give their feathers color. You'll see the greatest number of flamingoes here between March and August.

At the end of the long dirt road leading to the preserve, you'll find fishermen with small powerboats waiting to show visitors around. Even if none of your clan speaks Spanish, the natives have done this tour so often that they know exactly what you'd like to see. One of the highlights is a visit to **Bird Island**—or Isla de Pajaros, as the locals call it—to see the flamingoes nesting. As you approach a flock resting on the water, they'll spread their wings, revealing a silky black underside, and take flight like a bouquet of roses; it's quite astonishing! You can stop at a nearby freshwater spring for a swim and navigate through the **Petrified Forest** of dense mangrove that is generations old.

After a morning on the water, head to one of Celestun's great seafood restaurants overlooking the sea. If you still have energy after lunch, rent bicycles and travel out of town along the beach, where kids can see what an ungroomed beach in an authentic fishing village really looks like.

Celestun Tourist Office
+52 (988) 916-25-97
www.celestun.com.mx

yucatantoday.com/en/topics/celestun

Riviera Nayarit and the Pacific Coast

Riviera Nayarit is the lush coastal region of Mexico's **Nayarit** state, extending from the gated resort community of **Nuevo Vallarta** north to the **San Blas Peninsula.** Families will find diverse cultural and environmental riches as well as nice beaches facing the calm, shallow **Banderas Bay.** Although the region shares an airport with the established beach resort of Puerto Vallarta (see Chapter 31) farther south, Riviera Nayarit offers a greater abundance of eco-adventures.

Families with school-age kids will enjoy an excursion to **San Blas,** a picturesque and typically Mexican small town. Be sure to visit the main square, where colorfully painted bars and shops are tucked between the new city hall, church, and school. San Blas is a gateway to **La Tovara National Park,** where you can hire a small boat to tour the mangrove swamps. (Keep your hands tucked in so they're out of the crocodiles' way!) It's said this ecosystem hosts more than 250 species of birds, including the black-bellied tree duck, great blue heron, and roseate spoonbill on their migrations as well as the bumblebee hummingbird and Mexican woodnymph.

The sea turtle is the region's official mascot, and four protected species of sea turtle (leatherback turtles, Olive Ridley turtles, hawksbill turtles, and green turtles) make Riviera Nayarit their home. **Wildlife Connection,** an ecotour group based in Marina Vallarta, offers an evening tour in which you can participate in the release of baby turtles and learn more about their conservation. Wednesday nights during the nesting season, the **Grupo Ecológico de la Costa**

Verde marine turtle nursery in the town of San Francisco conducts an educational slideshow at the family-welcoming **Costa Azul Hotel,** often followed by the release of young hatchlings.

If you're visiting between November and April, you will likely be able to see hundreds of humpback whales as they migrate south from the Arctic to raise their calves in the protected waters of Banderas Bay. Several tour operators offer a variety of whale-watching tours appropriate for all ages and physical abilities.

> **VACATION PLANNING TIPS**
>
> Don't forget to get off your beach towels and explore! There are more than 20 towns in the Riviera Nayarit area, each with something unique and interesting to offer. If you prefer an organized tour of the region (and we do, because kids can learn much more), check out **Banderas Bay Travel** and **Vallarta Adventures**—two of the top tour operators. The former is known for its excellent guides and the latter for its adventure tours.

To really get out and explore more of the Nayarit wilderness, foothills, and pristine jungle, it's best to join an adventure tour. A good day-long expedition covering the Sierra Madre mountain region works well for less-active families, courtesy of a converted Mercedes diesel truck. En route, well-trained guides relate Mexico's history and the culture of its indigenous Huichol Indian tribes. There's usually a brief nature walk through forested land where guides talk about plant life, insects, and the forest ecology, and then a stop for a swim at one of the many beautiful and isolated beaches.

More energetic parents, 'tweens, and teens will enjoy one of the outdoor multi-sport days: they typically begin with a speed boat ride to a Banderas Bay beach, where you mount 4x4 Unimogs (similar to ATVs) to ascend to a mountainside base camp, hike a bit, hop on a mule, and journey into the subtropical forest for a zip line tour, some rappelling down waterfalls, and lots of wet fun.

Convention Visitor Bureau Riviera Nayarit
Nuevo Vallarta, Nayarit 63735
+52 (322) 297-25-16
www.rivieranayarit.com, www.visitmexico.com

Xcaret and Riviera Maya

Since the construction of major resorts began in the 1990s, many families have chosen to bypass **Cancun,** a long-popular beach destination and the region's gateway airport, to spend their holiday on the quieter **Riviera Maya.** White it's no longer as quiet as it used to be, the good news is that Riviera Maya's success depends on preserving the Yucatan Peninsula's distinctive environment and Mayan culture, and an increasingly sustainable style of tourism could ensure that. We love it, so go now if you can.

For tourists, the "Mayan Coast" of Quintana Roo extends about 100 miles south of Cancun to the town of Port Allen near the Belize border. Along the lush Atlantic coastline, where mangroves mingle with coral reefs interspersed with pockets of rampant overdevelopment, you'll find many miles of stunning beaches; numerous resorts; the well-known towns of **Playa del Carmen, Akumal,** and **Tulum;** several Mayan archeological sites; and the remarkable environment-themed parks of **Xcaret** and **Xel-Há.**

While many families prefer all-inclusive resorts, in **Playa del Carmen** and **Tulum** (still the most casual, New Age–style community) there are also a number of expensive boutique hotels and cheap, funky B&Bs offering some Mexican charm. We urge you to consider any accommodation as just a place to sleep; a fantastic world of exciting excursions beckons beyond the resort gates.

FELLOW TRAVELERS SAY ...

"We ventured to the natural water park Xcaret and snorkeled in the underground river tunnels. The fish mixed with plant life was breathtaking in their natural habitat. The beauty of nature struck me like it had not before ... especially when we watched the Native people perform a Mayan dance to the gods. I truly enjoy history, so being able to experience another culture's tradition thrilled me beyond belief."

—K. Q., www.travelBIGO.com

The justly famous **Xcaret**, an exotic ecological theme park, is the inspiration for parks such as Orlando's Discovery Cove (see Chapter 9). Taking advantage of the Yucatan Peninsula's underground sweet-water rivers, originally used by the native Mayan Indians for stealth warfare, Xcaret has created a subsystem of caves that your family can explore by floating along in life jackets. The water is relatively warm, the excitement is high (too high if your toddler's afraid of the dark), and the danger is nonexistent; it's a delight for all ages, with professional photographers poised to capture the thrill.

This remarkable 200-acre parcel of jungle has been hand-sculpted to show off its natural beauty. If you don't want to get wet, you can still get in on the fun by checking out butterfly, frog, and snake exhibits or hopping aboard a raft tour that floats through the tranquil jungle. Xcaret is committed to unusual educational activities that also happen to be tons of fun: **swimming with dolphins** or sharks (the vegetarian kind), snorkeling in a lagoon, studying a **Reef Aquarium** or a hydroponic garden, and trying the new quasi-scuba pastimes of **Sea Trek** ("You won't even spoil your makeup" claim the signs advertising this submersion in a fitted, air-filled helmet) or **Snuba** (a pre-scuba activity in which air is supplied to a group by a common source). Some of these activities require additional fees on top of the admission, and advance booking is recommended. When you're ready for a break, watch one of the regularly scheduled shows, such as the brisk display of equestrian skills or the Papantia Flying Men, who—secured by their ankles with ropes wound about a 90-foot pole—descend in flying formation in an ancient Mayan ritual seeking the blessings of fertility and bountiful harvests.

The park's after-sunset highlight is **Mexico Spectacular,** a wonderful extravaganza that begins with a game of pelota, the Mayans' legendary form of soccer played with flaming balls, followed by a costumed cast of 200 singers and dancers from each of the country's regions. It's a super-entertaining cultural immersion that's even more fun for kids if you spring for the special traditional dinner that's brought to your seat. With so much of real value to see and do, we suggest returning to Xcaret over two days so younger children aren't overwhelmed.

Xel-Há is a national park in the Riviera Maya that was given to the Xcaret management to guarantee its preservation, and it boasts the same pristine environment without the crowds. Creeks, lagoons, spring-fed natural caves (*cenotes*), and other waterways within this smaller park host a surprisingly varied collection of marine life; at certain times of year, sea turtles lay eggs on the beach. Its river, largely above ground, has enough current to feel like a lazy river ride. Roving Mariachis and other Mayan musical performers, as well as a naturalist with a huge iguana on his shoulder, mingle with kids. Dolphin swimming is also available for a fee, with reservations recommended.

Several tour operators offer versions of the eco-park experience that might include a trip to a traditional Mayan village, zip line experience, and rappelling into a cenote for swimming. For a non-structured experience, take the family farther south into the **Si'an Ka'an Biosphere,** the region's largest nature preserve of some one million protected acres.

To branch out from eco-adventures, there are two Mayan archeo-logical sites: **Tulum** (above the coastline and within the town) and **Coba** (45 minutes inland from Tulum); you can learn more about them in Chapter 30. For a fun shopping break suited to all ages, you can't do any better than Playa del Carmen (covered in Chapter 31).

Xcaret
Playa del Carmen, Q. Roo 77710
Cancun Reservations Office
+52 (998) 883-04-70
www.xcaret.com.mx, www.rivieramaya.com

Canada

Archaeologists believe the earliest Canadians were Inuit Indians or Eskimos, known as First Nations people, who thrived among such vast natural resources. Not until the end of the fifteenth century, when explorer John Cabot arrived from England, did the Old World appreciate how much fish, fur, timber, and other riches were to be found north of the territory that Columbus had found. After centuries of conflict between France and England over sovereignty, in 1849 Canada was recognized as its own country.

It was the coming of the railroad in 1885 that truly settled this vast country. Today, Canada is comprised of the 10 provinces of Alberta, British Columbia, Manitoba, New Brunswick, Newfoundland and Labrador, Nova Scotia, Ontario, Prince Edward Island, Quebec, and Saskatchewan, and the Northwest, Yukon, and Nunavut Territories. You'll be delighted to find that while maintaining very close ties with the British government and preserving French heritage east of Ontario, the 35 million Canadians are very much their own culture.

And, with such a variety of topography in a landmass larger than the United States, families can combine coastline, national parks, mountains, and exciting cities in one vacation.

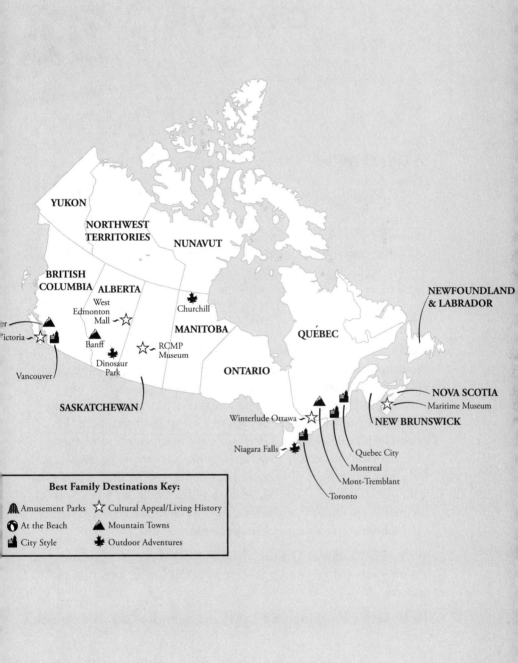

YUKON

NORTHWEST
TERRITORIES

NUNAVUT

BRITISH
COLUMBIA   ALBERTA

West
Edmonton
Mall

Banff

Dinosaur
Park

Churchill

MANITOBA

RCMP
Museum

SASKATCHEWAN

Victoria

Vancouver

QUÉBEC

ONTARIO

NEWFOUNDLAND
& LABRADOR

NOVA SCOTIA
Maritime Museum

NEW BRUNSWICK

Winterlude Ottawa

Niagara Falls

Quebec City

Montreal

Mont-Tremblant

Toronto

Best Family Destinations Key:

Amusement Parks ☆ Cultural Appeal/Living History

At the Beach ▲ Mountain Towns

City Style ✿ Outdoor Adventures

In This Chapter

- Embracing the European charm of Montreal's chic French culture
- Exploring historic Quebec City
- Eating and shopping in Toronto's multicultural neighborhoods
- Taking part in Vancouver's active urban lifestyle

Families flying into Canada will likely begin their vacation in one of the country's great cities. That seems fitting, as most are well run, affluent, heavily into high-tech, and very environmentally aware. A peaceful and liberal country (and one too large to make generalizations), many of Canada's social policies focusing on quality of life are on display in its cities. Social policies such as universal healthcare, generous maternity leave laws, ample vacation time, respect for a wide variety of cultures, and family rights—including legalized same-sex marriages—are held in high regard. Imagine a city where lifeguards are on duty at playground sprinklers and school systems teach childcare as a required subject—that's Canada!

We review Montreal, Quebec, Toronto, and Vancouver because they are international gateways to a myriad of cultural and recreational attractions.

Please keep a few things in mind as you plan your Canada vacation:

- Every family member of any age will need a passport to enter Canada, although children younger than 16 may cross a land border with only a government-issued photo ID and birth certificate.

- Canada is officially bilingual, but the locals will humor you whether you speak English, French, or neither.

- Credit cards are not always accepted at restaurants and shops, so carry some cash. ATM machines provide the best exchange rate.

Montreal, Quebec

Along the banks of the St. Lawrence River, the Quebecois city of **Montreal** has successfully balanced tradition and trend to become one of North America's most dynamic and fashionable destinations. It's here that towering Gothic cathedrals share the skyline with contemporary design; sidewalk café bars line time-worn cobblestone lanes; and family visitors relish a taste of Paris—minus the expense and hassle of a cross-Atlantic flight.

Old Montreal (or *Vieux Montréal* in French) should be the goal of your first neighborhood excursion. Stroll past restored and reused limestone Beaux-Arts buildings and down narrow lanes of tile-roofed stucco cottages, soaking in one aspect of residents' traditional way of life. A quick walk away is the innovatively designed **Pointe-à-Callière,** which encloses the **Montreal Museum of Archaeology and History** and the **Customs House** on top of a dig uncovering history from the 1700s. You don't have to read any labels; we just love walking down this living museum's glass and metalwork pathways to study the remains of the original city below our feet.

The eighteenth-century **Old Port** is a work in progress and a fun place to watch cyclists, inline skaters, and street performers in summer, or join **Ghost Tours** at night. Highlights here include **Marche Bonsecours,** a nineteenth-century public market capped by a silver dome with winged angels. As you walk down the waterfront, consider climbing the nearly 200 steps to the old **Clock Tower** to learn about the city's maritime history and take in a great view of the St. Lawrence. The **Centre des Sciences de Montréal,** a state-of-the-art interactive science museum on King Edward Pier, is fun both for kids who like to know how things work and for anyone else who needs a very entertaining shelter against the biting winds in winter.

In any season, the entire family will enjoy a stroll through **Mount-Royal Park,** designed by Frederick Law Olmstead, the architect behind New York City's Central Park. Because kids don't always appreciate cultural offerings, Montreal has plenty to keep young ones happy, too. At the **Montreal Botanical Garden,** one of the largest in the world, children can study the work of their peers in **Jardins-Jeunes.** A ride on the miniature sightseeing train makes it easy to see all that the gardens have to offer. Kids will love the nearby **L'Insectarium de Montréal,** where strange and creepy bugs are on display. Many of the creatures can be held and petted under the watchful eye of naturalists, and computer games and multimedia kiosks provide high-tech learning opportunities.

FELLOW TRAVELERS SAY ...

"Traveling with our eight-year-old grandson is an exciting experience and adds more fun and interest to any activity or place that we might visit. Montreal was the first destination of last summer's Canada trip. We visited the **Montreal Biodome,** a museum which explores four ecosystems in the natural environment. All types of animals—including beaver, alligators, and other animals—were shown in their natural habitat."

—D. B., www.FamilyTravelForum.com

Your teens will enjoy a stop at the **Redpath Museum,** a natural history museum that features exhibits on modern and prehistoric animals and offers an in-depth look at ancient cultures. Another must-do with kids who aren't afraid of the dark is the **SOS Labyrinthe,** located at the Old Port. This boat-shaped maze has almost a mile of corridors riddled with obstacles, traps, and dead-ends.

In 2006, Montreal was honored as a **UNESCO City of Design,** one of only three cities in the world to receive the title. On the streets, you may wander past the stunning nineteenth-century **Notre Dame Cathedral** near the twentieth-century **Olympic Stadium.** Kids will enjoy seeing the architecture that makes this city sparkle on a **Montreal Harbor Cruise** that transports your family through 20 miles of history and attractions ranging from the Old Port, where the cruise starts, to the **Parc des Îles.** The islands of Parc des Îles, **Notre-Dame,** and **Sainte-Hélène** were originally developed for the 1967 World's Fair, but now they host seasonal festivals—the summertime **Just for Laughs** comedy festival, the fun Fete des Enfants (Kids' Festival) each August, the renowned **International Jazz Festival,** and winter's **Montreal High Lights** celebration are among the most popular. There's also a posh **casino** featuring 2,700 slot machines and 105 gaming tables and **La Ronde,** an old-fashioned amusement park whose Ferris wheel can be seen from the old quarter. Small ferries leave regularly from the Old Port to these islands—a quick 10-minute ride.

VACATION PLANNING TIPS

Montreal is fun for all ages, but it's particularly special if you're traveling with older teens or adult kids who will love the sophisticated vibe. Museum-goers should consider a **Carte Musées Montréal;** the pass is valid at 30 museums, includes public transportation over a three-day period, and costs $45 Canadian plus tax. It's a bargain if you think you may be running in and out of several museums during your stay—a good possibility in winter. At most museums, young children can enter for free any time.

With more than 4,000 restaurants and a very French mentality, Montreal is a foodie city featuring cuisine from more than 80 countries. Even fussy eaters will understand why it has been voted the **Gastronomic Capital of the World** by AAA many times. And on a practical note, there's a wide variety of hotels ranging from classic B&Bs in Vieux Montréal to contemporary business hotels downtown. Budget travelers should search for one of the smaller motels outside town, because this is one of Canada's priciest cities.

Montreal Tourism
Montreal, Quebec H1V 1B3
514-873-2015
www.tourisme-montreal.org, www.quebecmusts.com

Quebec City, Quebec

A historic Old Town, nearby ski resorts, fun water parks, well-preserved monuments, and great food make Quebec City a fun, four-season family destination. And while 95 percent of the populace speaks French, almost everyone speaks some English and will be happy to hear you practice your "Bonjour" and "Merci beaucoup." Overlooking the **St. Lawrence River,** the capital of **Quebec province** has been influential in North American history since Samuel Champlain recognized its potential and founded a fur-trading post there in 1608. Viewed as a valuable prize in the colonial wars of the seventeenth and eighteenth centuries, it has become a tourist favorite with activities that remind visitors of its historic past.

Your first stop should be the **Old Quarter of Quebec,** divided into an upper and lower town connected by an inclined railway. This UNESCO World Heritage site will appeal to families, with highlights including **Artillery Park** and the **Citadel of Quebec** outlining the storied military past of Quebec.

FELLOW TRAVELERS SAY ...

"Onwards to Quebec City by train, and a new experience of watching the change of the Ceremonial Guard at the British-built Citadel. It houses a very interesting museum for the Royal 22nd Regiment. We all enjoyed a very interesting tour of the museums and the grounds with all the original cannons in place. There were many things of interest to an eight-year-old (or older) child. We all had a good time in the dress-up room in the Musée de la Civilisation. The city's historic architecture held our interest as well, particularly in Artillery Park and the Quartier Petit-Champlain. After a relaxing river cruise to view the development along the harbor, we went from the Old City to the New City by way of the Funicular. The Funicular was great fun."

—D. B., www.FamilyTravelForum.com

There are museums at every turn, too, such as the **Musée de la Civilisation,** which presents guests with thematic exhibitions concerning civilization, art, and society. Others are the **Musée du Fort,** whose original **Sound and Light** show explore the military past of the city, and the **Musée National des Beaux-Arts** in Battlefields

Park, representing 4,000 Quebec artists. Although not strictly a museum, the small **First Nations' Hotel** has an interesting exhibit about the local Huron-Wendat tribal culture.

Place Royale in the lower city is the site of New France's first settlement. This well-preserved square is full of shops and restaurants and is the heart of the city's artistic activities. Don't miss **La Fresque des Quebecois,** a 40-foot mural of Quebec depicting the 400 years of history in Quebec City. From here, explore **Maison Jean-Alfred Moisan,** the oldest grocery store in North America, which features some unique Canadian teas and products. A favorite for all is the **Erico Chocolate Economuseum,** a delicious place where everything is made onsite. Learn the history of chocolate, providing an educational delight for the entire family.

Among the city's frequent festivals and Catholic holiday events, two stand out. February is ruled by the **Carnaval de Québec,** a two-week-long winter event with a huge ice sculpture exhibit, snowmobiling, horse-drawn sleigh rides, and the loveable mascot **Bonhomme,** a fun-loving snowman. A unique opportunity for summer visitors is the fantastic summer festival, **Le Festival d'Été de Québec.** This festival features live music and street performers and has grown since its debut in 1968 to an 11-day event with more than 1,000 artists. The **Ice Hotel** celebrated its 10th anniversary in 2010 and is the only such hotel in North America. The blocks of ice are shaped into a new design each year, with themed suites, an Ice Slide, and the Ice Café.

In addition to the Ice Hotel, Quebec City has a variety of B&Bs and family-friendly accommodations to meet every budget. The elegant **Château Frontenac** is the most iconic hotel, a Loire Valley–style castle whose towers have dominated the skyline from a perch above the river for more than a century. In the surrounding countryside are many charming auberges, or inns, that include a meal in the price of a room.

While in Quebec City, you must pause to enjoy the French-influenced local cuisine. Kids of all ages love delicious crêpes—thin pancakes served with a variety of sweet and savory fillings. Be sure to stop in to small cafés and pâtisseries serving desserts. The ideal Quebecois dessert is Maple Pull or "Tire sur la Neige," a taffylike treat that's made by pouring heated syrup on a bed of snow, then rolling a popsicle stick in it to serve as a handle for the sticky treat.

VACATION PLANNING TIPS

Even families who hate culture won't want to miss the city's amazing free public events scheduled each summer through 2013. The circus masters at **Cirque du Soleil** have choreographed "Les Chemins Invisibles," a street event with their signature acrobatics, gymnastics, and innovative dance. The artists Robert Lepage and Ex Machina have programmed the **Image Mill,** the world's largest outdoor projection—a series of huge screens filled with remarkable imagery. If you plan to museum hop, investing in the **Quebec City Museum Pass** is a smart move. This three-day $50 Canadian pass includes two days of public transportation and access to all the museums Quebec City has to offer.

Don't miss the **Aquarium du Québec,** located in a wooded area crisscrossed by paths leading to picnic areas, near the popular **Quebec Bridge.** The aquarium features 10,000 specimens of fish, reptiles, and other marine mammals, incorporating educational cartoons and special children's exhibits during the summer. Another fun summertime activity with older children is a hot-air balloon ride. Next, visit the **Valcartier Vacation Village,** a popular water park during summers and a snow-tubing resort for families during colder weather. Twenty minutes outside Quebec City, this park also features horseback riding, rafting, and family river tours. In winter, the family-friendly Mont-Sainte-Anne or Le Massif ski resorts make for a great day trip.

If you have time to explore the surrounding area, **Montmorency Falls,** just 10 minutes outside the city, is worth a trip. The breathtaking waterfalls stand at 98 feet—higher than Niagara Falls. They are accessed by an aerial tramway ride that brings you to the top of the mountain, where you check out the museum chronicling the history of the area.

Quebec City Tourism
Quebec City, Quebec G1R 2L3
1-877-783-1608
www.quebecregion.com, www.bonjourquebec.com

Toronto, Ontario

For families who like to explore on foot, visit world-class museums and cutting-edge galleries, and browse unique boutiques, the gracious and manageable city of **Toronto** is hard to beat. It's a major business and government center that's cosmopolitan enough to thrill visitors from small towns without being overwhelmingly loud or pushy. In fact, Toronto and its multicultural citizens typically display the politely understated behavior of their former British rulers.

While young couples may see Toronto (or **T.O.,** as it's known) as a flashy weekend getaway, in fact there is much for a family to see and do. For a dose of culture, visit the **Art Gallery of Ontario,** which has a beautiful exhibit of medieval treasures from London's Victoria and Albert Museum. The **Royal Ontario Museum** features archeological finds and European decorative arts. Right next door is the **Bata Shoe Museum,** which features 12,500 of the most amazing shoes in history and is surprisingly fun for kids. For a day's outing, the **McMichael Gallery,** 45 minutes from Toronto, houses a great collection of Canadian landscape paintings and is surrounded by beautiful landscapes woven with nature trails.

FUN FACTS

The Canadian dollar (written CAD$ or $CND in English and French, respectively) is a coin called a loonie after the bird engraved on it; the two-dollar coin is a twoonie. American and Canadian coins worth less than one dollar are traded equally, a throwback to the days when both countries used Spanish dollars and cents as their currency.

More family-oriented, the wonderful **Ontario Science Center** is an interactive treat for anyone who loves their science to be hands-on. Staple exhibits include the Science Arcade, where the entire family can have a hair-raising experience jolted by (safe) electric currents, and the CA Planetarium, the only public stargazing experience in Toronto. With Kidspark to entertain children ages seven and younger and the Challenge Zone for teenagers, the entire family will be entertained.

Sports-loving families should make a stop at the **Hockey Hall of Fame.** You can browse the world's finest collection of hockey memorabilia and test your knowledge and reflexes at the many interactive exhibits. If you want to make it a complete sports day, go see a **Maple Leafs** game. Toronto's hockey team is immensely popular in the city, and the games are always a blast.

For a spectacular view over all of Toronto, you'll want to visit the **CN Tower.** Families can explore two observation decks: The Look Out Level at 1,136 feet and the Sky Pod at 1,465 feet, where a thick glass floor is cantilevered over the city streets. On the ground floor, there's a 4-D motion ride, Himalamazon, and a movie about the construction of the CN Tower.

In summer, nothing beats the **Harbourfront,** a 10-acre, fun-filled complex where you can play, feed the ducks, watch the boats, and even ice skate year-round on a new synthetic ice rink. Don't forget your camera; with Lake Ontario on one side and the city skyline in the background, Harbourfront is a hot site to take some postcard-like photos. If you can spare the better part of a day, another inexpensive outing is to take the short ferry ride to little **Centre Island,** a park with loads of shady spots and a breeze. **Centreville Amusement Area** has a Ferris wheel, waterslide, mini golf, and a nearby petting zoo. Pack your bathing suits; there's a wading pool and sandy beaches.

East of the long-established Harbourfront is **Polson Pier,** a lakefront development that 'tweens and teens love. Along the old Polson Quay is the **Sound Academy,** which hosts weekend parties for ages 19 and older (the drinking age here is 18) with bands such as Timbaland, M.I.A., and Bedouin Soundclash; the pier is also home to beach volleyball courts, mini golf, a pool, a go-kart track, and even a drive-in movie theater.

VACATION PLANNING TIPS

Get a **CityPass** as soon as you arrive in Toronto. It includes admission to the Art Gallery of Ontario, the CN Tower, the peculiar **Casa Loma** mansion, the Ontario Science Centre, the Royal Ontario Museum, and the fine **Toronto Zoo;** one pass, which is valid for nine days, costs half of what you would pay without the pass.

If the summer heat is too much to bear or the cold winds off Lake Ontario blow right through you, head downtown to visit the **Underground City.** This subterranean mall connects dozens of office buildings with 6.5 miles of covered marble walkways housing 1,100 restaurants, food halls, and shops. Drop by **Holt Renfrew,** a throwback to when merchandising in department stores was an art. The **Fashion and Entertainment District** around **Eaton Centre** is fun for shopping, as are any of the funky ethnic neighborhoods.

In this city where more than 100 languages and dialects are spoken, you're sure to have a multicultural family adventure. Experience delicious food in authentic Chinese restaurants in **Chinatown,** pretend you're shopping in Milan in Corso Italia or **Little Italy,** check out the specialty shops in **Greektown,** smell exotic herbs in **Koreatown,** try on traditional clothing in **Little India,** eat delicious desserts in the bakeries of **Little Poland,** or sample cheese in **Portugal Village.** Don't forget about some of the city's other neighborhoods, such as **Cabbagetown**—where parents with little ones must stop at the charming **Riverdale Farm** to pet the animals—the **Historic District,** and **Kensington Market.**

Families who like amusement parks should visit **Ontario Place** for bumper car rides, miniature golf, a motion-simulator ride, and the Cinesphere, which boasts the world's largest movie screen. In summer, there's **Soak City,** a water park with various slides and pools, and the offshore **Marina Village** at Lake Ontario. **Wild Adventure** offers paddle boats and a Wilderness Adventure log ride as well as the park's newest attraction: The Wild World of Weather. Another theme park in the Toronto area is **Canada's Wonderland,** which has waterslides, roller coasters, and 200 other fun rides, including the Behemoth, touted as the tallest and fastest coaster in Canada.

Fun in Toronto doesn't end when the sun goes down. With a bustling theater scene (much cheaper than Broadway for the same quality), your family is sure to find something worth seeing. You can often find last-minute, half-priced tickets at the **T.O. Tix Booth** in Dundess Square at Yonge Street, opposite Eaton Centre.

Tourism Toronto
1-800-499-2514
Toronto, Ontario M5J 1A7
SeeTorontoNow.com, www.toronto.ca

Vancouver, British Columbia

Vancouver, British Columbia's largest city and Canada's third largest,
is a beautiful family-friendly paradise bordered on three sides by
water. A major port, it has **Burrard Inlet** on the north separating
it from **North Vancouver, West Vancouver,** and the snow-capped
Coast Mountains rising 5,000 feet into view. To the west are the
lacy inlets of the Pacific Ocean, while the **Fraser River** separates
the city from its southern suburbs. Vancouver offers families a great
variety of museums and outdoor attractions, enhanced by exciting
new developments from the 2010 Winter Olympic Games. Few cities
combine such stunning vistas; gracious citizens; and a clean, safe
environment with so many kid-oriented activities.

VACATION PLANNING TIPS

Be prepared for rain! Bring raincoats and umbrellas, because Vancouver
is a fairly rainy city with a temperate climate. Vancouver's weather is best
from May to September, particularly during August and September.

A good place to start your trip is in the downtown area, where many
great shops, restaurants, and moderate-to-upscale hotels are located.
Here, you can find the **B.C. Place Stadium and Sports Hall of
Fame,** the world's largest air-supported dome stadium, which is the
home of the British Columbia Lions, one of the Canadian Football
League teams. The Hall of Fame's galleries feature British Columbia
sports from the early 1800s to the present. Evenings, your family can
choose between the busy **Robson Street** or **Gastown,** the city's
nineteenth-century quarter where cobblestone streets and Victorian
buildings are being taken over by stylish new boutiques and restaurants. Teens will enjoy perusing the eclectic shops, ethnic fashion

boutiques, thrift shops, antique furniture stores, and coffeehouses along south **Main Street** in Uptown.

While Vancouver's walkable downtown is a good base, your family will find that outlying areas—accessible by excellent public transport or taxi—also have much to offer.

Just north of downtown is **Stanley Park,** where you and your family can walk, inline skate, or cycle the 3-mile-long Seawall encircling this majestic 1,000-acre woodland park. Don't miss the path past totem poles representing the region's First Nations tribes. If you have tiny travelers aboard, head straight to the miniature train!

At the **Vancouver Aquarium Marine Science Centre,** located in Stanley Park, you can watch beluga whales, sharks, octopi, and much more. A cute facility named for the star of *Finding Nemo* is **Clownfish Cove,** an interactive play area where kids can get hands-on with horseshoe crabs. For rainy-day fun, head southeast of downtown to **Science World.** Housed in a giant "golf ball" (actually a geodesic dome), the museum offers hands-on exhibits and live demonstrations.

About 20 minutes north of Stanley Park is beautiful **Grouse Mountain.** Hop on the funicular for a 3,700-feet ascent and spectacular view of the city and bay, or join the hundreds of locals each day who make the rigorous 2,800-foot-long **Grouse Grind** hike to the peak for fitness. Winter visitors to Grouse can ski, snowboard, snowshoe, or take a sleigh ride. In summer, Grouse offers a lumberjack show, paragliding, mountain biking, hiking, and helicopter tours. Skiing enthusiasts should also visit **Cypress Mountain,** about 40 minutes from downtown. The mountain's facilities were renovated for the 2010 Olympics to host the freestyle skiing and snowboarding events.

Regardless of the weather, we love taking the short ferry ride to **Granville Island,** a fun place to walk around. Kids adore the little indoor farmer's market crowded with produce and bakery stalls and the many galleries, quality crafts shops, and street performers who bring it to life. Poke your heads into the Model Ships Museum, the Sport Fishing Museum, and the Model Trains Museum. Nearby is the **Vancouver Museum,** where families can enjoy displays about the Vancouver region and its natural history.

"The moment I stepped off the plane onto Vancouver soil, I knew Canada was much more than people made it out to be ... one could actually take deep, full breaths of air and enjoy its natural sweetness .... Outside of the natural purity of Canada, I was surprised by how urban the city of Vancouver was—huge buildings, community centers, restaurants, entertainment, and people. However, I immediately noticed the balance between nature and the city. Huge trees lined every street, and parks existed on almost every block. These natural elements beautified the city while cleaning the air and providing a relaxed environment."

—R. W., www.travelBIGO.com

Summer visitors can continue west to **Jericho** and **Ambleside Beaches.** A relatively quiet beach, Jericho has plenty of shade for picnics and a boardwalk for strollers. The sandy beach at Ambleside Park boasts a popular snack bar, playground, grass playing field, paved seawall, and—of course—the ocean for a swim on very hot days. Nearby is the **Museum of Anthropology,** which displays one of the world's largest collections of Northwest Coast aboriginal art. Kids learn about potlatch ceremonies and other aspects of the First Nations peoples' way of life.

To get in touch with Vancouver's beautiful natural scenery, take a day trip to mountainous North Vancouver—the self-appointed birthplace of mountain biking—where you can visit the **Capilano Suspension Bridge.** The 450-feet suspension bridge stretches 230 feet above the Capilano River Canyon, totally enveloped in a backdrop of majestic old-growth evergreens. Yes, it's Vancouver's oldest attraction and rather touristy, but floating on planks and cables above stunning scenery is an uncommon experience. If you'd rather avoid the crowds, check out the nearby **Lynn Canyon Suspension Bridge** instead. It swings 20 stories above the wild river, and you'll also find hiking trails through 100-year-old cedar forests and an **Ecology Centre,** where kids can manipulate hands-on displays such as animal puppets and discovery drawers.

In West Van, be sure to pay a visit to **Lighthouse Park** by the Point Atkinson Lighthouse; a 3-mile-long trail winds along the seaside with spectacular views of the trees and ocean. From here, there's a ferry that takes you to **Bowen Island.** Take the 20-minute scenic sail across Howe Sound to Snug Cove. Once there, you can hike to Killarney Lake. Along the way, watch for ducks, kingfishers, Canada geese, and swallows that inhabit the marshes around the lake.

Slightly farther from downtown Vancouver is **Westminster Quay.** Catch the SkyTrain from downtown Vancouver for the scenic ride to this waterfront development, where you'll find many activities for the entire family, including shopping, exploring the beautifully restored nineteenth-century architecture of B.C.'s first capital, **New Westminster,** and sightseeing along the Fraser River on a paddle wheeler.

Tourism Vancouver
Vancouver, British Columbia V6C 3L6
604-682-2222
www.tourismvancouver.com, www.hellobc.com

Mountain Towns

Chapter

34

In This Chapter

- Finding plenty of active family adventures in beautiful Banff National Park
- Seeking snow and sun at the world-class mountain resort of Mont-Tremblant
- Embracing the snow-filled fun at Whistler, the top-rated ski resort in North America

In a country that covers 41 percent of the North American continent, you would expect huge swaths of terrain to be covered by snow-capped mountains, dense evergreen forests, and rushing rivers. And in Canada, they are.

There are many, many mountain towns to choose from that will provide a wonderful, active family vacation at any time of year. In hundreds of small locales, citizens are actively committed to the environment and personal wellness—the same lifestyle that permeates the Mountain States of the American Rockies (covered in Chapter 18). In this chapter, we focus on the three best-known mountain resorts in Canada.

Banff and Lake Louise, Banff National Park, Alberta

While constructing the Canadian Pacific Railway in 1883, three workers discovered a cave that contained hot springs, marking the birth of the recreation area of **Banff National Park.** The park, the oldest and still one of the most beautiful in Canada, now encompasses more than 2,000 square miles of glaciers, ice fields, forests, rivers, valleys, and mountains. Part of the Rocky Mountain Range, Banff's alpine landscape makes it a perfect getaway for families looking for an active adventure.

Established as a UNESCO World Heritage Site in 1984, Banff matured from a Gold Rush town into one of Alberta's top tourist destinations with major attractions such as **Upper Hot Springs;** the beautiful golf course at the historic, castle-like **Banff Springs Hotel;** and the popular mountain resorts **Sunshine Village** (the very first in Banff), **Lake Louise Mountain Resort,** and **Mount Norquay Ski Resort**—all great for skiing and other snow sports.

The rugged mountain town of **Banff** is a small, efficient, and charming base for families to explore the enormous natural assets of the region. Banff serves as the commercial center, offering outdoor clothing stores, ice cream and fudge parlors, day spas, and cultural attractions such as the **Buffalo Nations Luxton Museum** and the **Whyte Museum.** The nearby **Cave and Basin National Historic Site** is where the first natural hot springs were discovered, and they can be seen flowing through the cave and outside into an emerald basin.

It seems everyone in this community of ski bums and New-Age families works for a tour operator offering guided tours through caves, up hills, or into the woods either on foot, horseback, mountain bike, snowmobile, or snowshoes. The tour options cater to every comfort level and range from motorcoach sightseeing to heli-skiing.

VACATION PLANNING TIPS

The "Greatest Outdoor Show on Earth," the **Calgary Stampede,** takes place in the nearby city of **Calgary** for 10 days each summer. The world's largest rodeo competition, it also features a midway, stage shows, and concerts. Book tickets early if you plan to vacation in Alberta during the stampede. If you're really in the spirit, pick up a driving map for the **Cowboy Trail** and see ranches, museums, real cowboys, and Western movie locations.

The **Banff Winter Carnival** is an off-slope event held each year featuring cross-country skiing, curling, and snowshoeing. During your visit, you'll pass by **Castle Mountain,** the summer internment camp for immigrants from Hungary, Austria, and Germany who were considered dangerous during World War I. There's little history left except for the roads and park infrastructure built by internees who were paid 25 cents per day for their labor.

Outside the town, a variety of wildlife and birds roam the snow-capped peaks and verdant valleys. Grizzly bears are just one of the numerous species wandering through the forests, although they are on the endangered list in the area. Other animals in the park, such as white-tailed deer, cougars, and the rare sightings of caribou, make this an exciting spot to watch for wildlife.

Nearby **Lake Louise** on the eastern edge of the park, just 32 miles from Banff, is a very small village serving the hotel guests at the Old-World **Chateau Lake Louise** and campgrounds. The stunning glacier-fed lake was named after Princess Louise Caroline Alberta, a daughter of England's Queen Victoria and wife of the provincial governor. If you are visiting during winter, check out the **Annual Ice Magic Festival** and the **Little Chippers Festival,** where the littlest ice carvers can learn the art and science of carving. The snow-capped peaks and (sadly, melting) glaciers comprising the **Icefields Parkway** are a must-see along a gorgeous road that extends for 143 miles from Lake Louise to the even wilder **Jasper National Park** to the north.

If you get to **Calgary,** stop by and view the site of the 1988 Winter Olympics. There, you can brave Skyline, the fastest zip line in North America; try Zorbing down the mountainside in a clear plastic sphere; or take in a superb **Calgary Flames** hockey game. Other attractions in the area include the **Calgary Zoo** and **Devonian Gardens,** the largest indoor garden in the world.

Parks Canada—Banff Information Center
Banff, Alberta T1L 1K2
403-762-1550
www.banffnationalpark.com, www.banfflakelouise.com

Mont-Tremblant, Quebec

Mont-Tremblant, a venerable mountain resort just a 90-minute drive from Montreal, is easily one of the best snow sports mountains on the East Coast—and, with more than 650 acres to ski, it's also one of the biggest. Legends about the freezing Canadian winter and ice storms, while partly true, shouldn't keep visitors away— temperatures are often comparable to Vermont and New Hampshire. Great skiing, wonderful food, a French flair, and numerous activities on and off the mountain will keep everyone in the family entertained.

For skiers and snowboarders, Quebec province's Mont-Tremblant has a more than 2,000-foot vertical drop, just under 100 trails, and a variety of terrain for different abilities. With half of all trails designated for experts, the daredevils in your group should be happy (although some experts won't feel challenged on this relatively small mountain). While snow sports attract most families to the region, it's a popular summer destination for lake sailing, fishing, hiking, and mountain biking.

VACATION PLANNING TIPS

Winter flights on Continental (with well-priced hotel and lift ticket packages) depart Toronto and New York and go directly to the tiny log cabin **Mont-Tremblant International Airport,** which is about a 45-minute drive from the resort.

Even if you don't ski or snowboard, you will find plenty to do in the European-style, pedestrian-only **Tremblant Village** base area. In winter, there's an ice-skating rink in front of the chapel and a fun sledding hill where all ages will enjoy sliding on an inner tube. The year-round **AquaClub La Source,** Tremblant's indoor and outdoor pool club, comes complete with waterslides, a Tarzan rope that swings across the pool, two hot tubs, and a fitness center. And there needn't be a disconnect between the family athletes and couch potatoes—the many fine restaurants that grace the central square of the village are easily accessible from both the mountain and nearby hotels and provide a great meeting spot at lunch. For après-ski, we enjoy watching families with pets (it's a very pet-friendly place) browsing the boutiques and preschoolers carrying baguettes back to their condos for supper.

On the sunnier south side of the mountain, Tremblant just completed a new base camp called **Versant Soleil,** complete with a casino, homes, hotels, and a lake for ice skating. In the nearby Quebecois towns of **Ville de Mont-Tremblant, Saint-Jovite,** and **Ste. Agathe,** you can make family-friendly outings to a syrup-making farm or snowmobile on the area's many abandoned railroad tracks—and don't worry, English is widely spoken.

Many families prefer to visit during the warmer months, when condo rates fall and the crisp mountain air beckons. Tremblant offers numerous lakes for canoeing, miles of mountain biking trails (and the requisite rental gear), panoramic gondola rides up to the mountain summit, and awesome alpine luge rides. There's also a car racing track and nearby whitewater rafting on the **Rouge River.** The ski mountain, which has children's programs for ages 12 months and older all winter, also runs summer nature day camps. Be sure to check out the resort's top-value Activity Passes and family specials.

Two beautiful championship courses, **Le Diable** and **Le Géant,** should keep the golfers in your family happy. For youngsters who aren't ready to play 18 holes, there's a mini-golf course. Animal-loving families should check out the **Birds of Prey** show, where you can see a slew of birds including horned owls, black vultures, and bald eagles, or sign up for one of the many naturalist-led nature walks—whether it's in sneakers or snowshoes.

Station Mont Tremblant
Mont-Tremblant, Quebec J8E 1S4
1-888-738-1777
www.tremblant.ca, www.tourismemonttremblant.com

Whistler, British Columbia

Consistently voted the number-one ski resort in North America, **Whistler-Blackcomb** towers above the international mountain town of **Whistler,** British Columbia. Just two hours from **Vancouver** along the scenic **Sea to Sky Highway,** its lively alpine village, restaurants, bars, and luxury accommodations were showcased during coverage of the **Vancouver 2010 Olympic and Paralympic Winter Games.**

FELLOW TRAVELERS SAY ...

"The reason I went to Whistler, Canada, was my love of snowboarding. I attended Camp of Champions. The most fun thing about snowboarding is seeing the look on people's faces when you are doing back flips or other difficult tricks that can be astonishing … my best friend Nick and I came running off the third and final chairlift to take a look at the mountain. It was a glorious moment. The mountain was absolutely beautiful, white snow, scenic background, and a smell of fresh mountain air. Next thing I knew, we were strapping up our snowboards and flying down."

—J. S. www.travelBIGO.com

The spotlight fell on Whistler when the huge resort hosted the world's top athletes for the Olympics alpine and nordic technical and speed events. However, Whistler is also known as one of the few mountains where visitors can ski in the morning and play golf in the afternoon. Chairlift access to 7,500 feet means there can be foggy, damp conditions in the spring, but it enables snow sports addicts to get their fix all year long.

The resort boasts 8,100 skiable acres, including more than 200 trails, 38 lifts, 3 glaciers, and 12 alpine bowls. Parents, never fear: the ski and ride schools require helmets for all students and affix GPS trackers to kids so that no one gets lost—and so you can figure out what trails they liked and may want to return to.

Shockingly, Whistler didn't have water or electricity until the 1960s, when legendary developers from **Intrawest** moved in to make it a top tourist destination. In 1966, Whistler opened to the public, and ever since it has been a favorite among snow bunnies and mountain bikers from around the globe. Before 2009, families had to choose whether they wanted to spend their day on the quiet, family-friendly Blackcomb slopes or at the slicker **Whistler Mountain,** but the **Peak2Peak Gondola** now links the two resorts with a new base village. Considered an engineering feat, the gondola transports guests nearly 3 miles in just 11 minutes, often at altitudes of more than 1,400 feet above the slopes—offering great views in any season.

Kick off your skis and check out off-slope activities such as ice skating and curling, then take a spin on one of the eight lanes at the **tube park.** All ages are welcome, but the 12-and-younger crowd must be accompanied by an adult. For a truly unforgettable experience, bundle everyone up for a horse-drawn sleigh ride or dog sledding to view the rugged beauty of the region.

FUN FACTS

Talk about Olympic dreams come true. Developed as a ski resort with the goal of hosting the 1968 Winter Olympics, Whistler didn't get the games that year. The town was then asked to be the 1976 host city after Denver backed out, but Innsbruck, Austria, was selected. Then, in 2010, Whistler was bestowed the honor of being the first-ever Host Mountain Resort for the Vancouver 2010 Winter Olympics.

The large pedestrian Village of Whistler is a shopper's dream, with hundreds of shops including **The Northface, Burton, Quicksilver,** and the **Olympic Store** offering the latest fashions at good prices. Other indoor, rainy-day activities might include a visit to the **Whistler Museum and Archives** or the newly opened **Squamish Lil'wat Cultural Center,** which celebrates the indigenous Squamish and Lil'wat First Nations peoples who inhabit Whistler Valley.

Village accommodations range from the highest-price, ski-in/ski-out luxury places to more moderately priced family-style condos. Year-round, there is on-mountain daycare, and at night the **Core Fitness** facility's supervised kids' programs teach rock climbing and other sports, giving parents some time to themselves. The **Magic Castle** at **Blackcomb's Adventure Zone** is another fun treat, great for indoor activities during inclement weather. Here, families can enjoy miniature golf, a climbing wall, and the Westcoast Luge at a majestic fun zone open from June through September. Year-round zip-lining is another not-to-be-missed adventure.

Whistler-Blackcomb Resort
Whistler, British Columbia V0N 1B4
1-866-218-9690
www.whistlerblackcomb.com, www.whistler.com

Cultural Appeal

In This Chapter

- Honoring seafaring culture at Halifax's Maritime Museum of the Atlantic
- Paying homage to Mounties at the Royal Canadian Mounted Police Heritage Center
- Embracing both traditional and cutting-edge culture in the port city of Victoria
- Shopping and playing 'til you drop at the West Edmonton Mall
- Partying in the snow at Ottawa's Winterlude Festival

We have heard Canada described as "dull" and listened while some American families asked how a trip "up north" could be any type of vacation at all. These naysayers couldn't be more wrong; each province in Canada offers a myriad of cultural traditions that families will enjoy.

In fact, in all our years reviewing family destinations and listening to the travel tales of FamilyTravelForum.com community members, we've heard some of the most astonishing facts and learned about some of the wackiest attractions ever—in Canada! After your Canadian vacation, let us know whether you agree that this country is among the most creative and imaginative on Earth.

Maritime Museum of the Atlantic, Nova Scotia

The sea defines **Halifax,** the capital of Canada's **Nova Scotia** province. The Old World city's authentic waterfront, featuring wooden wharves and working boats floating on the gentle swells, reflects the British ancestry of the region. Many families arrive in this city by cruise ship.

For a small seafaring city, Halifax has seen its share of maritime disasters. In 1912, the port witnessed the legendary end of the foolishly dubbed "unsinkable" *RMS Titanic.* The sinking of the *Mont Blanc* in World War I followed just five years later. Painful though these tragedies were, their stories make fascinating, interactive viewing and provide a wonderful way to learn about history. The best way for families to experience the nautical wonders of Halifax is to visit the **Maritime Museum of the Atlantic.**

One of Halifax's stellar attractions, the Maritime Museum is the oldest of its kind in Canada. Children interested in ship models will enjoy the Days of Sail Gallery, where reconstructions and small replicas of sailing vessels are on display. Military families can learn about the strong naval presence in Nova Scotia, which ranges from the earliest days of the Royal Navy dockyard in 1758 to the founding of the current Royal Canadian Navy in 1910. Other popular exhibits include the Age of Steam Gallery and Shipwreck Treasures of Nova Scotia.

A family favorite is the museum's *Titanic* exhibit. Although the famed ocean liner went down in the middle of the Atlantic Ocean, the shores of Halifax were only 700 miles away—thus, Nova Scotia had the first relief boats on the scene. The museum features an extensive collection of artifacts from the ship, including the only intact deck chair and shoes from an unknown child who was on board.

> **FUN FACTS**
>
> Outside the Maritime Museum, the local cemeteries in Halifax served as the burial ground for nearly half of the 300 recovered bodies from the *Titanic* wreckage of 1912. People think the grave marked "J. Dawson" belonged to Jack Dawson, the character played by Leonardo DiCaprio in the James Cameron movie, but actually it belongs to "James," a trimmer on the ship.

If you still want to learn more about the region's maritime history, there is plenty to do in town. Visit **Pier 21** where between 1921 and 1978, more than 1 million immigrants were processed. Now, the unique and interactive museum recreates the experience with pictures, posters, passports, and other displays that convey the hopes and fears of the foreigners starting their new life in Canada.

Also of interest is the **Halifax Citadel,** a working fort that offers fascinating tours, bagpipe presentations, and a very loud **Noon Gun** firing display around lunchtime. If you want to explore the sea itself, consider getting on the ocean with **Murphy's on the Water,** a sightseeing cruise and dining tour experience that operates on the **Cable Wharf** by **St. George.** Whale watching and other nature-oriented cruise experiences are also available.

Maritime Museum of the Atlantic
1675 Lower Water Street
Halifax, Nova Scotia B3J 1S3
902-424-7490
museum.gov.ns.ca/mma/index.html, www.novascotia.com

Royal Canadian Mounted Police Heritage Center, Saskatchewan

For more than a century, the **Royal Canadian Mounted Police** have kept crime to a minimum across Canada. In 2007, they were honored with the **Royal Canadian Mounted Police Heritage Center** in Regina, Saskatchewan, which explores the role of the red-clad Mounties.

Housed in an elegantly designed stone and glass building on the grounds of the **RCMP Academy** (where most Mounties train), the new Heritage Center uses art exhibits, multimedia presentations, and special programming and tours to tell the story of the RCMP.

If you're in Saskatchewan, drop by and visit the center's famed horses, Pepper, Salute, and Falcon—allowing for great photo ops. Depending on when you visit, you may also be able to catch the RCMP Musical Ride at the **RCMP Academy Depot Division,** where nearly 55,000 cadets have trained on their way to becoming policemen. The RCMP Musical Ride showcases intricate cavalry drills performed by 32 highly skilled equestrian Mounties and horses that have been trained to stand patiently for hours of petting and photo-taking.

The **Sergeant Majors Parade** is held weekdays at 12:45 P.M. in Parade Square. Another fun event is the **Sunset-Retreat,** held on Tuesday evenings during July and August; the event includes a troop drill, military music, and the lowering of the Canadian flag. The fanfare is more than enough to keep the kids quiet for the entire ceremony!

The capital city of Regina has much to offer in the cultural spectrum, including performances at the **Regina Conservatory of Music** at Regina College. Annual civic festivals include the **Regina Folk Festival,** the **Cathedral Village Arts Festival,** and the **Regina Dragon Boat Festival.** Held each Labor Day, the Dragon Festival draws 20,000 spectators who watch the racing in **Wascana Lake** and enjoy martial arts demonstrations, Chinese folk dancing, and a children's fair. A major highlight of Regina is **Wascana Centre,** a park built around Wascana Lake that includes concert and theater halls, educational facilities, and a skateboarding park.

VACATION PLANNING TIPS

The lowest temperature ever recorded in Regina, Saskatchewan, was -58°F, and the highest temperature was 110°F. The semi-arid continental climate brings hot summers and cold winters. Be prepared for extreme temperatures no matter what time of year you visit.

Royal Canadian Mounted Police Heritage Center
5907 Dewdney Avenue
Regina, Saskatchewan S4T 0P4
1-866-567-7267
www.rcmpheritagecentre.com, www.regina.ca

Victoria, British Columbia

With the mildest climate in Canada, half the rainfall of neighboring Seattle and Vancouver, and a stunning setting pressed between the mountains and shore of **Vancouver Island,** Victoria is a year-round, picture-postcard destination. The capital of British Columbia, this pretty and very civilized waterfront city is small and manageable yet offers many family-friendly events and cultural attractions.

All ages will enjoy the **Royal British Columbia Museum.** You can easily spend a day here taking in the wide array of permanent and temporary exhibits as well as catching a movie at the IMAX theater. **Ocean Station** allows visitors to experience the underwater world of the West Coast with an aquarium full of sea stars, fish, sea urchins, and more. The Royal British Columbia's **First People's Gallery** has one of the finest collections of native Indian arts and handcrafts in the country, while the large **Modern History** and **Natural History Galleries** are known for their life-size replicas of items ranging from Captain George Vancouver's eighteenth-century ship *HMS Discovery* to grizzly bears and sea lions. Ask at the Information Desk for children's activity sheets to keep your young ones engaged as you make your way through the museum.

Another fascinating find is the **Royal London Wax Museum.** This kid-friendly museum features more than 300 political, royal, and historical wax figures, including William Shakespeare, Walt Disney, Princess Diana, and Babe Ruth. Also on display are wax replicas of the Crown Jewels of England, enhanced by audio-visual technology. Kids will also love **Miniature World,** "The Greatest Little Show on Earth," which is home to 80 mini attractions such as the world's smallest operating sawmill and a variety of dollhouse styles.

When you're ready to get outside, you can head out to **Bear Mountain** for some hiking or dress up to visit the classic **Empress Hotel** on the harbor and stay for high tea. If you want to tour the city from a different perspective, saddle up with **Tally Ho Carriage Tours,** a horse-drawn carriage company that has carted folks around Victoria since 1903. The entertaining tour guides relate Victoria's rich history peppered with humorous anecdotes.

FUN FACTS

Every year in early spring, citizens of Victoria participate in **Flower Count,** a tradition of counting all the flowers in the city. Each municipality competes to win the title of "Bloomingest Community" by having the most flowers. More than a billion flowers are counted every year.

Nature lovers will flock to Victoria's indoor tropical rain forest at the **Butterfly Gardens.** This little piece of paradise includes 35 species of free-flying butterflies, including the exotic Blue Morpho and Giant Owl. Waterfalls, trees, orchids, and even carnivorous plants are part of the display. Before you enter, be sure to watch the video preview that explains the cycle of a butterfly's life; tours and access to the more in-depth Learning Center are also available. Kids can learn about and play with many animals, including peacocks, at the **Beacon Hill Children's Farm** in **Beacon Hill Park.**

Victoria embraces its fashion, cuisine, and arts. Adults in your family will want to follow the **Ale Trail,** a map leading to local microbreweries where tours and samples are free. Canada's oldest **Chinatown** wraps around Fan Tan Alley, its narrowest street, and is a great place for collectibles and cuisine. Fashion boutiques have permeated the hipper neighborhoods of **Lower Johnson,** the **Design District,** and **North Fort,** where you can also find contemporary furniture, handcrafts, and home décor.

Of course, the Victorians are very into food and sustainable agriculture. **Terralicious,** located on the scenic Saanich Peninsula, is a gardening and cooking school that hosts five-day programs during spring and summer for kids ages 5–13 (broken down into age-appropriate groups) who commune with farm animals and grow their own produce while learning how to cook. Grownups are welcome, too.

Tourism Victoria
Victoria, British Columbia V8W 1T3
1-800-663-3883
www.tourismvictoria.com, www.canada.travel

West Edmonton Mall, Alberta

Edmonton, about two hours north of Calgary, Alberta, is best known to Canadians for what was once the world's largest indoor entertainment complex: the **West Edmonton Mall.** Begun in 1981 and expanded in three phases, it now encompasses more than 5.3-million square feet. WEM, under the same ownership as Minnesota's Mall of America (reviewed in Chapter 12), is an indoor entertainment and retail complex built on superlatives. There is a 217,800-square-foot indoor water park considered "the largest in the world"; the "world's largest" indoor amusement park; and myriad other indoor delights, including a skating rink, nightclub, mini-golf course, aquarium, a replica of one of Columbus' sailing ships, and a billiards center. And don't forget about the more than 800 shops and 100 eateries. **West 49,** a skateboard store in the mall, features an indoor skate park between aisles of baggy jeans and flat-soled "Sk8r" shoes. And then, there are the amazing attractions that require buying a ticket.

The **World Waterpark** encompasses 5 acres of water play, including a wave pool, and keeps its water at a balmy 84°F. Warm water also runs through more than 20 activities and several slides, with something fun for even the youngest swimmers. Nonswimmers can look for the Wakeboard Festival or attend Dive-In movies at night. Bungee jumping dangles over one end of the wave pool, and thrill seekers who sign up for the jump may elect to "hit" the water at the bottom of their fall or just bounce crazily above it. The friendly staff attends to visitors with rental towels, chaise lounges, lockers, and several fast-food outlets; lifeguards abound.

With more than 24 rides and attractions, **Galaxyland Amusement Park** is the world's largest indoor amusement park, and it's fascinating just to see how they fit everything in. There's Mind-bender, the world's largest indoor triple-loop roller coaster curled around and above Galaxy Kids, four stories of space-themed play area for younger children.

The mall features other family-friendly adventure areas as well, including a lagoon that's home to three bottlenose dolphins, an interactive marine life touch pool, four submarine voyages in the world's largest indoor lake, a bowling alley, a chapel, a petting zoo, Chinatown with groceries and restaurants, and **Professor Wem's Adventure Golf Course.** Families who want a more out-of-this-world themed golf experience should check out **Putt 'N' Glow,** where you can play miniature golf on a phosphorescent course.

Be sure to take a free daily tour of the mall's famous **Fantasyland Hotel.** Each of the hotel's rooms is unique and reflects a theme done to the max: the Wild West family room has a king bed and saddle, with the kids' bunks inside a jail cell; the Artic Room has a life-size polar bear sculpture reclining in the living area. WEM also offers Toddler Time for kids age five and younger (with a chaperone) who are shopping in the mall. This baby-friendly area offers storytelling, face painting, and coloring.

If you'd rather not spend your entire vacation in the mall, Edmonton has much of interest including the top provincial art museums. **Fort Edmonton Park** is a living-history museum with several streets of shops, each devoted to a different era between 1846 and 1920. Kids will love the period trolley, steam train, 1920s-era mini-golf, and classic carousel spinning in a fun midway. **TELUS World of Science** is an interactive learning space with a cool Body Fantastic exhibit. Summer visitors can take advantage of the many festivals; the annual summertime **Capital EX** at the Exposition Grounds is a huge celebration of Alberta's agricultural industry and is well worth a visit on its own.

West Edmonton Mall, Alberta
1755, 8882 170 Street
Edmonton, Alberta T5T 4J2
1-800-661-8890
www.wem.ca, www.travelalberta.com

Winterlude in Ottawa, Ontario

Every February, thousands flock to Canada's capital to join in on Winterlude, three weekends of every snow activity imaginable and one of the most family-friendly events in the northern hemisphere.

Despite the cold weather, locals and visiting families participate in a range of vigorous outdoor activities such as ice skating on the world's largest skating rink. While this 4.8-mile-long natural rink known as **Rideau Canal Skateway** will be sure to keep your tootsies warm, there are plenty of other heart-pumping activities. Downhill skiing, for example, is designed for younger novices, and the festival provides qualified instructors. For those with shaky legs, try the easy—but fun and fast—**Sun Life Giant Slide** in **Jacques-Cartier Park.** Kids can also go ice fishing, in which case they'll also receive a certificate and fishing rod. (Parents should register their kids well in advance for such activities.)

Throughout the festival, ice and snow sculptors delicately chisel away at massive blocks of ice, in **Centennial Park.** Visit the **Rogers Crystal Lounge,** which is full of hands-on sculptures and carvings and even a lounge with family board games—made of ice, of course.

FUN FACTS

Winterlude's **H2Orchestra** generates all its music by using some form of water. The concerts feature water-based instruments such as the hydrau-lophone, which creates a unique sound from water, ice, and steam.

At **Place Gatineau,** in the huge Sun Life Snowflake Kingdom play area, counselors are on duty to keep the fun flowing. Each Winterlude weekend features a number of family-welcoming educational tours, including one led by the **Canadian Rangers,** who teach kids about the work they do.

You can take part in an array of Winterlude food tastings, such as a mass stew cook-off at **ByWard Market** downtown, then return to ByWard to see the many wonderful gift items, handcrafts, and gourmet delicacies for sale. If you have little ones in tow, be sure to visit with Winterlude's mascots, the **Ice Hog Family**—a group of furry animals that crossed an ice bridge to arrive in Alaska long ago. Every winter they make their appearance at Winterlude and even put on a show, **Topsy-Turvy,** themed after an acrobatic circus.

Families visiting Ottawa at other times of year or just wanting to get out of the cold will appreciate many of the **Capital Region** attractions found in both Ottawa (Ontario Province) and **Gatineau,** across the Ottawa River in Quebec Province. Surely, the kids will want to drop into the luxurious lobby of the **Fairmont Chateau Laurier,** a castle-like hotel whose green copper towers and turrets embellish many Ottawa vistas.

Also, be sure to visit the **Canadian Museum of Civilization** and its amazing collection of First Nations totem poles, and the **Canadian Museum of Nature,** where all ages can get tips from the area's hardy animals about how they survive during the harsh winter season. On the historic grounds of **Rideau Hall,** visit the state rooms of the governor general's residence and discover the unique collection of art showcasing Canadian diversity. Families who want to learn more about this bilingual, very Canadian city can board a double-decker bus for a hop-on/hop-off tour of more than a dozen stops, including the seat of government at **Parliament Hill,** the country's finest art collection at the **National Gallery of Canada,** and the **Canadian Aviation Museum,** among others.

NCC/Winterlude
Ottawa, Ontario K1P 1C7
1-800-465-1867
www.canadascapital.gc.ca, www.ottawatourism.ca

Outdoor Adventures

In This Chapter

- Getting in on the fossilized fun at Dinosaur Provincial Park
- Seeing Niagara Falls' beauty by air, land, and sea
- Gawking at Hudson Bay polar bears and whales in Churchill, Manitoba

Canada's varied geography has defined the country, not only throughout the course of its history but also in the experiences of the people who came to live or travel there. Perhaps that's why the Canadian government has been so active in protecting its land in national parks. At present, Canada's 39 national parks represent almost every type of terrain and ecosystem on the North American continent, and Parks Canada offers many instructional activities to help visitors appreciate—and interact safely with—the natural environment.

Canada is also highly regarded for its commitment to the environment on a local level, and many municipalities provide visitors with opportunities to contemplate nature at its finest. We think you'll find that in Canada, a country devoted to the great outdoors, a family outdoor adventure is truly something special.

Dinosaur Provincial Park and Dinosaur Valley, Alberta

Dinosaur Provincial Park, about one and a half hours from the oil boom town of **Calgary,** is best known for its wealth of dinosaur fossils. Equally recognized for its unusual badlands topography, Dinosaur Park has been designated a UNESCO World Heritage Site to protect its rare treasures. It should come as no surprise that parents from around the world, including celebrities such as Brad Pitt and Angelina Jolie, take their kids here.

FUN FACTS

The **Canadian Badlands** are similar geographically to the Badlands of South Dakota (see Chapter 13) in the United States and cover part of southern and eastern Alberta province. They got their name from the early settlers who complained about how difficult it was to cross this unusual landscape, with its extreme swings in temperature, high winds, and little water. The appearance of the smoothly deformed rocks, or **hoodoos,** results from compressed marine mineral deposits that have been carved by the movement of glaciers, then later eroded into peaks, deep valleys, and rolling prairies. Along with dinosaur fossils came rich coal deposits, making the Badlands a destination for generations of fortune seekers.

Most people come for the dinosaur fossils, and they are rarely disappointed. Forty dinosaur species have been discovered in the park, and more than 500 specimens have been extracted and are now in exhibits around the world. Children will love how close they can get to the actual fossils—they're allowed to tiptoe in the footsteps of the dinosaurs and see where complete dinosaur skeletons have been unearthed.

About two hours from the Park in **Drumheller,** center of the so-called "**Dinosaur Valley**" region, families can ogle the world's largest collection of Triceratops, Allosaurus, and other dinosaur fossils at the state-of-the-art **Royal Tyrrell Museum of Paleontology.** The museum offers an extensive display of dinosaur skeletons and a huge roster of special programs for kids. Prized for its Cretaceous-era fossils, the museum opened in 1884 with Albertosaurus bones excavated nearby by Joseph Burr Tyrrell, a geologist looking for coal deposits. His discovery brought waves of paleontologists to the site, including the American Museum of Natural History's colorful Barnum Brown, star of the 3-D IMAX film *T-Rex, Back to the Cretaceous*, which was filmed at the museum. There are many other dinosaur-related sites in the area, including the continuing fossil bed excavations near Medicine Hat that are shown in the **Devil's Coulee Dinosaur Heritage Museum.**

Kids ages 14 and older will have a blast joining an actual crew excavating in Dinosaur Provincial Park. **Bonebed 30 Guided Excavations** allows small groups to work on an actual dig with an experienced paleontological technician as guide. After an orientation to the park and the research project, you work in a real quarry and prospect for new fossil finds that contribute to research going on at the Royal Tyrrell Museum. Numerous camping areas in and around the park make this a budget family vacation; there's even a campground under the shadow of the **World's Largest Dinosaur,** one of those long-ago erected statues that served as a roadside attraction to lure passersby to the town.

For non-dinosaur-related activities, we recommend the **Atlas Coal Mine National Historic Site,** where you can explore the 210-foot-deep underground conveyor tunnel, hike up to the newly restored Blacksmith Shop, and ride on the 1936 mine locomotive. In **Drumheller,** you can rent bikes and ride the town's path along the Red Deer River. For a taste of local culture, go see a performance of the **Canadian Badlands Passion Play,** which portrays the life and death of Jesus Christ in drama. It is shown during summer in a natural 2,500-seat outdoor amphitheatre.

Dinosaur Valley
Drumheller, Alberta T0J 0Y3
403-823-6300
www.dinosaurvalley.com, www.travelalberta.com

Niagara Falls, Ontario

A natural wonder straddling the Ontario and New York State border, **Niagara Falls** and its offshoot Horseshoe Falls (named after its "U" shape) generate a loud roar as more than 600,000 gallons of water fall nearly 170 feet every second. From one end to the other, the brink of Horseshoe Falls measures 2,500 feet—and with mist emerging from the surface inspires awe from all onlookers. The second largest waterfall in the world (beaten only by Victoria Falls in Zimbabwe), the Canadian side of Niagara attracts millions of visitors every year who come to see the majestic waters for themselves.

FELLOW TRAVELERS SAY ...

"We stood next to the falls and watched as the crystal clear waters roared. It was breathtaking! I was instantly captivated by the sight and sound of Niagara Falls ... certainly a wonder to visit. It's more than just a waterfall; it's a breathtaking example of the work of God. I discovered on this trip that the world has its select few gems that it holds precious and wants us all to see."

—H. L., www.travelBIGO.com

For a closer look, hop on the **Maid of the Mist,** which has been ferrying visitors to and from the base of the falls since the 1950s. Warning: although rain slickers are provided, you will get drenched. A slightly drier option is the 30- to 45-minute tour called **Journey Behind the Falls,** where you descend 150 feet by elevator through the earth's bedrock and walk through tunnels that lead to various portals and observation decks. The brave can actually stand at the very foot of the Horseshoe Falls in the basin.

For an aerial tour of the falls, **Niagara Helicopters**' six-seater choppers take off every 15 minutes. Seeing the falls and its source from above offers an unparalleled experience. For another spectacular adrenaline rush, ride a 1,500-horsepower jet boat full on into the Class V rapids created by the falls.

VACATION PLANNING TIPS

Although 90 percent of the water flowing down the Niagara River falls over Canada's Horseshoe Falls, families shouldn't forget that New York State is home to the less-powerful, but still just as splendid, **American Falls** and the **Bridal Veil Falls**.

Although the falls are beautiful during the day, evenings—especially after a snowfall or ice storm—are also a great time for taking in their splendor. For another look at this aquatic spectacle from above, enter the **Skylon Tower** (775 feet) or the 25th floor Observation Desk of the **Konica Minolta Tower.** From these heights, kids will love watching the wild spectrum of colors cast by the nightly **Falls Illumination.** Plus, a few times a week, there is a fantastic fireworks show at **Queen Victoria Park.** For more water-based fun, book a room at the **Great Wolf Lodge,** an indoor water park hotel that is bound to satisfy your kids' curiosity about going over the falls in a barrel.

Niagara Falls Tourism
1-800-563-2557
www.niagarafallstourism.com, www.ontariotravel.net

Whales and Polar Bears of Churchill, Manitoba

Churchill, a small town on the **Hudson Bay** in **Manitoba,** has a history dating back to the ancient Inuit tribes. Once a main post in the fur trade, the region has wide-open spaces and wilderness untouched by humans. Located at the convergence of three ecosystems (marine, tundra, and boreal forest), Churchill's awe-inspiring natural wonders await any adventurous family looking to kayak, hike, and bike the surrounding lands and waters.

During summer, when frigid temperatures subside, more than 3,000 **Beluga Whales** congregate in the **Churchill River** to feed, mate, and give birth. As these "sea canaries" frolic, socialize, and shed their winter skin, families with older children (ages 12 and older) can dive in and get up close to these majestic creatures. A variety of local outfitters take groups on excursions where, in wetsuits and snorkels, you can jump right into the river and play with the belugas.

Not only is Churchill "Beluga Central," it's also the self-proclaimed **Polar Bear Capital of the World.** As the cold climate returns, polar bears begin to swim ashore. They arrive at the coast as early as mid-July, but it's not until October that their numbers explode. During November, you can spot more than 40 of this threatened species (their numbers are dwindling due to shrinking sea-ice habitats) on any given day. Families can join naturalists on organized tours to the Hudson Bay tundra to view the glorious polar bears.

FELLOW TRAVELERS SAY ...

"Churchill's population is almost 1,000. It's located on the Hudson Bay, where polar bears wait for winter's ice ... All of Churchill can be seen on foot. We meandered through downtown, passing the polar bear jail that holds wandering bears until the ice forms. We passed homes with nail doormats that keep polar bears out."

—S. D., www.travelBIGO.com

Churchill has more once-in-a-lifetime opportunities for the nature-loving family. The town lies underneath the **Auroral Oval,** an ideal viewing location for the beautiful **Northern Lights.** When the Hudson Bay freezes over completely in late January, the days become shorter and the clear, long nights make it easier to see nature's lightshow. Let the kids stay up late for this special performance—they will be in awe of the purple and green light waves that fill the sky. During the spring, you might see some of the more than 200 species of migratory birds that pass through Churchill.

To learn more about the region's indigenous people, the famous **Eskimo Museum** contains a vast number of artifacts and sculptures from three of the major Canadian aboriginal groups—the Cree, Dene, and Inuit.

Town of Churchill
204-675-8871
www.churchill.ca, www.travelmanitoba.com

The Bests

Best Cities and Mountain Towns for Families

The Northeast

Baltimore, Maryland

Boston, Massachusetts

New York, New York

Philadelphia, Pennsylvania

Pittsburgh, Pennsylvania

Washington, D.C.

The South

Atlanta, Georgia

Memphis, Tennessee

Miami, Florida

New Orleans, Louisiana

Orlando, Florida

The Midwest

Chicago, Illinois

Kansas City, Missouri

Indianapolis, Indiana

St. Louis, Missouri

Minneapolis and St. Paul, Minnesota

The Southwest

Albuquerque, New Mexico

Houston, Texas

Phoenix and Scottsdale, Arizona

The Mountain States

Aspen-Snowmass, Colorado

Breckenridge and the I-70 ski corridor

Jackson Hole, Wyoming

Park City and Utah Olympic Park

The West

Las Vegas, Nevada

Los Angeles, California

San Diego, California

San Francisco, California

The Northwest

Anchorage, Alaska

Portland, Oregon

Seattle, Washington

Mexico

Cancun, Quintana Roo

Mexico City, D.F.

Oaxaca, Oaxaca

Canada

Montreal, Quebec

Quebec City, Quebec

Toronto, Ontario

Vancouver, British Columbia

Banff and Lake Louise, Banff National Park

Mont-Tremblant, Quebec

Whistler, British Columbia

Best Cultural and Historical Attractions for Families

The Northeast

Baseball Hall of Fame, New York

Ben & Jerry's Factory Tour, Vermont

L.L. Bean of Freeport, Maine

Mystic Seaport and Essex, Connecticut

Pennsylvania Dutch country's Amish heritage

The South

Colonial Williamsburg, Virginia

Louisville horse country, Kentucky

Nashville's country-western scene, Tennessee

Pirates of Key West, Florida

The Midwest

Automobile Heritage Trail, Michigan

Branson, Missouri's showplace

Mall of America, Minnesota

Rock and Roll Hall of Fame, Ohio

Iowa State Fair

Mackinac Island, Michigan

Mt. Rushmore, The Badlands, and the Black Hills, South Dakota

National Underground Railroad Freedom Center, Ohio

The Southwest

National Cowboy & Western Heritage Museum, Oklahoma

UFOs and Roswell, New Mexico

The Southwest (continued)

Santa Fe, New Mexico, Museum of International Folk Art

Schlitterbahn, New Braunfels, Texas

San Antonio and The Alamo, Texas

The Wild West in Fort Worth, Texas

The Mountain States

Buffalo Bill Museum and Cody, Wyoming

Colorado Springs, Pike's Peak, and Garden of the Gods

Dinosaur National Monument, Colorado-Utah

Historic Steam Railways of the Rockies

The West

Big Island of Hawaii

Hoover Dam, Nevada

Napa Valley and California wine country

Hollywood, California

Virginia City, Nevada

The Northwest

Leavenworth, Washington's Bavarian village

Lewis & Clark Trail, Washington-Idaho-Oregon

High Desert Museum and Bend, Oregon

Mexico

Campeche, Yucatan

Chichen-Itza and the Mayan World of Yucatan

San Miguel de Allende, Guanajuato

Canada

Maritime Museum of the Atlantic, Nova Scotia

Royal Canadian Mounted Police Museum, Saskatchewan

Victoria, British Columbia

West Edmonton Mall, Alberta

Winterlude Ottawa, Ontario

Best Beaches for Families

The Northeast

Cape Cod National Seashore, Massachusetts

The Jersey Shore, New Jersey

Rehoboth Beach, Delaware

The South

Clearwater to Naples on Florida's West Coast

Beaches of the Florida Panhandle

The South (continued)

Gulf Shores, Alabama

Myrtle Beach, South Carolina

Outer Banks and Kitty Hawk, North Carolina

Virginia Beach, Virginia

The Midwest

Favorite Great Lakes beaches

The West

California beaches

Maui, Hawaii

North Shore's Banzai Pipeline, Oahu

The Northwest

Columbia River Gorge, Oregon-Washington

Florence, Oregon, and Sand Dunes National Recreation Area

Mexico

Cozumel and Isla Mujeres, Quintana Roo

Playa del Carmen, Quintana Roo

Puerto Vallarta, Jalisco

Zihuatanejo and Ixtapa, Guerrero

Best Amusement Parks for Families

The Northeast

Hershey Park, Pennsylvania

Lake Compounce, Connecticut

Sesame Place, Pennsylvania

The South

Dollywood and Pigeon Forge, Tennessee

Sea World and Discovery Cove, Florida

Universal Orlando, Florida

Walt Disney World, Florida

The Midwest

Cedar Point and Sandusky, Ohio

Cuyahoga Valley, Ohio

Holiday World, Indiana

Wisconsin Dells

The West

Disneyland and Anaheim, California

Legoland, California

Universal Studios Hollywood, California

Best Outdoor Adventures for Families

The Northeast

Acadia National Park, Maine

Deep Creek Lake, Maryland

Lake Placid and the Adirondack Mountains, New York

Pocono Mountains, Pennsylvania

White Mountains, New Hampshire

The South

Blue Ridge Parkway and Appalachians

Great Smoky Mountains National Park, Tennessee

Swimming with manatees in Florida

The Southwest

Fredericksburg and Texas Hill Country

Grand Canyon, Arizona

Sedona, Arizona

The Mountain States

Bryce and Zion Canyons, Utah

Glacier National Park, Montana

Mesa Verde National Park, Colorado

Rocky Mountain National Park, Colorado

Yellowstone National Park, Wyoming

The West

Kauai, Hawaii

Lake Mead, Nevada

Lake Tahoe, California-Nevada

Yosemite National Park, California

The Northwest

Denali National Park and Preserve, Alaska

Glacier Bay National Park, Alaska

Olympic Peninsula, Washington

Mexico

Cabo San Lucas and Baja California Sur

Celestun Flamingo Preserve, Yucatan

Riviera Nayarit and Pacific Coast, Nayarit

Xcaret and the Riviera Maya, Quintana Roo

Canada

Dinosaur Provincial Park and Dinosaur Valley, Alberta

Niagara Falls, Ontario

Whales and Polar Bears of Churchill, Manitoba

Family Travel Resources Guide

The FamilyTravelForum.com community is constantly sharing advice, information, and the latest online and offline resources to make travel with family of any age easier, less stressful, and a better value. We hope you'll drop by the site and do more research on these topics and anything else you need to know about.

In addition, we'd like to share some resources that may be helpful to you and your family as you make your travel plans.

Airports These days of enhanced security mean longer airport waits, but many airports have fun children's play areas and even nurseries. Check out www.eskyguide.com/reference to learn about the amenities available before you fly.

Allowance Money is serious business, and there are many teachable money moments during family vacations. Establish a base allowance for each child so you won't be nagged to death for souvenirs; augment it with quarters given for good behavior in the car/on the plane.

Baby gear You don't need to take everything; many hotels have loaner strollers, playpens, highchairs, and more. If not, whatever you need can be delivered by Babys Away (www.BabysAway.com) or any of the many other local equipment rental places.

Babysitting If you're interested in some adult time, call your hotel in advance and try to arrange for childcare, either through a local service used by the hotel or by a trusted staff member. For days away, ask whether the resort has a state-licensed daycare facility or a branch of a childcare chain such as La Petite Academy (www.lapetite.com).

Backseat diversions Many kids have their own electronics these days, but we love old-fashioned games. Look online for rules to classic car games such as I Spy, The Alphabet Game, and others; having silly dollar-store gifts to hand out as prizes works well. Klutz Press and Rand

McNally make great backseat atlas books. Our favorite time-passers are Etch-a-Sketch, AutoBingo, and books on CD borrowed from the library. Keep an inflatable ball handy for rest stops.

Camping   Each regional Outdoor Adventures chapter provides resources for camping information. For commercial campgrounds, Yogi Bear's Jellystone Park Camp-Resorts (1-800-558-2954; www.campjellystone.com), located in 70 U.S. and Canadian destinations, is our favorite chain for families.

Car seats   Companies such as Hertz offer free car seat rental promotions in summer so you may not need to take your own. If you're flying, be sure your car seat is rated for aircraft or you'll have to check it. NHTSA.gov has comprehensive safety information if you have any questions about installing car seats or booster seats.

Climate   Most of us take family vacations when our kids are out of school, which means most families travel during the summer. We urge you to consider making winter or spring holidays your main vacation period, as prices are generally much lower, crowds are gone, and many of these destinations are truly at their best.

Condos   Many families prefer to stay in a condo, vacation villa, or rental house with kitchen facilities to save money on meals and lodging. Of the hundreds of websites devoted to this topic, we like VRBO.com, ResortQuest.com, and Zonder.com. Don't forget that all the hotel chains have condo units for rent at most of their resort properties so you can have the best of both worlds.

Cruises   We don't review any family cruises in this book, but they're more accessible than ever. For example, Carnival (1-800-522-7648; www.carnival.com) now sails from 20 different home ports in the United States, Canada, and Mexico, so you might want to combine a cruise and land vacation.

Currency and credit cards   ATMs are available everywhere; find out which regional banks will accept your card without an additional fee. Inform your credit card company if you will be using your card outside the country. An ATM in Canada and Mexico will provide the best exchange rate; be sure you have a four-digit PIN, because many foreign banks don't accept more than four. Travelers' checks are not always easy to cash, but you will be able to pay for most purchases outside the U.S. in U.S. dollars.

Documents Be sure to carry copies of identification and health insurance coverage for yourself and any kids traveling with you. If kids younger than 18 are traveling to Mexico or Canada without both birth parents or legal guardians present, they will need a notarized Permission to Travel Letter to present at border crossings.

Electricity Mexico and Canada have the same electricity standard as the U.S.—120 V; 60 Hz. Be sure to bring a plug adaptor kit because foreign plugs may vary from U.S. standards.

Electronic entertainment Be sure each child packs his or her own entertainment and is responsible for it. All you have to do is download some TV shows onto your iPod, smartphone, or laptop for emergencies. If you're flying, drop by an InMotion store (located in 50 U.S. airport terminals) and rent a DVD player and the latest flicks to keep everyone happy.

Emergencies Throughout the United States, dial 911 in case of emergency. Throughout Mexico, dial 01-55-800-903-9200 for toll-free tourist assistance or 066, 060, or 0808 in case of emergency. Throughout Canada, visit www.canada.travel for a directory of regional tourist offices, or dial 911 in case of emergency.

Health/hygiene Carry your own wipes and hand sanitizer and use them frequently to minimize germs. Be very cautious about raw fruits, vegetables, and drinking water while you're on the road. If you need medical assistance, check with your hotel front desk, call 1-800-Doctors, or look online at doctor.webmd.com for a physician directory by zip code.

Hotels All the major brands court the family market with promotions and perks, such as 50 percent off a connecting room and a welcome gift, especially during summer. Some of the best international hotel chains for families include:

- Hilton's Embassy Suites (1-800-EMBASSY; www. embassysuites.com) and Homewood Suites (1-800-CALL-HOME; www.homewoodsuites.com) brands, both have large rooms, pullout sofa beds, and perks such as free breakfast.

- Many Hyatt Hotels (1-888-591-1234; www.hyatt.com) have excellent kids clubs for a fee.

- Full-service Westin and Sheraton Hotels (1-800-325-3535; www.starwoodhotels.com) and Fairmont Hotels & Resorts (800-257-7544; www.fairmont.com) offer family perks such as Kids Eat Free deals.

- Luxury brands Ritz Carlton (1-800-542-8680; www.ritzcarlton.com) and Four Seasons (1-800-819-5053; www.fourseasons.com) have many family amenities and free kids clubs.

- Presidente Intercontinental (www.intercontinental.com) and Camino Real (www.caminoreal.com) have luxury resorts in Mexico with terrific kids clubs and lots of family amenities.

- Among U.S. small boutique chains, we especially like the family- and pet-welcoming Loews Hotels (1-866-LOEWS-WB; www.loewshotels.com) and the friendly, super-stylish Kimpton Hotels (1-800-Kimpton; www.kimptonhotels.com), all of which have family rates and special perks.

- Holiday Inn (1-888-Holiday; www.holidayinn.com) and Candlewood Suites (1-888-233-0369; www.candlewoodsuites.com) are two of the top budget chains. Delta Hotels (1-888-890-3222; www.deltahotels.com) is a very family-oriented budget chain across Canada. Best Western (www.bestwestern.com) has more than 40 locally owned hotels in Mexico that welcome families.

- Youth Hostels (www.hihostels.com) are a great place to stay and always a bargain. Hundreds of them in the United States, Mexico, and Canada have family rooms with private facilities.

Insurance   Travel insurance is an essential part of any prepaid vacation with kids. If you're booking non-refundable airfare, hotel stays, or tours, insure your trip against Timmy making it to the playoffs or Sally breaking her leg in gymnastics. Life happens.

Maps   Google Maps and Mapquest.com provide excellent online and printable maps and directions. Even if you have a GPS, buy an atlas, get maps from the local tourist office, or print route maps and laminate them so the kids can learn to navigate.

Phone   To make calls to Canada from outside the country, dial "1" before the local area code. To make calls to Mexico from outside the country, dial "52" before the local area code. If you aren't traveling with an international cell phone, it is much cheaper and easier to use a locally bought prepaid calling card (widely sold at newsstands and gift shops) to stay in touch.

Restaurants   We think every traveling family should carry a half-day food supply at all times, including water bottles for each family member and some treats. Also, keep in mind that a vacation is a great time to introduce the kids to new kinds of cuisine, especially those items they might not like at home. If you're dining on the road, Red Lobster and Denny's are two chains that get relatively high marks for healthy road food in the United States. In Canada, Lick's Homeburgers is a favorite chain, as is the VIPs chain throughout Mexico. If you want to splurge for a nice meal (and we love to do that), remember that many places have lunch specials.

Road trip survival kit   Carry paper towels, garbage bags, extra batteries or a car-lighter-to-AC converter, flashlight, masking tape, and a cooler. Make sure your car insurance covers road trips into Mexico and Canada.

Safety   On any vacation, remain alert and aware of your surroundings and your kids. Be sure that every child has the name of your hotel and its address with them at all times. Carry photocopies of all passports or photo IDs for the kids. Before wandering around a new town, ask your hotel staff for their safety advice. When making foreign travel plans, visit http://travel.state.gov and look for any country alerts.

Snacks   Carry plenty of snacks for everyone. They don't have to be bulky or unhealthy; several companies make freeze-dried fruit treats and small energy bars that kids like.

Trip planning   The Internet is a great trip-planning tool, and at www.FamilyTravelForum.com, you can fill out a Custom Trip Plan form and ask our staff to help you. Don't forget to contact the tourist office of your intended destination for their brochures and maps. Many tourist offices produce great kids' guides with historical information, coloring books, and even downloadable games filled with factoids that kids will enjoy en route. Others can arrange pen pals for your kids or book tours with free local guides, such as New York's Big Apple Greeters service.

Index

J

K

Maritime Museum of the
Atlantic, Nova Scotia, 347-348
Market Days, 291
Martin Luther King Center, 56
Marvel Cave, 124
Maryland
city attractions, Baltimore,
3-6
Deep Creek Lake, 45-46
Massachusetts
city attractions, Boston, 6-9
beach destinations, Cape Cod,
31-33
Mattress Factory museum, 17
Maui, Hawaii, 233-235
Mauna Kea mountain, 222
Mayan civilizations (Chichen-
Itza, Yucatan), 296-299
Mazatlan, 307
McCormick-Stillman Railroad
Park, 153
McMichael Gallery, 331
McNay Art Institute, 166
Métreon, 218
Medieval Times, 85
Mel Fisher Maritime Heritage
Museum, 75
Melrose Avenue, 214
Memaloose State Park, 271
Memphis, Tennessee
city attractions, 58-60
Memphis Rock 'N' Soul
Museum, 59
Menil Collection, The, 151
Mennonite Information Center,
29
Mercado Benito Juarez, 290
Mercado de la Merced, 287
Merry-Go-Round Museum, 137
Mesa Verde National Park,
197-199

Mesquite Championship Rodeo,
170
Metropolitan Museum of Art, 10
Mexican Riviera, 307
Mexico destinations
beach destinations, 302-312
city attractions, 283-292
historical attractions, 294-301
outdoor adventures, 314-321
safety tips, 282-283
Mi Tierra restaurant, 166
Miami, Florida, 61-63
Michigan
Automobile Heritage Trail,
121-123
Mackinac Island, 130-131
Upper Peninsula, 131
Mill City Museum, 119
Millennium Park, 111
Miniature World, 350
Miniland U.S.A., 240
Minneapolis, Minnesota,
118-120
Minnehaha Falls, 119
Minnesota
city attractions, 118-120
Mall of America, 125-126
Miracle Mile, 211
Mirage Hotel, 208
Mirror Lake, 251
Mismaloya, 308
Mission Bay Park, 215
Mission Beach, 215
Mission San Jose, 165
Mississippi River, 117
Missouri
cultural attractions, Branson,
123-125
city attractions, 111-118
Mobile Bay, 82
Monongahela River, 17

P

S

W

Z

X-Y